e-Mergers

Merging, Acquiring, and Partnering e-Commerce Businesses

JIM KEOGH

Prentice Hall PTR
Upper Saddle River, NJ 07458
www.phptr.com

ISBN 0-13-031390-4

90000

9 780130 313904

Library of Congress Cataloging-in-Publication Data

Keogh, James. Edward, 1948–
    E-Mergers : merging, acquiring, and partnering e-Commerce businesses / James Keogh.
        p. cm.
    Includes index.
    ISBN 0-13-031390-4
        1. Internet industry--Mergers. 2. Internet industry--Law and legislation. 3. Electronic
    commerce--Management. 4. Electronic commerce--Law and legislation. 5. Consolidation
    and merger of corporations. 6. Consolidation and merger of corporations--Law and
    legislation. 7. World Wide Web. I. Title.

HD9696.8.A2 K46 2001
658.1'6—dc21   2001045141

Editorial/Production Supervision: *Vincent Janoski*
Acquisitions Editor: *Mark Taub*
Marketing Manager: *Bryan Gambrel*
Manufacturing Buyer: *Maura Zaldivar*
Composition: *Sean Donahue*
Cover Design: *Anthony Gemmellaro*
Cover Design Director: *Jerry Votta*

© 2002 by Prentice Hall
Published by Prentice Hall PTR
Prentice-Hall, Inc.
Upper Saddle River, NJ 07458

Prentice Hall books are widely used by corporations and government agencies for training,
marketing, and resale. The publisher offers discounts on this book when ordered in bulk quan-
tities. For more information, contact Corporate Sales Department, phone: 800-382-3419; fax:
201-236-7141; email: corpsales@prenhall.com; or write Corporate Sales Department, Prentice Hall PTR, One Lake Street, Upper Saddle River, NJ 07458.

All products or services mentioned in this book are the trademarks or service marks of their
respective companies or organizations.

All material from Tim Miller at Webmergers.com is copyright © 2001 by Webmergers.com.
Reprinted by permission of Tim Miller and Webmergers.com (*www.webmergers.com*).

All rights reserved. No part of this book may be reproduced, in any form or by any means,
without permission in writing from the publisher.

Printed in the United States of America

10 9 8 7 6 5 4 3 2 1

ISBN 0-13-031390-4

Pearson Education LTD
Pearson Education Australia PTY, Limited
Pearson Education Singapore, Pte, Ltd.
Pearson Education North Asia Ltd.
Pearson Education Canada, Ltd.
Pearson Educatión de Mexico, S.A. de C.V.
Pearson Education—Japan
Pearson Education Malaysia, Pte. Ltd.

This book is dedicated to Anne, Sandra, and Joanne, without whose help it could not have been written.

CONTENTS

PREFACE

Dotcom companies are regrouping for the next battle in the war to stake a claim to a piece of the cyber market. The first battle depleted the financial ammunition many dotcoms had stored from rounds of private and public financing.

Those financial sources are drying up, and dotcoms must develop a new strategy before the next battle begins. The strategy many dotcoms are adopting is to join forces with other corporations to create a sizable onslaught against the competition.

Dotcoms are merging with other dotcoms and with firms outside of cyberspace to form a strong, formidable cyberspace business. Others are acquiring weaker players who have valuable assets but lack the financial wherewithal to enter the fray of one more battle.

Mergers and acquisitions is new to players in the dotcom industry. Most dotcoms are in the "startup.com" class, where entrepreneurial drive, fueled by an influx of enthusiastic capital from Wall Street, brought ideas written on napkins to reality.

I've written this book for dotcom managers who are contemplating merging their company with another company or who are considering acquiring a company. Mergers and acquisitions is a complex process. I wrote this book to help dotcom managers understand the mergers and acquisitions process and how to work efficiently with mergers and acquisitions professionals.

The mergers and acquisitions process begins by identifying and prequalifying targets. A target is a company that is the focus of the merger acquisition. Identifying and prequalifying targets is the topic Chapter 1, where you will learn about the various types of mergers and acquisitions transactions and how to identify targets of opportunity. Chapter 1 shows you how to search and contact targets either directly or by using brokers and finders. You'll also explore legal considerations that influence your search.

Once a target is found and prequalified, you must conduct due diligence. Due diligence is a process by which you investigate the target in an effort to substantiate financial and legal records and other information pertaining to the target. Chapter 2 walks you through this process.

Due diligence is a long and detailed process that lasts nearly the entire length of the deal. During this period, you'll be expected to arrange financing for the deal. Chapter 3 shows you the various types of transactions that are available and explores your financing options. In Chapter 3 you'll learn about debt structuring, leaseback financing, take-back financing, bridge financing, and other financing methods. You'll also explore the legal considerations that impact financing.

Taxes can have a dramatic effect on a merger or acquisition. Chapter 4 introduces you to the tax implications of a deal. You'll learn tax basics, valuation methods, and tax accounting methods that can lower the tax liability of a deal.

Critical aspects of every merger or acquisition are employees. Chapter 5 explores issues that must be addressed before dotcoms can join forces. These issues include compensation, benefits, retirement, health plans, stock ownership, and terminations.

In Chapter 6 you'll learn various mergers and acquisitions techniques that are unique to public corporations and others that are unique to private corporations. You'll learn about tender offerings, public disclosure, the duties of the board of directors, defensive strategies, and how to avoid insider conflicts.

Cyberspace has no national boundaries and neither do mergers and acquisitions. Chapter 7 explores factors that must be considered when doing a deal in the international arena. You'll learn about how to deal with a United States-based dotcom and how to do a similar deal with a foreign-based dotcom. Special attention is given to domestic and foreign taxing issues and international financing considerations.

After you have settled on a target, you must decide a fair price to pay to merge with or acquire the target. Chapter 8 shows you how to price the deal. You'll learn about pricing basics, buying strategies, forecasting cash flows, risk assessments, and pricing models.

With a price set in your mind, the challenge of doing a deal begins when you enter into negotiations with the target. You'll learn everything that you need to know about negotiations in Chapter 9. You'll learn how to set the stage for negotiations, how to develop a negotiations strategy, how to use a letter of intent and the acquisition agreement to your advantage, and how to establish closing procedures that assure that the deal closes on schedule.

The deal isn't done until you close the deal and integrate your company with the target. Chapter 10 shows you the critical points of how to close the deal and how to consolidate both companies. You'll learn what to do before and on closing day, how to pay for the deal, and how to make your company and the target one company.

Chapter 11 explores the techniques of creating business alliances, which is another way dotcoms can join forces without formally merging or acquiring a business. A business alliance is a strategic arrangement whereby complementary dotcoms enter into a combined effort to fight the next battle in cyberspace.

The war over who controls cyberspace is far from over. We've only seen the first of many battles to come. Dotcoms are poised to regroup through mergers, acquisitions, and business alliances. The techniques and strategies discussed in this book are the primary intelligence you require to form a company that can conquer all competitors.

Tim Miller, president of Webmergers.com, has provided insights into the mergers, acquisitions, and strategic partnerships taking place in the e-commerce arena. Webmergers.com is a leading marketplace for analysts and services for buyers and sellers of Web properties. Webmergers.com's knowledge base is frequently used for identifying M&A trends and for valuing Web companies.

CHAPTER 1

Identifying and Prequalifying Targets

Done deals make everyone happy.
—Anonymous

In This Chapter

- Mergers and Acquisitions and Targets
- Types of Transactions
- Planning
- Identifying Opportunities
- Searching for Targets
- Contacting Targets
- Using Brokers and Finders
- Using Investment Bankers and Commercial Bankers
- Legal Considerations

Consider the impact of the Internet. A major online book reseller discovered an obscure book on poisonous insects in New Mexico and offered the book online. Fifteen thousand copies were sold the first day. The reason for this success is that the Internet focused a dispersed niche market to a single location.

The Internet is a disruptive technology that is revolutionizing the way we normally do such things as communicate with each other, find information, and make purchases. No longer are consumers limited by their location, for shopping online crosses natural and national boundaries. The Internet gave birth to a new economy.

1

The new economy has its foundation anchored in electronic commerce, where there are proprietorships, partnerships, and corporations who have pioneered online markets. These are known as *dotcom* companies. Some dotcom companies are well positioned to capture and retain a market segment. Others stake a claim to markets too small to support their venture.

Behind dotcom companies is an electronics industry that provides infrastructure and technical tools necessary for the new economy to flourish. These include manufacturers of computers, components, cables, wireless transmitters, and software. Collectively they enable the dotcom companies to compete for consumers against established brick-and-mortar companies.

Some ventures are strong and have a long-term prospect for success. Others lack the wherewithal to survive on their own, even if they seem to dominate a market. These organizations are targets for mergers or acquisitions and are the subject of this book.

Once pioneers proved that the new economy is viable, investors financed upstart companies to establish online markets for each brick-and-mortar market. Firms who moved quickly and established a strong online presence had an opportunity to take over markets held by brick-and-mortar industry leaders. As consumers move their business online, the brick-and-mortar market is being left behind.

The new economy is following the trail of the birth of any new industry. First, innovative technology is developed and perfected. Next, fledging entrepreneurs exploit the technology to provide new goods and services to consumers. Consolidation follows, where successful organizations are combined.

Consolidation of dotcom and supporting companies is underway and provides new opportunities to reorganize the new economy into powerful units that can rejuvenate fledgling but promising companies. In this chapter you'll explore how to develop a plan for identifying candidates for merger or acquisition.

MERGERS AND ACQUISITIONS AND TARGETS

Consolidation occurs when companies combine through a merger or acquisition. There is a subtle but distinct difference between a merger and an acquisition. A merger occurs when one company's stock is exchanged for another company's stock. The company that gives up its stock, called a *target,* is considered the decedent, and no longer exists. The remaining company is called the survivor. I'll call targets dotcom throughout this book, because many merger and acquisition deals involve the acquisition of dotcom companies.

Let's say Al Company and Bob Company agree to a merger that results in Bob Company as the survivor. An agreement is reached as to the number of shares of Bob Company that stockholders will receive for their shares in Al Company. For this example, two shares of Al Company are exchanged for one share of Bob Company.

Stockholders in Al Company exchange their shares, which are voided and placed in a vault. At that point, Al Company ceases to exist, and assets of Al Company are transferred to Bob Company. Stockholders of Al Company still retained ownership of those assets and gain the assets of Bob Company.

A *merger* is a legal matter and has nothing to do with the operations of either company. Al Company can function as an operating unit of Bob Company, although, legally, Al Company does not exist.

In the previous example, companies exchanged shares of stock to consummate the merger. Mergers in real life follow a formal transaction process that is outlined in the laws of the state (or states) where the companies are incorporated.

The corporation that survives a merger is determined by a number of factors, some of which are subjective. These include the number of employees, the selection of the chairman, net worth, and the size of the operation.

An *acquisition* occurs when one corporation buys the stock or assets of another corporation. Both corporations exist after the acquisition. Let's see how this works with Al Company and Bob Company.

Bob Company acquires Al Company for $10 a share. Stockholders of Al Company transfer ownership of their shares to Bob Company in exchange for $10 per share. Al Company remains a legal corporation that is owned by another corporation. Therefore, Al Company becomes a legal subsidiary of Bob Company.

After a corporation acquires shares, corporate officers can merge the two corporations without approval of stockholders. This is called a *short form* merger. In the previous example, officers of Bob Company can merge with Al Company after acquiring shares of Al Company. In many states, stockholders of Bob Company do not have the right to approve the merger.

Another acquisition technique is for Bob Company to purchase the assets of Al Company. Al Company sells its brand name, Web site, servers, and other assets of the firm to Bob Company in exchange for cash. Al Company still exists as a shell company and remains owned by the stockholders of Al Company, which own the cash exchanged for assets by Bob Company.

Tech Talk

Short Form Merger: A company acquires the stock of another company, after which the acquired company is merged with the acquirer.

Corporations acquire assets rather than stock of another corporation as a way to limit liability and to simplify the transaction. A corporation has assets and liabilities. An acquiring corporation desires the assets of another corporation, and not its liabilities (except in certain tax situations). Both assets and liabilities are transferred when a corporation buys shares of the acquired corporation. No liabilities or limited liabilities are transferred when a corporation buys the assets of an acquired corporation (except those normally associated with the asset).

Stockholders must approve all mergers and acquisitions, including the sale of assets, except in the short form merger.

Tech Talk

Shell Company: A corporation that no longer functions as a business.

From Tim Miller, Webmergers.com

While Waiting for a Suitor

On the constructive side, several "Internet Survival" speakers offered these suggestions for Internet companies in search of financing in current tough times. Among the suggestions:

- Customer financing: Getting major customers to help front costs is often the least costly in the long run.
- Equipment leasing: A way to spread out equipment costs.
- Strategic financing: Funding from a corporate partner is very attractive, but difficult to find; often involves bureaucratic processes.

- Merger with companies that have positive cash flows: Often the best alternative if management interests are aligned.
- Asset/technology sales or licensing: Often a desperate measure and often involves fire sale prices.
- Flat or "down" rounds: Unattractive option, but still keeps startups in the game.
- Restructuring or recapitalizations: Ugly, but it's survival.
- "Unlikely sources": Try local or state government or economic development sources of funding.
- International sources: Several speakers said European investors may be currently more receptive to B2C and B2B financing at better terms than in North America. At least one speaker and several Europe-based attendees demurred, citing the traditional conservatism of European (and Japanese) investors.
- Revisit former contacts: Try VCs that once turned you down. It's not unheard of for VCs to have a change of view, particularly if the business plan has evolved and proof-of-concept has been achieved.
- In-kind funding: When startups are seeking in-kind funding in the form of advertising or other services, panelists strongly encouraged startups to separate the commerce deal from the equity deal, even going so far as to negotiate the two deals separately with a separate team.
- Commercial lenders: Another long-shot option.

And, some suggestions to stretch cash and brush up the business:

- Trim payroll, advertising, second-priority projects and all unnecessary travel (typically sales-related travel is spared).
- Change the business model. Don't fall in love with a particular business model.
- Set achievable milestones and hit them; have milestones for both finance and operations and hit both.

TYPES OF TRANSACTIONS

There are generally two types of acquisitions: friendly acquisition and hostile acquisition. A friendly acquisition is a transaction in which both the buyer and seller agree to the acquisition. A hostile acquisition, which is commonly referred to as a *hostile takeover,* is a transaction in which the seller is against the acquisition.

Let's say that Bob Company owns an e-village Web site and Al Company owns an auction Web site. Bob Company needs a way to expand the offering of the e-village Web site by offering an auction. There are three alternatives available to Bob Company: create its own auction Web site, form a strategic alliance with an existing auction Web site, or acquire an existing auction Web site.

Creating an auction Web site is probably the most costly option, since Bob Company lacks the technology and the expertise to operate an online auction. A strategic alliance is the least costly option, but also is the less profitable, since revenue from the auction flows to the strategic alliance partner and not to Bob Company.

Tech Talk

Strategic Alliance: A contractual arrangement between two companies, where one company provides a service to another for a percentage of each transaction.

Acquiring an existing auction Web site is desirable. Al Company seems a likely target to acquire. The CEO of Bob Company needs to devise a plan that convinces the CEO of Al Company that stockholders and employees of both companies are better off joining forces than operating independently.

A friendly acquisition is transacted if the CEOs of Al Company and Bob Company agree on terms for either a merger or acquisition. However, the CEO of Bob Company must reconsider the strategy if the CEO of Al Company is not amenable to the terms. Bob Company could look for another target or institute a hostile acquisition.

A hostile acquisition occurs when the board of directors of a public company rejects the offer of a buyer and the buyer pursues the acquisition. Stockholders must approve an acquisition or merger and can overrule the board of directions.

The buyer in a hostile acquisition communicates directly with stockholders, convincing them to sell their stock to the buyer. The acquisition goes forward once a majority of stockholders agrees to transfer their stock.

From Tim Miller, Webmergers.com

Microsoft's M&A Diet

In the ongoing search for smart Internet M&A strategies, it's always helpful to look at the feeding habits of market leaders. In that light, let's take a look at Microsoft, which has been very selectively picking up tidbits from the amply stocked watering holes of the Internet.

Microsoft has bought infrequently, spending a little over an estimated billion dollars on eight Web deals. By contrast, Yahoo! has spent $10.5 billion on a half dozen deals, and AOL has spent $4.4 billion on a dozen deals, not counting the Time Warner acquisition.

Microsoft acquired MongoMusic for a reported $56 million. MongoMusic is an online music recommendation engine that enables users to match their favorite music with similar artists. MongoMusic's technology also enables users to listen to tune segments immediately over the Internet and to purchase music they like.

The key word in the above description is "engine." The fact that it deploys a software-driven application to create value for users over and over makes MongoMusic a classic acquisition for Microsoft. The following table contains Microsoft's Web deals.

Microsoft Web Acquisitions

Target	Description
Hotmail	Web email
Firefly Network, Inc.	Collaborative filtering software
Link Exchange, Inc.	Advertising network
CompareNet, Inc.	Product comparator
Jump Networks, Inc.	Online calendar
OmniBrowse, Inc.	Wireless content delivery services
DriveOff.com	Auto e-tailer
MongoMusic	Music recommendation engine

Most of Microsoft's targets have two or more of the following characteristics in common:

- Online applications that enable users to DO something
- Self-perpetuating "content" created by an application or by user interactions
- Viral spread to other users
- Ability to be leveraged across Microsoft Internet properties

For example, Jump Networks' calendaring program enables visitors to perform multiple tasks related to scheduling and reminders. In so doing, users create their own content that they are compelled to revisit from time to time. And users send invitations to others, virally encouraging them to join.

Some time ago in a magazine article, we coined the word "aptent" (applications + content) to describe services like Jump, Hotmail, and other online applications that perform much the same role as traditional words-and-picture content.

In other words, these applets draw and retain visitors, who are exposed to advertising and e-commerce opportunities. Many of these properties, for example, shopping comparison "bots," produce their own content, over and over again with little editorial involvement. Firefly's group collaboration is another perfect example of an application that self-perpetuates content.

Perhaps the ultimate Microsoft aptent acquisition was that of Hotmail, which it bought in 1997 for about $400 million, when it had about 12 million subscribers. While that price may have seemed steep at the time, Hotmail today has about 70 million subscribers, all of whom signed up in large part on word-of-mouth spread virally by emails themselves.

While its initial price came out to about $33 per subscriber, the current price paid per subscriber is just under $7, a bargain by any definition, given that Microsoft has been making money from each of the billions of emails sent by its users.

While Microsoft is far from being a wild spender, it will pony up when it sees the right aptent opportunity. The company first offered Hotmail owner Sabeer Bhatia $160 million for the property. According to the Industry Standard, the 20-something Bhatia, to the horror of his VC investors, countered with an audacious $700 million, but Microsoft finally agreed to pay about $400 million.

AOL, of course, has also seen the aptent light. It spent about $400 million to buy Israeli company Mirabilis for its Web-based instant messaging technology (AOL already had its own IM technology for its proprietary service). Mirabilis now has about 73 million registered users and it appears that AOL intends to join it up with IM, which has about 65.5 million registered users.

Buyers have spent close to $10 billion on nearly 100 aptent acquisitions since 1998, according to Webmergers.com data. Aptent has an interesting dynamic with regard to startups and their exits. Buyers tend to buy outright, rather than license, these properties.

This has created a sort of "me-too" bidding war for the best properties, often creating the investor's dream scenario—liquidity at reasonable rates even for fifth, sixth and seventh-tier players.

Aptent is a perfect example of how the medium shapes the content. In the case of the Internet, the happy union of computing and communication enables online applications such as calendars, discussion forums, chats, and bots to exist where they couldn't exist before.

The value and economies of aptent may seem obvious, but if they are, why do we have so many online companies that are struggling (and the use of the word struggling is intentional) to recreate old-economy content models such as daily news publishing on the Web?

Maybe the Internet is simply not the place to create new content, but rather to aggregate and add value to existing content or to create new kinds of content that leverage the Web's interactivity.

Speaking of old content models, it may be no coincidence that the one property that Microsoft has sold outright (for $240 million to Ticketmaster Online-CitySearch) was Sidewalk, a regional information guide that may epitomize the editorially intensive site.

> So, if buyers and sellers of Internet companies are to take a lesson from the gorilla's eating habits, what is it? In the case of Microsoft, the observation may be that the way to think about creating value through online content has less to do with "viewing" and more to do with "doing."

PLANNING

The merger and acquisition process begins by identifying the strengths and weaknesses of your company, then finding a dotcom company that compensates for those weaknesses. The objective is to systematically analyze opportunities rather than haphazardly pursue dotcoms that may not enhance your company's profitability.

First, establish criteria for dotcoms. The criteria are used to quickly identify if a dotcom is a candidate worth pursuing. Companies that fall outside the criteria are immediately rejected from further conditions. Criteria involve hundreds of variables that relate to the current and future operations of your company. Each element, such as market share, cash flow, and market growth, is quantified, enabling candidates to be rank based on desirability.

It is critical that guidelines be established before any effort is made to acquire a dotcom company. Otherwise, unnecessary funds are spent for a dotcom that does not complement your company.

Your board of directors can avoid common failures in the merger and acquisition process by creating a group of executives to develop and monitor the use of planning guidelines. Here are some of the items that should be included in the guidelines:

- List the responsibilities of each person in the corporate planning hierarchy.
- Identify decision-makers in the process.
- Create a technique used to compare external investments against developing similar opportunities within the company.

Special care must be taken to assure that managers objectively compare in-house development with external acquisition because, intuitively, managers opt for in-house development. The reasons for this approach are many. Managers have more control over a venture if they develop it themselves. They also see this as more challenging than acquiring a business. Furthermore, acquiring a business invites competition from the management team running the dotcom company, which may not be advantageous to the manager.

Tech Talk

In-House Development: Using corporate resources to develop a business without acquiring an existing company in the desired market.

Cash Flow

At the center of every merger and acquisition strategy is the efficient use of cash flows by redeploying cash flows from low to high yielding investments. Here's how this works. Capital is invested into a business operation to generate cash. Let's say a book reseller acquires services and equipment to create an online bookstore. The online bookstore operations return a predictable level of cash each month. The cash can be reinvested into the online bookstore operations or invested in other opportunities that return a higher yield.

In addition to the cash flow from operations, the strategy must also consider the cash flow generated by the sale of a business unit. Your company can realize a premium by selling off the unit, especially if there is low growth potential in the current industry. Proceeds from the sale can be reallocated to operations that have higher growth potential and yield a higher return.

Planning occurs at five levels:

- Enterprise level
- Corporate level
- Business unit level
- Product line level
- Functional level

At the enterprise level, the board of directors reviews the use of cash flows and decides if a change in is order. They consider alternatives to re-investing cash flows into their core business, which should include acquiring a competitor to expand their business and to sell off business units to use the proceeds for a higher yielding venture.

The corporate level realigns similar business units into groups. Each group is treated as an enterprise that collectively provides a cash flow to the parent company. Group presidents are responsible for maximizing long-term return of the group by redistributing cash flows generated by operating units under their control. Their strategies can include selling off or acquiring business units.

The business unit level organizes similar product lines into a business unit. The business unit manager is responsible to assure a predictable cash flow from the unit by reinvesting returns into existing products, new products, and/or acquired products.

The product line level devises ways to continue a cash flow from a particular line of products by carefully monitoring the product life cycle. Products have a predictable life span over which product managers are able to extract the highest possible return by using various marketing techniques. Product managers must introduce new products to replace existing products before cash flows from their existing products dwindle.

The functional level addresses how to increase cash flows from a product by modifying the product's manufacturing process and by relocating facilities to areas of lower rent and labor rates.

Managers at each level of the planning process should be aware of the net present value of its unit. The net present value is the current value of future cash flows and is used to determine the market value of the unit.

The market value is the criteria used by managers to determine if continuing operations, acquiring a new unit, and/or selling the unit can enhance a unit's cash flow. A unit is an enterprise, a subsidiary, a business unit product, or a component of a product.

Tech Talk

Net Present Value: The value of tomorrow's cash flows in oday's dollars.

From Tim Miller, Webmergers.com

Vertical Acquisition Strategy

A common practice used to gain a stronghold in an industry is to acquire businesses that collectively form a fully integrated organization. A good example of this strategy is the Healtheon/WebMD Corp.

Healtheon/WebMD Corp. integrated the entire spectrum of the health care marketplace by acquiring everything from business-to-business to business-to-consumer companies. On the B2B front, the company acquired its leading competitor, Careinsite, Inc. (CARI) and its parent Medical Manager Corp. (MMGR) for about $5 billion. In the B2C arena, the company bought Web MD's main health information rival, OnHealth Network Co. (ONHN) for about $300 million.

Acquisitions include health information companies Direct Medical Knowledge, Sapient Health Network, WebMD, Inc., OnHealth Network Co., and Greenberg News Network, which is a medical news service. On the operations side of the industry, they acquired the healthcare transactions company MEDE AMERICA Corporation, Kinetra, which processes medical claims, and Careinsite/Medical Management that manages practices.

IDENTIFYING OPPORTUNITIES

The fit chart (see Figure 1–1) guides you through the process of identifying dotcoms that complement your company. The chart helps you to pinpoint the strengths and weaknesses of your company, identify dotcom companies, and rank dotcoms based upon their needs.

There are three strategies that you should consider when identifying opportunities:

- Horizontal integration
- Vertical integration
- Diversification

Horizontal integration is when a company expands its current business by acquiring a competitor or by moving existing operations into new territories. For example, an Internet service provider (ISP) in New Jersey can expand the business by either acquiring an ISP in New York or opening operations in New York. In either case, the ISP horizontally expands the business.

The advantage of horizontal integration is that the company knows the business and can maintain or enhance the operation of the dotcom. The drawback is that the company can overextend the capabilities of its existing operations and that of the dotcom by consolidating redundant tasks. For example, the ISP may seek to consolidate network and server operations by reassigning tasks from the dotcom to the company. However, this might overwhelm the existing staff and lead to operational errors that affect customers of both businesses.

Vertical integration is when a company expands by acquiring a supplier or customer. Acquiring a supplier is called *backward integration* and acquiring a customer is called *forward integration.*

Let's say an owner of an online shopping mall wants to vertically expand operations. The company has a strategic alliance with a company that provides online transactions for storeowners on the site. The online shopping mall can vertically integrate operations by acquiring the online transaction company. Likewise, one or more stores on the mall can be acquired. Stores are customers of an online shopping mall.

Vertical integration is an advantage if the dotcom's profit margin is rolled into the company's cash flow or if the acquisition provides a competitive advantage in the market. The drawback is that the company is acquiring a business operation that it knows little about, which could erode the value of the acquisition.

Diversification is expansion into a different business that extends existing offerings to customers or operates in an entirely different industry. For example, an ISP might expand into IP telephony and offer existing customers telephone service over the Internet. Another alternative is for the firm to expand into network design and installation. Both of these options diversify the company's operations.

Company		Dotcom	
Strength	Weakness	Strength	Weakness

Figure 1–1   The fit chart can be used to list the strengths and weaknesses of your company and of the dotcom.

Creating the Fit Chart

The process of creating the fit chart begins by assembling top executives of the firm who are involved in strategic planning for the company to form a planning committee. Typically, these are the chief financial officer, chief executive officer, and appropriate operating unit managers. The planning committee is asked informally to determine the key factors that can be used to identify the strengths and weaknesses of the company. Their input is listed on the fit chart.

Next, the planning committee is asked to identify the strengths and weaknesses of the company. The facilitator of the meeting must encourage a frank discussion and avoid the dangers of each executive protecting his or her turf; otherwise, this exercise does not present a realistic picture of the organization.

Once the strengths and weaknesses of the company are identified, the planning committee is asked to identify new opportunities. The discussion should focus on industries, then move toward dotcom companies within an industry. For example, growth opportunity might exist in hosting high-demand Web sites in an area that complements the company's current operations.

The planning committee must decide on a market segment that is in an attractive industry, and then focus on identifying dotcoms within that industry. Each dotcom is placed on the fit chart. It is important that no dotcom be dismissed at this stage because there is insufficient objective information with which to base a decision. Instead, all candidates must be considered as equals.

The planning committee identifies and records on the fit chart the strengths and weaknesses of each dotcom. Dotcoms must not be rated at this stage. The objective of this process is to familiarize the planning team with targets.

The most important factor to determine at this stage is how a dotcom generates profit. Typically, profits are derived from margin or turns in inventory. Also note a dotcom's return on investment. Other financials are reviewed once a dotcom is ranked high on the fit chart.

Here's how to use the components of the fit chart. List the following:

- Your geographical market, competitors within the market, and each share of the market and its growth rate in the horizontal integration component
- Potential new geographical markets and potential growth rates in the market extension component
- Suppliers and your purchases from each supplier in the vertical backward integration component

- Your customers and their purchases from your company in the vertical forward integration component
- All products and services that are not offered by your company, but are purchased by your customers in the product/service extension component
- Opportunities that don't fit in other components in the free form component

Once information is entered into the fit chart, it is used to identify those dotcoms that have the best synergy with the company. Be sure to include your company's operating units in the fit chart. You'll then able to rank your business units with dotcoms. The results might indicate that it is in the best interest of the company to sell a business unit, then redirect the proceeds to acquiring a higher valued dotcom.

Here's how this is done:

- Review the fit chart for dotcoms that complement the company's weaknesses or supplement the company's strengths.
- Weigh the complements and supplements according to importance to the company.
- Rank dotcoms based on the complements and supplements they offer to the company.

From Tim Miller, Webmergers.com

Winner Take All Strategy

Online one-to-one marketplaces tend to have a "winner-take-most" dynamic. The player that is first to assemble the largest base of buyers and sellers is the one most likely to win. That dynamic in part explains the billions of dollars that investors are spending to seize the juiciest B2C and B2B niches. E-marketplaces are still so fragmented that we seldom stop to think about what happens if and when a winner-take-most becomes a reality.

However, we have somewhat of a case study in the online marketplace for residential real estate. Here, one gorilla, Homestore.com, Inc., has almost from its debut dominated home sales online listings.

How? Homestore leveraged its relationship with its majority owner, National Association of Realtors, which with 750,000 members, bills itself as the world's largest trade group.

Thanks to its NAR relationship, Homestore gets exclusive access to Multiple Listings Services systems that list properties for sale. The company has also recently said it will invest heavily on electronically integrating the backend transaction process to further tighten its hold on the niche. Competitors like Microsoft Corp's HomeAdvisor.com, Inc. and HomeSeekers.com, Inc. do not have nearly the reach of Homestore.

The absence of big home marketplace plays seems to have pushed real estate-related deal-making into non-core areas such as e-mortgages, relocation services, data and appraisal services, and rentals matching.

Only several deals relate to home listings. Rather, the typical transaction looks more like last the purchase of online appraisal software provider Day One by real estate information provider Appraisal.com.

Few transactions involve the core "sweet spot" of actual home listings. Homestore has exclusive online access to the listings of the three major real estate brands that Cendant owns. Homestore also gets some of the relocations services that Move.com has assembled. Move.com has been an active acquirer itself.

We can only speculate about scenarios when and if gorillas rule nearly every electronic niche. But the Homestore case gives us some visibility on what we might expect in the future, both in marketplace dynamics, impact on M&A, and last, but not least, involvement of government antitrust entities.

SEARCHING FOR TARGETS

The fit chart identifies the strengths and weaknesses of your company and becomes the basis from which to identify dotcoms that will buttress weaknesses. The two common approaches used to locate dotcoms are using outside resources and using in-house resources. Outside resources are finders and brokers, which are discussed later in this chapter. In-house resources are corporate staff used to find dotcoms.

There are two major objectives of finding prospective dotcoms. First, search a dotcom that complements your company's objectives of horizontal integration, vertical integration, or diversification. After dotcoms are identified, they must be screened to assure there is prima facie evidence to seriously consider the dotcom.

Tech Talk

Prima Facie Evidence: Facts that at first glance lead you to believe a dotcom is a fit for your company.

The planning committee must form a search committee comprised of corporate and operational unit executives along with specialists in areas of legal, finance, and engineering. They must work cohesively for six months to over a year to objectively examine dotcoms that meet the criteria established by the planning committee.

The type of expansion (horizontal integration, vertical integration, or diversification) dictates the starting point for the search. Horizontal integration focuses on competitors, which are likely to be well known by corporate executives. Vertical integration directs the search committee's attention to customers and suppliers. Diversification takes the search to a broad level where the search committee explores industries outside that of the company.

In all three cases, the search begins with a literature search. Literature is any publication that discusses competitors, customers, and suppliers, and covers news of industries that are targeted for expansion by the company.

Tech Talk

Literature Search: The task of reviewing all written, audio, and video documents pertaining to a dotcom or the dotcom's industry.

The literature search must be goal-oriented. The first goal is to understand a dotcom industry, including economic indicators that affect the industry and the industry structure. The next goal is to identify companies within the industry and rank them by importance. In doing so, the search committee gathers information about each company. The final goal is to identify key people in the industry. These are typically specialists that are recognized experts in various aspects of the business.

Identifying key people in the industry can seem difficult to achieve, especially if members of the search committee are not familiar with facets of the targeted industry. However, these specialists are published in the trade press, appear as speakers at trade shows and conferences, and are typically quoted in the media.

The objective of a literature search is to gather qualitative and quantitative information, such as profits, margins, sales, and the source of profit, about an industry and about particular dotcoms. The search committee needs to understand how targeted industries work and how significant companies within the targeted industries work.

Information is available from trade association publications, trade magazines, trade shows, corporate publications, filings if the dotcom is a public company or in a regulated industry, and credit reports. Standard and Poor's as well as Dun and Bradstreet are excellent sources of information. Of special interests are publications that focus on mergers and acquisitions, since this is where the search committee learns of consolidations within an industry. Table 1.1 contains Internet Web sites that will help in a literature search, and Table 1.2 lists related published resources.

A literature search helps the search committee to piece together an image of an industry and a dotcom. However, the literature is rarely comprehensive; it leaves gaps that must be filled in through other search methods, such as contacting the dotcom, customers, suppliers, and competitors.

Caution

Contacting the dotcom and related companies is a delicate matter, since the search is in a preliminary phase and the target is unaware of your interest. In addition, the search committee does not want to tip its hand, because a premature announcement could make negotiations difficult if the target is later desirable.

Search committees have been known to probe dotcoms by assuming the role of a potential customer. In that way, the committee can elicit general information necessary to complete its picture of the dotcom without disrupting the dotcom's business operation. More penetrating questions are left to the due diligence process, which is discussed in Chapter 2, "Due Diligence."

Caution

Always question the information gathered during the search. Don't assume the information is accurate until it is independently confirmed. This is especially true when using news reports. A news report summarizes complex business information into several paragraphs of easy-to-read text. In doing so, facts can easily become inadvertently distorted without the reader's knowledge.

Caution

The mindset of the search committee is that of an opportunity maker and not of an opportunity taker. An opportunity maker is someone whose purpose in finding a dotcom is to enhance the operations of a company. In contrast, an opportunity taker sees the target as an investment and seeks to enhance a financial position.

Table 1.1   Internet Web Sites Used for Literature Searches

www.bizbuysell.com	www.maol.com
www.bizlist.com	www.masource.org
www.cbex.com	www.mergernetwork.com
www.dialog.com	www.mergers.net
www.findex.com	www.netpreneur.org
www.firstlist.com	www.nvst.com
www.fourleaf.com	www.researchers.com
www.innostar.com	www.snlnet.com
www.instituteofe-commerce.com	www.wallstreettranscript.com
www.lexisnexis.com	www.worldm-anetwork.com

Table 1.2   Sources for Corporate Information

Organization	Service Provided
Thomas Register	Organizes companies by products and services
Frost & Sullivan	Industry research
findex.com	Financial information
Dialog Corporation (www.dialog.com)	Industry databases
Predicasts	Databases available through libraries
Nelson's Directory of Investment Research	Wall Street research reports
Dun and Bradstreet Directories	Information about public and private companies
Harris Infosource	Information about manufacturing companies
Hoover's Handbook of Private Companies	Information on large private companies
Washington Researchers (www.researchers.com)	Information on public and private companies and markets and industries
The Wall Street Transcripts	Wall Street research reports
Value Line Investment Survey	Information on public companies
Directory of Corporate Affiliations	Corporate affiliations
Lexis/Nexis (www.lexisnexis.com)	Database of general business information
Competitive Intelligence Professionals (www.scip.org)	Information about industries
Business Periodicals Index (BPI)	Business and technical article listing
Standard and Poor's Publications	Industry surveys and corporate records

When the literature search is completed, the search committee should have a file of information on targeted industries and companies that at this early stage are considered dotcoms. These files should contain

Per Industry

- Trade associations
- Trade shows and conferences
- An overview of unique government regulations
- Economic report on the industry
- Significant companies within the industry
- Issues facing the industry
- Market definition
- Market forecast
- Market share
- Market financials
- Key industry specialists
- Media reports on the industry
- Government reports on the industry
- Industry forecasts

Per Company

- Market share
- Company profile
- Company financials
- Company strategy
- Profiles of key personnel
- Company strengths
- Company weaknesses
- Company suppliers
- Company customers
- Dependencies on each supplier and customer
- Company's catalogs
- Company's press releases
- Media reports on the company
- Company's regulatory filings
- Competitive advantages and disadvantages
- Company forecast

Estimating Information about
Private Companies

Private companies are not required to provide any information to the public unless the company is in a regulatory industry, such as telecommunications, where there are various filings with state and federal agencies.

The lack of public information presents a problem when gathering information about a private company, especially since few private companies voluntarily make available marketing and financial data.

Although exact information is difficult to obtain, the search committee can use ratio analysis to estimate data about a private company. Ratios of key indicators, such as sales:headcount, are first determined for the industry using data available from industry associations and sources described in the literature search. Ratios can be developed using data from public companies in the industry if industry ratios are unavailable.

Ratios can be applied to estimated data regarding the private company. Here's how this works. Let's say that it is recognized within the industry that $1,000 of sales is generated for each employee. If the search committee can estimate the number of persons employed by a private company in the industry, then the ratio can be applied to estimate the sales volume.

In this case, the private company's employee headcount might be derived from company, industry, and government sources. Some companies go to the extreme of counting cars in the employee parking lot.

From Tim Miller, Webmergers.com

A Bold Strategy

Most B2C e-tailers have hunkered down to ride out the dotcom shakeout storm. But not HealthCentral.com (HCEN). This online health superstore is flying directly into the eye of the hurricane. It's trying to buy its way to profitability by snapping up its competitors.

HealthCentral has acquired three other e-tailers—that despite having its own stock price hammered as much as 95 percent off its modest high of $14. HealthCentral acquired the assets of More.com and its Comfort Living unit for 5 million shares worth roughly $6 million based on HCEN's stock price at the close of market the day before the deal was announced. The company had previously acquired Vitamins.com and certain assets of DrugEmporium.com, the Internet subsidiary of Drug Emporium, Inc., an Ohio-based pharmacy chain. HealthCentral also bought several online firms.

Once HealthCentral sees an acquisition that fits strategically, it asks the big question, "Does it accelerate our path to profitability?" says CEO Al Greene, who was involved in 39 acquisitions in his previous life as an executive in several health care companies. Added Greene, "They can't contribute to cash burn; they have to alleviate cash burn."

Since buying your way to profitability might sound about as logical as eating your way to slenderness, we asked Greene to explain how acquisitions might decrease cash burn. His responses are summarized below.

Buy vs. Build

Acquired infrastructure can save on development expenses. For example, in buying Drug Emporium, Greene acquired a technology platform that cost $13 million to build. Greene said he was preparing to spend nearly that amount to build a similar system from scratch. The deal also brought a Kentucky distribution center right near to a FedEx hub (as well as $3 million in inventory). Gaining the distribution center allowed HCEN to cancel its costly distribution deal with Bergen Brunswick, Greene said.

Procurement Economies

HealthCentral inherited Drug Emporium's purchasing deals. "We immediately achieved an eight percent decrease in our cost of goods," said Greene.

Marketing

Again, HealthCentral believes it gains by inheriting traffic flows, brand names, and marketing relationships. In the More.com purchase, for example, HCEN inherited a promotional relationship with the PharMor drugstore chain.

Shift Product Mix

The Comfort Living unit of More.com brought in a line of high-priced, high-margin back massagers, ergonomic office chairs, and other goods that create a more profitable profit mix.

Add Throughput

Adding new products to an existing distribution system increases optimization so long as it doesn't overwhelm the facilities.

Not surprisingly, another of the key questions HealthCentral.com asks while considering an acquisition is, Can it be easily integrated? Cultural and physical integration problems have killed more than one merger, but Greene claims to have integrated all of his deals in less than six weeks. Greene said what surprised him most about integrating Internet companies is "how easy it was compared with the health care distribution and services business," where he did nearly 40 deals in the past.

To be sure, HealthCentral didn't have to do much integration of cultures for the simple reason that most employees were laid off. "One of the reasons [merger integration] went so quickly is that we didn't do a lot of personnel integration—and that's the secret to getting value out of these deals," Greene said.

For example, HealthCentral laid off 75 of More.com's 100 employees and 110 of Drug Emporium's 150. Senior management is typically first to get the axe.

Other integration issues involve merger of multiple acquired brands. HealthCentral has taken the risky step of combining all of its brands under yet another new single brand, WebRX.

Greene sees the current climate for acquirers as somewhat of a buyers' market. "For a lot of these sellers, it's any port in a storm," he said. "Despite the fact that our stock is in the tank, venture capitalists and other investors see that they're converting their investment into another investment—in this case, Health Central—and continue to go along for the ride."

Has HealthCentral been getting bargains in its acquisitions? It's hard to use previous valuations as a benchmark, because those valuations were often exaggerated by Internet exuberance. But here are some benchmarks.

HealthCentral bought More.com for about $6 million in stock. The deal included Comfort Living, whose higher margin products expect to generate $8 million in sales, a promotional deal with the PharMor drugstore chain, and some 400,000 customers. By way of comparison, More.com raised $30 million at pre-money valuation of more than $200 million, Greene said.

Greene paid just over $7 million in stock for Drug Emporium. In return, he got $3 million in inventory, a $13 million technology platform; a bricks-and-mortar distribution center, ability to sell prescriptions, and an eight percent cut in cost of goods, thanks to Drug Emporium's purchasing contracts.

CONTACTING TARGETS

The literature search narrows the field to a manageable number of dotcom companies. At this stage, the search committee still avoids discounting candidates other than those that are obvious misfits. The literature search typically leaves information gaps about companies that can only be filled by contacting each dotcom.

The initial contact is a delicate procedure, since the merger or acquisition proposal is likely to be unsolicited. First, approach the chief executive officer, the chief financial officer, corporate directors, or owners of the dotcom. These contacts have a financial interest in the dotcom and are likely to benefit from a deal.

Avoid contacting anyone who may feel that your proposal is not in his or her best interest. These include heads of business units, counsel, and auditors who could lose their relationship with the dotcom should the deal be consummated.

Begin the conversation by stating that your firm intends to become a player in the dotcom's industry and you are unsure if your board of directors intends to acquire an existing company or create a startup company. This brief statement is sufficient to capture the dotcom's attention. Three possibilities will stir in the mind of the representative from the dotcom.

1. You've identified yourself as a new competitor, which the dotcom knows little or nothing about. This will surely generate questions from the dotcom representative, even if his or her company is not interested in selling.

2. You also implied that there are opportunities in your firm for someone who is experienced in the industry. The representative will be very eager to hear more about your plans if he or she is contemplating leaving the dotcom.

3. You've suggested that your firm may be interested in acquiring the dotcom, in which case the representative can financially gain from the deal, assuming he or she has a financial interest in the dotcom.

Follow up by inquiring if the representative knows if any firm in the industry is for sale. Your request can be taken in two ways: as a request for advice from an industry expert or as a direct inquiry as to whether or not the dotcom is for sale. In either case, you give the representative a polite way to reject or explore your overture.

Rarely can you expect a positive response because the dotcom knows nothing about you. Instead prepare yourself for hesitation and cautious inquires. Your objective is to make the dotcom feel comfortable about exploring your proposal.

Two important barriers to further discussions are the dotcom representative's lack of knowledge about your company and the role he or she will play after the deal is completed. Anticipate these issues, then take measures to address them before the dotcom raises the issues.

Be frank about your company. Volunteer financial, operational, and background information about yourself and the officers and board of directors of your company. Make it clear that your intention is to retain the expertise of any dotcom; however, use general terms to avoid any misrepresentation. For example, "retain the expertise" is achieved by keeping management in place or by hiring management as consultants. Such statements convey that your firm is capable of pulling off the deal and that it is an unlikely threat to key personnel in the dotcom. Avoid mentioning price or any merger or acquisition, since these items are covered in negotiations.

Move discussions to the next stage by suggesting a meeting. Exploring the possibilities of a merger or acquisition is a sensitive operation for the dotcom. Any outward sign of a deal has a ripple effect with employers, vendors, customers, and stockholders, especially if either or both companies are public corporations.

Choose a meeting place carefully. Find a neutral ground so both parties feel confidentiality is maintained. A hotel conference room is the best choice for the first meeting. Subsequent meetings can move to the offices of an investment banker, once the formal merger and acquisition process begins.

Create a written agenda that starts with a review of your company, followed by your understanding of the industry and the dotcom. Give the dotcom the opportunity to present its operations and correct any misunderstandings in your statements. The third agenda item is information you require, addressing the gaps in your literature search. Title this as "question and answer period." Keep the actual questions off the written agenda.

Expect to sign a nondisclosure agreement prior to the meeting. A nondisclosure agreement stipulates that information revealed during the meeting cannot be disseminated. You too should request that the dotcom sign a nondisclosure agreement to protect your information.

Share the agenda with the dotcom prior to the meeting and invite the company to include topics they'd like to cover. Price and terms of the deal should not be on the agenda of the first meeting.

Speak in general terms at first, then in more detail as the meeting progresses. Your objectives are to assure that the facts you elicited from your literature search are correct and that both companies feel there is a potential deal.

Conclude the meeting by highlighting how a merger or acquisition benefits both companies, if this remains true. You may discover there isn't a fit because of personalities or cultural differences between the firms.

If both sides feel there is a potential fit, then discussions move to the next phase, in which additional information is gathered to form the foundation for negotiations. These steps are discussed throughout this book.

Be prepared to spend months working on the deal. It is common for both sides to lose interest, so you must take steps to keep the deal alive. During that time, you and the dotcom will build a paper trail of representations of fact, which is used to support negotiations and as evidence in the event of a lawsuit brought by either party. It is not uncommon for deals to wind up in court over a verbal misrepresentation of material fact that inhibits the successful operation of the dotcom after the deal.

From Tim Miller, Webmergers.com

Why Aren't More Dotcoms Acquired Before They Fold?

Webmergers.com has been asking M&A experts to help explain why 130 Internet companies have shut down without finding merger partners, even at fire-sale prices. Here are some of the explanations:

- There's no there there.

Some Internet companies simply don't have a sustainable business model. Others simply have not yet built up assets of value, such as a strong team, proprietary technology, customer lists, intellectual property, brand or domain names, or other assets.

- The company put all its eggs in the funding basket.

Many of the failed companies were expecting second- or third-round funding that appeared always to be just around the corner. By the time they realized their investors had fled, they were already facing shutdown.

- They waited too long.

Some companies began trying to sell themselves after cash began to run out. In that desperate condition, they lost all leverage with buyers and any ability to hire a good intermediary. Most advisors recommend that an M&A strategy be implemented early on, while cash is plentiful—if not with the very first draft of the business plan. For example, Chase H&Q put Evite, the online invitations company, on the auction block while Evite still had $17 million in cash.

- VCs don't have time to play matchmaker.

Venture capitalists and incubators are currently overwhelmed with simply tending to the basic needs of their portfolios. They don't currently have resources for the time-consuming business of shopping a company. In some cases it's easier for them just to shut it down.

- Buyers no longer need to "buy talent."

The Internet explosion has caused the rapid education of thousands of technical and marketing professionals. With a much larger employee base to choose from, acquirers find it less necessary to buy companies just to obtain scarce Internet expertise.

- Bricks-and-mortar companies are sitting on the sidelines.

According to Webmergers.com's Q2 Web M&A Report, non-Internet companies accounted for only nine percent of total dollars spent to acquire Internet destinations in Q2. As one analyst said, "It might be just more fun for bricks-and-mortar companies to watch these dot-coms die."

USING BROKERS AND FINDERS

An alternative to searching for a dotcom is to enlist the services of a broker or finder. Brokers and finders perform similar functions in that they do the legwork to locate dotcoms that fit the needs of a company. However, they differ in their responsibilities.

A broker represents the company during the search and in the subsequent deal, and follows prescribed rules when negotiating the best deal for their client. A broker is an agent who has a fiduciary responsibility to represent one party to the deal, but is not permitted to represent both parties. The client he or she represents compensates the broker. Some jurisdictions require brokers to be licensed by the government.

A finder introduces both parties without representing either party and does not negotiate the deal. There is no fiduciary responsibility, and one or both parties compensate the finder. Typically, finders are not regulated and therefore don't require a license to operate.

The act of negotiations determines if a finder is acting as a broker. Courts view a finder as a broker if the finder discusses price or any terms of the deal. The mere lack of a broker's license does not exclude a finder from becoming a broker, although the finder is open to legal consequences in such cases.

Laws governing brokers and finders are based on state or local law rather than regulated by a federal agency. These regulations vary by state and locality. For example, some states make a distinction between a broker and finder, while other states treat a finder as a broker.

Another variation is with fees. Some states recognized nonwritten fee agreements, while other states prohibit fees that are not agreed upon in writing. Still other states prohibit fees paid to unlicensed brokers or finders.

Caution

Whenever you receive a solicitation from a broker or finder, respond in writing, especially if you reject their services. Make sure fees and terms of a broker or finder agreement are also in writing should you decide to employ the broker or finder. Keep a written record of all phone conversations and meetings with a broker or finder. Written records are used in court if the broker or finder makes claim to fees that you feel are unearned. Pay special attention to deals that cross state and national boundaries because laws in each locality might apply to your relationship with the broker or finder.

Caution

Avoid volunteers, finders who make unsolicited contact with a broad range of companies, proposing mergers and acquisitions. They don't represent anyone, yet stand to collect a fee if you contact a dotcom they identify and the prospective deal is within a jurisdiction that recognizes a verbal fee agreement.

Caution

Don't avoid paying fees to a broker or finder if, as a result of their effort, you consummate a deal. Your company could be exposed to action under the Racketeer Influenced and Corrupt Organizations Act (RICO), which imposes triple damages if successfully prosecuted.

Brokers and Finders Fees

Fees are based on the price of the deal. Historically, the Lehman Scale was used, in which the fee was five percent of the first million, four percent of the second million, three percent of the third million, two percent of the fourth million, and one percent of additional millions.

Two problems exist with the Lehman Scale. First, the deal price is difficult to determine because of the structure of the deal. Simply said, there isn't a clear and distinct price upon which to apply the Lehman Scale.

The other concern is the size of deal. Prices have escalated since the Lehman Scale was implemented, which leads to outrageous fees when the percentages are applied to today's prices.

Many companies bypass the Lehman Scale and negotiate a flat fee, regardless of the ultimate price of the deal. There are three types of fees addressed in the negotiation: the base fee, the closing fee, and the extraordinary fee. The base fee is the amount paid regardless of whether the deal is consummated. The closing fee is an additional sum paid when the deal is consummated. The extraordinary fee is paid if unusual circumstances occur, such as in a hostile takeover.

USING INVESTMENT BANKERS AND COMMERCIAL BANKERS

Investment bankers and commercial bankers have overlapping roles in mergers and acquisitions. Both firms provide advisory services to companies and offer temporary financing, called *bridge loans,* to facilitate a transaction. Investment bankers and commercial bankers differ in that an investment banker underwrites securities for the deal, which commercial banks are prohibited to do by the Glass Seagall Act. However, subsidiaries of commercial banks can underwrite securities within very strict guidelines.

Tech Talk

Bridge Loan: An obligation that finances a merger or acquisition to consummate the transaction before permanent financing is in place.

Advisory services include opinions on financing deals, restructuring debt, and the fairness of an offer. You'll learn more about how these services play a role in the due diligence process in Chapter 2. Investment bankers and commercial bankers are in the position to render an objective opinion on every aspect of a deal. These services are often utilized to balance the workload of working through a deal between in-house staff by using a team of experts provided by banks.

These bankers also provide an independent view on any aspect of the deal required by the company. A few companies involved in a merger or acquisition enlist the services of multiple bankers, asking each to render an opinion on the same issue. The collective opinion provides a consensus, which the company uses to address the issue.

Companies should be concerned when dealing with an investment banker or commercial banker, because bankers can advise many suitors of the dotcom, although this is avoided to prevent the impression of conflict of interest.

Likewise, bankers cannot tie in deals that require you to use more services than you require from the bank. This means that a banker cannot link an advisory opinion to using the bank for a bridge loan.

Tech Talk

Tie-In: An arrangement by which a banker links more than one service and requires a client to use the linked services, regardless of whether these services are necessary.

In addition to offering advisory and loan services, bankers also fulfill the role of a broker and finder. It is not at all uncommon for a banker to seek a buyer for a division of a client's company. A banker becomes a finder if a buyer is found through the banker's efforts. The banker earns a broker's fee if the banker negotiates all or part of the deal. In such cases, rules governing brokers and finders apply to bankers.

Caution

Contracts for services must be in writing and clearly identify deliverables and fees. Bankers receive different fees for each service. For example, there is a fee for an advisory opinion and another for brokering the deal.

Caution

Bankers might employ the services of brokers or finders for your deal. It is critical that bankers reveal such arrangements, let you qualify the broker or finder, and clearly identify who pays the broker or finder fee. You must authorize everyone working on your behalf during the deal.

From Tim Miller, Webmergers.com

Emergency Triage for Dotcoms

The Internet train wreck this year created huge demand for emergency room doctors to save the victims—or to at least salvage some vital organs. Now, a new breed of advisors is stepping in to fill the need. They have names like the Internet Recovery Group and the Internet Workout Group.

They specialize in a wide variety of tasks, including disposing of assets; advising on cash flow management; managing creditors and funders; finding merger partners; identifying and selling assets; literally moving in and taking over management of the company; and buying distressed companies outright.

The need is enormous. "You are never going to see again for a long period of time such a huge proliferation of businesses that are going to collapse—or collapse into one another," said Brian Millman, a vice president at Gertzler & Co. Gertzler & Co is a 30-year-old New York City turnaround firm that started an internal Internet practice. "And the only way you're going to see them collapse into each other is through M&A transactions."

Depending on the source of the estimate, there are anywhere from several thousand to tens of thousands of Internet startups and publicly traded companies in existence. Some experts, like Merrill Lynch analyst Henry Blodgett, have predicted that as many as 75 percent of these companies will be forced to close or merge with other companies in coming years.

A number of shops are positioning themselves to meet the coming deal frenzy.

- New York City-based Gertzler is a traditional "crisis management" firm that is switching some resources from widgets to Web sites. It has two Internet companies under its wing. The 11-person boutique typically takes over management of a firm until it's turned around, focusing on triage of debt, helping determine which bills to pay and which units to sell off.

- Across the continent from Gertzler, just north of the Silicon Valley accident scene, Steve Gerbsman of Gerbsman Partners has formed The Internet Recovery Group (IRG) to assist in selling assets, restructuring, and otherwise acting to salvage "under-performing, under-capitalized and under-valued" Internet companies. With six Internet deals live or completed, Gerbsman says he can typically recover 30 to 60 percent of investors' dollars, given the right combination of buyer dynamics, assets, and deal currency. Gerbsman has been doing traditional turnaround work for the past 25 years.

- Down in Austin, Texas, a venture capital firm and an investment group have teamed up to invest in 10 to 12 "distressed e-commerce" companies by the end of the year. The new group, Eco Associates, is a joint venture of investment bank Capstar Partners, LLC and venture capital firm Interfase Capital, L.P. Eco Associates has already provided an undisclosed amount of financing to Mall.com, an online shopping and entertainment site. The group's model is a modified-incubator approach—perhaps best described as an "intensive care" unit for dotcoms. The intensive care comes in the form of plans to cut 50 to 75 percent out of development costs at its targets and outsourcing that development to an affiliated fleet of Internet services firms.

- On an island off the North Carolina coast, Wall Street veteran Jim Nesfield has founded The Internet Workout Group, which has been buying up bargains among DSL resellers and Internet security companies. "We're owners," Nesfield says. "We're vultures, true vultures, and we try to buy it as cheaply as possible...we're buying for good reason—the assets are temporarily undervalued." Nesfield doesn't do asset sales because he thinks selling in the current climate often leaves money on the table. "I've seen companies with $26 million invested sell for $1 million," he said. "We believe there's value in some of these companies."

- Even online auction and trading sites are getting into the vulture action. Bid4Assets.com, an online marketplace for distressed assets, recently put on sale the domain name, office furniture, and other assets of collapsed Washington, DC-area Web site CivicZone.com, which is in Chapter 7 liquidation.

The current Internet carnage is nothing new to technology, says Gerbsman. "This is not unlike any new frontier in technology," he said. "You first have the wild, wild West, only this was more wildly exuberant than most. Then you have consolidation, which is the phase we're in now. Then comes stabilization and, finally, regrowth."

Gerbsman and others point to the unique challenges in working with troubled dotcoms compared with working with manufacturing and other hard-asset companies that have typically been the targets of turnaround specialists.

- Typically, there are few hard assets like drill presses, factories or raw materials.
- Typically, there's no senior lender or debt source.
- Company executives are often inexperienced and lack operating experience.
- Executives are often saddled with a strong sense of "denial" that they're in trouble—sometimes not waking up to the truth until it's too late.
- Some companies simply have flawed business models that don't generate cash and can't get to cash breakeven.

Perhaps most startling to veterans is the sloppiness of business discipline among many dotcom startups. "Basically, these companies went public on the fact that their revenue growth was going to be exponential," said Millman, "but even with some significant marketing expenses, these companies are still exhibiting stagnating or even declining growth. A lot of guys were proud they did a deal with AOL, but never did an analysis on whether it's profitable to pay AOL $10 million to get 2 million customers a year."

Gerbsman says he can reclaim 30 to 60 percent of an investment, depending on the amount of competitive bidding, the quality of the assets, and the appreciation potential of any paper being issued to buy the company.

The tech wreck has also produced a new breed of buyout firm that specializes in Internet and other technology companies. More recently, players such as Francisco Partners LP, the $1.8 billion fund headed by Robertson Stephens cofounder Sanford Robertson, have moved into the space, with one of its target "fallen angels." Francisco Partners in February spent $55 million to buy foundering technology concern XcelleNet and is looking at numerous others. New York investment bank Wasserstein Perella Group also dispatched its chief surgeon, President Frederic Seegal, to San Francisco to head up its dotcom clinic, whose aim is to help out in Internet consolidation.

One of the challenges in selling an Internet company is assessing and packaging assets that are often "squishy" compared with traditional widget companies. Dotcoms offer a few computers, desks, and promotional Frisbees, of course, but the real assets are difficult-to-assess things like software, traffic, user loyalty, brand equity, human knowledge, and of course customer lists. Customer lists often emerge as a core asset, but even they often are difficult.

For one, they lose value with age at about the same rate as croissants. In addition, privacy concerns have crimped the sale of individual customer lists that are not part of a company sale. Here are the assets that Steven Gerbsman of the Internet Recovery Group looks for in an Internet company.

- Customer and vendor lists
- Patents and trademarks
- Intellectual capital of the people
- Strategic relationships
- Code and domain name
- Process for developing the technology

LEGAL CONSIDERATIONS

Corporations are governed by reams of regulations that must be considered whenever a company is considering a merger or acquisition. Failure to identify and address such concerns can have a far-reaching effect on the deal, which in some situations can nullify negotiations.

The legal aspects of a deal become complex because the arrangement might fall within the jurisdiction of federal, state, and local regulatory authorities, each of which must be explored to assure the merger or acquisition is in compliance.

Some regulations, such as employee benefits, antitrust, and security laws, pertain to all corporations. Other regulations, such as transmission licenses used to create a wireless Internet connection, are focused on the nature of the business.

Let's say you thought about acquiring an ISP. Intuitively, you assume the ISP industry is an unregulated, since fundamentally, the ISP retails bandwidth supplied by a telecommunications carrier and provides ancillary services such as Web hosting.

However, the ISP might own real estate, which falls under local building, zoning, and fire code. Federal and state environmental protection agencies become involved if the building contains asbestos as electrical wrapping or insulation, or if it has an underground oil tank used for heating. The tank could leak, polluting neighboring property and resulting in an order to remove the contaminated soil and replace it with clean fill.

Attorneys who specialize in mergers and acquisitions are attuned to identifying these regulations and how they apply to a particular deal. Therefore, it is highly recommended that such a specialist become involved early on in the negotiations and due diligence process to assure the deal will not run afoul of the law.

Your attorney must provide a list of regulations that need to be reviewed, then identify those regulations that influence the deal. This is called a *regulatory audit,* which clearly specifies

- Regulations with which the deal is in compliance
- Regulations with which the deal is not in compliance
- Steps necessary to bring the deal into compliance
- Regulatory authorities who must approve all or part of the deal
- Timeline for the regulatory authorities' approval process
- Material required by the regulatory authorities to support the approval process
- Pending regulations that affect the deal

The timeline is critical to planning a merger or acquisition, for some regulatory agencies require six months before your deal reaches their agenda. Incorporating the timeline in the plan assures that all regulatory issues are addressed at the time of closing.

Tech Talk

Regulatory Audit: A list of laws and regulations that cover the deal.

The regulatory audit provided by your attorney should be shared with the dotcom, since its management might be required by law to address regulatory issues prior to the transaction. In addition, environmental and other similar issues should be resolved before transfer occurs; otherwise, the expense of achieving compliance falls on the buyer.

Antitrust

You need to be sensitive to antitrust concerns, especially in segments of the industry where there are few significant competitors. Regulatory authorities must answer this question: Will the merger or acquisition create a company that has the resources to discourage or eliminate competition in its industry?

There are three aspects of a deal that are considered. These are conglomerate acquisitions, horizontal acquisitions, and vertical acquisitions. A conglomerate acquisition occurs when the company and dotcom are in different industries. A horizontal acquisition occurs when the dotcom is a competitor of the company. A vertical acquisition occurs when the dotcom is either a customer or supplier of the company.

The Clayton Act and the Hart Scott Rodino Antitrust Improvements Act establish federal regulations overseeing antitrust matters and are enforced by the Federal Trade Commission and the Department of Justice.

The Clayton Act specifies, among other factors, that members of the board of directors cannot sit on the board of a competing company. An exception exists for representatives of banks and other financial institutions who have fiduciary interests in both companies.

The Hart Scott Rodino Antitrust Improvements Act requires the company and the dotcom to provide the Federal Trade Commission and the Department of Justice with notice of an impending merger or acquisition. However, there are exceptions to the notification rules of the Hart Scott

Rodino Antitrust Improvements Act; generally, companies required to send notifications must have

- Gross assets of $100 million or more
- $10 million in gross assets or annual sales prior to the transaction
- 50 percent or more of the voting stock of the dotcom
- Contractual power to designate a majority of the new company's directors

Notification involves providing the Federal Trade Commission and the Department of Justice information about both companies, including financials grouped by the North American Industrial Classification code. Filings are exempt from the Freedom of Information Act and therefore are not made public unless the information is necessary for judicial or administrative action. The information is reviewed to determine if the deal will have an anticompetitive effect if allowed to proceed. The review takes about 30 days to complete and can be extended another 20 days if the agency requires additional information about the deal. Any violations are reported to the companies, who must remedy the agency's concerns before closing the deal.

Deals involving companies in industries where the four largest companies control less than half the market are unlikely to run afoul of antitrust regulations. Agencies also look at factors that make companies unlikely to become involved in collusion. These include

- Companies are not direct competitors in the same market.
- Products are significantly different.
- Price is not the only deciding factor regarding purchase.
- Products are significantly different.
- Rapid change in technology within the industry.
- The lack of previous collusion by companies involved in the deal and within the industry as a whole.

SUMMARY

Consolidation occurs when companies combine through a merger or acquisition. A merger occurs when one company's stock is exchanged for another company's stock. The company that gives up its stock, called a target, is considered the decedent, and no longer exists. The remaining company is called the survivor. A merger is a legal matter and has nothing to do with the operations of either company.

An acquisition occurs when one corporation buys the stock or assets of another corporation. Both corporations exist after the acquisition. After a corporation acquires shares, corporate officers can merge the two corporations without approval of stockholders. This is called a short form merger.

Corporations acquire assets rather than stock of another corporation as a way to limit liability and to simplify the transaction. Stockholders must approve all mergers and acquisitions, including the sale of assets except, in the short form merger.

There are two types of acquisitions. A friendly acquisition is a transaction in which both the buyer and seller agree to the acquisition. A hostile acquisition, also known as a hostile takeover, is a transaction in which the seller is against the acquisition.

The merger and acquisition process begins by identifying the strengths and weaknesses of your company, then finding a dotcom company that compensates for those weaknesses.

The board of directors creates an executive committee to develop and monitor the planning guidelines. The planning guidelines identify each person in the corporate-planning hierarchy, decision makers, and how investments are compared with developing similar opportunities within the company.

At the center of every merger and acquisition strategy is the efficient use of cash flows by redeploying cash flows from low to high yielding investments. Capital invested in a business operation generates cash. The cash can be reinvested into the operations or invested in other opportunities that return a higher yield.

Planning for a merger or acquisition occurs at five levels. These are the enterprise level, corporate level, business unit level, product line level, and functional level. The enterprise level is where the board of directors reviews the use of cash flows and decides if a change in is order. The corporate level realigns similar business units into groups. Group presidents are responsible for maximizing long-term return of the group by redistributing cash flows generated by operating units under their control. Their strategies can include selling off or acquiring business units.

The business unit level organizes similar product lines into a business unit. The business unit manager is responsible to assure a predictable cash flow from the unit by reinvesting returns into existing products, new products, or acquired products.

The product line level devises ways to continue a cash flow from a particular line of products by carefully monitoring the product life cycle. Product managers must introduce new products to replace existing products before cash flows from those products dwindle. The functional level addresses how to increase cash flows from a product by modifying the product's manufacturing process.

Managers at each level of the planning process must calculate the net present value of its unit. The net present value indicates the current value of future cash flows and is used to determine the market value of the unit. The market value is the criteria used by managers to determine if continuing operations, acquiring a new unit, and/or selling the unit can enhance a unit's cash flow.

The fit chart guides the planning team through the process of identifying dotcoms that complement the company by pinpointing the strengths and weaknesses of the company and of dotcoms; the results of the fit chart are used to rank dotcoms.

The fit chart considers three strategies: horizontal integration, vertical integration, and diversification. Horizontal integration is when a company expands its current business by acquiring a competitor or by moving existing operations into new territories. Vertical integration is when a company expands by acquiring a supplier or customer. Acquiring a supplier is called backward integration and acquiring a customer is called forward integration. Diversification is expansion into a different business that extends existing offerings to customers or operates in an entirely different industry.

Two common approaches used to locate dotcoms are using outside resources and using in-house resources. Outside resources are finders and brokers. In-house resources are corporate staff.

There are two major objectives in finding prospective dotcoms. First is to find a dotcom that complements your company's objectives of either horizontal or vertical integration or diversification. Next, dotcoms must be screened to assure there is prima facie evidence to consider the dotcom.

The search begins with a search of the literature. Literature is any publication that discusses competitors, customers, and suppliers, and covers news of industries that are targeted for expansion by the company.

The literature search must be goal-oriented; the first goal is to understand a dotcom industry, including economic indicators that affect the industry and the industry structure. The next goal is to identify companies within the industry and rank them by importance. The final goal is to identify key people in the industry who are recognized experts in various aspects of the business.

The literature search gathers qualitative and quantitative information, such as profits, margins, sales, and sources of profit, about an industry and about dotcoms. The search committee uses this information to understand how targeted industries and significant companies within the industry work.

The literature search narrows the field to a manageable number of dotcom companies, but leaves information gaps about companies that can only be filled by contacting each dotcom.

The initial contact is a delicate procedure. First, approach the chief executive officer, the chief financial officer, corporate directors, or owners of the company. These contacts have a financial interest in the dotcom and are likely to benefit from a deal. Avoid contacting anyone who may feel that your proposal is not in his or her best interest.

Begin the conversation by stating that your firm intends to become a player in the dotcom's industry and you are unsure if your board of directors intends to acquire an existing company or create a startup company. Follow up by inquiring if the representative knows of any firm in the industry that is for sale.

Two important barriers to further discussions are the dotcom representative's lack of knowledge about your company and the role he or she will play after the deal is completed. Anticipate these issues, then take measures to address them before the dotcom representative raises them.

Volunteer information about your operations, financing, company officers, your board of directors, and yourself. Make it clear that your intention is to retain the expertise of any acquired company; however, use general terms so as not to make any misrepresentation.

Move discussions to the next stage by suggesting a meeting. Choose a meeting place carefully, since any outward sign of a deal has a ripple effect with employers, vendors, customers, and stockholders, especially if either or both companies are public corporations.

Find a neutral ground so both parties feel that confidentiality is maintained. A hotel conference room is the best choice for the first meeting. Subsequent meetings can move to the offices of an investment banker, once the formal merger and acquisition process begins.

Create a written agenda that starts with a review of your company, followed by your understanding of the industry and the dotcom. Give the dotcom the opportunity to present its operations and correct any misunderstandings in your statements. The third agenda item is information you require, addressing the gaps in your literature search. Title this as "question and answer period." Keep the actual questions off the written agenda.

Expect to sign a nondisclosure agreement prior to the meeting. A nondisclosure agreement stipulates that information revealed during the meeting cannot be disseminated. You too should request that the dotcom sign a nondisclosure agreement to protect your information.

Share the agenda with the dotcom prior to the meeting and invite them to include topics they'd like to cover. Price and terms of the deal should not be on the agenda of the first meeting.

Speak in general terms at first, then in more detail as the meeting progresses. Your objectives are to assure that the facts you elicited from your literature search are correct and that both companies feel there is a potential deal.

Conclude the meeting by highlighting how a merger or acquisition benefits both companies, if this remains true. You may discover there isn't a fit because of personalities or cultural differences between both firms.

An alternative to in-house searches is to enlist the services of a broker or finder. A broker represents the company during the search and in the subsequent deal. A broker is an agent who has a fiduciary responsibility to represent one party to the deal, but is not permitted to represent both parties. A finder introduces both parties without representing either party and does not negotiate the deal. There is no fiduciary responsibility, and one or both parties compensate the finder.

Investment bankers and commercial bankers have overlapping roles in mergers and acquisitions. Both firms provide advisory services to companies and offer temporary financing, called bridge loans, to facilitate a transaction. They differ in that an investment banker underwrites securities for the deal, which commercial banks are prohibited from doing by the Glass Seagall Act. However, subsidiaries of commercial banks can underwrite securities within very strict guidelines.

The legal aspects of a merger and acquisition are complex, because the deal might fall within the jurisdiction of federal, state, and local regulatory authorities, each of which must be explored to assure the merger or acquisition is in compliance.

Attorneys who specialize in mergers and acquisitions must provide the company and the dotcom with a regulatory audit that lists regulations that might influence the deal.

QUESTIONS

1. Explain how to begin the merger and acquisition process.

2. Explain the role of regulatory agencies in a merger and acquisition.

3. Explain the importance of cash flow in a merger and acquisition.

4. Explain the role of investment bankers in a merger and acquisition.

5. Explain why government agencies investigate mergers and acquisitions for antitrust violations.

6. Explain the difference between a broker and a finder.

7. Explain why business units must be continually measured in net present value.

8. Explain how cash flows in a product line can be redirected.

9. Explain why large corporations organize business units into groups.

10. Explain how you would approach a dotcom.

CHAPTER 2

Due Diligence

A careful examination avoids costly mistakes.

—Anonymous

In This Chapter

- Due Diligence Basics
- Investigation Checklist
- Legal Investigation
- Environmental Investigation
- Evaluating the Results of Due Diligence

A gentleman's agreement has its place in a game of cards, but it has no place in a merger or acquisition, because a deal is a complex arrangement that contains many twists and turns, each of which can lead to a misunderstanding.

Emotions play an important role in a deal, especially when the company is anxious to consummate the agreement so it can realize the expected benefits of the merger or acquisition. However, emotions work against the best interest of the company, since emotions are founded on perceptions and perceptions are not necessarily fact.

A clever CEO of an Internet telephony company used an interesting technique to entice private investors to discuss opportunities to become a part of her firm. She leased office space in a modern but modest high-rise office building. For a premium on her lease, she had the exclusive right to place the name of her company on the office building.

Whenever customers or potential investors visited her offices, they assumed her company owned or leased the entire office building. This gave the impression that her company had substantial cash flow and assets, which was not the case.

In another case, a dotcom company that created an online community boasted to potential strategic partners of having 30,000 registered members who were programmers. The company supported its claim with an audit report, prepared by a reputable accounting firm, that verified the count.

The numbers were modest to say the least, but sufficient to attract firms who wanted a presence before this niche audience. However, a careful examination of the audit report showed that the information contained on the member registration forms had not been verified. Therefore, the dotcom company wasn't sure itself if any of its 30,000 members actually were programmers.

Strategic partners in this case anticipated that 30,000 programmers frequently visited the Web site and participated in features, such as technical roundtables, offered on the site. However, the audit report never made such claims. The auditors simply counted the number of names in the Web site's member database. They never explored the number of times a typical member visited the site or the accuracy of the membership registration forms.

No deception exists in either the Internet telephony company or the dotcom company examples because the owners of these companies did not make any misrepresentations. Instead, they presented only the best side of their offerings and left investors and strategic partners to discover the downside for themselves.

Expect a dotcom to highlight aspects their business that strengthen your company's operation. Don't expect a dotcom to voluntarily mention its weaknesses. It is your responsibility to ask the proper questions that probe every area of the dotcom's business and challenge any implicit or explicit claims that are made to you by the dotcom. This is called the *due diligence process,* which is the topic of this chapter.

DUE DILIGENCE BASICS

Experts in mergers and acquisitions recommend that due diligence focus on three areas of interest to the company.

1. Is the dotcom advantageous to the company's stockholders?
2. What is the value of the dotcom?
3. Can the company fund the deal?

Before answering these questions, your management team must verify all information known about the target industry and information that the dotcom represents about itself. The assumption when beginning the due diligence process is not to assume anything. The objectives are to identify misrepresentations and to identify underutilized resources that can, if properly managed, increase cash flow.

Tech Talk

Target: A term that describes the company that is being merged or acquired.

Approach the process with a clean slate, disregarding positive and negative opinions that you received regarding the dotcom. Positive and negative opinions are likely to be based on a combination of fact and perception—and maybe misperceptions.

The main purpose of due diligence is to separate fact from fiction, then to arrive at a clear and honest presentment of the dotcom and the proposed deal. Failure to achieve this result could lead to decisions and strategies founded on misinformation and later unraveled when the facts are known—sometimes after the deal agreement is signed.

Tech Talk

Deal Agreement: The document agreed to by the company and dotcom that specifies details of the merger or acquisition.

Whether or not a deal is in the best interest of your company depends on how well you and your management team can predict future earnings of the target. Forecasting isn't a precise science. Therefore, there is no guarantee of future performance. The best any management team can expect is to review the past, identify significant factors that influence earnings, and then extrapolate data to glimpse into the future.

A key component to a forecast is the past performance of a dotcom; historical events can be used by the management team to identify significant earning factors. Historical events about a dotcom are contained in the dotcom's records.

Due diligence recreates the dotcom's history from its incorporation to each facet of its current operations. It is only after the due diligence process is completed that your management team is assured that they "know" the dotcom. A majority of problems that occur after a merger or acquisition is completed can be traced to a poor execution of the due diligence process.

For example, the CEO of a dotcom may voice a rosy future for growth of its industry. The company may accept the CEO's forecast at face value, especially if the CEO is a recognized industry expert. However, the company's trust could be unfounded unless the CEO supports his claim with an industry survey conducted by an independent, unbiased, respectable firm. Even if such a survey exists, the company needs to verify that the survey addressed the CEO's claim and that it is current. The survey could be three years old, trying to forecast an industry that dramatically changes every year and a half.

If the company accepts the CEO's claims, then the company is basing its industry forecast on expert speculation of the CEO, based on outdated information. Although the CEO in this case isn't intentionally misrepresenting facts, the CEO is giving an insufficiently founded opinion.

From Tim Miller, Webmergers.com

Sick Stocks Mean Buyout

Buyout funds, many of which have been hungrily eyeing the Internet, are salivating over the collapse in Internet stock prices. To them, the market slump spells one thing—the buffet line.

"Every tragedy creates an opportunity," said Scott Kelly, the 35-year-old CEO of M&A West, Inc., who bought its third Internet company. Even though his company is smarting from a nearly 50 percent market hit of its own, he says the downturn "does give us the opportunity to acquire some private, and in some cases, public, Internet companies at better valuations. Some of these companies have spent a lot of money building a base of users—now we can buy those [customer] databases and make money with them."

Traditional LBO funds and a range of buyout/incubator hybrids have been flocking to the Internet gold rush. Players range from old-line LBO firms like KKR, Forstmann Little, and Hicks Muse Tate & Furst to new hybrids like Silver Lake Partners LLC and incubators such as Idealab!, CMGI, and Divine Interventures, Inc. (DVIN). These funds are similar to LBOs without the "L"—they typically aren't using leverage, but tend to be much more willing than VCs to take majority stakes and get involved in managing and combining the properties they acquire.

Kelly said he is looking to buy profitable companies that are immediately accretive to M&A West earnings. M&A West then aims to build additional revenue through organic growth and by seeking synergies among its portfolio.

It then plows cash flow back into marketing and development. Kelly cited Faludi as a good example of what he looks for. He said the company has been profitable for eight years on the strength of consulting with a blue-chip customer base. Its applications, which provide front-end technology for e-commerce applications, are synergistic with existing M&A West portfolio companies.

"The idea," explained Kelly, "is that we use a traditional 'growing a business' approach to the nontraditional Internet." A prime example of the nontraditional approach, he said, is an e-commerce company that "did its first round of VC funding and blew a third of it on Super Bowl advertising. That's really playing into the VC game. [VCs] are like the drug dealer in the schoolyard. They give you a little bit to get you hooked, and after that they charge you an arm and a leg."

For Kelly, the crash in tech stocks is a two-bagger. Not only does it bring takeover prospects into shooting range, it also lowers the expectations of private sellers. "Everybody has been thinking they ought to be a billionaire," he said. Looking forward, Kelly sees potential opportunities in the e-grocer arena and financial services, where M&A West already has a position with VLDC Technologies, venture capital portal VentureList.com, stock research engine InvestorPackages.com, and LinuxFunding.com.

The Beginning

Due diligence starts when you assemble the strengths and weaknesses of an industry and dotcoms, as described in Chapter 1, "Identifying and Prequalifying Targets." Each piece of information learned is listed, along with the source of the information and a confidence level.

Tech Talk

Confidence Level: An indication of how sure you are that the information accurately represents the dotcom. A confidence level is noted as a percentage of confidence, where 100 percent represents total confidence in the information.

Let's say you are exploring the online flower retail industry as a potential area to expand your firm's product line. You obtain industry data from an industry association that estimates the size of the market. This information is noted, then you assess the accuracy of the information.

Is the data reliable? Is the association a major player in the industry? Is the estimate based on a proven statistical method? Was the survey conducted by a reputable, unbiased organization? Is the estimate current? These are the common questions you need to ask when validating the information. Validation techniques are discussed throughout this chapter. Next, assign a confidence level to the information, based on your evaluation. The confidence level is 100 percent if a reputable organization was hired by a major industry association three months ago to conduct the survey, using a widely accept statistical method. You can say that you are 100 percent confident that the survey result is correct.

In contrast, a two-year-old survey produced by the same organization and association should be assigned a confidence level of 75 percent depending on how rapidly changes occur in the industry. You can say that you are 75 percent confident that the survey result is correct.

The confidence level assigned to information gathered in the due diligence process is subjective rather than statistically accurate, and it represents your management team's best assessment of the data.

Appraising Assets

The fit chart and other methods discussed in Chapter 1 are used to address the issue of whether or not the dotcom is a good addition to the company. Once the company settles on a dotcom, the next step is to evaluate the dotcom, beginning with an appraisal of its assets.

Assets are divided into two general categories, *used* assets and *unused* assets. A used asset is something used in the business operations. An unused asset is something owned by the dotcom but not used in running the business. For example, an Internet service provider (ISP) owns several high-end servers that are used to host Web sites. These are used assets. The same dotcom owns a facility acquired in a previous merger that is rented to another firm. The facility is the original site of an acquired ISP whose business was combined with the ISP's existing facility. The original facility is an unused asset because, although rented, revenues from the property are not material to the ISP's business.

Within the used and unused categories of assets, assets are divided into *tangible* and *intangible* assets. A tangible asset is a building, server, and other things that you can touch. An intangible asset is goodwill, trademarks, copyrights, and patents. These are things you cannot touch, but that have a value to the dotcom.

Tech Talk

Goodwill: is an intangible asset that takes into account the value added to a dotcom as a result of patronage and reputation.

The due diligence process must identify assets of a dotcom and determine each asset's market value. For example, the process must decide the current value of each server owned by an ISP. Likewise, a value must be assigned to the goodwill of the dotcom.

Evaluating the assets of a dotcom is a complex issue that is fraught with controversy. Accountants from both the company and the dotcom are likely to agree on the value of tangible assets such as a server, because both use standard accounting rules to establish the asset's current value. However, assessing the value of goodwill and other intangible assets is less precise than evaluating tangible assets. How much is the dotcom's name and reputation worth? It varies in each case. The name and reputation of amazon.com is far more valuable than Jim's e-bookstore. Yet assigning a dollar value to either is subjective.

The best approach when evaluating the assets of a dotcom is to employ a professional appraiser who specializes in assessing the kinds of assets found in a dotcom. Actually, many appraisers are needed because each has different expertise. For example, a real estate appraiser sets a value on real property while an appraiser specializing in software engineering places a value on the dotcom's software.

Always choose an appraiser whose qualifications are verifiable, since the appraiser's recommendations become a major component of negotiating the deal. Ideally, the appraiser is sanctioned by a government agency or trade association, and has passed a qualifying examination. Some areas of expertise, such as software engineering, are not sanctioned. In this case, find an appraiser whose experience, qualifications, and reputation are recognized in the industry.

Both the company and the dotcom should employ their own appraisers, each of who will have their client's best interest in mind. Expect that no two appraisers will reach the same value for an asset. They will differ; however, the differences define a range within which to negotiate a fair market value for the asset.

There are two steps in the appraisal process of due diligence. First, appraisers render a tentative value for each asset, the sum of which determines the tentative value of the dotcom. Keep in mind that there is likely to be more than one tentative value, depending on the stage of the deal.

The initial tentative value is when the company narrows the field to a handful of dotcoms. A rough appraisal is often made without the intentions of the company known to the dotcom. The initial tentative value gives the company a ballpark value that is used to estimate the affordability of the dotcom.

A formal tentative value is determined when the company begins pursuing a dotcom. The deal is still in the preliminary phase, although the dotcom is aware of the company's interest and is likely to assist the company with information during the evaluation process. The formal tentative value is sufficient for the company to devise a financing plan and to initiate formal negotiations with the dotcom. Both the company and the dotcom conduct a thorough appraisal as negotiation progresses. The result of the thorough appraisal becomes the basis for determining the price of the deal.

It is advisable that the company also appraise its own assets, especially if the intent is to merge the company and the dotcom. The value of the company's assets is material to stockholders in the dotcom. Lenders who will finance the deal use the appraisal of the company's assets, as is discussed in Chapter 3, "Structuring and Financing the Deal."

From-Birth Investigation

Due diligence requires the company to perform a *from-birth* investigation of the dotcom. This means going back to when the dotcom was formed and documenting each event that has led to the dotcom's current status.

An intense investigation can seem to be overkill, especially if the dotcom is well respected in the industry. However, reputations can be misleading and are sometimes concocted by manipulation of the press. In addition, facts assumed to be true are sometimes not true on close examination. For example, it isn't unheard of that a well-known product name has not been protected because the dotcom failed to register the appropriate documents. Yet the product name is a valuable intangible asset that is presumed to be owned by the dotcom. However, no one legally owns the product name. A from-birth investigation quickly reveals such problems.

Begin the investigation by searching public records to verify that the proper documents were filed to form the corporation. Typically, the Secretary of State of the state of incorporation is the repository of these papers. Public records indicate the date of incorporation, whether or not the corporation continues to exist in good standing, and the articles of incorporation. Although a corporation might be properly formed and registered with the state, the corporation is obligated to abide by laws and pay an annual franchise fee. Failure to do either of these could negate or suspend the right of the corporation to operate within a jurisdiction. You need to know of any such problems and give the dotcom an opportunity to resolve these issues before closing the deal.

The articles of incorporation is a public document that explicitly defines the corporation's purpose and rules under which the corporation operates. For example, the articles of incorporation could state that the corporation is created to auction merchandise over the Internet. The articles of incorporation must be amended if the corporation also chooses to become an e-tailor of merchandise.

The laws of the jurisdiction prohibit the corporation from conducting business outside the scope of the articles of incorporation. However, it is a common practice to word the articles of incorporation in such a way as to permit the corporation to conduct any kind of business.

The articles of incorporation also provides a history of any material changes that have occurred over the life of the corporation, such as a name change. It is important to ascertain all the names under which the corporation conducted business, because recorded activities in other public records might use names other than the current corporate name. Therefore, you must search all the names used by the corporation to assure you have a complete corporate history.

Corporate law in many jurisdictions requires corporations to file minutes of board of directors meetings with the Secretary of State. The minutes reflect material action taken by the board of directors, including election of directors and officers and approval of corporate policy.

The Line of Authorization

A chain of authorization extends from voters in a state and follows through into the corporate policies that define a business operation. In a sense, registered voters give authority to a corporation to conduct business. Here's how this works.

The Line of Authorization

State voters approve a state constitution that creates the three branches of state government (judicial, executive, and legislative). The constitution also authorizes the legislative and executive branches to create laws, called statutes. Statutes authorize the formation of corporations and specify rules for the corporation, which are administrated by the Secretary of State.

Statutes authorize the Secretary of State to certify articles of incorporation proposed by stockholders. The certification grants authority from the state to the corporation to operate within terms specified in the articles of incorporation, which includes the power to create stock certificates.

The articles of incorporation also defines how the board of directors and officers are elected and defines the powers of directors and officers. Stockholders elect directors and the board of directors elects corporate officers.

The board of directors is authorized by the articles of incorporation to create policies, called corporate policies, that cover a breadth of topics. These include human resource, accounting, and the organization's structure. Directors and officers must conduct business within corporate policy.

The certificate of incorporation authorizes the corporation to exist. However, additional authorization is likely required for the corporation to conduct business in other jurisdictions. Let's say a corporation was formed in California and has operations in three other states. The corporation is required to comply with the various statutes of all four states, which probably require tax certification and business registration in each state. Due diligence requires you to obtain relative documents that permit the dotcom to operate in each state where the dotcom has a business presence. A business presence is defined as an office, warehouse, or other facility and is not defined as where their customers reside. For example, a California-based e-tailer has warehouses in Ohio, Texas, and Florida and sells to customers throughout the United States. A company seeking to take over the e-tailer needs to examine documents filed in California, Ohio, Texas, and Florida. No documents are required to be filed by the corporation in other states.

Caution

State sales tax regulations are in flux. At this writing, corporations must have a presence in a state to collect sales tax for a state. Efforts are underway by states to require e-tailers to collect sales tax on sales made to each state that has a sales tax.

Certified copies of each document relating to the dotcom must be obtained during the due diligence process. Copies are noted as received, then stored with other documents pertaining to the merger or acquisition.

The focus of the due diligence investigation turns towards restrictions imposed on the dotcom through judgments and liens on property the dotcom owns. Judgments, liens, and bankruptcies are filed in jurisdictions where legal action is taken or where the corporation resides. Undisclosed action can affect the dotcom's balance sheet.

A thorough examination of all relevant legal filings in all jurisdictions must be completed before closing the deal. Restrictions imposed by legal actions might be passed to the company once the dotcom is acquired. For example, a supplier in Florida might have won a judgment against the California-based e-tailer. The judgment is recorded in the county where the judgment was issued. Likewise, a lien on a corporation's Florida warehouse, which is used as collateral for a loan, is recorded in the county where the property is located.

At this point in the due diligence process, you will be assured that the corporation does exist and is in good standing with all jurisdictions where business is conducted. You'll know that the stockholders, directors, and officers involved in the deal are duly authorized to represent the corporation. The details of all judgments and liens, if any, against the corporation are known.

Next you need to verify that the dotcom owns the assets it claims to own. You need to obtain certified copies of copyrights, patents, deeds, trademarks, and bills of sale. Verification should be made independent of the dotcom. Many of these documents are found in filings with the appropriate government agency. Some documents, such as bills of sale, can only be provided by the dotcom; however, the seller must verify the document.

A Balanced Approach

The due diligence process must use a pragmatic approach that balances the corporation's need for information with cost and time constraints imposed by a from-birth investigation. A thorough investigation requires an investigative staff composed mostly of outside consultants, who charge the company an hourly fee. Outside consultants include attorneys, auditors, and specialists such as engineers.

Once momentum builds towards a deal, it is advantageous to the company that the deal close in a relatively short time frame because a delay tends to allow time for the dotcom to second-guess its decision to move forward on the deal. However, a thorough due diligence investigation can extend the closing and therefore becomes a hindrance more than a benefit, as well as a costly venture.

A from-birth investigation is intrusive and can have a detrimental effect on the dotcom. Although a dotcom realizes verification of its representations is necessary, the company must appreciate that the investigation exposes the dotcom's confidential and strategic information to a company that in the end may not consummate the deal.

Concerns about revealing sensitive information is uppermost in the minds of the dotcom's management. Aside from information available in the public record, a probe into the inner operations of the dotcom creates opportunities for exploitation by competitors if the deal collapses.

The issue then becomes how much information is necessary for the company to close the deal without risking its relationship with the dotcom. Likewise, the dotcom must determine what information it can provide to the company without compromising the deal or future business operations should the deal fail.

The depth of an investigation is determined, for all practical purposes, by the reputation of the dotcom and the quality of initial supportive information provided to the company by the dotcom. A dotcom that is highly respected in the industry, with a proven track record and stable management, requires a limited investigation before closing the deal.

The company must require the necessary credit checks, a recent audit, and a review of operational reports. In addition, the investigation must identify any significant changes that occurred in the industry and with the dotcom that invalidates representations by the dotcom.

A from-birth investigation must be conducted regardless of the reputation of the dotcom, but the bulk of the probe occurs after the deal closes. In place of a from-birth investigation prior to closing, the dotcom must make representations regarding the its operations and provide a warranty in the deal agreement that investigators can substantiate at a later time. Any substantive misrepresentations can substantially reduce compensation to the dotcom or negate the deal entirely, although reversing a deal is costly.

However, a dotcom whose reputation is tarnished or is not firmly established in the industry is likely to require an intense from-birth due diligence before the deal is closed. Not doing so exposes the company to potential liabilities that make the deal unprofitable.

Financial institutions that the company uses to finance the deal will also conduct due diligence before presenting the company with a commitment letter (see Chapter 3). However, financial institutions limit their investigation to information required to secure financing obligations. For example, title and lien searches are all that is necessary for real estate property to be used as collateral for a loan. Therefore, the company shouldn't rely on a creditor's assessment of the dotcom as the basis for consummating the deal, since a financial institution's due diligence is limited in scope.

Caution

Don't expect a dotcom to fully cooperate with due diligence. A from-birth investigation is not in the dotcom's best interest, because it might expose problems that are expensive to remedy or problems that become deal-breakers. Likewise, making factual representations in the deal agreement and providing the company with warranties is not favorable for the target, since it exposes the target to future liabilities. The company is able to reopen the deal after the deal is completed if factors covered under the warranty prove to be false.

Many problems regarding a company's investigation of a dotcom are avoidable by both parties signing a letter of intent. A letter of intent states the company's desire to consider the dotcom for a merger or acquisition— and the dotcom agrees to be considered.

The letter of intent contains language that outlines the due diligence process required by the company. These terms are negotiated before parties sign the letter of intent. Either within the letter of intent or in a separate document, both parties sign a nondisclosure agreement that restricts the use of any information that is uncovered during due diligence. Here are the more common items included in the letter of intent:

- How the company accesses the dotcom's facilities
- How the company meets and discusses the deal with the dotcom's personnel
- How the company meets and discusses the deal with the dotcom's customers and suppliers
- How the company disposes of the dotcom's confidential information

- Restrictions on outside investigators to prevent information they gather from being used by them with other clients

---

Tech Talk

Nondisclosure Agreement: A document stating that information revealed during the due diligence process will be maintained confidential. Disclosure of information is actionable through litigation.

From Tim Miller, Webmergers.com

Seller Self Protection

The downturn in technology stock prices has cast a bit of a shadow over the red-hot Internet M&A sector. The enormous volatility of Internet stocks makes the M&A process fairly harrowing for employees and founders of target companies, particularly when they face delayed registration periods. "It's not real until it's cash," says Tom Bentley, managing partner of Alliant Capital, a fast-growing technology M&A firm based in Silicon Valley.

Fortunately, Bentley and others supplied several suggestions on how sellers can protect themselves. There are several stages at which sellers should think about self-protection:

1) Before Signing the Deal

Clearly, the deal structure itself is the best way to put in place a safety jacket. Some options:

- Skew the ratio toward cash. Webmergers.com data shows that when cash is involved at all, the cash-to-stock ratio for Web deals is almost always much less than 20:80. Sellers can negotiate for more cash, but they then may have negative tax consequences and may erect barriers to getting the deal done.

- Build in a price "collar." Such protections allow sellers to walk away from the deal if the buyer's price falls outside a preset range, or "collar."
- Structure the deal in "fixed dollars," with the number of shares adjusted to equal a set dollar amount regardless of movement in the buyer's shares. For example, when newly IPO'd Andover.Net, Inc. sold itself to VA Linux Systems (LNUX) for about a billion dollars, Andover received $3.81 in cash for each share and about .4 of a share of VA common stock. However, the deal fixed VA's stock price at its average closing price over a ten-day trading period bracketing the deal date. Good thing, that. VA Linux stock dropped 68 percent since its close the day before the purchase was announced. However, buyers may be understandably reluctant to ink such deals.
- Structure an earn-out relationship based on future performance. An earn-out provides upside in stock or cash, based on performance. For example, Excite/AtHome's acquisition of Bluemountain.com requires Excite to kick in another $270 million in stock plus some options if Bluemountain meets performance goals. The risk in performance-based pricing is that the buyer often has a hand on the scale because it controls the marketing and development dollars that often determine the performance of the acquired unit.

2) Between Signing and Closing

The 2-week to 4–5-month period before closing is when collars and other legal techniques are typically exercised. However, Alliant's Bentley points out that collars are losing favor, especially in the technology world, where both buyer and seller are valued with sky-high "concept" valuations. "A lot of Internet buyers and sellers are strategically related," he explained. "If Kana and Epiphany did a deal, for example, they'd probably rise or sink together. So, is it fair to say the seller's dollar level should stay the same if the buyer's is falling? We're seeing buyers and sellers participate equally in both the upside and the downside." Bentley said that collars may be more appropriate for the "old world" in which companies were valued on a somewhat more tangible discounted cash flow basis and a seller needed to be protected against an unanticipated bump in the road for the buyer. "But now that the discounted cash flow model has been kind of thrown out the window, the need to protect the dollar value is probably not as important," Bentley said. "You need to protect the relative value."

3) Between Closing and Liquidity

After closing, sellers who've accepted stock have several other options to protect the value of their volatile booty. States such as California in many cases allow for a "fairness hearing" that often results in a seller being allowed to register stock as early as 30 days after close of deal, subject to insider restrictions or other company policies. In addition, employees or founders who have restricted stock that they can't sell for a year can protect themselves with options or hedging techniques, the latter requiring no up-front outlay of cash.

Timing

Due diligence is a strategic factor in a deal that motivates the dotcom to work towards closing the deal only if the due diligence process is completed in a timely fashion. Here's how to keep the due diligence process moving along.

First, complete the substantive portion of due diligence before making an offer. A substantive portion values the dotcom's tangible and intangible assets and identifies the liabilities of the deal. It is at this point when the company is in a position to determine the dotcom's worth.

A substantive evaluation requires less time than a from-birth investigation, yet the results are sufficient to know if the deal is mutually advantageous to both parties. The initial offer based on the substantive evaluation includes contingencies that nullify the offer should a contingency fail to materialize. This strategy gives the dotcom a flavor of the deal if the contingencies are addressed during the due diligence process.

Tech Talk

Contingency: A condition specified by the company that, if met by the dotcom, enables the company to consummate the deal.

Let's say a company is acquiring a dotcom that builds search engines. As part of a thorough due diligence process, the company requires a software engineer to evaluate the condition of the search engine code. The company can make an initial offer to the dotcom contingent on a positive opinion rendered by the software engineer. The offer is negated if the engineer's opinion is not positive. It is in the dotcom's best interest to cooperate with the software engineer's evaluation. Failure to do so will result in the contingency not being met.

Contingencies also serve as a "to-do" list that leads to a done deal and tends to expedite the due diligence process, which could otherwise be bogged down in procedural issues. A long due diligence process raises the cost of pursuing the deal for both parties and risk straining relations between the company and the dotcom.

Risks

There are two concerns that must be considered whenever both sides of a potential deal begin due diligence. These are business operations and competitive suitors.

Due diligence informally announces that the dotcom will be merged or acquired either by the company or by another suitor if the deal fails. Employees, suppliers, customers, and competitors reassess their positions once they learn the dotcom is on the market.

The ramifications can be staggering and can dramatically affect the business operations of both the company and the dotcom. Speculation causes employees to wonder about their roles after the deal closes. Anticipate that key employees will explore other opportunities, which could impact conditions at both organizations. For example, key marketing and sales personnel could join a competitor and bring along important clients. Likewise, the success of the dotcom might be based on the skills of a few managers. Failure of those managers to continue with the dotcom after the deal is completed is likely to reduce the dotcom's future success.

Suppliers and customers also recognize the potential change in status quo and can be expected to hedge their positions by developing stronger relationships with other firms. This can lead to reduced availability of supplies and reduced business from key customers.

Due diligence places the dotcom in play and inadvertently invites other bidders for the dotcom, which increases the dotcom's price. In essence, your company is telling the industry that the dotcom is for sale.

Competition may or may not be advantageous to the dotcom. Ideally, the dotcom merges or is acquired by a company whose culture and management style enhances that of the dotcom. However, an undesirable suitor who undertakes a hostile takeover may pursue the dotcom, especially if the dotcom is a public company.

Tech Talk

Hostile Takeover: The term used to describe a company (in this case, a dotcom) being acquired by a company without the consent of the target's management.

INVESTIGATION CHECKLIST

Due diligence is a complex process that separates fact from fiction and raises more questions than the process answers in many cases. This is especially true when a company undertakes a from-birth investigation of the dotcom, because of the multifaceted operations of the business.

Before the investigation begins, the company must establish guidelines for investigators. Guidelines must include areas to focus the investigation and procedures to record and distribute information gathered during the investigation.

First, the company, in conjunction with the dotcom, must develop an investigation checklist that clearly itemizes areas of the dotcom's operation that will be probed. The checklist should be organized to include seven areas.

1. Corporate pedigree
2. Corporate assets
3. Corporate agreements
4. Personnel issues
5. Financials
6. Litigation issues
7. Debt analysis

Each area is subdivided into focus points of the investigation. Table 2.1 contains a sample investigation checklist.

Next, the company must devise a way to make the investigation non-intrusive to minimize the effect on the dotcom's operation and to maintain a low profile within the industry. This is achieved by limiting the overt gathering of information in the dotcom's offices during normal working hours. For example, the company and the dotcom can agree to rent office space outside of each other's facilities for the due diligence process. Many times, an outside consulting firm can be enlisted for this purpose and can provide staffing for the investigation.

The dotcom can deliver documents, files, and other material to the off-site location, where investigators make copies and return the information immediately to the dotcom. In this way, the staff of neither the company nor the dotcom sees investigators in their offices.

Next, documents must be organized and protected. Documents that support or counteract claims by the dotcom should be numbered sequentially so they can easily be referenced during discussions regarding the investigation. Some companies number documents sequentially, while others group documents into areas the investigation will probe, then number documents sequentially within the group. Either technique is sufficient as long as investigators, the company, and the dotcom can track and identify each document.

The company and the dotcom must agree on the number of copies of each document that are to be produced. At least two copies should be made: one copy for the company and the other for the dotcom. Additional copies increase the risk that confidential information might fall into the wrong hands.

Each copy should identify the recipient of the copy to assure an audit trail exists. Some companies use the watermark feature of word processing software to inscribe the recipient's name on each copy. It is difficult to tamper with the watermark on a copied document.

Next, establish a priority and threshold for each item on the investigation checklist. This helps to reduce due diligence expenses and focus investigators on meaningful areas. Keep in mind that due diligence expenses are frequently borne by the company.

The dotcom is likely to underwrite its out-of-pocket costs, especially in the case of a friendly takeover. However, the due diligence process benefits the company and is not necessarily advantageous to the dotcom.

Expect that a dotcom will also conduct due diligence on the company, especially in a merger and when take-back financing (in which the dotcom extends a loan in lieu of cash payment for all or part of the deal) is involved. The dotcom underwrites the cost of this due diligence process.

The checklist must be prioritized and each item assigned a deliverable date. Priority is determined by the relevant importance an item has on a deal. For example, verifying incorporation documents has a higher priority than verifying a vendor contract, because an invalid incorporation document (indicating that the corporation doesn't exist) negates a vendor contract.

A threshold should be established that defines significance for areas being investigated. For example, assets under $150,000 can be excluded from the investigation because their value is insignificant to the magnitude of the deal. Of course, the level of significance varies based on the nature of the deal. Thresholds reduce the scope of the investigation to higher priority items and make efficient use of investigators.

Table 2.1   Items to Include on an Investigation Checklist

Area to Investigate	Comments
Corporate Pedigree	
Certificate of incorporation	Certifies that the corporation exists.
Articles of incorporation and amendments	Defines the scope of the corporation.
Bylaws	Look for poison-pill provision that makes acquisition less desirable.
Board of directors minutes	Policies, election of officers, and material transactions.
Ownership	Identifies the material stockholders.
Corporate Assets	
Real estate	Title search, property evaluation, and inspection reports.
Licenses	Verify issuance, duration, transferability, and terms.
Patents, trademarks, trade names, and copyrights	Verify proper filings and ownership.
Personal property	Verify ownership or lease documents, assure transferability and inspection reports.
Inventory	Valuation, inspection reports, consignment arrangements reviewed.
Software systems	Valuation, inspection reports, ownership and transferability.

(continued)

Table 2.1   Items to Include on an Investigation Checklist *(continued)*

Area to Investigate	Comments
Corporate Agreements	
Suppliers	Validation, terms, compatibility with your business operations, market comparison.
Customers	Validation, terms, compatibility with your business operations, and market comparison.
Key employees	Validation, terms, compatibility with your key employee agreements, market comparison, and transferability.
Consultants	Validation, terms, compatibility with your business operations, and market comparison.
Leases	Validation, terms, compatibility with your business operations, market comparison, and transferability.
Loans obligations	Validation, terms, compatibility with your business operations, market comparison, and transferability.
Asset purchasing agreements	Validation.
Insurance	Validation, terms, compatibility with your business operations, market comparison, and transferability.
Shareholder agreements	Validation, terms, compatibility with your business operations, market comparison, and transferability.
Personnel Issues	
Pension	Validation, terms, compatibility with your business operations, market comparison, and transferability.
Profit sharing	Validation, terms, compatibility with your business operations, market comparison, and transferability.
Deferred compensation	Validation, terms, compatibility with your business operations, market comparison, and transferability.

(continued)

Table 2.1 Items to Include on an Investigation Checklist *(continued)*

Area to Investigate	Comments
Personnel Issues	
Stock options	Validation, terms, compatibility with your business operations, market comparison, and transferability.
Health and insurance benefits	Validation, terms, compatibility with your business operations, market comparison, and transferability.
Financials	
Financial statements	Validation, compatibility with your business operations, and market comparison.
Inventory reporting	Validation and compatibility with your business operations.
Accounting method	Validation, compatibility with your business operations, and market comparison.
Tax considerations	Determine tax liabilities and advantages.
Pricing policies	Validation, compatibility with your business operations, and market comparison.
Capitalization	Determine outstanding stock and stock validation.
Litigation Issues	
Previous litigation	Determine impact on business operations, cause of litigation, likelihood of repeated litigation, cost of litigation.
Pending litigation	Determine impact on business operations, cause of litigation, likelihood of repeated litigation, cost of litigation, likelihood of success, transferability.
Prospective litigation	Determine impact on business operations, cause of litigation, likelihood of repeated litigation, cost of litigation, likelihood of success, transferability.
Consent degrees	Determine impact on business operations, cause of litigation, likelihood of repeated litigation, cost of litigation, likelihood of success, transferability.

(continued)

Table 2.1 Items to Include on an Investigation Checklist *(continued)*

Area to Investigate	Comments
Litigation Issues	
Settlements	Determine impact on business operations, likelihood of repeated litigation, cost of settlement, transferability.
Government decisions	Determine impact on business operations.
Pending legislative/regulatory changes	Determine impact on business operations.
Debt Analysis	
Current debt	Determine impact on business operations, terms, termination date, pre-payment penalty, transferability.
Pending debt	Determine impact on business operations, terms, initiation date, termination date, prepayment penalty, transferability.
Terminating debt	Determine impact on business operations, terms, termination date, prepayment penalty, transferability.
Lien search	Validate liens, determine impact on business operations, terms, transferability.
Credit check	Determine impact on business operations, effect on your company, recent changes in credit rating.

From Tim Miller, Webmergers.com

Finding Value in the Dotcom Debris Field

Austin, Texas-based Eco Associates is making one of the bolder forays into scorched Internet territory. The VC/buyout hybrid, with a strong belief that the market has overreacted on the down side, plans to buy majority stakes in 10 to 12 distressed e-commerce companies before it's finished. Eco has bought into such scorned B2C properties as Mall.com and led a group that put $27.5 million in struggling consumer health site DrKoop.com. Eco acquired Chip Shot Golf Corp. (Chipshot.com), a bankrupt golf products e-tailer. Eco, with about a $200 million fund, is a joint venture of investment bank Capstar Partners, LLC and venture capital firm Interfase Capital, L.P.

Eco and Interfase principal Scott Hyten believes an "overreaction in the market" that knocked 95 percent or more off Internet valuations has created some pockets of value. And believe it or not, he's already feeling nostalgic about the good old days of "real" Internet bargains. "The amount of interest [from competing investors] is definitely picking up," lamented Hyten, "The cheap bottom-feeding days are probably behind us...the bottom was about three weeks ago. Back then, we could really just cherry-pick."

Indeed, most of Eco's buyout targets were in desperate shape. DrKoop.com had nearly run out of cash and ChipShot, having burned through some $50 million in funding, had filed for Chapter 11 bankruptcy protection. Eco and Interfase also own Urban Box Office, a multimedia company focused on the urban marketplace.

Eco's strategy is to buy leading e-commerce companies, carve out operating costs, leverage technology, and put marketing and product mix into intensive care. Chipshot is one example. "With Chipshot, you had a company with a good set of technology, one of the best we've seen," said Hyten, who cut his teeth on technology in his previous life as a founding employee of Perot Systems.

"They'd built a nationwide brand and had a pretty stable customer base in excess of a million shoppers that were relatively loyal.... It turns out their biggest problem is distribution and fulfillment—they were receiving orders and fulfilling only half of them." Eco will cover debtor and possessor financing while it outsources most of Chipshot's IS and product distribution and builds up marketing relationships.

The jury is very much still out on the Eco approach—DrKoop.com is currently considering a reverse stock split to avoid a Nasdaq delisting, and Urban Box Office has filed for bankruptcy protection after Interfase withdrew funding because of what it said was the startup's failure to adhere to turnaround execution hurdles. However, with nearly every Internet e-tailer, large or small, still in pre-profits stages, Hyten says it's too early to call the game. "The difference between a successful and a failed dotcom right now is largely a matter of perception," he said. "Maybe we are absolutely crazy, but we're capitalizing these companies for a couple of years."

Hyten said the shakeout has in some ways made it easier to build businesses. For example, he said, Mall.com is seeing 40 percent week-to-week traffic increases, much of it thanks to a giant fire sale in online advertising. "It's amazing that at the same time we're going to have the largest growth in a retail market in history, we're also seeing marketing and advertising costs falling through the floor," said Hyten, who said he'd just finished writing a $100,000 check for 75 million banner advertising impressions.

Selection Criteria: How Eco Identifies Value

Eco currently has about 600 investment prospects on its list, with more waiting in the wings. "Almost every day, we talk with companies that have a gun to their head, " said Hyten.

In evaluating deals, Eco looks for the following:

One of the top 3–5 providers in a major B2C e-commerce sector.

- Strong marketing and technology people who are willing to step up and "make their career" (senior management need not apply)
- A company that has over-extended its product mix and can easily cut back to a focused set of high-volume, higher-margin products
- Health and other focused e-commerce verticals.
- Infrastructure that complements existing portfolio companies

Pet and home furnishings e-tailers need not apply.

LEGAL INVESTIGATION

A dotcom is likely to be the subject of various legal actions, each of which must be carefully reviewed to determine its effect on the deal and the possibility that the company might inadvertently become a party to the action. Pending litigation may substantially influence the dotcom's assets and financials to a degree that makes the dotcom unattractive.

Expect the dotcom to categorize pending and threatened litigation as material or immaterial to the its operation. However, this opinion should not be accepted without independent confirmation performed by an attorney appointed by the company to conduct a litigation analysis.

Tech Talk

Material Litigation: Legal action, the success of which will
influence business operations.
Immaterial Litigation: Legal action, the success of which will
not influence business operations.

Due diligence will discover previous and pending legal action, independent of the dotcom's statement. However, uncovering potential action against the dotcom requires a careful investigation by attorneys representing the company. Although the dotcom is likely to acknowledge threats, it is not in their best interest to reveal more than necessary to satisfy requests by the company.

Your company must be alert to half-truths and optimistic opinions based on broad assumptions. For example, the company might ask the dotcom to present all potential material litigation that has yet to be filed. Although attorneys for the dotcom use a reasonable definition of the term *material,* the term is defined by the dotcom, whose interest is not to expose litigation that might destroy the deal.

Request information about litigation directly from the dotcom's attorney rather than through management, because the corporate attorney represents the shareholders of the dotcom and not the management of the firm. Revealing litigation might not be in the best interest of management, but is favorable to the shareholders if such acknowledgement leads to a rewarding deal for the shareholders. Therefore, due diligence requires that the company search correspondence from customers, employees, vendors, suppliers, and government agencies, looking for indications of possible legal action. It is common to find a threat of legal action amidst correspondence, since the dotcom has "deep pockets," which attracts litigation. However, the company, not the dotcom, must evaluate the merits of each potential action. Those deemed a substantial risk need closer examination to assess the likelihood of successful litigation and potential damages. The assessment must also evaluate the cost of litigation and how it would impact the dotcom's operation.

Don't underestimate the impact litigation could have on the business. Besides the potential drain on cash flow, substantial legal action diverts management attention from running the business. Litigation also could influence the relationship the dotcom has with customers and suppliers, especially if the action is followed closely in the press. This is regardless of whether the action reaches court.

Salomon, Inc.'s government bond scandal illustrates this point. The government accused Salomon of misusing the bidding process to acquire government bonds. The accusations alone forced some customers to stop doing business with Salomon until the matter was adjudicated. This included state pension funds that are prohibited by law to do business with anyone who is under a cloud of suspicion.

Historical and current litigation could indicate future, similar legal action. Let's say a customer sued because someone she met in a chat room operated by the dotcom harassed her. In fact, a frequent visitor to the chat room also harassed others who participated in chats. A successful action is likely to attract similar action that could occur after the merger, requiring the company—not the dotcom—to litigate.

Litigation analysis must explore litigation involving other firms in the industry too. You might discover that an industry practice is in the crosshairs of the Association of Trial Lawyers, whose members might be using a competitor as a test case, which if successful will be repeated for each company in the industry—including the dotcom.

A similar concern involves any case brought against management by an employee. Many jurisdictions recognize the dotcom's management as an agent for the dotcom and therefore combine the accused manager and the dotcom as the defendant. A successful case is likely to bring additional action from other employees and former employees.

Litigation Analysis

An attorney who specializes in investigating the legal environment of a corporation should be hired to oversee the litigation analysis. It is common to have an attorney direct the litigation search performed by a team of attorneys, each of whom has experience in a particular aspect of litigation. For example, the litigation analysis team typically consists of specialists in contract litigation, employee litigation, tax litigation, environmental litigation, and other areas that require special knowledge, such as case law and administrative law.

Expect the team to consult experts whenever a particular action or potential litigation is reviewed. Expert opinions are used to assess the merits of the case and the impact the case has on the dotcom both during litigation and if litigation is successful.

Once the litigation analysis team is assembled, the attorney for the company asks the attorney for the dotcom to identify previous, current, and threatened litigation against the dotcom and against firms within the industry. The dotcom's attorney is asked to render an opinion on the merits of each case.

The dotcom's attorney is also asked to provide all documentation for cases. Case documents include charges, pleadings, legal research, evidence, depositions, and testimony. Any information used by the dotcom's attorney in the case should be made available for litigation analysis. Likewise, the dotcom must provide insurance policies that cover the dotcom's liabilities in these cases.

The litigation analysis team will determine the scope of insurance policies—that is, whether a policy covers reported action or all actions that occurred while the policy is enforced. A policy that covers reported action might not cover litigation started after termination of the policy, even if the libelous action occurred during the coverage period.

Insurance coverage might terminate when the deal agreement is signed, depending on the type of deal. In that case, the company might be exposed to future legal expenses incurred by ongoing cases involving the dotcom. The dotcom's insurance coverage can be extended if the dotcom or the company purchases a tail policy.

Tech Talk

Tail Policy: Insurance that continues the coverage of an existing policy.

The litigation analysis team must assess the coverage given by each policy. The review includes the deductible and compensatory and punitive damages. A high deductible might materially affect the dotcom's financials. Some policies cover compensatory damages, but exclude punitive damages, which could be substantially higher than compensatory damages.

Don't assume that because an insurance policy exists, liabilities are covered. The litigation analysis team must determine if the insurance company consistently rejected claims made by the dotcom in the past. If so, then claims made regarding current litigation may too be rejected, exposing the dotcom to material financial losses.

A survey of information provided by the dotcom is sufficient for the litigation analysis team to prioritize cases, then schedule a systematic review of each case. While the opinion of the dotcom's attorney is valuable input, the litigation analysis team must arrive at its own conclusion, independent of the dotcom's attorney.

Liability Transfer

Of particular concern to the litigation analysis team is the exposure to the company after the deal is consummated. This is called *successor liability.* Although the company and the dotcom are separate entities, a merger or acquisition combines their business operations. The litigation analysis team must determine what debt or torts, if any, transfer to the company following a done deal.

Generally, an asset transfer in which the company purchases assets of the dotcom does not transfer liability associated with the asset. However, there might be inherent problems with the assets that could cause new litigation to be filed. Let's say the company takes over the dotcom's chat room and no action is taken to prevent a chat room participant from harassing other participants. Harassment occurs prior to the transfer of the asset, which causes pending litigation, and continues after the transfer, which exposes the company to additional complaints.

There are three situations in which the company assumes litigation from the dotcom:

1. The two companies consolidate business operations through a merger.
2. The company agrees to accept the liabilities of the dotcom, as specified in the deal agreement.
3. The courts determine the sole purpose of the deal is for the dotcom to avoid liability.

Liability in some jurisdictions seems to center on continuation of an existing practice, regardless of the type of deal agreed to by the company and the dotcom. The legal profession refers to this as the *duck rule.* If it walks like a duck and talks like a duck, then it is a duck, regardless of what you call it. For example, a company's operation of the dotcom's Web site without material changes is considered a continuation of the dotcom's offering and therefore could infer litigation associated with the Web site transfers to the company.

Another common transfer is legal obligations with employees of the dotcom. A company who retains the services of the dotcom's employees also retains agreements made with employees. Labor attorneys frequently recommend that termination notices be given to employees of the dotcom company, followed by an employment offer to work for the company under new terms.

The exception to this technique is if a labor contract exists between the dotcom and its employees. In such a situation, some jurisdictions conclude that the labor contract is transferred to the company and any changes to the labor contract must be renegotiated.

Material Litigation

Only material litigation affects the deal. Some areas that present material litigation are

- Antitrust
- Breach of fiduciary duty
- Contract disputes
- Deceptive trade practices
- Discrimination
- Fraud
- Patent infringement
- Product liability
- Restraint of trade
- Severance
- Wrongful termination

Personnel matters—specifically, wrongful termination and severance—seem to be receiving increased litigation interest. Wrongful termination occurs when, after a consolidation, an employer (such as the dotcom or the company) dismisses an employee for unjustifiable reasons, such as age discrimination.

Likewise, severance becomes the concern of stockholders if key employees of the dotcom receive large severance, commonly called a *golden parachute*. Stockholders might perceive such an arrangement as compensation for arranging the deal rather than as compensation justified by prior service to the dotcom.

The litigation analysis determines whether or not each case or threatened case is material by establishing guidelines before undertaking the analysis. A threshold of material loss is set, below which legal action is not considered substantive to change the financials or business operation of the dotcom.

The threshold is dependent on the size and business of the dotcom. For example, a $100,000 potential loss through litigation cost and judgment is not material to a dotcom with a net worth of $100 million. The litigation analysis team, in conjunction with your company's management and the dotcom, decide on the threshold. It is important for the dotcom to recognize the threshold before the analysis begins; otherwise, a disagreement might arise if, before moving forward with a deal, the company requires the dotcom to resolve a case that the dotcom believes is immaterial.

A threshold is not the only factor that determines the materiality of litigation. A case that falls below the threshold could have far-reaching ramifications that affect business operations. Sales tax action against the dotcom by a local jurisdiction is a prime example. The damages might be insignificant; however, success through a judgment or settlement could invite litigation from tens of thousands local jurisdictions.

Likewise, information revealed about the dotcom during the discovery process of litigation might be used in other litigation, especially those filed after the deal, when the company—not the dotcom—is liable.

In assessing the liability of a case, the litigation analysis team considers the cost of litigation. The cost includes attorneys' fees, filing fees, investigating fees, expert witness fees, and the disruptive cost imposed on business operations. The accumulative expense may warrant the litigation analysis team to recommend that a case is material and require the dotcom to resolve the issue before the deal agreement is signed. Litigation can be disposed of expediently, without a trial, by an out-of-court settlement or by using alternative dispute resolution, where parties to the litigation agree to accept the decision of an arbitrator.

ENVIRONMENTAL INVESTIGATION

Although dotcoms operate in the virtual world, they do have brick-and-mortar operations that might be exposed to environmental litigation issues. For example, a facility might have a large fuel tank leak that pollutes a neighboring waterway or the ground water used for drinking water. Similarly, waste products produced from a chip manufacturer may contain pollutants and must be disposed of, using specified procedures. Failure to do so is actionable by federal, state and local government agencies.

Due diligence must consider environmental factors that can influence the dotcom and carry through to the company after the deal agreement is signed. Failure to perform a comprehensive environmental analysis exposes the company to liabilities that could have profound effects on the business operations of both the dotcom and the company after the deal. An environmental analysis considers regulations on the federal, state, and local levels, each of which can take action that affects a dotcom's current and future operation.

Some common environmental concerns include

- Toxic waste on the site possibly caused by a prior owner
- Existence of asbestos on the facility
- Hazardous materials used by the dotcom, such as in manufacturing circuit boards and chips
- Underground fuel tanks

Let's say that a dotcom is found to inadvertently cause a fuel spillage, such as from a leaky oil tank used to heat a facility. The dotcom is likely to incur the expense to remove the contaminant and to restore all properties to their original condition. Furthermore, the dotcom is exposed to litigation for personal injuries that arise from the contamination. The cleanup and ensuing litigation is costly and affects the dotcom's financials, especially if the liability is not fully covered by insurance. Liability for an environmental problem can also penetrate the corporation veil and hold stockholders, directors, and officers personally accountable.

A company should not reject a dotcom if the environmental analysis uncovers conditions that might cause government agencies to bring action. Instead, an assessment must be made to determine the expenditures necessary to bring the dotcom in line with government environmental regulations. The assessment must be comprehensive, for once the deal is penned, the environmental problem becomes a liability for the company as well as the dotcom: the dotcom for causing the problem and the company for permitting the problem to continue.

Except in rare circumstances, many environmental problems are addressable if properly funded. The company has several options in such cases. The dotcom can be rejected. The dotcom can be required to remedy the problem before the deal moves forward. The company can use the cost of rectifying the environmental problem as a bargaining chip in negotiations.

The company may find that a better deal can be made if the company underwrites the cleanup, assuming of course that full impact of the environmental problem has been thoroughly assessed. A dotcom is likely to be amiable to reducing the price to reflect cleanup cost and the cost of unforeseen litigation. This arrangement should only be pursued if the company's environmental and legal experts conclude that this is an acceptable risk.

Caution

The environmental analysis must research the history of property owned by the dotcom to determine if any hazardous materials were removed from the facility. Hazardous materials must be disposed of by licensed vendors and stored in certified dumpsites. Failure to do so exposes the target to cleanup of the entire illegal dumpsite, regardless of the amount of the target's hazardous material that is dumped at the site. Acquiring the target is likely to bring your company into such litigation.

Caution

Environmental laws can be retroactive. Actions taken by the dotcom might be legal at the time the action occurred, but could become illegal in the future, at which time the company is liable for the environmental cleanup. Your company can offset potential environmental exposure by requiring the target to provide a warranty that covers the future exposure.

Caution

The environmental analysis must identify governmental regulations that require an environmental inspection of facilities before title can transfer from the dotcom to the company. These rules might be found at all levels of government, not simply at the federal level.

EVALUATING THE RESULTS OF DUE DILIGENCE

The objective of due diligence is to identify all pertinent information about the dotcom before initiating formal negotiations. Due diligence reveals much about a dotcom's operation, assets, liabilities, and ownership. However, it is the responsibility of the company's management to decide if the dotcom should be pursued, based on the results of the due diligence investigation.

Due diligence results are presented in many reports prepared by investigators, and each covers a different aspect of the dotcom. Each report should contain five sections:

1. Facts uncovered independently by investigators
2. Facts that substantiate representations made by the dotcom
3. Facts that refute representations made by the dotcom
4. Representations made by the dotcom that cannot be substantiated
5. The investigators' opinions

The three areas of a report that require special attention by the company's management are

1. Representations refuted by the investigation
2. Unsubstantiated representations
3. The investigators' opinions

Refuted representations need further examination, since due diligence contradicts knowledge provided by the dotcom. This conflict could arise from a misunderstanding of the dotcom's statement, which can be remedied by the dotcom clarifying the issue, followed by corroboration by the company's investigators.

However, the conflict might be a sign of a serious problem. For example, perhaps the dotcom's management does not closely monitor its operations, or management may have outright misrepresented facts to mislead the company. In either case, a creditability issue is raised that could seriously impact further dealings with the dotcom.

The company must follow up on any unsubstantiated representations made by the dotcom and ask the dotcom's management to provide the company with the foundation for its claim. Failure to comply also raises a creditability issue.

Opinions rendered by investigators sum up the investigators' views of particular aspects of the dotcom and should be given serious consideration by the company. Investigators tend to avoid giving a simple recommendation in their opinions. That is, you cannot expect to see a buy or pass recommendation on the deal.

Instead, investigators interpret each fact uncovered during the investigation and indicate the importance each fact has on the operations of the dotcom. For example, the opinion of the litigation investigator will highlight pending and potential litigation, then describe the impact each case is likely to have on the dotcom, both before and after the deal.

The company's management is responsible for determining how much the deal will be influenced by factors that receive negative opinions from investigators. That is, the litigation investigator might say an employee's discrimination suit has merit and could result in compensatory and punitive damages of $50 million. The company's management must decide if the litigation is material to the deal.

The investigation checklist (see Table 2.2) used to organize the due diligence process should also be used to record negative and unresolved issues that were uncovered during the process. Negative and unresolved issues from each investigative report should be listed beneath the related category on the investigation checklist.

One of three ranks—irrelevant, negotiating point, and showstopper—should be placed alongside each issue to indicate the relevancy the issue has on the deal. The company's management must carefully consider the investigator's opinion before a consensus is reached regarding the relevance of an issue.

A special effort needs to be made to assure rankings are based on fact, and not on emotions. It is not at all uncommon for the company's management to have a "gut feeling" that the dotcom is a fit, then discount the importance of negative issues that would lead a reasonable person to reject the dotcom.

Issues that are likely to have little or no bearing on the successful operation of the dotcom, from the time the intent letter is issued to the signing of the deal agreement and after the deal is consummated, should be ranked as irrelevant.

Issues that may have marginal, or at least perceived, impact on the deal and that are addressable by either the company or the dotcom, should be ranked as negotiating points. Let's say the dotcom's e-commerce site experiences serious performance problems during high-volume periods. This gives some customers a bad experience, which can impact future sales. Both parties recognize this problem as an issue that affects business operations. The company could play up this negative issue during negotiations in an effort to decrease the purchase price. The problem, however, can be remedied by relocating the Web site to a high-performance hosting service and tweaking the Web site application. The expense to address the problem is immaterial to the company, yet can be leveraged in negotiations.

Showstoppers are issues that must be resolved by the dotcom before the deal agreement is signed. Let's say a class action suit is filed by competitors, charging the dotcom with unfair trade practices. This is a showstopper, if the case has merit.

The dotcom cannot remedy all showstoppers, and therefore a show-stopper can transform into deal breakers. The company management must suspend the deal whenever an item is marked as a showstopper.

An assessment is then made to determine if the showstopper is addressable by the dotcom within a reasonable time period. If it is, then the deal remains alive and the company and the dotcom establish a deadline for when the showstopper must be repaired. Failure to do so will kill the deal. If the company deems that the dotcom cannot resolve the showstopper within a reasonable time period, then the dotcom is no longer considered a candidate for a merger or acquisition.

Dotcoms that pass due diligence become serious merger or acquisition candidates and require the company to develop a formal bid, and then to devise a structure for the transaction (both of which are discussed later in this book).

Table 2.2 Results of Investigation Assessed by Relevance to the Deal

Area to Investigate	Issues	Ranking IR = Irrelevant N = Negotiable S = Showstopper
Corporate Agreements		
Leases	Lease for headquarters nontransferable	IR
Loans obligations	Balloon loan payment due after deal deadline	N
Insurance	No tail policy on any insurance policy	N
Personnel Issues		
Pension	Dotcom has pension plan and company does not have pension plan	S
Litigation Issues		
Pending litigation	State sales tax claims rejected by dotcom	S

SUMMARY

Experts in mergers and acquisitions recommend that due diligence focus on three areas of interest to the company: Is the dotcom advantageous to the company's stockholders? What is the value of the dotcom? Can the company fund the deal?

Before answering these questions, your management team must verify all information known about the dotcom's industry and information that a dotcom represents about itself. The assumption when beginning the due diligence process is not to assume anything. The objectives are to identify misrepresentations and to identify underutilized resources that can, if properly managed, increase cash flow.

The main purpose of due diligence is to separate fact from fiction, then to arrive at a clear and honest presentment of the dotcom and the proposed deal. Failure to achieve this result could lead to decisions and strategies founded on misinformation and later unraveled when the facts are known—sometimes after the deal agreement is signed.

Each fact is assigned a confidence level, based on your evaluation. The confidence level is 100 percent if you can say that you are 100 percent confident that the fact is correct. The confidence level is subjective rather than statistically accurate and represents your management team's best assessment of the data.

Evaluation of the dotcom begins with an appraisal of the dotcom's assets. Assets are divided into two general categories: used assets and unused assets. A used asset is something used in the business operations. An unused asset is something owned by the dotcom but not used in running the business.

Within the used and unused categories of assets, assets are divided into tangible and intangible assets. A tangible asset is a building, server, and other things that you can touch. An intangible asset is goodwill, trademarks, copyrights, and patents. These are things you cannot touch, but that have a value to the dotcom.

The due diligence process must determine each asset's market value. The best approach when evaluating the assets is to employ a professional appraiser who specializes in assessing the kinds of assets found in a dotcom. Always choose an appraiser whose qualifications are verifiable, since the appraiser's recommendations become a major component of negotiating the deal. Ideally, the appraiser is sanctioned by a government agency or trade association, and has passed a qualifying examination. Some areas of expertise, such as software engineering, are not sanctioned. In this case, find an appraiser whose experience, qualifications, and reputation are recognized in the industry.

There are two steps in the appraisal process. First, appraisers render a tentative value for the each asset, the sum of which determines the tentative value of the dotcom. The initial tentative value is used to narrow the field to a handful of dotcoms and gives the company a ballpark value that is used to estimate the affordability of the dotcom. The initial tentative value can be determined without the knowledge of the dotcom.

A formal tentative value is determined when the company begins pursuing a dotcom. The deal is still in the preliminary phase, although the dotcom is aware of the company's interest and is likely to assist the company with information during the evaluation process. The formal tentative value is sufficient for the company to devise a financing plan and initiate formal negotiations with the dotcom.

Due diligence requires the company to perform a from-birth investigation of the dotcom. This means going back to when the dotcom was formed and documenting each event that has led to the dotcom's current status. Begin the due diligence investigation by searching public records to verify that the proper documents were filed to form the corporation. Typically, the Secretary of State of the state of incorporation is the repository of these papers.

Public records indicate the date of incorporation, whether or not the corporation continues to exist in good standing, and the articles of incorporation. The articles of incorporation is a public document that explicitly defines the corporation's purpose and rules under which the corporation operates, and provides a history of any material changes that have occurred over the life of the corporation, such as a name change.

Due diligence requires you to obtain relative documents that authorize the dotcom to operate in each state where the dotcom has a business presence. A business presence is defined as an office, warehouse, or other facility, and is not defined as where its customers resides.

A thorough examination of all relevant legal filings in all jurisdictions must be completed before closing the deal. Restrictions imposed by legal actions might be passed to the company once the dotcom is acquired.

You need to verify that the dotcom owns the assets it claims to own. You need to obtain certified copies of copyrights, patents, deeds, trademarks, and bills of sale. Verification should be made independent of the dotcom.

The due diligence process must be pragmatic and balance the corporation's need for information with cost and time constraints imposed by a from-birth investigation. The depth of a due diligence investigation is determined for all practical purposes by the reputation of the dotcom and quality of initial supportive information provided to the company by the dotcom.

A dotcom that is highly respected in the industry and has a proven track record and stable management requires a limited investigation before closing the deal. A from-birth investigation must be conducted, regardless of the reputation of the dotcom, but the bulk of the probe occurs after the deal closes. However, a dotcom whose reputation is tarnished or not firmly established in the industry is likely to require an intense from-birth due diligence before the deal is closed. Not doing so exposes the company to potential liabilities that make the deal unprofitable.

Many problems regarding a company's investigation of a dotcom are avoidable by both parties signing a letter of intent. A letter of intent states the company's desire to consider the dotcom for a merger or acquisition— and the dotcom agrees to be considered.

The letter of intent contains language that outlines the due diligence process required by the company. These terms are negotiated before parties sign the letter of intent. Either within the letter of intent or in a separate document, both parties sign a nondisclosure agreement that restricts the use of any information that is uncovered during due diligence.

It is important that the due diligence process move swiftly: otherwise, it could impede the deal. Due diligence places the dotcom in play and inadvertently invites other bidders for the dotcom, which increases the dotcom's price. In essence, your company is telling the industry that the dotcom is for sale.

Speculation of a pending deal also causes employees to wonder about their roles after the deal closes. Anticipate that key employees will explore other opportunities, which could impact conditions at both organizations. Therefore, a prolonged due diligence investigation places the company at a disadvantage.

Here's how to keep the due diligence process moving along.

First, complete the substantive portion of due diligence before making an offer. A substantive portion values the dotcom's tangible and intangible assets and identifies the liabilities of the deal. At this point, the company is in a position to determine the dotcom's worth.

A substantive evaluation requires less time than a from-birth investigation, yet the results are sufficient to know if the deal is mutually advantageous to both parties. The initial offer based on the substantive evaluation includes contingencies that nullify the offer should a contingency fail to materialize. This strategy gives the dotcom a flavor of the deal if the contingencies are addressed during the due diligence process.

The due diligence investigation must follow an organized procedure that begins with an investigation checklist that clearly itemizes areas of the dotcom's operation that will be probed. Guidelines are established to assure the investigation is not intrusive on the dotcom's operation and to maintain a low profile within the industry.

Documents gathered by investigators must be organized and protected. Each item on the checklist must be prioritized and a threshold created. This helps to reduce due diligence expenses and focus investigators on meaningful areas. Priority is determined by the relevant importance an item has on a deal.

A litigation analysis must be undertaken to uncover previous, current, and threatened litigation. Litigation is divided into material and immaterial litigation. Of particular concern is the exposure the company might have after the deal is consummated. This is called successor liability. Although the company and the dotcom are separate entities, a merger or acquisition combines their business operations. The litigation analysis team must determine what debt or torts, if any, transfer to the company following a done deal.

Due diligence must consider environmental factors that can influence the dotcom and carry through to the company after signing the deal agreement. Failure to perform a comprehensive environmental analysis exposes the company to liabilities that could have profound effects on the business operations of both the dotcom and of the company, following the deal. An environmental analysis considers regulations on the federal, state, and local levels, each of which can take action that affects a dotcom's current and future operation.

Due diligence results are presented in many reports, prepared by investigators, and each covers a different aspect of the dotcom. Each report should contain five sections: facts uncovered independently by investigators; facts that substantiate representations made by the dotcom; facts that refute representations made by the dotcom; representations made by the dotcom that cannot be substantiated; and the investigators' opinions.

The company's management is responsible for determining how much influence factors that receive negative opinions from investigators have on the deal.

QUESTIONS

1. Explain the purpose of due diligence.

2. How could environmental issues affect a dotcom company?

3. Explore the steps required to conduct litigation analysis.

4. How can a company become a defendant of litigation involving a dotcom?

5. Explain how experts are likely to render a decision on an aspect of the dotcom.

6. How should thresholds be established?

7. How can you avoid delays caused by the due diligence process?

8. What role does a dotcom's warranty plan in the liability of a company?

9. How can you prevent disagreements between the dotcom and the company over a due diligence investigation?

10. How do you handle a substantial misrepresentation made by the dotcom?

CHAPTER 3

Structuring and Financing the Deal

Careful borrowing makes dreams a reality.
—Anonymous

In This Chapter

- Types of Transactions
- Financing Options
- Structuring Debt
- Leaseback Financing
- Take-Back Financing
- Bridge Financing
- High Yield Bonds
- Refinancing
- Financing Through Insurance Companies
- The Financing Process
- Legal Considerations

TYPES OF TRANSACTIONS

Three kinds of transactions are used to acquire a business. These are asset purchase, stock purchase, and a merger of both businesses. The choice of transaction depends on the capitalization of the buyer, tax implications, and the degree of liability the buyer is willing to accept. A buyer that is well capitalized might choose an asset purchase to simplify the acquisition without the liability exposure presented in a stock purchase or merger. In a stock purchase or merger, the buyer assumes the assets and liabilities of the seller.

A stock purchase or merger is preferred whenever the buyer assumes the seller's business operation, because negotiations are based on the valuation of the entire business rather than limited to the value of particular assets. A stock purchase or merger is more complicated than an asset purchase because of the complex nature of a business operation. However, there are legal and tax advantages to the buyer, because titles to assets don't change necessarily. Only title to stock changes.

The advantages and disadvantages of asset purchase, stock purchase, and merger are discussed in this section.

Asset Purchases

An asset purchase occurs when the buyer acquires all rights of the seller in an asset in exchange for consideration. Consideration can consist of cash, stock, or a combination of both, as negotiated between the buyer and seller.

Assets are classified as tangible assets and intangible assets. Tangible assets are physical property such as software to run a Web site, real estate, and computer equipment. Intangible assets are domain names, copyrights, trademarks, and leases. Both tangible and intangible assets are transferred from the seller to the buyer when the negotiated consideration for the asset is paid by the buyer to the seller and the seller provides the buyer with appropriate documents that demonstrate title has transferred. These documents include a bill of sale and a deed.

An asset purchase is advantageous over other kinds of acquisitions whenever a transaction involves a portion of the seller's business rather than the entire business. An asset is a well-defined component of a business that has a value and can easily be transferred to the buyer. In contrast, an entire business is a complex organization of assets and business operations that may not be divided into concise units that can be sold individually.

Let's say a dotcom company operates two Web sites, each with its own well-known domain. One Web site is an auction site and the other is a retail travel site. A buyer is interested in acquiring the auction site. However, there isn't a clear division between the operations of each site. Each Web site has its own servers and software, but share the same management team, facilities, and support staff. Spinning off the auction site through the sale of stock is a complex undertaking, because the two Web sites are not operated as independent businesses.

A simpler acquisition method is to acquire the assets used in the auction site. In this case, the seller transfers to the buyer servers, software, and intangible assets such as domain names and trade names used in the auction Web site. The buyer relocates these assets to the buyer's own facilities and offers employment to management and staff who operate the auction—at the same or better terms than they currently receive from the seller (see Chapter 6, "Public and Private Corporations," for a full discussion of personnel issues).

Once the buyer agrees to move forward with an asset purchase, the buyer must receive approval from 50 percent of the owners of common stock for the sale of substantially all assets of the seller. This assumes the corporation falls under Delaware law or a derivative. Many states use Delaware corporate law as a model for their own corporate laws.

Liabilities

Limiting liability is a primary reason a buyer makes an asset purchase rather than a stock purchase. Generally, business liabilities incurred by the seller do not transfer to the buyer when assets are purchased, although there are exceptions. The buyer can agree to accept specific liabilities as part of the sales agreement. In this case, specified liabilities transfer from the seller to the buyer.

Liability might transfer with the asset under other circumstances, including if the asset is inventory and the seller has outstanding obligations to creditors, if the sale price is materially below the market value of the asset, or if all the assets of a seller are purchased.

Asset purchases are governed by a form of the Uniform Commercial Code (UCC), which has been adopted by every jurisdiction except Louisiana. A critical component of the UCC is the bulk sales law. The bulk sales law focuses on inventory transfer to the buyer and requires that if the asset is inventory, notice of the transfer be sent to creditors of the seller ten days prior to the transfer. The notice identifies the party to the transaction and states whether or not the seller's obligation to the creditors will be satisfied prior to transferring title to the asset.

The buyer must be assured that the seller's obligations to creditors are addressed. Failure to do so could transfer the seller's liability to its creditors to the buyer. Buyers typically place a portion of the purchase price in escrow to satisfy the seller's creditors and avoid pass-through liability.

Fraud statutes in local jurisdictions must be reviewed carefully before an asset purchase is consummated to avoid unexpected liability. A buyer in some cases can be held liable to the seller's creditors if the price of the asset is well below market value and the seller cannot meet its financial obligations—even if no fraud has occurred.

A buyer must also be alert to the de facto merger doctrine whenever a buyer purchases all the assets of a seller. Local jurisdictions might declare an asset purchase a de facto merger if, after the acquisition of a business's assets, stockholders of the seller's business become stockholders of the buyer's business. In this case, the liabilities of the seller are transferred to the buyer, because the asset purchase had the same effect as a merger of the seller and buyer.

Tech Talk

Uniform Commercial Code: A set of rules created by the National Conference of Commissioners of Uniform State Laws that govern the conduct of business.

From Tim Miller, Webmergers.com

Incubator as Acquirers

Incubators and venture capitalists out of necessity, and sometimes desperation, are constantly adapting to the dizzying rate of change in the new economy. Back in the days of Internet euphoria, we saw new varieties of incubators and accelerators emerge. Now we're seeing these entities morph into new financial creatures designed to take advantage of the new realities of the Internet marketplace. As they adapt, some incubators find themselves getting into M&A, like it or not.

Incubators and VCs have increasingly found themselves in the role of buyers of Internet companies. In most cases, the deals have been by relatively obscure incubators, although Idealab has purchased such companies as music site Spun.com and the remnants of content push company Pointcast. Also, Idealab company PetJungle.com merged with PETsMART.com.

In a European example, e-auctioneer Bid2Day Scandinavia AB, which is backed by UK incubator NewMedia SPARK, acquired Tradera AB, its Swedish counterpart. And of course large Internet holding companies like CMGI, Inc. have been active buyers, with CMGI buying 34 Internet companies.

It remains to be seen whether incubator-as-buyer will persist in current market conditions. Idealab, for one, appears to have lost its appetite, with founder Bill Gross recently telling *The New York Times* that past acquisitions have not panned out and that he doesn't plan future acquisitions. Just weeks ago, Idealab pulled its planned IPO due to market conditions.

For most incubators, buying new companies takes a back seat to marrying off the squawking hatchlings that presently crowd their nests. CMGI, for example, pared its flock of some 50 companies down to 15 through internal mergers, divestitures, and shutdowns.

To this end, equity sponsors are frantically arranging shotgun weddings, either within their own portfolios or with their fellow VCs. Idealab has already been quite active in coupling its portfolio companies. For example, Idealab—backed by Paymybills.com—acquired fellow Idealab personal payments company Payme.com.

VCs and incubators are also reaching out to each other for matchmaking prospects. We have noticed an increasing number of mergers in which both buyer and seller are backed by VCs, incubators, or angels. Perhaps the most dramatic example of VC-to-VC matchmaking occurred in what turned out to be a six-way marriage of venture-backed firms. Bidcom, Inc., a construction industry e-commerce exchange, acquired competitor Cephren Inc. to form a new company named Citadon. Cephren itself was formed by the merger of yet two other venture-backed firms, eBricks.com and Blueline Online. And to cap it off, Bidcom had acquired Cubus Corp.

All of the players in this six-way merger were venture backed. Blueline took its money from Telos Venture Partners, Bay Partners, and others. eBricks.com had seed investment from E. M. Warburg, Pincus & Co.

Bidcom, Cephren's acquirer, had $63 million in venture financing from such funders as Internet Capital Group, GE Corporation, Partech International, and Oracle. Cubus was backed by angel group The Band of Angels and Credit Suisse First Boston Technology Group.

The merger of Bidcom and Cephren was accompanied by a $41.5 million mezzanine infusion from Cephren funders, including GE Equity Investments, GE Power Systems, Goldman Sachs & Co., and Grupo Picking Pack (GPP).

There's one big morsel left for this merger juggernaut. The remaining major competitor in the online construction space is Buzzsaw.com. That San Francisco-based firm has raised a total of $90 million to date, with its latest $75 million injection arriving from Bank of America, Impact Ventures, and Morgan Stanley–Dean Witter.

Expense

In an asset purchase, each asset is handled as a single transaction, unlike in a stock purchase, where all assets are transferred in one transaction. Many buyers find that an asset purchase is more expensive and has greater tax implications than a stock purchase, because it involves multiple transactions.

Let's consider an online retailer that has warehouse facilities throughout the United States. Each facility is treated as a separate purchase. Laws governing jurisdictions of each facility must be reviewed to assure that the asset transfer is in compliance. Typically, this requires the services of attorneys who practice in each jurisdiction, both for the seller and the buyer.

Transfer of these facilities to the buyer will likely involve a transfer tax, sales tax, and other fees that add to the cost of the deal. Furthermore, the transfer could cause each facility to be revalued for tax purposes, resulting in higher property taxes.

The transfer of ownership might trigger enforcement of other local law. Some jurisdictions require a facility to be inspected and brought up to current building and zoning regulations whenever title to the property changes hands. This can expose the buyer to unexpected expenses.

Further complications arise whenever intangible assets, such as leases and licenses, are purchased, requiring third-party approval before the title to the asset is transferred. The buyer is never assured that a third party will approve the transfer. For example, a lease typically contains a clause requiring the seller to obtain the property owner's permission to transfer a lease to the buyer. The online retailer, in our example, might have to negotiate permission with owners of warehouses if the warehouses are leased. The deal is in jeopardy should negotiations with property owners fail.

However, a stock purchase avoids these issues, because title to the asset remains in the seller's name. Title of the stock in the seller's corporation is the only title that transfers to the buyer.

Stock Purchases

A stock purchase occurs when the seller exchanges stock in the seller's corporation with a buyer for a negotiated payment. The seller's corporation ceases to exist after the deal is consummated. Special regulations must be followed if the seller is a public corporation (see Chapter 6). Private corporations are exempt from these regulations.

A stock purchase is an indirect way by which a buyer acquires the seller's rights to assets. Assets revert to the buyer without tax implications and other drawbacks realized in an asset purchase because title to the assets remains in the name of the seller's corporation.

Before a buyer enters into a stock purchase, the buyer must carefully examine the seller's liabilities and the seller's agreements with third parties to assess their impact on the deal. Unlike an asset purchase, a stock purchase transfers both the assets and liabilities of the seller to the buyer.

The seller's liabilities fall into two general classes. These are liabilities the seller discloses to the buyer and liabilities that are undisclosed. The buyer must review disclosed liabilities and determine which liabilities seem proper for the buyer to inherit. The seller, as part of the acquisition agreement, should indemnify liabilities that impose an unacceptable risk to the buyer. Likewise, the seller should agree to indemnify the buyer from undisclosed liabilities.

Agreements with third parties are also potential problems if an agreement contains an approval clause. An approval clause grants a party who has an agreement with the seller the right to renegotiate terms whenever control of the corporation changes. The approval clause negates the advantage a stock purchase has over an asset purchase, especially where intangible assets such as leases are concerned.

A third party might block transfer of a crucial asset; therefore the buyer must determine if an approval clause exists prior to consummating the stock purchase. If there is an approval clause, then the buyer has an opportunity to renegotiate or abandon the deal.

The buyer must also assess the availability of all the seller's stock before pursuing the deal. Unlike an asset purchase that requires 50 percent stockholder approval, a stock purchase requires 100 percent stockholder approval. The buyer needs to be assured that all stockholders will sell their stock to the buyer. The deal can collapse if one share remains outstanding.

From Tim Miller, Webmergers.com

Dangers of Acquisitions

Depending on your point of view, Neoforma.com picked a good or a bad time to make a series of acquisitions. On a Monday, the company, which creates B2B marketplaces for new and used medical products, bought EquipMD, Inc., a privately held company that provides procurement services for physicians.

On Friday, it bought two companies, Eclipsys (ECLP), a company that provides health care information technology solutions, and its affiliated company HEALTHvision, Inc., whose services connect health care companies with their local constituents.

Neoforma bought in stock, paying well over $2 billion for all three firms. However, its stock has since slid dramatically, caught in a crossfire of a stock meltdown and announcements from major competitors.

Neoforma provides a case study of the risks of all-stock transactions. The company's "currency" has declined some 70 percent since its acquisition of U.S. Lifeline and some 50 percent since its acquisition of Eclipsys and HEALTHvision, Inc., knocking a stunning billion dollars of value out of the last deal.

While sellers can sometimes be protected by a variety of agreements, Neoforma told Reuters there was no protective "collar" surrounding the Eclipsys/HEALTHvision deal, which carries a breakup fee of around $43 million.

For well over a decade, the online industry has struggled with one big problem when it comes to health care-related services. The problem: getting physicians to change the way they do business and to pay money to participate, not necessarily in that order.

Neoforma, like others in the health care world, has decided to buy docs. Its chairman, president and chief executive Bob Zollars described its EquipMD deal as "the first of several steps we are taking to aggregate buyers" in various health care segments. In buying EquipMD, Neoforma got access to 15,000 physician customers in about 4,000 practices. The last two acquisitions brought in another 25,000 doctors.

Mergers

A merger occurs when two corporations combine assets and liabilities and only one corporation survives. The boards of directors of both corporations agree to merge by adopting a resolution, then the resolution is presented to stockholders for approval. Once approved, the merger is consummated and a certificate of merger is filed with the appropriate state agency.

A merger provides an advantage over a stock purchase in that the buyer—the corporation seeking the merger—does not deal with each stockholder in the dotcom (until after the merger). Instead, the buyer must reach terms with a majority of the dotcom's stockholders, who must approve the merger. Dissenting stockholders are required by law to participate in the merger.

However, a merger of subsidiaries of a holding corporation requires only the board of directors' approval. Stockholders are not required to vote on the merger. A subsidiary merger occurs when assets of a subsidiary of a holding corporation are transferred to another corporation. Subsidiary mergers are discussed later in this section.

Tech Talk

Subsidiary: A corporation that is solely owned by another corporation.

Types of Mergers

There are seven types of mergers. Each type of merger differs from the others by the way cash and stock transfer from the dotcom to the buyer.

Taxable Forward Merger. A taxable forward merger occurs when the buyer gives compensation, usually in the form of cash, to stockholders of the dotcom. The dotcom transfers title to its assets to the buyer. Stockholders of the dotcom are exposed to capital gains tax and the buyer is exposed to applicable asset transfer taxes and fees, as discussed previously in this chapter.

Taxable Reverse Merger. A taxable reverse merger occurs when the buyer gives cash to stockholders of the dotcom. Shares of the dotcom are distributed to stockholders of the buyer. The capital gains tax exposure remains for the dotcom's stockholders.

Taxable Forward Subsidiary Merger. A taxable forward subsidiary merger occurs when a buyer gives cash to stockholders of the dotcom and the dotcom's assets are merged with a subsidiary of the buyer. Let's say A-Holding Corporation has a solely owned subsidiary called A-Dotcom. A-Holding Corporation wants to merge B-Dotcom with A-Dotcom, and enters into a taxable forward subsidiary merger. A-Holding Corporation gives stockholders of B-Dotcom cash. B-Dotcom transfers the assets of its corporation to A-Dotcom. Stockholders of the dotcom are exposed to capital gains tax because they received cash for their stock in the dotcom.

Tax-Free Forward Merger. A tax-free forward merger (known as an *A-reorganization*) occurs when the buyer's stockholders give the dotcom's stockholders stock in the buyer. The dotcom transfers its assets to the buyer. This transaction is tax-free because the stockholders of the dotcom retain title to the assets, since they own shares of the buyer. A tax-free forward merger is commonly referred to as a *corporate reorganization*.

Tax-Free Forward Triangular Merger. A tax-free forward triangular merger is a type of subsidiary merger that occurs when the buyer gives the dotcom's stockholders shares in the buyer's holding corporation and the dotcom's assets are transferred to the buyer's subsidiary. Here's how it works. A-Holding Corporation has a solely owned subsidiary called A-Dotcom. A-Holding Corporation wants to merge B-Dotcom with A-Dotcom. Stockholders of A-Holding Corporation give stock in A-Holding Corporation to stockholders of B-Dotcom. B-Dotcom transfers its assets to A-Dotcom. Stockholders in B-Dotcom retain ownership of assets formerly held by B-Dotcom because they hold stock in A-Holding Corporation.

Tax-Free Acquisition of Stock Merger. A tax-free acquisition of stock merger (known as a *B-reorganization*) occurs when corporations exchange stock. Let's say that A-Dotcom wants to merge with B-Dotcom, where A-Dotcom is the survivor. Stockholders of A-Dotcom give stockholders of B-Dotcom shares of A-Dotcom in exchange for their shares of B-Dotcom. Stockholders of B-Dotcom retain ownership of assets of B-Dotcom after the assets are transferred to A-Dotcom because B-Dotcom stockholders now own A-Dotcom. Therefore, the merger is tax-free.

Acquisition of Property for Stock Merger. An acquisition of property for stock merger (known as a *C-reorganization*) occurs when a corporation exchanges stock for assets of another corporation. For example, A-Dotcom wants to merge with B-Dotcom, where A-Dotcom is the survivor. Stockholders of A-Dotcom give stockholders of B-Dotcom stock in A-Dotcom. In return, B-Dotcom transfers its assets to A-Dotcom.

In addition to the A-reorganization, B-reorganization, and C-reorganization mentioned here, there is a D-reorganization. A D-reorganization is not a merger. Instead a D-reorganization occurs when a holding company transfers assets to a subsidiary.

Stock Purchase-Merger Strategy

A majority of stockholders of the dotcom must approve a merger. However, approval in some situations might be difficult to achieve because of dissenting stockholders in the dotcom. In such a case, the buyer can use a combination of stock purchase and merger to circumvent dissenting stockholders. This is called the *stock purchase-merger strategy.*

The initial phase of the stock purchase-merger strategy is for the buyer to make a stock purchase of a majority of stock in the dotcom before announcing merger plans. Once the controlling block of stock is acquired, the buyer proposes the merger, then votes the block of stock in the dotcom to approve the merger. The dissenting stockholders of the dotcom must follow the decision of the majority stockholders.

Caution

A premium is typically paid to stockholders in the dotcom in order to acquire the majority of stock. The premium is not paid to the minority stockholders in the dotcom once the merger is approved. However, some federal regulations may prohibit this price differential, so counsel should investigate federal regulations before initiating the stock purchase.

The stock purchase-merger strategy is also implemented whenever the buyer wants to vary compensation paid to stockholders of the dotcom. For example, a major stockholder in the dotcom may accept a note rather than cash for his or her position in the dotcom. The note might be important to the financing strategy of the buyer. Therefore, the stockholder and the buyer consummate a stock purchase, the arrangements of which are not available to other dotcom stockholders.

From Tim Miller, Webmergers.com

Incubator as Intermediary

While some financiers are playing internal yenta, at least one incubator has gone the next step, transforming itself into an M&A brokerage of sorts.

Santa Monica-based incubator NetCatalyst positioned itself as a "liquidity engineering" outfit that takes a hands-on approach to fix sellers' business models before taking them to the auction block. Its activist role might well be dubbed "M&A accelerator."

NetCatalyst believes activism is necessary. "You can no longer just go out there and sell an Internet company," says NetCatalyst managing director and startup veteran Riggs Eckelberry, "You have to do something in order to get a decent valuation."

In the dotcom battlefield, Eckelberry sees NetCatalyst as a field hospital for companies that still have some life—and cash—left. "VCs and incubators can only handle one or two of their wounded at a time, so in a way we're an outsourced resource for them, " he said. "We'll be their extension into that company.... We identify what's needed and have a strong CEO-level team come in and take immediate action while we pursue opportunities."

Is NetCatalyst just engaged in high-end window-dressing? No, says Eckelberry. "It's like shocking a pool; your only option is to shock it when it gets green and gross." And, he added, "It's a lot more than most merchant bankers do."

For example, NetCatalyst might do an instant makeover of a client's customer relations management system to goose revenue from added upsell or cross-sell of products.

The firm has a half dozen active engagements, Eckelberry said. In one non-M&A-related engagement, NetCatalyst worked with Email Shows, a dotcom that enables users to eavesdrop on fictional email exchanges between actors from Hollywood features—an effort to "monetize" fan clubs.

For this company, NetCatalyst acted as virtual business development resource, bringing them deals with a number of Tinseltown fan sites. In another deal earlier this year, NetCatalyst helped roll up about three dozen music fan sites into a portal for music fans called Musicfans.com.

NetCatalyst doesn't have its own fund but rather relies on funding partners on an as-needed basis. The firm has three revenue models. For active advisory work, which in many ways resembles a traditional venture capital role, the company usually receives equity. When it sends in a "strike team" for two to four months, NetCatalyst usually asks for a hybrid fee-plus-incentive deal. An M&A deal works on a success fee basis, with fee commensurate to the amount of "liquidity engineering" that takes place.

Netcatalyst emerged out of the union of two incubators run by technology executive Ron Posner and former financial executive Chris Karkenny. Eckelberry said it is the union of Karkenny's financial skills with Posner's operating experience that gives NetCatalyst an activist edge. "Financial organizations can do great deals, but they are powerless when it comes to dealing with a broken company," he said.

Posner is an active investor and former CEO or senior executive at such companies as Peter Norton Computing, WordStar, and Ashton-Tate. Karkenny is former treasurer of Quarterdeck Corp. and Eckelberry started an Internet direct marketing company and had previously helped sell several Internet companies.

NetCatalyst is aggressively creating offices and partnerships around the world to enable portfolio companies to expand or merge globally. It has partners in England, France, Italy, Sweden, and Asia and recently took a stake in London-based Mindship, a networking outfit that attempts to link global Internet accelerators to aid in cross-border collaboration.

FINANCING OPTIONS

There are four common methods used to finance a deal. These are cash, stock, notes, or a combination. The cash financing method is when a buyer exchanges cash for stock or assets of the dotcom. Cash is raised through accumulated excess revenue from current operations, new issues floated by the buyer, liquidation of the buyer's assets, and/or debt incurred by the buyer.

The stock financing method is the exchange of the buyer's stock for assets or stock of the dotcom. Stockholders in the dotcom become stockholders in the buyer. The number of shares that are exchanged is negotiated.

The note financing method requires the dotcom or a third-party lender to accept a note from the buyer in lieu of cash or stock. In exchange, the dotcom transfers its assets or stock to the buyer.

Each method has advantages and disadvantages that must be weighed carefully before deciding the appropriate financing method to use for a deal. The cash financing method is the simplest, since no ongoing financial commitments exists between the buyer, the dotcom. and third parties once the deal is consummated. Third parties are lenders.

However, the buyer's acquisition of the cash might have unexpected disadvantages. Let's say that cash used to acquire a dotcom is realized through the issuance of new shares of the buyer to the public. The new shares dilute existing stockholder positions and could alter control of the buyer. Similarly, the sale of the buyer's assets could expose the corporation to unforeseen liabilities, such as taxes and labor strife.

The stock financing method conserves cash resources and enables the cash to be used to generate additional cash flows from other investments. However, the buyer must acquire the stock in the buyer's corporation that will be used in financing the deal. The buyer's stock can be treasury stock that is either purchased from the market or that the treasury has not as yet issued.

The note financing method also conserves cash resources, but redirects some cash flow to retired debt. Note financing might impose terms that restrict business operations. For example, the buyer may need to maintain a specified debt-to-asset ratio. Failure to do so might give the lender the right to call in the note. Restrictions are discussed later in this chapter.

Tech Talk

Treasury Stock: Shares of a corporation owned by the corporation.
Cash Flow: A series of cash payments generated by business operations and/or investments.

Maximum Leveraged Strategy

At the extreme end of the financing scale is the maximum leveraged strategy, also known as a *leveraged buyout,* where the acquiring company's capital structure is substantially more debt than equity. The maximum leveraged strategy requires the buyer to borrow as much of the acquisition cost as possible from lenders.

The concept of the maximum leveraged strategy is easy to understand. Typically, the buyer uses the assets of the dotcom as collateral for loans, the proceeds of which are used to purchase the assets or stock of the dotcom. However, there is a wrinkle in the strategy, because the buyer needs title to the dotcom's assets to collateralize the loan. Title does not transfer from the dotcom to the buyer until the deal is consummated, which doesn't occur until the buyer compensates the dotcom. This becomes a catch-22.

One of two solutions is used to overcome this obstacle. However, before either solution is implemented, lenders and the dotcom need to understand that the buyer is using the maximum leveraged strategy and to understand the nature of the collateralization problem that is associated with this strategy.

The first solution is for the acquisition agreement and the loan agreement to be executed simultaneously. Documents for both agreements are signed in the same room at the same time. This means the transfer of title to the asset, cash payment for the asset, and lien on the asset also occur simultaneously.

Technically, however, the dotcom and/or the lender are exposed to risk for a few minutes during the signing. For example, the buyer might sign the loan agreement before the dotcom signs the title transfer agreement. Technically, the buyer signed an agreement to use assets it does not own as yet as collateral for the note.

If any party to the deal becomes uncomfortable with such a risk, then a second solution can be used to avoid this timing problem. The second solution requires the buyer to give the dotcom a promissory note in exchange for title to the asset. At that point, the buyer possesses title to the asset and can execute the loan agreement with the lender. Proceeds from the loan agreement are used to retire the promissory note. The execution of all agreements occurs within minutes of each other.

Before embarking on the maximum leveraged strategy, the buyer must be sure that debt service is comfortably funded through cash flows generated by the acquisition. Avoid using the maximum leveraged strategy if there isn't a steady, predictable cash flow, such as is the case in a startup dotcom. Failure to meet this requirement will have a negative effect on performance. The primary advantage of the maximum leveraged strategy is that cash flows used for debit service can be redirected for other purposes, including profit as loans are paid down.

A buyer can reduce debt service caused by the maximum leveraged strategy by selling all or some of the dotcom's assets after the deal is consummated. It is common for a buyer to negotiate the sale of the dotcom's assets prior to the deal with dotcom. Shortly after the acquisition, the buyer sells the assets.

Minimum Leveraged Strategy

The minimum leveraged strategy requires the buyer to minimize compensation paid for a dotcom. Compensation must take into consideration ancillary expenditures that include administrative costs and fees, refinancing expenses, operating capital, and exposure to current and potential litigation.

The minimum leveraged strategy begins by identifying the expenses involved in the deal, then determining if the dotcom or the buyer is responsible for the expense. It is to the advantage of the buyer to shift as many expenses as possible to the dotcom, thereby reducing the ancillary expenditures that are necessary to close the deal.

Pass-Through Liabilities

Next, the buyer examines the dotcom's debt structure to identify the dotcom's liabilities that might be inherited by the buyer. Where possible, the dotcom's liabilities should be satisfied from the proceeds of the deal rather than become an ongoing drain on cash flow for the buyer. This means a minimum of the dotcom's liability is passed through to the buyer.

An alternative to retiring the dotcom's liability is for the buyer to adjust the acquisition price downward to compensate for carrying forward existing liabilities. This might be advantageous to the buyer, because terms of inherited liabilities may be renegotiated with the lender to the favor of the buyer.

In some situations, the buyer is in a better financial position than a dotcom to accept risks such as current litigation against the dotcom. The buyer could forego the dotcom indemnifying the buyer for those risks in lieu of a lower acquisition price.

Partial Acquisition

Next, the buyer determines if it is sensible to acquire a portion of a dotcom's operation rather than the dotcom's full operation. Acquiring only the parts of the dotcom that are beneficial to the buyer tends to reduce the cash requirements for the deal.

For example, A-Dotcom wants to expand its auction Web site. B-Dotcom has an auction Web site, along with a retail Web site. A-Dotcom can lower the acquisition cost by acquiring only B-Dotcom's auction Web site. As an alternative, A-Dotcom might purchase the entire B-Dotcom, then sell off the retail Web site, effectively lowering the acquisition price of the auction Web site.

Sell-Offs

Before considering the sell-off option, a buyer must carefully examine the marketability of sell-off candidates. No assumption should be made that a component of the dotcom can be sold. The buyer needs to locate potential buyers for each component prior to consummating the deal to determine the market value of a component. Ideally, an agreement to sell off the component is signed in advance of closing the deal with the dotcom. A sell-off agreement typically contains a contingency clause that makes the sell-off agreement invalid if the deal with the dotcom fails.

Hidden Cash

Next, the acquiring corporation needs to examine the dotcom closely to determine if the dotcom has potential cash. Potential cash consists of cash and near-cash assets that are not obvious during the initial examination of a dotcom's books and records. Potential cash can be used to lower the acquisition price by assigning those funds to the dotcom, or it can be liquidated and used to offset the price. Here are areas to search for potential cash:

- Real estate recorded far below market value
- Pending lawsuits that can quickly settled and bring in a one-time cash flow
- Overfunded pension plans, where an adjustment results in cash to the dotcom
- Tangible property, such as art, that has appreciated significantly
- Substantial receivables that have become the property of the buyer

Incentives

Finally, the buyer can offer the dotcom incentives to consummate the deal at a favorable price. Incentives include a fast closing because financing is in place; favorable treatment of employees who the buyer retains and of those who terminate employment; and favorable arrangements with key managers, including bonuses and profit-sharing.

Keeping Existing Debt and Leases

Inheriting a dotcom's debt and lease liabilities is at times a strategy that minimizes leverage of a deal if the terms of the obligation are more attractive to the buyer than is the market price for comparable agreements. Terms of an obligation are transferable if the debt or lease agreement does not restrict assignment of the obligation to a third party. A restriction could prevent or severely limit assignment by requiring a penalty for early termination of the obligation. For example, a lender might require extra consideration to assign the debt to the buyer. Likewise, the lender may require the buyer to pay a penalty if the buyer prepays the loan. In contrast, other obligations may have generous restrictions or none at all. A lender may honor the terms if the buyer passes the lender's approval process, such as a routine credit check.

It is critical that the buyer perform a market-to-market analysis of the dotcom's existing debt and leases to assess whether or not terms of these obligations are favorable. Market conditions fluctuate; therefore, terms of older obligations rarely reflect current market conditions unless a variable rate is used.

Lenders are in tune with the debt and lease market and will apply or waive restrictive clauses in the debt or lease, depending on whether conditions are favorable to the lender. Let's say an existing loan is three points higher than the current market. Transferring the loan to the buyer is an advantage to the lender, because the loan returns a higher cash flow than is available in the current market.

Alternatively, a lender might encourage early termination of the loan and forego prepayment penalties if current rates are appreciably higher than the interest rate of the loan.

Caution

The buyer can negotiate a better acquisition price by accepting liabilities for a loan carrying a high interest rate if the loan carries a minimal or no prepayment penalty. The buyer can refinance the loan once the deal is consummated and realize a higher cash flow than if the loan remained enforced.

Caution

An asset purchase may have hidden restrictions that prohibit the dotcom from transferring title to the buyer, even if a debt or lease obligation is transferable. Unsecured debt incurred by the dotcom may be contingent upon the continued operation of the enterprise. The asset may be a critical component of the dotcom's operation and therefore nontransferable without an arrangement with the lender of the unsecured obligation.

Caution

Be sure regulations of local jurisdictions are examined carefully to assess whether or not a merger constitutes a transfer of ownership. Restrictions in debt and leases whereby the debt or lease lender must approve transfer of control in the dotcom may or may not apply in a merger. Some jurisdictions don't consider a merger a change of ownership, because the buyer inherits the obligation of the dotcom.

The Lender's View

Once the buyer determines that maintaining a debt or lease is a favorable financing method, the lender of the debt or lease must be contacted by both the buyer and the dotcom and informed of the deal.

The lender reviews the financials of the buyer to assess the credit risk of transferring the debt or lease to the buyer. Depending on the results of the assessment, the lender may permit the transfer, renegotiate terms, or recall the debt or lease. Recall is possible if the debt or lease agreement contains a clause giving the lender the right of refusal.

Renegotiations have advantages and disadvantages, depending on market conditions. For example, a low market demand for the debt or the leased equipment gives the buyer an advantage, since the market place provides the lender with limited recourse. The opposite is true if there is heavy demand in the market place for capital or the leased equipment.

A high credit risk does not automatically forego the opportunity for the buyer to continue the debt or lease. The lender may transfer the obligation if the dotcom becomes a guarantor of all or part of the obligation. In such a case, the buyer compensates the dotcom for its cooperation when negotiating the acquisition price.

Maintaining Relationships

The buyer should explore whether or not it is desirable and feasible to maintain agreements with the dotcom's financial institutions and vendors, since they are both comfortable financing an aspect of the business.

Financial institutions typically provide the dotcom with revolving credit as working capital, and letters of credit to vendors. These relationships are maintainable, although terms probably need to be renegotiated.

Vendors provide financing when they deliver goods, then extend payment for 10 to 90 days. Floating payment might be at favorable rates or interest free. These terms too might require renegotiation, although it is in the best interest of vendors to continue a relationship with the buyer.

Intercorporate financing is other financing that might be in place and can be inherited by the buyer. Intercorporate financing occurs when a holding corporation directly finances a subsidiary. The buyer examines the possibility that an intercorporate financing obligation might be transferred to the buyer, assuming the buyer acquires the subsidiary of the holding corporation. This is a form of take-back financing in which the dotcom accepts a note in lieu of cash as part or all of the compensation for the deal.

From Tim Miller, Webmergers.com

The Rollup Strategy

The Internet is a potential fun fair for rollup artists. The Net has spawned tens of thousands of specialized startups that are often relatively simple to buy and integrate. Here's why we believe there is an untapped market for rollups of certain kinds of Internet destinations, such as Internet content properties:

Rollups Make Business Sense

- The Internet is inherently a narrowcast medium. Unlike any medium in history, the Web enables the creation of highly specialized content sites, newsletters, and services. These micro-niches are often financially viable even at very low volumes, but total revenues for any given property are usually quite small.

- Thousands of passionate entrepreneurs have taken advantage of the Web's low entry barriers to build such specialized Web properties. A founders' vision, passion, and hard work are often key to the success of the site.

- In order to build a substantial business within niches, it is necessary to aggregate a number of such related vertical sites.

- Once aggregated, a "virtual circle" begins to kick in: The network can bring new traffic to acquired sites and the acquired sites in turn contribute traffic to other network sites.

- It's often quicker to buy rather than build niche sites.

- Prices have tended to be reasonable.

- Retention can be high. Founders often stay happily on board because the deal frees them to focus on their original passion—the content—and foist off the hosting, ad sales, and other infrastructure details to the buyer.

- Dealmaking is partly virtual: Much of the deal can be done via email and phone, without a series of costly onsite meetings. Internet.com, for example, has purchased a number of sites without ever having met in person with the principals. Also, new tools are emerging at the back end to support online collaboration and dealmaking.

- Integration can be "lite": Some sites, notably content sites and some e-commerce sites, lend themselves well to very light integration that consists mainly of transferring the site to a new server, switching advertising servers, and setting up some financial and administrative reporting systems. Of course for e-commerce and other transactional properties, integrating back ends gets much more complex.

> • Encrustation has not set in: Most Web properties are young, small, and relatively malleable. They're not so set in their cultures as to be unable to mesh with an acquirer. Besides, in a true "network," too much homogenization is not even wanted or needed, because it might well destroy the unique look and feel of a site that drew its users in the first place.

STRUCTURING DEBT

Debt is a typical component of every acquisition, except when a deal involves total cash or stock compensation. Debt extends the cash flow generated by business operations by borrowing additional cash that is used to take advantage of opportunities to increase cash flow in current or future operations. The buyer negotiates a loan agreement that guarantees the lender a return of principal and interest. Interest is the sum paid to the lender for the risk of losing the principal should the buyer fail to repay the principal.

Risk Assessment

A lender determines the risk of a loan by assessing the creditworthiness of the buyer. The objective of this assessment is to ascertain the buyer's ability to repay the principal and interest. The assessment method differs among lenders; however, ratios are typically used to compare the buyer with corporations in the same industry.

Various financial ratios are used to assess the creditworthiness of the buyer. Two of the most common are the current ratio and the quick ratio, which are called *liquidation ratios* because they indicate the solvency of the buyer. The current ratio determines the number of times total current assets of a buyer cover total current liabilities.

Tech Talk

Current Ratio: Total current assets:total current liabilities.

For example, a dotcom that has $600 million in total current assets and $400 million in total current liabilities has a current ratio of 1:1.6. This means that for every dollar in liability, the dotcom has 1.6 dollars in assets should the dotcom liquidate.

The quick ratio is another commonly used financial ratio and gives a lender an indication of how well a buyer can meet obligations if there is a downturn in business. The quick ratio is similar to the current ratio, except that inventory is removed from the current assets because the value of inventory depreciates substantially if the market for the product diminishes.

Tech Talk

Quick Ratio: Total current assets (less inventory):total current liabilities.
Current Assets: Assets that can be converted into cash within a year.
Current Liabilities: Liabilities due within a year.

Let's say a dotcom reseller of books has total current assets of $650 million and that $220 million of those assets is in inventory. Current liabilities amount to $400 million. This gives the dotcom reseller a quick ratio of 1:1.07, meaning that it barely has enough assets to cover outstanding obligations should the dotcom need to liquidate.

Each lender determines a satisfactory ratio based on common business practice and on the buyer's industry. For example, common business practice may rank a buyer as a high risk if the quick ratio is 1:1, because there is no margin for error. In contrast, a quick ratio of 1:5 might be a high risk if the industry quick ratio average is 1:2, where assets overwhelmingly cover liabilities.

From Tim Miller, Webmergers.com

Rollups in Practice

Alan Meckler has bought 67 Web sites in the past five years. He's rolled them up into Internet.com, Corp., an Internet-industry-focused content company that now sports 122 Web sites split out into more than a dozen "channels," eight million page views per weekday, and 3.5 million subscribers to 250 email newsletters.

And amid the troubled world of dotcom content, Internet.com is doing quite well, thank you. The company sports a market cap of close to $730 million, has more than $80 million in cash, and currently maintains a stock price around $27, which, while certainly well below its 52-week high of $72, is more than double its low of $12.25 and much healthier than many of its content peers.

Internet.com spent $16 million plus for ClickZ Network, which offers online and offline content about Internet marketing. Previously, the average deal was about $900,000.

Meckler is feeling quite good about his rollup strategy, which focuses solely on content and e-commerce sites that relate to Internet technology, marketing, finance, and other Net topics. Although sites range from topics as diverse as Application Service Providers (ASPs), *www.aspwatch.com,* to PDAs, *www.pdastreet.com,* in the final analysis, they still have a common appeal to people who are intensely interested, for personal or business reasons, in new technology. In Meckler's view, this very focus is a secret to his success.

"The fatal flaw is not being totally focused," he said. "And we're damn focused." A laser focus on Internet-related topics, he said, causes synergies across the Internet.com network. "We know that anything we buy is going to jump in page views immediately," Meckler explained, "because the topics are so closely related." In addition, he points out, marketing is much easier and inexpensive to do when portfolio companies have a high audience overlap.

Conversely, Meckler believes that rollups of nonrelated dotcom businesses create undue marketing burdens on the owner. He points to VerticalNet, which has made 20 acquisitions to help build a collection of 57 B2B exchanges in sectors ranging from meat and poultry to water quality. "The only connection between water pollution and poultry is that chickens drink water," Meckler said.

Meckler likens Internet publishing to newsletter publishing gone wild. Indeed, several decades ago as a fledgling publisher, he cut his narrow-casting incisors on a motley collection of profit-free newsletters and journals. "My great fortune was that I didn't make any money for 20 years, but that I learned verticality," Meckler said. He says the "father of verticality" in specialty academic journals was media baron Robert Maxwell, who built Pergamon Press into a highly profitable collection of specialized journals.

Meckler says another secret to Internet content is keeping the audience qualified. Because his audience is focused and highly involved, Meckler can charge advertisers average CPMs of $40 for banners and $60 for newsletters, far above the highly eroded CPMs that now lie south of $5 or $10 in many other less refined audience sectors.

Don't go to *www.internet.com* looking for an impressive home page splash. The home page isn't the destination, which, Meckler says, is exactly the point. "A lot of people don't know Internet.com as a brand," he said proudly, "but there are millions of people who know one of our little newsletters and rely on it every day." Meckler said that of his eight million weekday page views, only about 40,000 come to the home page. "That's a heinous thing to most Internet people," he said, "but that's exactly how we want it."

In his first Internet acquisition in late 1994, Meckler paid two guys in Chicago about $50,000 for an ISP directory known as "The List." Since then, he's been refining his integration technique with each successive deal. Now, the minute a deal is done, Internet.com's integration team springs into place.

Duties range from such technical tasks as transferring the site to Internet.com hosts and plugging in a new advertising server to such administrative tasks as setting up financial reporting and getting business cards issued.

Deals are short and snappy. Meckler signs off on each one and is famous for making quick—and final—decisions. "We can do editorial due diligence in ten seconds," he said, noting that his team relies on only four to five metrics and can typically get a contract signed in two to three days, based on preliminary metrics, with detailed traffic log file analysis taking a couple of additional weeks.

Once the deal is done, Meckler says, his team can integrate a property in 30 to 60 days. Integration is very "lite" and typically involves placing an Internet.com banner and, more importantly, a cross-network directory, on the home page of the acquired site.

Internet.com fields a team of 10 financial people and 18 accounting professionals, who split their time between doing M&A and investing Internet.com's small venture funds, which specializes in, not surprisingly, highly vertical content and e-commerce plays.

Meckler also claims high retention of principals. Of the first 45 acquisitions, he said, only two owners have left—and even when they do leave, the sites have achieved enough momentum to keep growing. "They're happier than a clam," he said. "We come in and say, do it [content] full time...and here's another $150,000 a year—go out and hire a couple of writers."

Debt Layers

In addition to ratio analysis, a lender examines the existing debt structure of the buyer. Debt structure consists of how existing obligations are associated with assets and other obligations.

Debt can be unsecured or secured. Unsecured debt is backed by the good faith of the buyer. Secured debt is backed by collateral. In the absence of liens on specific assets such as real estate, a lender has claim to corporate assets, based on loan agreements between the buyer and lenders.

Debt is divided into two layers called *senior debt* and *subordinate debt*. In the event of a liquidation of the buyer, obligations of senior debt are satisfied before obligations of subordinate debt.

Senior debt is less risky than subordinate debt and therefore carries a lower interest rate than subordinate debt. However, with each layer, there are sublayers, each specifying the order in which debts within the layer are paid back. For example, subordinate debt has senior-subordinate, junior-subordinate, mezzanine, and take-back sublayers. Mezzanine debt is high yield bonds, commonly known as junk bonds. Take-back debt is an obligation a dotcom accepts in lieu of cash or stock payment for an acquisition. Both are discussed later in this chapter.

The objective of the buyer is to assemble a layered debt structure that provides an acceptable average cost of the debt service while providing the opportunity to expand cash flows.

Lenders of senior debt typically require specific performance by the buyer, measured by various ratios in addition to the liquidity ratios, depending on the nature of the business. However, lenders of subordinate debt accept a broader performance tolerance than senior lenders and therefore incur a higher risk and higher interest rate.

As the buyer accepts senior debt obligations, performance ratios are likely to fall below the threshold required by lenders of senior debt. Therefore, the buyer must look toward the subordinate debt market for additional capital.

Senior Debt

Senior debt is commonly used to finance the acquisition and to provide working capital as a revolving loan agreement. A revolving loan is a note that specifies a maximum amount that can be drawn at any time by the buyer.

Senior debt plays a crucial role in financing a deal. Therefore, lenders of senior debt, who are usually banks, must be presented with the proposed acquisition, once preliminary terms are reached with the dotcom. The presentation to senior lenders is time-sensitive and can make or break a deal. Avoid approaching senior lenders before details of the deal with the dotcom are in place; otherwise, senior lenders might conclude it isn't worth their expense to review the deal.

An objective of the presentation is to address foreseeable concerns a lender may have about issuing senior debt to finance a substantial portion of the capital required to close the deal. Ideally, the lender is in a position to offer a commitment letter soon after the presentation concludes.

Caution

Buyers who seek senior debt might be exposed to fees from lenders to absorb expenses lenders incurred when reviewing the deal agreement, especially if debt is not eventually provided by the lender.

Caution

Failure to secure a commitment letter from a senior lender is likely to break the deal, since senior debt is a major component of the financing structure of any deal.

The presentation to senior lenders must substantiate the project's viability and the success of the buyer once the deal is consummated. The buyer must prove to the lender that cash flow projections are realistic and include servicing both senior and subordinate debt. Failure to address these issues could hinder the creditability of the buyer in the eyes of the lender and therefore lose financing.

Senior debt can take the form of a demand note. A demand note is a loan agreement whereby the lender tightly controls the distribution of funds. Failure to comply with those controls exposes the buyer to the risk that the debt will be called.

Typically, the lender must approve of actions that are not standard business practice for the buyer. For example, drawing from a revolving loan might require the lender's approval rather than an automatic draw at the discretion of the buyer. Likewise, the use of cash flows might be restricted by the terms of the demand note to repay the note before the cash flows can be utilized for other purposes.

Protection to Lenders

Although terms of a demand note limit the discretion of the buyer, the terms give additional protection to a lender, who is likely to be a greater risk than other participants in the deal. However, the lender must be reasonable when using its discretion and have a sustainable rationale for its actions. Failure to do so exposes the lender to litigation by the buyer.

Senior lenders may insist on a structure before providing a commitment letter. Let's say A-Dotcom is an online sporting goods retailer and Brick-And-Mortar is a chain of sporting goods stores. Brick-And-Mortar agrees to acquire A-Dotcom. After the deal is consummated, A-Dotcom is deceased.

The senior lender may object to blending the operations of A-Dotcom with Brick-And-Mortar because A-Dotcom is more valuable as a separate operation than if its assets are merged with Brick-And-Mortar. The lender is concerned about retaining maximum liquidation value.

However, a restructure of the deal could address the lender's concerns. Here's how this works. Brick-And-Mortar forms a holding corporation called Brick-And-Mortar Holdings. Brick-And-Mortar Holdings is the sole stockholder in both Brick-And-Mortar and A-Dotcom.

Senior debt is issued to Brick-And-Mortar Holdings, using A-Dotcom shares as collateral. The lender retains the right to sell all shares in A-Dotcom should Brick-And-Mortar Holdings default on the debt. This is more advantageous to the lender than liquidating assets of A-Dotcom.

The lender is concerned that cash flows are directed toward debt services rather than used for other purposes, such as cash distributions to stockholders. To this end, lenders include a cash leakage clause in the loan agreement. The cash leakage clause restricts the use of excess cash flows by the buyer to the retirement of debt. For example, dividends are prohibited, compensation is limited, and loans by the buyer are prohibited. All excess cash must be used to prepay debt.

The cash leakage clause also stipulates how a prepayment is applied to the debt. A prepayment retires payments due at the end of the loan schedule rather than the next payment. In this way, the loan schedule is shortened and the lender receives principal sooner, which is reinvested. Applying the prepayment to the next loan payment keeps the length of the loan schedule intact and gives the buyer a payment holiday.

Subordinate Debt

Subordinate debt is a loan that has secondary rights to the buyer's assets should be buyer become insolvent. Primary rights are reserved for senior debt. Subordinate debt contains clauses as part of a loan agreement that restrict buyers and lenders in financing the deal.

There are at least six common clauses found in a subordinate loan agreement:

Substantive and Procedural Clause. The substantive clause stipulates the order of payment among lenders. Let's say that cash flows fail to maintain a level necessary to satisfy payments to lenders. The substantive clause defines how the buyer and lenders resolve this problem. Payments covered by the substantive clause include fees and penalties, in addition to principal and interest. The procedural clause delineates steps lenders follow to initiate litigation if the buyer defaults on the debt.

Hold and Pay Clause. Subordinate debt is exposed to a payment blockage if the buyer becomes insolvent. Any cash remaining after liquidation is used to fully pay senior lenders. Residual cash, if any, is use to satisfy subordinate lenders. That is, a buyer that defaults senior lenders is prohibited from paying subordinate lenders until the senior debt is no longer in default. It is common business practice to include a hold and pay clause in subordinate loans as a way to protect payment to senior lenders. The hold and pay clause requires subordinate lenders to hold in reserve amounts paid by the buyer to satisfy the debt until the senior lenders are paid. Let's say the buyer paid subordinate lenders before paying senior lenders. Furthermore, assume there were no excess funds to pay senior lenders. This condition triggers the hold and pay clause and enables the senior lenders to recover funds paid by the buyer to subordinate lenders to cover the buyer's obligations to senior lenders.

Prepayment Clause. Generally, payment on principal to subordinate lenders is defined in a payment schedule that begins following retirement of the senior debt. Exceptions to the payment schedule are defined in a prepayment clause. A prepayment clause is typically included in subordinate loans that prohibits prepayments except when cash flows earmarked for dividends are redirected to prepay subordinate debt. Prepayment is also allowed in conjunction with a refinancing plan, where proceeds from new issues or new subordinate debt are used to prepay existing subordinate debt.

Refinancing Clause. Subordinate loans typically contain a refinancing clause that stipulates that subordinate debt remain subordinate to senior debt in any refinancing plan instituted by the buyer. The purpose of this clause is to assure the buyer can refinance senior debt in a highly leveraged acquisition in an effort to lower debt services.

Subordinate Limitation Clause. A subordinate limitation clause is sometimes included in subordinate loans to limit the level of subordination to senior debt. For example, it is feasible for the buyer to continue to incur senior debt after subordinate debt is issued. This increases the exposure that subordinate lenders will not receive payment in the event of insolvency. The limitation clause sets the subordination level to 150 percent of senior debt set at the time the subordinate debt was issued. This means that subordinate debt is subordinate to no more than 150 percent of the senior debt value. Subordinate lenders receive payment before senior lenders once the 150 percent limit is exceeded.

Trade Debt Clause. The trade debt clause specifies the subordination of vendor debt. Vendor debt, sometimes referred to as trade debt, is cash or merchandise loaned to the buyer as part of normal business operations. For example, a publisher delivers books to an online bookseller and foregoes payment for 30 days. The online bookseller has incurred vendor debt for the net value of the books. Typically, vendor debt is placed at a higher level in the subordinate debt priority list than is take-back debt. Take-back debt is an obligation issued by the dot-com in lieu of payment for the acquisition.

Blockages and Suspensions

Loan agreements contain complex issues that must be negotiated among all lenders and the buyer. Negotiations are delicate when dealing with lenders who have opposing agendas. For example, senior lenders need assurance they will receive payment ahead of subordinate lenders. However, subordinate lenders need to be assured that they are not so far down the subordination ladder that they will not receive compensation in the case of insolvency.

Senior lenders block subordinate lenders from receiving payment whenever the buyer's cash flows fall below a level to satisfy all senior debt obligations. Blockages have a far-reaching effect for the buyer. Since the buyer is contractually blocked from paying subordinate lenders, the buyer defaults on the subordinate debt and triggers an acceleration clause. An acceleration clause gives the subordinate lender the right to call the entire debt.

Furthermore, subordinate lenders can force the buyer into involuntary bankruptcy, which can have a negative effect on all lenders. All lenders are better served if the buyer remains out of bankruptcy, because more cash flow is likely to be generated from an ongoing operation than from one that is bankrupt.

Senior lenders typically limit their right to block payment to subordinate lenders to only extraordinary situations, such as if the buyer is on the verge of insolvency. This limitation is coupled with a suspension clause that restricts the right of subordinate lenders to take action if the subordinate debt is declared in default. This suspension lasts for a specific duration, or until senior debt is paid.

Blockage and suspension of rights to take action on a debt that is in default places senior lenders and subordinate lenders at opposing positions. In the event of default, both senior lenders and subordinate lenders want cash to remain with the buyer while a workout is arranged between lenders and the buyer. A workout is an arrangement whereby the buyer is able to fulfill its debt obligations, although loans are technically in default.

Typically, senior lenders want to control subordinate lenders by blockage and suspension clauses and to control every facet of a workout. Subordinate lenders want to minimize suspension and become equal participants in a workout. Conflicts in their positions are resolved by lenders agreeing to terms that place reasonable limits on blockage and suspensions, while subordinate lenders continue to receive interest payments.

Cross-Default Clause

Senior lenders and subordinate lenders have a tendency to include a cross default clause in all loan agreements. A cross-default clause stipulates that default on any debt is default on all debt. This clause addresses the situation in which the buyer makes payment to senior lenders, but foregoes payment to subordinate lenders, placing the subordinate debt in default. In this scenario, only the subordinate lenders can take action against the buyer. The senior lenders have no standing to take any recourse because the senior debt is not in default. Therefore, subordinate lenders could cause a workout without senior debt lenders having a right to participate.

Caution

Although this section addresses lenders collectively, terms with each lender are negotiable and can differ even within the same class of lenders (i.e., senior and subordinate).

Caution

Subordinate lenders may prefer to use a separate subordination agreement to define blockages and suspensions rather than include these terms in the loan agreement. A separate subordination agreement enables the subordinate lender to associate terms to specific senior debt rather than apply terms to all senior debt.

LEASEBACK FINANCING

A buyer can finance tangible assets of a dotcom by entering into a leaseback arrangement with a third party. Leaseback financing, sometimes referred to as *sales leaseback,* is where a third party purchases the asset, then leases the asset to the buyer. The buyer provides a cash flow to the third party that covers all or a portion of the purchase price, plus interest.

Leaseback financing is similar to a collateralized loan for an asset in that a third party provides the purchase price of the asset and the buyer pays the third party a scheduled series of cash flows. However, leaseback differs from a collateralized loan in that title to the asset is transferred from the dotcom to the third party rather than to the buyer.

The buyer can use leaseback financing as a way to minimize expensive debt, such as unsecured debt, and to reduce cash expenditures, because the third party—not the buyer—purchases the asset.

There are three types of leaseback financing agreements:

- Operating lease
- Installment contract
- Finance lease

The primary difference among leaseback types is how each is treated for accounting and tax purposes.

An installment contract is where the sum of payments over the term of the lease is less than the residual value of the asset. This is sometimes referred to as a *partial pay-out lease*. The buyer has the right to purchase the asset from the third party according to terms in the leaseback agreement.

A finance lease is similar to a collateralized loan. The buyer makes claim to ownership of the asset, which might have accounting and tax advantages to the buyer.

An operating lease is similar to an installment contract, except that the asset is returned to the third party at the conclusion of the lease period. The third party then sells the asset on the open market to recover the residual value of the asset.

There are three factors that are negotiated in leaseback financing:

- The current value of the asset
- The percentage of the asset that is leased
- The interest rate paid to the third party

The buyer must have the asset appraised to determine the asset's current value and the residual value of the asset.

The liquidation value or the book value of the asset might be used to establish the current value of the asset. The liquidation value might be substantially higher than the book value. Once the buyer and the third party agree on the asset's current value, they agree on the percentage of the remaining useful life of the asset that will be expended during the term of the lease. This percentage is applied to the asset's current value to determine the value of the lease.

The buyer and the third party then negotiate the interest rate for the lease and develop a payment schedule. This too is negotiable; however, third parties tend to expect monthly payments.

Tech Talk

Liquidation Value: The expected proceeds of the sale of the asset in the open market.
Book Value: The depreciated value of the asset, used for accounting procedures.

Caution

The leaseback agreement must stipulate whether the third party or the buyer holds title to the asset, since title becomes a factor in senior and subordinate loan agreements. Lenders do not have claim to leaseback assets where a third party holds the title.

TAKE-BACK FINANCING

Take-back financing occurs when the dotcom provides funding for a portion of the acquisition and should be looked upon by the buyer as a favorable source of financing. The buyer benefits from take-back financing because the dotcom shares the risk in the future operations of the acquisition. Take-back financing may be the keystone to the financial structure of the deal should other lenders be unavailable. That is, without take-back financing, the deal might be killed.

The dotcom benefits from a take-back financing because the buyer provides incentives to the dotcom to participate. Incentives include a higher price for the acquisition and an equity kicker. An equity kicker can take the form of a warrant, which is the right to purchase stock in the buyer some time in the future at a predetermined price.

Take-back financing takes the form of a loan or preferred stock in the buyer. If a loan, take-back financing is a subordinate debt and ranks lower than other subordinate debt.

Preferred Stock

Preferred stock is equity in the buyer rather than debt. Preferred stock confers certain preferences to dividend payments and distribution of corporate assets. The buyer is required to paid dividends in full to preferred stockholders before any cash distribution is made to common stockholders. Furthermore, the buyer must pay cash or distribute other assets at least equal to the stated value of the preferred shares before any assets are distributed to common stockholders.

Let's say that the stated value of a share of preferred stock is $100. The dividend is specified as a percentage of the stated value, such as 7 percent. This means that the preferred stockholder is promised a $7.00 dividend for each share of preferred stock that is held.

Dividends on preferred stock are paid quarterly, but the buyer is not required to approve payment of dividends. Dividends are cumulative, however. This means that unpaid dividends must be paid before any cash distributions are made to common stockholders.

Preferred stock offers a number of advantages to the buyer:

- Preferred stock does not negatively impact the buyer's liquidation ratios, because preferred stock is equity, not debt.
- The buyer has a right to skip a dividend payment without fear the dotcom will take action. In contrast, a missed debt payment places the debt in default and becomes actionable by the lender.
- A dividend payment to preferred stockholders can be skipped, even in profitable years, and therefore additional cash flow can be redirected toward other opportunities rather than paid dividends.
- Holders of preferred stock do not have voting rights and therefore cannot control the buyer although they hold an equity position in the buyer.
- Preferred stock makes the deal more attractive to lenders because preferred stock provides capital to finance the deal without incurring debt obligations.

The primary disadvantages of preferred stock to the buyer are

- Preferred stock restricts dividend payments and cash distributions to common stockholders.
- The dotcom may require the buyer to issue mandatory redeemable preferred stock that specifies a future time when the buyer is forced to retire the shares. This has the same effect as paying a balloon note, which is a note that requires a substantial amount—if not all—of the principal be paid in one payment sometime in the future.
- Loss of tax benefits if the buyer is profitable. Interest payments for debt service are tax deductible. Payments to preferred stockholders are considered dividends, not interest.

Caution

The Securities and Exchange Commission (SEC) considers mandatory redeemable preferred stock as debt, not equity, and therefore might impact the balance sheet of the buyer.

Caution

The issuance of preferred stock prohibits the buyer from becoming an S corporation and therefore loses the pass-through tax advantage. See Chapter 4, "Tax Implications," for more information about tax considerations.

The advantages of receiving preferred stock by the dotcom are

- Returns that are more favorable than those of a loan.
- Dividends are paid to preferred stockholders before dividends are paid to common stockholders.
- Dividends are a fixed percentage of the stated value of the preferred issue. There isn't any fixed dividend to common stockholders.
- Unpaid dividends accumulate; therefore missed dividends are recouped as long as dividends are eventually declared.
- Preferred shares might be mandatorily redeemable, assuring that the dotcom would recover the stated value of the shares. Common stockholders are not guaranteed the value of their shares.
- Preferred shares are liquid and can be sold at any time in the secondary market.

The disadvantages of receiving preferred stock by the dotcom are

- Preferred stockholders' recovery rights are below those of subordinate lenders. They are one of the last obligations to receive any distribution should the buyer become insolvent.
- There is no contractual obligation that requires payment of dividends and principal.
- Preferred stockholders cannot take action against the buyer should dividends be missed.

- Preferred stockholders have no influence in the operation of the corporation, although they hold an equity position in the corporation. The business might be mismanaged following the deal, yet the dotcom has no right to influence management's decisions.
- The dotcom retains equity interest in the acquired operation, rather than severing the relationship.
- A loan may prove to be of greater value in the secondary market than in preferred stock.
- Preferred stock is unsecured in comparison to a loan that might be secured by collateral.

A dotcom may be reluctant to accept take-back financing because of the drawbacks, especially if the dotcom is seeking to cash out of their business, as is the case for many dotcoms. Incentives might sweeten the deal, and if pushed, the dotcom might retain a token take-back financing.

There is a greater opportunity for take-back financing when a dotcom seeks to sell a division of the corporation rather than the entire corporation. In this scenario, the dotcom has revenue sources other than the division to provide a steady cash flow and is in a more flexible position than a dotcom looking to cash out.

Warrants

Warrants are used as an equity kicker to offer a dotcom an incentive for participating in take-back financing. A warrant is an agreement that specifies the number of shares in the buyer that can be redeemed by exercising the warrant. In addition, the warrant agreement contains clauses that set the redemption price, and restrictions on redemption and transferring the warrant to a third party. Warrants typically have a dilution clause that adjusts the number of shares that can be redeemed if adjustments, such as stock splits and new issues, are made to common stock.

Caution

Initially, warrants do not jeopardize the tax pass-through feature of S corporations, because the dotcom does not own shares of the buyer. Instead, the dotcom has rights to own shares in the future. However, the S corporation status, if it exists, can be affected when the warrants are exercised. An S corporation must be an individual, and not a corporation.

BRIDGE FINANCING

Bridge financing is short-term debt used to finance an acquisition until a permanent debt is in place. Buyers use bridge financing whenever a deadline to close a deal is shorter than the time necessary to arrange long-term financing. The lender of bridge debt runs the risk that the buyer is unable to place long-term financing and thereby presents a longer term exposure than originally negotiated.

The term of bridge financing varies and can be as short as a few days and as long as 90 days. Interests rates and fees are the normal expenses involved in bridge financing. Interest rates are quoted as a percentage above the Federal Funds rate. Fees are a percentage of the principal.

Tech Talk

Federal Funds Rate: The interest the Federal Reserve Bank charges banks for loans.

Let's say A-Dotcom makes an asset purchase of B-Dotcom. A-Dotcom uses proceeds from a new issue of common stock to finance the deal. However, the new issue will not be released until 30 days following the close of the asset purchase.

A-Dotcom arranges bridge financing with A-Bank to cover the $100 million cost of acquiring assets of B-Dotcom. The Federal Funds rate is 6 percent, and A-Bank sets the bridge-financing rate at 14 percent. A-Bank also charges A-Dotcom a 1 percent fee of $1 million for the commitment letter and another 1 percent when A-Dotcom funds the loan.

However, A-Bank automatically increases the bridge-financing rate to 16 percent if A-Dotcom does not retire the loan within three months from the date the loan was funded. The higher interest rate is designed to discourage A-Dotcom from using the short-term bridge financing as a long-term financing solution. Also, the fee for the commitment letter is not refundable if A-Dotcom decides not to use the funds.

Bridge financing is negotiable, and the agreement typically contains clauses that protect the interests of the lender. The objective of the lender is to recover principal and interest in the shortest time frame. Therefore, the agreement will contain clauses that penalize the buyer for not refinancing the bridge loan within the deadline set in the bridge-financing agreement.

The buyer's objective is to make the agreement flexible and have the option to roll over the bridge loan to a long-term loan should other financing become unavailable when the bridge loan is due.

A clause common to bridge-financing agreements specifies that proceeds from refinancing must be used to retire the bridge loan. This assures the institution that cash flows from refinancing will not be redirected toward other opportunities.

Caution

Failure to repay a bridge loan by the deadline specified in the bridge-financing agreement places the bridge loan in default. A loan in default raises creditability issues with institutions that provide long-term financing.

Caution

Avoid overly restrictive terms that could easily be violated and that could place the bridge loan in default.

HIGH YIELD BONDS

High yield bonds are subordinate, unsecured debt that is classified by the market as below investment grade. These are commonly referred to as *junk bonds*. High yield bonds return a high interest rate when compared with investment grade issues because of the risk taken by the bondholder.

Typically, high yield bonds contain a clause that prevents the buyer from calling the bond for a specific period. Afterwards, the buyer must pay a premium as a penalty for prepaying the bond before the maturity date.

The high yield bond takes the form of an indenture agreement, which details the terms of the bond. The indenture agreement is between the buyer and the financial institution that represents the bondholders.

Terms contained in the indenture agreement place restrictions on the buyer and limit the sale of assets by the buyer. For example, the buyer is prevented from selling an asset unless the proceeds are used to retire debt.

Other clauses contained in the indenture agreement restrict the buyer from creating new debt and distributing cash to stockholders prior to the retirement of the high yield bond. Restricting the buyer's ability to create new debt can become too constricting. Attempt to loosen the restrictions by negotiating into this clause a liquidity ratio test that permits taking on new debt so long as the buyer maintains a specified liquidity ratio.

Likewise, negotiate a test to determine when the buyer can distribute cash to stockholders. For example, disbursements can be withheld until the net worth of the buyer exceeds a specified amount, after which time disbursements can be limited to a specified percentage of net worth.

Still another clause specifies that the obligation to repay the high yield bond is inherited by the buyer should the buyer merger or itself be acquired.

Caution

The buyer should attempt to negotiate out any restrictive clause that could easily lead to default. A high yield bond in default exposes the buyer to costly penalties and is likely to have repercussions with other lenders.

Treat all terms in a high yield indenture agreement as negotiable. Prepare for negotiations by obtaining previous indenture agreements from the financial institution. These agreements typically contain clauses the financial institution expects to use in a new indenture agreement.

Also obtain indenture agreements from other financial institutions and compare clauses within the agreements. Highlight those clauses that are too restrictive, then find similar but less restrictive clauses in the other indenture agreements. Expect financial institutions to insist on their restrictive clauses. Plan to counter by proposing less restrictive clauses found in other indenture agreements.

Caution

Conflicts may arise between senior lenders and high yield lenders when addressing the issue of disposing of assets. The high yield indenture agreement might have a clause specifying that the proceeds from selling an asset that isn't applied to senior debt must be applied to high yield debt. However, senior lenders may prefer that the proceeds remain as operating capital. Attempt to address such a concern when negotiating the high yield indenture agreement.

A buyer wishing to issue a high yield bond will negotiate terms of the indenture agreement with a financial institution such as a bank, investment bank, or insurance company. The high yield bond is then placed privately or publicly by the financial institution. Publicly held high yield bonds must be registered according to securities law. Once registered, the bond can be traded in the market.

REFINANCING

Periodically, the buyer should assess the ongoing cost of a loan agreement and compare the cost with the expense to secure new financing. The buyer should consider refinancing the loan agreement when new financing is appreciably less expensive than a current loan agreement.

Refinancing also should be considered whenever a buyer determines that an existing loan is too restrictive. Terms of the original loan agreement might hinder the buyer's attempt to comply with the loan agreement should business conditions change after the deal is finalized. Negotiations must begin with the lender quickly, before the loan becomes in default; otherwise, relationships with other lenders will be affected.

Although a loan agreement is a binding contract, refinancing can modify the agreement. Refinancing alters a loan agreement so that new terms become more favorable than existing terms to the buyer.

There are two general strategies used when refinancing a loan agreement: renegotiating terms with lenders and retiring debt before maturity. The choice of strategies to use depends on the situation.

Renegotiations

Refinancing begins when the buyer surveys other lenders to determine interests rates and conditions for replacing existing debt. The survey result is compared with each loan agreement to determine if another lender offers favorable terms.

Next, current loan agreements are categorized as favorable, marginally unfavorable, and substantially unfavorable as compared to terms offered by other lenders. Loan agreements in the favorable or marginally unfavorable categories should not be refinanced. Financing available in the current market is not substantially different from terms of these loan agreements. However, loan agreements in the substantially unfavorable category are candidates for refinancing.

Next, the buyer determines the expense that would be incurred to prepay loans in the substantially unfavorable category. In some cases, prepayment penalties and other fees makes it uneconomical to retire the loan. Gains realized by lower interest rates might be offset by prepayment penalties and fees.

Finally, the buyer approaches the lender of the current loan and requests to renegotiate the loan agreement, using the survey results as leverage in the renegotiations. Continuing with the current lender can be advantageous because a working relationship has been established and the lender is knowledgeable about the buyer and about the deal.

Changing the terms of an existing loan agreement is more expedient than creating a new loan agreement, so long as the buyer's operations has substantially remained unchanged. The buyer can always enlist the services of another lender if renegotiations fail.

Retiring Debt

A refinancing is also used to redirect cash flows from debt service to business operations by retiring debt before maturity. The buyer requires new sources of cash to fund refinancing debt if business operations do not produce excess cash. Two commonly used means of generating cash are to liquidate an asset and to issue new equity.

Nonencumbered assets that are not productive should be liquidated and the proceeds used to retire debt. However, before proceeding, the buyer must examine clauses in existing loan agreements that restrict the disbursement of assets.

Permission of the lender is required to liquidate assets that are used as collateral. The lender may grant permission if the lender is assured the proceeds of the sale are used to retire the lender's loan.

Lenders, as a matter of protocol, should be notified prior to liquidation of any material asset of the buyer, because liquidation could be perceived as a sign of financial trouble for the buyer. In addition, some loan agreements require a lender's permission to liquidate any material asset, even if the asset is not used as collateral for the loan.

Caution

Lenders expect prepayment fees and penalties to be paid when a debt is retired prematurely, even if the lender gives permission for the buyer to sell an asset to cover the debt.

The issuance of new stock to raise cash is at times an advantageous way to refinance debt, because the buyer receives cash from new stockholders and does not incur any new debt. However, the buyer must consider the disadvantages of issuing new equity. These are the dilution of existing stockholders, a change in the control of the corporation, and the impact the change will have on the corporation's earnings per share ratio.

The positions of stockholders are reduced whenever new common stock is issued and current stockholders don't increase their positions. Let's say that a buyer issues 10,000 shares and Stockholder A owns 5,100 shares, thereby owning controlling interest in the corporation. Through a new issue, the buyer increases outstanding shares to 20,000 shares. Stockholder A's position is reduced to 25.5 percent of the shares unless Stockholder A acquires an additional 5,100 shares.

A loan agreement might use the buyer's earnings per share ratio as a test to trigger whether or not a loan is in default. Issuing new stock might place the buyer's earnings per share ratio below the acceptable level for a lender. Let's say the buyer had earnings of $500,000 and there are 10,000 shares outstanding. The buyer's earning per share ratio is $50 per share. However, the ratio drops to $25 per share when a new issue of 10,000 shares are placed, bringing the outstanding shares to 20,000.

FINANCING THROUGH INSURANCE COMPANIES

A buyer should consider an insurance company as a source for financing an acquisition because insurance companies traditionally divert cash flows from insurance premiums to fund mergers and acquisitions. Terms in loan agreements created by an insurance company are fairly standard within the insurance industry. However, the risk tolerance varies among insurance companies. Therefore, a buyer will find it advantageous to assess the offerings of many insurance companies rather than to focus on a few insurance companies.

Acquisitions funded by an insurance company typically require a bridge loan to close the deal, because insurance company financing requires more time to get in place than does other financial institution financing. This is primarily caused by the lengthy loan approval process used in the insurance industry.

The process begins by the buyer, either directly or through an investment bank, opening negotiations on loan terms with an insurance company. Deals that involve large amounts typically require that a syndicate of insurance companies be formed to finance the deal. The insurance company that underwrites the largest portion of the loan is designated the lead lender of the syndicate and takes the lead in negotiations.

Terms of the loan are listed on a term sheet, which is reviewed and approved by members of the syndicate, after which the term sheet is used by the lead lender's counsel to draft the loan agreement. The loan agreement is then reviewed and approved by each member of the syndicate and by the buyer.

Caution

The buyer should avoid multiple drafts of the loan agreement because succeeding drafts tend to encourage syndicate members to include additional restrictive clauses, which are not in the best interest of the buyer.

Caution

Insurance companies are less likely than other financial institutions to renegotiate restrictive clauses once a loan agreement is signed. Requests to renegotiate these terms will incur a fee to cover the expense to review the request.

The buyer must give special attention to any prepayment clause in the insurance company loan agreement because of restrictions it places on the source of funds used to retire the debt. Typically, the prepayment clause prevents the buyer from using new debt that has an interest rate lower than the existing loan to prepay the loan.

In addition, the prepayment clause typically contains a formula used to calculate the penalty the buyer incurs when the note is prepaid prior to maturity. The formula uses a declining penalty calculated on a percentage of the outstanding balance of the note.

Let's say that note is for $1 million, with a maturity date of 10 years. The prepayment penalty is calculated at 10 percent of the outstanding balance for the first year. This percentage declines by 1 percent each year. Therefore, the prepayment penalty in the fifth year is 5 percent of the outstanding balance.

Caution

The loan agreement may allow a partial prepayment that is penalty free.

THE FINANCING PROCESS

The financing process consists of steps the buyer takes to finance an acquisition. The process begins with the creation of the bankbook. A bankbook is a financing proposal created by the buyer and used to attract financial institutions and insurance companies into financing the deal.

The bankbook is the buyer's plan for the acquisition and stipulates facts that the prospective lender needs to assess the deal and determine if the lender wants to participate in financing the deal. The bankbook should include

- Background on the buyer
- Background on the dotcom
- Description of the proposed deal
- Financials of the buyer
- Financials of the dotcom
- Projections of the financials after the deal
- Price of acquisition
- Proposed financing structure
- Project cash flows
- Project earnings
- Identification and estimated value of assets that can be used as collateral (include formal appraisals and estimated liquidation value)
- Proposed payback schedule for debt

Next, the prospective lender reviews the bankbook and determines if the deal meets the lender's minimum requirements. If so, the prospective lender begins a month-long background check that includes

- Review of 10Ks
- Review of 10Qs

- Review of independent audit reports that certify financial information and tax returns
- Review of proxy statements
- An independent appraisal
- Review of facilities
- Interview of key personnel in the buyer and in the dotcom

Once this information is collected and reviewed by the lender, the lender's loan officer determines if the institution should become a participant. If so, a recommendation is sent to the lender's credit committee for approval.

A commitment letter is issued once the credit committee approves of the loan. A commitment letter specifies the general terms within which the lender will loan funds to the buyer. The commitment letter is not the loan agreement but instead is the lender's positive response to the buyer's request for a loan. The commitment letter contains

- The type of loan (e.g., term or revolving credit)
- Loan amount
- Interest rate
- Maturity date
- Amortization schedule
- Required collateral
- The structure of the loan (e.g., senior or subordinate debt)
- Use of funds
- Fees and related expenses
- Default and prepayment penalties
- Restrictive clauses
- Expiration date
- Information required at closing (e.g., legal opinions)

Caution

Lenders expect to receive a fee for evaluating a deal and another fee to generate a commitment letter. The evaluation fee must be paid even if the financial institution does not participate in the financing. Likewise, the commitment letter fee must be paid even if the buyer does not proceed with the loan.

Caution

A commitment letter typically expires 30 days after the commitment letter is issued. The buyer can expect that finance terms might change and another commitment letter fee may be incurred should the buyer want to extend the expiration date of the commitment letter.

Timing is critical whenever a bankbook is submitted to prospective lenders. It is in the best interest of the buyer to evaluate each lender's terms before commitment letters are delivered. This provides the buyer time to evaluate the proposal from each lender without the pressure imposed by the commitment letter expiration date.

The evaluation period is the time when the buyer can negotiate terms with prospective lenders, because the terms have not been presented to the credit committee. Furthermore, the buyer can leverage favorable terms from other prospective lenders during negotiations.

Financing Agreements and Terms

There are three aspects of a loan agreement that a buyer can negotiate with a lender: interest rate, fees, and terms of the loan.

The interest rate reflects market conditions and risks of the deal. The most secured investment for a lender is a U.S. Treasury obligation in which the lender receives a low interest rate relative to other loans and has minimal risk. In contrast, high yield bonds pay lenders a very high interest rate but are highly risky because these bonds are subordinate, uncollateralized loans, rated below investment grade.

Rates quoted by lenders are based on the prime rate. The prime rate is the lowest rate that a lender charges borrowers. For example, the interest rate for a loan might be quoted as prime plus 2 percent. This means that if the prime rate is 8 percent, then the interest rate for the loan is 10 percent.

It is to the advantage of the buyer to negotiate the loan rate based on a publicly set rate rather than on the prime rate established by the lender, since the lender is at liberty to set the prime rate to any interest rate. A publicly set rate is one that neither the buyer nor the lender can influence.

Publicly set rates are the Federal Reserve rate (Federal Fund rate) and the London Interbank Offered Rate (LIBOR). These rates reflect the current market rate, whereas the prime rate reflects the lowest rate the lender wants to charge borrowers. The difference in rates becomes relative if the loan is based on a variable rate rather than on a fixed rate. The interest rate on a variable rate loan is reviewed at agreed-upon intervals, at which times adjustments in the interest rate might be made. Any change in interest rate is based on the prime rate, Federal Fund rate, or LIBOR, depending on the loan agreement.

Fees

Fees are charged to reimburse the lender for expenses incurred in servicing the loan. Fees tend to become a valuable source of cash flow for lenders, and therefore lenders are noted for charging fees for minor services.

Fees are negotiable and can be waived by the lender if the buyer feels that fees are unreasonable and not a common business practice in the industry. Here are categories of fees that can be expected when dealing with a lender:

- Typical fee
- Bankbook review fee
- Commitment letter fee
- Extension (of deadline) fee
- Waiver fee
- Opinion fee
- Appraisal fee
- Outside counsel fee
- Letter of credit fee
- Closing fee
- Syndicate management fee (if the financial institution is the syndicate manager)
- Termination fee

Multiple Lenders

Multiple lenders can be direct or indirect parties to a financing agreement, especially when the loan has a substantial principal that exceeds the risk tolerance of any one lender. There are three ways in which multiple lenders can participate in financing the deal: as a member of a syndicate, directly with the buyer, and through indirect financing.

Lenders to a multilender financing agreement form a group called a syndicate. One lender is designated the syndicate manager and coordinates negotiations between other lenders and the buyer. Negotiations result in a single loan agreement signed by each syndicate member and by the buyer. Each lender is a direct party to the loan agreement.

Rather than form a syndicate, lenders can directly enter into a loan agreement with the buyer. In this case, the buyer coordinates the terms of the loan agreements among all the lenders. The buyer must resolve conflicts among lenders.

Lenders might decide to indirectly participate in financing the deal by acquiring a portion of another lender's obligation. Here's how this works. One lender signs a loan agreement with the buyer, then transfers a portion of the loan agreement to other lenders. The other lenders are indirectly a party to the buyer's loan agreement.

There are two common ways in which a buyer's loan agreement can be partial to other lenders. The lender transfers its right to receive payment from the buyer to other lenders in exchange for compensation. This effectively makes those financial institutions the lender to the buyer. The buyer makes all payments directly to the other lenders.

Another way in which the loan agreement is partial to other lenders is for the lender to issue its own loan, secured by payments made by the buyer to the other lenders.

Let's say Financial Institution A loans A-Dotcom $100 million. Financial Institution B and Financial Institution C each loan Financial Institution A $50 million. Financial Institution A receives payment from A-Dotcom, then makes Financial Institution B and Financial Institution C payments towards the $50 million loan.

The difference between these methods is which corporation is in debt. In the first example, the loan agreement is partial and sold to other lenders. The buyer is in debt to the other lenders. The buyer is no longer in debt to the lender that signed the loan agreement. In the second method, the buyer is in debt to the lender who is the signator of the loan agreement. The lender is in debt to the other lenders.

Caution

Every effort should be made to avoid dealing with multiple lenders who are not acting in concert with each other. Always try to have lenders speak with one voice, especially when negotiating restrictive clauses in the loan agreement.

The loan agreement must specify the decision process used by the lenders to amend the loan agreement. Typically, the percentage of the loan determines voting rights. That is, one or more financial institutions that hold

51 percent of the loan amount determine if terms in the loan agreement can be modified after the loan agreement is signed.

Closing Terms

The buyer can expect lenders to forestall closing the deal until certain issues are addressed. Of particular concern are liens on collateral used for the loan. An asset can be used to collateralize more than one loan if the liquidation value of the asset exceeds the principal of one of those loans. The excess liquidation value is available to cover other loans.

However, lenders typically prefer a perfect lien, which is where a single lender has claim to an asset. A lien search is necessary to verify that a perfect lien is available before closing on the loan agreement. A lien search documents previous liens on the asset, if any, and dates when those liens were removed from the asset. Failure to provide this information before or at closing might delay execution of the loan agreement.

Another concern when closing a loan agreement is certifications provided by the buyer's outside auditors. Lenders prefer to have auditors' comments on the buyer's financial projections and solvency. However, auditors rarely offer such opinions. Therefore the buyer, its auditors, and lenders must agree on the language of the auditor's certification before closing.

Material litigation is another concern of lenders during closing. The buyer must assure the lender that no material litigation has been initiated between the date the lender issued the commitment letter and the date the loan agreement is signed. Typically, the buyer's attorney confirms the absence of new material litigation at closing.

The buyer is expected to provide lenders at closing with warranties that all statements and documents submitted to the lender are accurate and have not materially changed since the statements and documents were delivered to the lender. Warranties cover the following areas of the loan agreement:

- The acquisition is in compliance with laws, regulations, and existing contractual agreements.
- No liens exist on assets used to collateralize the loan, except as agreed upon with the lender.
- The buyer's and dotcom's financial statements are accurate and reflect assets owned.
- The buyer is solvent.

Misrepresentations, whether made knowingly or inadvertently, are a serious matter. The lender is likely to withhold funding should misrepresentations surface after the loan agreement is signed. Misrepresentations might place the loan in default should the loan have already been funded by the lender. A loan in default gives the lender the option to call the loan, which is also known as *accelerating* the loan. That is, the lender demands full payment of the outstanding principal along with applicable penalties and fees, if any.

The buyer should attempt to modify the default clause in the loan agreement to give the buyer latitude if the lender declares the loan in default. First, redefine events that trigger default as only material events. For example, the buyer might warrant that an asset is free of any liens. However, a minor lien is discovered against the asset after the loan agreement is signed and the loan is funded. Technically, the lender can declare that the loan is in default, unless materiality is included in the loan agreement. The asset still has sufficient liquidation value to cover the loan. Therefore, the loan should not be placed in default because the lien has not materially changed the warranty.

Next, include a grace period within which time the buyer can remedy the event that caused the loan to be in default. For example, a 30-day grace period gives the buyer time to remove the minor lien on an asset, as mentioned in the previous example.

Registration Rights

A loan that is privately placed is prohibited by federal and local regulations from being sold in the secondary public market, although the lender can transfer the loan to another party through a secondary private placement. The inability to access the secondary public market limits the liquidity of the loan should the lender decide to liquidate its position. The lender is likely to require that a registration rights clause be included in the loan agreement.

A security issued by a buyer (such as loans, stocks, and warrants) can be exchanged in the secondary public market if the security is registered in accordance with applicable federal and local regulations. The registration rights clause grants the lender the right to require the buyer to register the security. Loans issued with a registration rights clause are more liquid than unregistered loans, and therefore the lender is likely to consider a loan that can be registered less risky, which might be reflected in the interest rate applied to the loan.

The buyer must be fully aware of the expense and impact that exercising a registration rights clause has on the buyer. The registration rights clause gives the lender the right to force the buyer to register securities and therefore become a public corporation. The buyer typically wants to determine for itself whether or not to go public and, if so, when to go public. This is especially true when warrants, preferred stock, and common stock are issued to lenders as an equity kicker to a loan agreement.

The registration process and subsequent files are time consuming and costly to the buyer. Substantial fees to accountants and attorneys are incurred, and key personnel must divert attention from the business to the registration process. Likewise, the buyer is exposed to ongoing expenses, regulations, and potential liabilities that are avoided by not becoming a public corporation.

A compromise position between the need for the lender to receive registration rights and the concerns of the buyer to avoid prematurely becoming a public corporation is to include restrictions in the registration rights clause. The buyer can restrict which securities are covered by the registration rights clause. Some securities can be publicly available while other securities remain privately held. Securities covered by the registration rights clause are defined by demand registration rights and piggyback registrations rights inclusions in the registration rights clause.

The demand registration right limits the registration rights clause to securities held by a particular lender. Let's say that Financial Institution A loans A-Dotcom $100 million and receives 1,000 shares as an equity kicker. Financial Institution A requires that a registration rights clause be included in the loan agreement.

A-Dotcom does not want to grant a registration rights clause because A-Dotcom does not want to incur the registration expense and associated exposure, especially since Financial Institution A is just one of many lenders that participate in A-Dotcom's financing.

Financial Institution A suggests the inclusion of demand registration rights rather than blanket registration rights. The demand registration right limits registration rights to only the loan agreement with Financial Institution A.

While the demand registration right satisfies Financial Institution A's concerns, it does not address the concerns of A-Dotcom, who is especially interested in keeping the equity kicker privately placed rather than making equity available in the secondary markets.

A-Dotcom might counter the demand registration right by suggesting the inclusion of a piggyback registration right. A piggyback registration right restricts registration rights to a single security or to a class of securities.

In this example, A-Dotcom might use the piggyback registration right to limit registration rights to the note held by Financial Institution A and not to the equity kicker. This piggyback registration right could be expanded to include debt securities and exclude equity securities. In this way, only debt is exposed to the exercise of the registration rights clause. The buyer retains the right to determine if and when equity is offered to the public.

Negotiate More Restrictions

It is advantageous to the buyer to include other restrictions to the registration rights clause. These are a waiting period, termination triggers, and a position threshold.

A waiting period prevents the financial institution from exercising the registration right until a specified length of time has passed from the date the loan is funded. The waiting period gives the buyer sufficient time to integrate the acquisition with its own operation.

Registration rights should terminate once the buyer establishes stability and the risk of insolvency is substantially lowered from the time the loan agreement is signed. Termination can be triggered by a date or by events such as material pay-down of the principal.

Registration rights transfer control over an aspect of the buyer's future from the buyer to the lender that receives the registration rights. Exercising this control might have a dramatic impact on other lenders as well as on the buyer. Therefore, the buyer should establish a position threshold that triggers a lender's authority to exercise the registration rights.

Let's say A-Dotcom's capitalization consists of only $100 million in loans. No funds are raised from the equity market. Financial Institution A holds a $10 million loan; Financial Institution B holds a $20 million loan; and Financial Institution C holds a $70 million loan. All three financial institutions required registration rights clauses in their loan agreements.

However, granting the registration rights clause to all lenders will result in an unbalanced control over the buyer and its debt. Financial Institution A holds 10 percent of the outstanding debt, but has the same rights as Financial Institution C, which holds 70 percent of the debt, to force A-Dotcom to offer the loans in the secondary public market. Registration of the loans may not be advantageous to other lenders.

A position threshold restores a balanced control by requiring 51 percent of the lenders of the outstanding debt to approve the exercise of a registration right. In the previous example, neither Financial Institution A nor Financial Institution B can exercise its registration right unless Financial Institution C approves. This is because Financial Institution C holds more than 50 percent of the outstanding debt.

Caution

Be sure that the same position threshold clause is included in all loans; otherwise, terms of the registration rights clauses will be in conflict and might trigger default in one or more existing loans.

Conflicts Among Lenders

Each lender that participates in financing the acquisition seeks to minimize its exposure to risk presented by the deal. Risk is assessed differently by each lender and minimized by the inclusion of restrictive clauses in the loan agreement.

Conflicts arise whenever restrictive clauses of two or more loan agreements are at opposing positions and when abiding by one loan agreement triggers default in another loan agreement. A common area of contention is with assets used as collateral for loans. For example, two loans may be collateralized with the same asset, which might impede liquidation should one of the loans be in default. The lender whose loan is in default may want the asset liquidated. However, liquidation violates terms of the loan agreement that is not in default.

Other contentious areas are rights of lenders of senior and subordinate debt. Senior lenders require reassurance that terms in subordinate loan agreements don't overshadow or block their rights to assets should the buyer become insolvent.

The buyer must expect conflicts to arise among creditors and should become proactive to resolve differences among them. Here are a few guidelines that minimize these conflicts:

- Identify opposing issues during negotiations with lenders prior to the loan being recommended to the credit committee. This resolves differences before the buyer incurs expenses associated with commitment letters.

- Avoid lenders negotiating terms with each other. Instead, the buyer should negotiate with each lender independently. Loan agreements tend to become overly restrictive and the negotiation period extended once lenders negotiate with each other.

- Obtain copies of inter-creditor agreements lenders have signed in other deals, if possible. These inter-creditor agreements contain terms and language that are acceptable to each lender.

- Determine if the conflicting issues might be negotiable. The buyer must be willing to abandon a lender if the conflicting issues prevent other lenders from issuing a commitment letter.
- Require lenders to sign an inter-creditor agreement that details the terms of each conflicting aspect of each loan and defines terms that resolve these conflicts. Each loan agreement is between the buyer and a lender, and therefore a lender might not be privy to terms proposed by other lenders. Use the language contained in previous inter-creditor agreements as the basis for creating the inter-creditor agreement for the deal.

LEGAL CONSIDERATIONS

Attorneys for lenders and for the buyer resolve nearly all the legal concerns that surround financing an acquisition with documents signed at closing. Documents include loan agreements, inter-creditor agreements, and liens that are soon after registered with the appropriate authorities.

However, lenders remain exposed to fraudulent conveyance. Fraudulent conveyance occurs when title to assets, used as collateral for a loan, is not free and clear. Courts typically nullify such liens by declaring a fraudulent conveyance, which leaves the loan unsecured. An unsecured loan becomes valueless should the buyer become insolvent.

Fraudulent conveyance can also occur if the buyer has not received a reasonable value for the price paid for the dotcom. Let's say A-Dotcom acquires B-Dotcom for $10 million, financed by a combination of secured and unsecured loan.

The value of A-Dotcom should be reasonably $10 million. Unsecured lenders can claim fraudulent conveyance if the value of A-Dotcom immediately following the acquisition is materially less than $10 million.

Unsecured lenders loan funds based on the perceived value of the buyer rather than based on the liquidation value of particular assets. If the deal didn't result in equivalent value, then unsecured lenders are exposed.

One of three conditions must be proven to have existed shortly after the deal before a court declares fraudulent conveyance:

- The buyer is not able to repay creditors.
- The buyer is insolvent.
- There is insufficient operating capital to maintain operations.

If plans presented by the buyer to lenders were fair and reasonable, these conditions should not exist shortly after the deal closes.

Caution

A conflict exists in the definition of solvency. Generally accepted accounting principles (GAAP) define solvency as having sufficient assets to repay debts according to a loan schedule. An alternative GAAP definition is that the book value of liabilities is less than the book value of assets. However, solvency for fraudulent conveyances requires that the probable liabilities be less than the fair and salable liquidation value of assets.

Caution

Attorneys rarely give opinions on fraudulent conveyance issues because to do so requires attorneys to predict the actions of the courts, something attorneys don't do.

Fraudulent conveyance might occur whenever assets held by a subsidiary are used as collateral for a loan made to another subsidiary or for the holding corporation by a lender. The problem arises because the subsidiary that has title to the asset is not receiving equivalent compensation.

When a subsidiary provides collateral for a loan given to the subsidiary's holding corporation, the transaction is called *upstreaming*. The lender issues the loan to the holding corporation and receives a lien against an asset held by the subsidiary.

Similarly, when a subsidiary provides collateral for a loan given to a subsidiary of its holding corporation, the transaction is called *cross-streaming*. The lender issues the loan to the sister subsidiary and receives a lien against an asset held by the other subsidiary.

Fraudulent conveyance can be avoided in these situations by executing a *downstream* transaction. A downstream transaction occurs when assets of the holding corporation are used as collateral for loan made to a subsidiary. The holding corporation owns both the asset and the subsidiary and therefore receives equal value in the transaction.

SUMMARY

There are three ways in which a buyer can acquire a dotcom. These are asset purchase, stock purchase, and a merger of both businesses. The choice of transaction depends on the capitalization of the buyer, tax implications, and the degree of liability the buyer is willing to accept.

An asset purchase is cash-intensive and limits liabilities. A stock purchase or merger transfers both a dotcom's assets and liabilities to the buyer. However, a buyer might be in a better position than the dotcom to satisfy those liabilities.

There are seven types of mergers:

- Taxable forward merger
- Taxable reverse merger
- Ttaxable forward subsidiary merger
- Ttax-free forward merger
- Tax-free forward triangle merger
- Tax-free acquisition of stock merger
- Acquisition of property for stock merger

Each type of merger differs from the others by the way cash and stock transfer from the dotcom to the buyer.

A buyer can take advantage of both a stock purchase and a merger in the same deal by using the stock purchase-merger strategy. This strategy requires the buyer to acquire a majority of the dotcom's stock, then vote that stock to merge the dotcom with the buyer. This strategy works around the problem of dissenting stockholders' stopping a merger from occurring.

There are four common methods used to finance a deal: cash, stock, notes, or a combination of all three. The cash financing method is when a buyer exchanges cash for stock or assets of the dotcom. Cash is raised through accumulated excess revenue from current operations, new issues floated by the buyer, liquidation of the buyer's assets, and/or debt incurred by the buyer.

The stock financing method is the exchange of the buyer's stock for assets or stock of the dotcom. Stockholders in the dotcom become stockholders in the buyer. The number of shares that are exchanged is negotiated. The note financing method requires the dotcom to accept a note from the buyer in lieu of cash or stock. In exchange, the dotcom transfers its assets or stock to the buyer.

At the extreme end of the financing scale is the maximum leveraged strategy, also known as a leverage buyout, where the acquiring company's capital structure is substantially more debt than equity. The maximum leveraged strategy requires the buyer to borrow as much of the acquisition cost as possible from lenders.

The minimum leveraged strategy requires the buyer to minimize compensation paid for a dotcom. Compensation must take into consideration ancillary expenditures that include administrative costs and fees, refinancing expenses, operating capital, and exposure to current and potential litigation.

Inheriting a dotcom's debt and lease liabilities is at times a strategy that minimizes leverage of a deal if the terms of the obligation are more attractive to the buyer than is the market price for comparable agreements.

A buyer structures debt according to debt layers. These layers of debt are senior debt and subordinate debt. Subordinate debt is subdivided into senior subordinate debt, junior subordinate debt, and take-back debt. The buyer must retire senior debt before subordinate debt, should the buyer become insolvent.

Lenders reduce the risk of a loan by including restrictive clauses in the loan agreement. Restrictive clauses limit the buyer's business practices to activities that will not impede the buyer's ability to repay the loan.

The financing process begins with the creation of the bankbook. A bankbook is a financing proposal created by the buyer and used to attract financial institutions and insurance companies into financing the deal.

The bankbook is the buyer's plan for the acquisition and stipulates facts that the prospective lender needs to assess the deal and determine if the lender wants to participate in financing the deal.

Once a lender agrees to participate in financing the deal, the lender issues a commitment letter that contains the terms and conditions of the loan. A loan agreement is drawn up once the buyer agrees to the terms in the commitment letter.

Conflicts arise in multilender financing when restrictive clauses in loan agreements are at opposing positions. The buyer is responsible to resolve conflicts before commitment letters are issued. Lenders are expected to sign an inter-creditor agreement that specifies how disagreements are to be resolved.

QUESTIONS

1. How can a buyer overcome dissenting stockholders of a dotcom when the buyer wants to acquire the dotcom through a merger?

2. What is the purpose of a bankbook?

3. What information is contained in a commitment letter?

4. What is the purpose of a trade debt clause?

5. What is a common difference between a repayment clause in a loan agreement issued by an insurance company and in a loan agreement issued by a bank?

6. What is the purpose of a bridge loan?

7. What are the advantages of leaseback financing?

8. How does fraudulent conveyance affect a deal?

9. What is the purpose of refinancing?

10. What ratios are used to determine if a buyer is solvent?

CHAPTER 4

Tax Implications

Taxes are unavoidably taxing.

—Anonymous

In This Chapter

- Tax Basics
- Taxable Issues
- Adjusted Basis
- Tax Accounting Methods
- Taxes and Organizational Structure
- Taxes and Financing
- Tax Free Transactions
- Tax Strategy

TAX BASICS

Whenever assets of a corporation are disbursed during an acquisition or to stockholders, both the corporation and stockholders are exposed to tax liabilities that might be avoidable by following a properly designed tax strategy.

Two factors determine whether or not a disbursement of assets is taxable: the book value and the sale price of the assets. The book value of an asset is the depreciated value of the asset as recorded on the books and records of the corporation. Let's say a dotcom purchases a server at a cost of $11,000. The server has a useful life of five years based on standard accounting practices. Each year, the value of the server depreciates $2,000. At the end of five years, the server has a residual value of $1,000 after the asset is fully depreciated.

Tech Talk

Residual Value: The value of a fully depreciated asset that can be realized by selling the asset.

Let's say that the dotcom is sold at the end of three years and the sale includes the disbursement of the server to the buyer. The server is sold at its book value, which is $4,000. Some assets appreciate in value, and therefore the purchase price of the asset, which is the market value, is higher than the book value. However, in this example a server rarely appreciates, and therefore the value of the server is assessed at book value.

Tech Talk

Market Value: The value an asset will realize if sold in the current market.

The disbursement has no tax implications to the dotcom because the market value is at or below the book value of the server. That is, the dotcom does not realize a gain or loss in the sale of the asset to the buyer. However, the buyer might be exposed to sales tax liabilities, depending on state and local tax regulations.

The dotcom might be exposed to tax liabilities should the market value of the asset be greater than the book value. Suppose the dotcom developed online consumer-tracking software at a cost of $11,000 and the software had a five-year useful life. The same depreciation considerations apply to the software as applied to the server.

Three years after the software is developed, the dotcom is acquired. The book value of the software is $4,000. However, the dotcom negotiates a sale price of $20,000, which is the market value of the software. The software appreciated in value.

Whenever an appreciable asset is disbursed, the dotcom might be taxed on the gain, which in this example is $16,000. The rate at which the gain is taxed will vary with each deal and with each taxing authority.

Assets can also be disbursed to stockholders when a dotcom is liquidated. The dotcom liquidates by transferring title to the asset to another party, such as a buyer, in exchange for consideration, which usually is in the form of cash.

Cash is the only asset remaining in a dotcom. A portion, if not all, of the cash is transferred to creditors in exchange for retiring the debt. Excess cash is used to purchase stock from stockholders, causing the dotcom to be dissolved.

Disbursing cash to stockholders in exchange for outstanding shares does not incur a tax liability for the dotcom. However, stockholders might realize a gain if the cash they receive is higher than cash paid for the shares. This gain is a taxable exposure for the stockholder.

Double Taxation

Stockholders of some dotcoms might experience double taxation on disbursed assets, especially if the asset appreciates in value. The initial tax liability is incurred when the dotcom sells the asset above book value.

The second tax liability incurs when the dotcom disburses excess cash generated by the sale to stockholders in the form of a dividend or in exchange for shares. Dividends are treated as regular income, and cash received in exchange for shares might be treated as a capital gain if the value exceeds the purchase price of the shares.

Double taxation is avoided if stockholders are lenders and not equity holders, if the dotcom is declared a Subchapter S corporation (see the section "Taxes and Organization Structure"), or if the stockholder is a holding corporation.

Disbursement of cash can be made to lenders in the form of principal and interest. The dotcom is not exposed to tax liabilities, and reduces tax liabilities on earnings with a tax deduction equal to interest payments. The lenders, on the other hand, might be liable for taxes on interest payments, but there are no tax liabilities on the principal.

Subchapter S Corporation

The board of directors of the dotcom might declare the corporation as a Subchapter S corporation if the dotcom qualifies under Internal Revenue Service regulations, which are discussed later in this chapter. Subchapter S corporation regulations eliminate double taxation to stockholders by passing through gains realized by the dotcom directly to its stockholders. Let's say the dotcom sells its software, as in the previous example, for a gain of $16,000. The $16,000 becomes excess cash. That is, the cash is not used for operating expenses or for debt service. This gain is passed through to stockholders without being taxed at the corporation level if the corporation is declared a Subchapter S corporation.

Holding Corporation

A holding corporation is a corporation that is a stockholder holding at least 80 percent of the shares in affiliate corporations, which are known as subsidiaries. A subsidiary can pass through gains and losses to its holding corporation, which files a consolidated income tax return. However, subsidiaries do not need to file separate income tax returns, except for some state and local jurisdictions. A consolidated income tax return also enables gains and losses to be shared among subsidiaries.

Let's say A-Holding owns 100 percent of the outstanding shares in A-Dotcom and B-Dotcom. A-Dotcom is an online book retailer and B-Dotcom is an online auction. A-Dotcom shows a gain of $10 million, which is fully taxable if A-Dotcom was not a subsidiary of A-Holding. B-Dotcom reported a loss of $5 million. A-Holding can use the $5 million loss to offset the $10 million gain and therefore realizes a tax liability on $5 million rather than on the original $10 million gain.

Caution

Internal Revenue Service regulations permit pass-through gains and losses to holding corporations. However, state regulations vary. Some regulations prohibit pass-through, in which case the subsidiary is liable for taxes as if it were an unaffiliated corporation.

TAXABLE ISSUES

Federal, state, and local taxes have a critical influence on a deal, from both the buyer's and the dotcom's perspective. At times, the buyer's and the dotcom's tax objectives are at opposing positions. The buyer takes a long-term tax strategy that focuses on three areas of a deal. These are to minimize tax liabilities to acquire the dotcom, to operate the corporation following the acquisition, and to minimize tax liability when the acquisition is ultimately sold by the buyer to another buyer.

In contrast, the dotcom has a short-term tax strategy, with the objective to minimize tax liability incurred by the deal. For example, the deal might be the last phase in the dotcom's long-term tax strategy, which is to sell the dotcom to the buyer. The dotcom can employ various strategies before the acquisition to minimize the tax exposure following the deal. These strategies include arranging for deferred compensation from the buyer and changing the tax structure of the dotcom.

The deferred compensation strategy disperses the realization of the gain from the acquisition over several tax years, during which the dotcom's stockholders may be in a lower tax bracket. Receiving full compensation for the acquisition in one lump payment may place stockholders in a higher tax bracket. Stretching payment over several years may place stockholders in a lower tax bracket.

Changing the tax structure of the dotcom requires the dotcom to declare itself as a Subchapter S corporation to avoid double taxation on the acquisition. Careful attention must be given to appropriate tax regulations to assure that the dotcom is qualified to become a Subchapter S corporation.

A Compromise Tax Strategy

Whenever the tax strategies of the buyer and dotcom are in conflict, both parties should develop a compromise tax strategy that minimizes tax liabilities for the entire deal—not a strategy that favors one party over the other. Typically, a compromise is reached by structuring the deal to realize maximum aggregated tax savings to both the buyer and the dotcom. An aggregated tax saving still exposes either the buyer or the dotcom to a higher tax expense that would not have been realized if the deal were structured to favor one or the other side. However, adjustments are made to the price to reflect this higher tax expense.

Federal, state, and local tax regulations are in constant flux; therefore both the buyer and the dotcom must request that an independent tax analysis of the deal be performed by qualified tax professionals. Here are the areas that are likely to be included in the tax analysis:

- Elections of a taxable year
- Credit carry-forwards and carry-backs
- Net operating loss
- Accounting method
- Foreign tax credits

- Tax implications of each jurisdiction in which the dotcom operates
- Exposure to retroactive tax obligations of the dotcom after the deal is closed
- Amortization of goodwill
- The impact management participation in the deal has on tax obligations
- The structure of the transaction as a stock purchase or asset purchase
- The structure of both the buyer and the dotcom as a Subchapter C corporation, Subchapter S corporation, or partnership
- Method of compensation for the acquisition—equity, debt, or a combination
- Post-deal distribution of the dotcom's assets
- Distribution of earnings and profit of the dotcom after closing the deal

---

Caution

The buyer or the dotcom can request a private letter ruling on any tax issue that is unclear based on the facts in the deal. Private letter rulings are issued by the national Internal Revenue Service office and are binding. However, a request should be made only with explicit recommendations by a tax advisor, because the request might expose issues that might be more favorable if treated in other ways.

ADJUSTED BASIS

The adjusted basis of an asset is used to calculate the tax liability that results from an acquisition. The adjusted basis is calculated by subtracting depreciation, amortization, and related charges from the initial basis of the asset.

The buyer might be exposed to sales tax on the adjusted basis value of an asset following an asset purchase. The dotcom might be exposed to capital gains tax if the sale price of the asset is higher than the adjusted basis value of the asset.

Once the asset is acquired, the buyer steps up the adjusted basis to reflect the acquisition price and expenses. The acquisition price plus expenses becomes the new adjusted basis for the asset. The buyer then applies depreciation or amortization tax credits gained from the new adjusted basis to reduce tax liabilities of operating income. However, the step-up adjusted basis exposes the transaction to higher sales tax if applicable and exposes the dotcom's stockholders to double taxation. The higher price for the asset is recorded as a gain for the dotcom and is taxed accordingly. The gain is again taxed as the gain is passed through to stockholders as dividends or as part of liquidation, unless the dotcom is a Subchapter S corporation.

Carryover

In contrast, sales tax is not applied to a stock purchase because title to assets of the dotcom remains in the hands of the dotcom's stockholders, which is the buyer after the deal. The value of assets transfer to the buyer on a carryover basis.

Tech Talk

Carryover Basis: The adjusted basis of an asset is transferred without change to the buyer following a stock purchase or merger.

A stock purchase or merger transfers assets of the dotcom and other factors that have tax implications to the buyer. These include tax credits, tax losses, earnings, and profits. The buyer must carefully examine tax implications before consummating the deal, because some implications may result in a negative effect on the buyer. The acquisition price can be adjusted to reflect any negative tax effects.

However, carryover basis offers a less favorable tax position to the buyer at times, because the carryover basis is typically less than an asset's fair market value. The carryover basis is determined by depreciation and amortization methods used for tax purposes and does not necessarily reflect the asset's real economic depreciation, which is determined by the sale of the asset.

Caution

The transaction type alone does not determine if an asset is recorded on an adjusted basis or on a carryover basis. The value of an asset after the deal is the deciding factor. A change in the asset's value requires that the asset be recorded on an adjusted basis; otherwise, the asset is recorded on a carryover basis.

The buyer and dotcom must look at the fine details of a deal before determining the deal structure; otherwise, the deal is exposed to unnecessary tax liabilities. Two areas of particular concern are the de factor merger (see Chapter 3) and the step-down basis.

A de facto merger occurs when a buyer acquires all the assets of a dotcom through an asset purchase. The buyer and dotcom consider a de factor merger as an asset purchase and expect to receive appropriate tax treatment. However, the transaction might be treated as a merger for tax purposes should the asset purchase be declared a de facto merger by the courts.

There are times when the economic value of an asset drops below the asset's adjusted basis. Let say customer-tracking software is depreciated over five years, but new products make the software obsolete in two years. Therefore, the software's adjusted basis does not reflect the market value of the software. In this case, the buyer and dotcom should consider a stock purchase or merger rather than an asset purchase. Stock purchases and mergers carry over the value of the asset, enabling the buyer to continue to depreciate the asset.

The buyer should determine the value of the dotcom's net operating losses, if any, since net operating losses can be used by the buyer to reduce the buyer's net operating income and thereby reduce the buyer's tax liability. Net operating losses can be carried forward (up to 20 years) or carried back (two years) to offset future or previous net operating income.

Federal tax regulations limit carryover tax losses to the buyer. These regulations are complex and a buyer requires a tax professional to assess the deal based on the carryover tax loss regulations. However, the buyer must continue a material portion of the dotcom's business operations for the buyer to realize any carryover losses from the dotcom.

Caution

Federal and state tax regulations differ, so net operating losses that are carried forward and carried back may apply differently between federal and state tax liabilities.

TAX ACCOUNTING METHODS

Taxes are calculated based on the way in which the buyer and dotcom record assets and liabilities on the day the deal closes. There are two ways in which assets and liabilities are recorded: the purchase method and the pooling of interest method. Both are recognized as generally accepted accounting practices.

Once assets and liabilities are recorded and financial records are adjusted to reflect changes (i.e., step-up adjustment basis), the buyer must disclose the transaction to the Security and Exchange Commission (SEC) regardless of whether either the buyer or the dotcom is a public or private corporation. The disclosure must include

- Name and description of the dotcom
- Identification of the accounting method as purchase method or pooling of interests method
- Number of shares issued by the buyer after the acquisition (pooling of interests method only)
- Financial reports of the buyer and dotcom prior to the acquisition (pooling of interests method only)
- Impact of a change in the fiscal year on the financial statement (pooling of interests method only)
- Adjustments to the net assets (pooling of interests method only)
- Impact of the buyer's and dotcom's operations on financial reports issued prior to the acquisition that are consolidated to reflect the acquisition (pooling of interest method only)
- Cost of acquisition
- Consolidated financial reports before and after the acquisition

Purchase Method

The purchase method requires accountants to prepare a closing financial statement that describes assets, liabilities, earnings, and losses of the dotcom as of the day the deal closes. These are the values that are carried over and recorded on the buyer's books and records.

There are five major components that are carried over from the dotcom to the buyer:

- assets
- liabilities
- goodwill
- earnings
- losses

Assets are recorded under the purchase method by allocating the purchase price and acquisition cost to each asset of the dotcom. Liabilities are recorded at their fair values.

Goodwill is the sum paid above the net asset of the dotcom. The net asset is the net worth of the dotcom and is calculated by subtracting liabilities from assets. The dotcom's earnings and losses are carried over to the buyer as stated in the dotcom's closing financial statement.

The purchase method is advantageous when the buyer wants to enhance its value following the acquisition, because assets are adjusted to the current market value rather than the book value. The adjusted value of the assets makes the buyer more attractive to lenders than if the pooling of interest method is used, where assets are valued at book value.

Furthermore, the performance of the buyer is not diluted by consolidation of financial reports of the dotcom. An underperformance of a dotcom has no influence on the buyer. In contrast, the performance of a dotcom is combined with the buyer if the pooling of interest method is adopted.

The major disadvantages of the purchase method are that the price of acquiring assets reduces operating income of the buyer after the acquisition, and there is imprecision when setting the price for the assets.

The price of an asset is based on the current market for the asset adjusted for exposure to liabilities, such as pending litigation, that carry over after the deal and the cost of acquiring the asset.

The initial step in setting the price of an asset is to determine the asset's current value by reviewing the sale price of similar assets or by enlisting the services of an appraiser. Typically, the buyer and dotcom agree on three appraisers, then accept the average appraisal as the current value of the asset.

Next, an assessment is made to determine liabilities and expenses associated with acquiring the asset. These include any warranties associated with products and uncollectable receivables. Adjustments for liabilities and expenses are made to the current value of the asset to arrive at the adjusted, or net, value of the asset, which is the price paid by the buyer to the dotcom.

Pooling of Interest Method

The pooling of interest method treats the deal as a stock purchase or merger, and combines assets, liabilities, earnings, and losses of both the dotcom and the buyer. Once these values are combined, accountants for the buyer recreate previous financial statements to reflect the combination of both corporations.

There are two primary advantages of using the pooling of interest method. These are continuity of reporting financial results and higher reportable income. Both factors are critical should the buyer want to increase the value of the buyer's stock or issue new stock.

The pooling of interest method restates financial statements, thereby providing continuity of financial records from before and after the deal. Investors are able to identify patterns in the buyer's financials that enables them to forecast future performance.

Higher reportable income is achieved because there are no costs involved in acquiring assets, which offsets carryover earnings from the dotcom. Investors determine the price of a stock based on the earning abilities of the corporation. A high reportable income translates into high earnings and should also translate into high stock price.

The is a major disadvantage of the pooling of interest method. The results of combining the dotcom's and the buyer's financial statements may have a negative effect, especially if one of the corporations is in financial trouble. For example, outside auditors traditionally include comments in financial reports that highlight unusual and exceptional factors that influence the dotcom's business operations. These comments must be included in consolidated financial reports once the deal is consummated. This means the buyer's financial reports that were free of auditor's comments now contain auditor's comments, which might raise concerns of the buyer's stockholders.

A consolidation of assets carries over the current value of assets, which might be lower than the fair market value of those assets. Therefore, the buyer might be more valuable after the deal than the value reported on the consolidated financial statements.

The dotcom and the buyer must meet specific accounting standards before the pooling of interest method is permitted. These standards include:

- The buyer and dotcom must be independent corporations, and neither can be a subsidiary of another corporation for at least two years prior to the acquisition.
- All assets and liabilities must combined. Neither the buyer nor the dotcom can combine selected assets and liabilities.
- The acquisition must be made in a single transaction. No issues can be pending.
- The buyer must offer 90 percent of the voting class of stock and not restrict the right of holders of these stocks.
- No special terms for stockholders of either the buyer or dotcom can be enacted after the acquisition.
- Assets must be retained for two years except when disposal of the asset is part of normal business operations or is done to streamline the combined corporation.

- The buyer and the dotcom must have material business operations rather than assets and minimal business operations.
- No disposition of material assets is allowed in the six months before the deal.

Caution

Acquisition expenses are allocated to the consolidated corporation following the acquisition rather than to the buyer and the dotcom separately.

TAXES AND ORGANIZATIONAL STRUCTURE

Tax liabilities are assets based on the type of organizational structure adopted by the buyer, dotcom, and consolidated business operations after a stock purchase or merger. There are four types of organizational structures that can be adopted:

- Subchapter C corporation
- Subchapter S corporation
- Partnership
- Limited liability company (LLC)

Partnerships are subdivided into a general partnership and a limited partnership. The letters C and S refer to subchapters in the Internal Revenue Service code that regulates corporation taxes.

A Subchapter C corporation is considered by taxing authorities as a taxpaying entity and is taxed on earnings, and stockholders are taxed on distributions such as dividends. The other types of organizational structures are not considered taxpaying entities by taxing authorities. Instead, these are referred to as *pass-through entities,* since earnings of Subchapter S corporations, partnerships, and LLCs are passed through to stockholders and partners.

Pass-through entities avoid double taxation commonly found in Subchapter C corporations. A Subchapter C corporation pays taxes on earnings, and stockholders also pay taxes on earnings that are distributed as dividends.

There is an exception to the pass-through entities rule that applies to partnerships. Any partnership created under state law is eligible for pass-through earnings. However, earnings of a partnership can avoid double taxation only on distributions to partners who are not corporations. Double taxation, and possibly triple taxation, occurs when a corporation is a partner in a partnership.

Earnings from a partnership distributed to a corporate partner are taxed at the partnership level and at the corporation level. Furthermore, earnings are taxed at the stockholder level of the corporate partner if the corporation is organized as a Subchapter C corporation.

Triple taxation could also occur if a corporation is a holding corporation and has not taken acceptable tax avoidance measures. For example, a subsidiary of the holding corporation is taxed on earnings. Earnings are then distributed to the holding corporation, where they are taxed again. The holding corporation distributes earnings to its stockholders, and they too are taxed.

The holding corporation avoids taxes on earnings from subsidiaries by filing a consolidated income tax return that reflects earnings of both the holding corporation and its subsidiaries. The holding corporation must own 80 percent of the stock and votes in a corporation to be considered a subsidiary for tax purposes.

Earnings remain exposed to double taxation when earnings are distributed to stockholders of the holding corporation. A holding corporation is prohibited from being organized as an Subchapter S corporation.

A Subchapter S corporation is defined as a corporation that has fewer than 76 stockholders who are residents of the United States and are not a corporation. A Subchapter S corporation is restricted to one class of stock. For example, a Subchapter S corporation can issue voting common stock, but cannot issue nonvoting common stock and preferred stock.

Caution

Subchapter S corporations might not be recognized for preferential tax treatment for state and local taxes. All stockholders, regardless of their residence, might be required to pay state and local taxes on earnings distributed by Subchapter S corporation to the state and locality where the Subchapter S corporation resides.

Choice of Organizational Structure

There are three important factors that determine the choice of organizational structure:

- Reducing the pass-through of business liabilities to the owners
- Minimizing taxes
- Passing through losses

The buyer must weigh the importance of these options, then select the choice that is best suited for the deal.

Both the Subchapter C corporation and Subchapter S corporation limit pass-through liabilities to stockholders. With few exceptions, liability stops at the corporation level. The exception to this rule occurs if the courts declare that the corporation was formed to fraudulently avoid creditors, in which case the courts remove the corporate veil. Partnerships, however, pass through liabilities to partners in the business, although liabilities of the partnership are limited by the creation of a limited partnership.

A Subchapter S corporation and a partnership are the two organizational structures that eliminate double taxation. However, a corporation that is disqualified from becoming a Subchapter S corporation and acquires a dotcom should consider operating the dotcom as a subsidiary and file consolidated taxes. This technique avoids the possibility of double taxation.

Losses realized by a business are used to offset earnings from previous or future years, but are not passed through to owners except if the business is organized as a partnership. At the end of the tax year, a partnership passes through earnings and losses to partners who then use the earnings or losses to adjust their personal exposure to taxes. Let's say that two people are partners in a dotcom retail business. The first year of operations, the partnership losses total $20,000. The loss is passed through to each partner as $10,000 each. One partner received earnings of $100,000 from other sources in the year the partnership realized the loss. The $10,000 can be used to reduce the $100,000 earnings and thereby reduce the partner's tax liabilities.

In contrast, a dotcom retail business organized as a Subchapter S corporation or a Subchapter C corporation cannot pass through the $20,000 loss to stockholders. Stockholders can only realize a loss from the business under two circumstances:

1. When the stockholder sells shares at a lower price than the stockholder paid for those shares, the difference in price is realized as a loss, which can generally be used to offset earnings from other sources.
2. If the corporation is insolvent and is liquidated, stockholders lose the entire value of the price they paid for the stock, which is a loss that is used to adjust other earnings.

TAXES AND FINANCING

Tax liabilities are impacted by the method used to finance a deal. A deal can be financed through debt, equity, or a combination of debt and equity, as discussed in Chapter 3. Debt by its nature is where a lender loans the buyer cash in return for repayment of the cash and interest. Generally, the lender does not take an equity position in the deal unless equity is used as an incentive to loan the cash.

Straight debt can be structured into debt/equity financing by the buyer offering the lender an equity kicker or a clause enabling the lender to convert the debt into equity. An equity kicker is either a warrant to acquire shares in the buyer at a specific price or a transfer of stock to the lender.

Both the courts and taxing authorities have difficulty defining debt and equity in cases where the buyer and lender appear to use other than straight debt to finance a deal. Courts and taxing authorities use intent when deciding if a loan agreement is straight debt or equity. A definition of intent requires both the buyer and lender to prove that the loan agreement

- Defines a principal
- Defines an interest rate equal to market rates
- Defines a reasonable payment schedule
- Does not define conditions within which the loan does not have to be repaid
- Does not use shares in the buyer as collateral
- Defines the lender's rights should the buyer become insolvent
- Declares that it is not inevitable that the lender will exercise conversion debt to equity should such a clause exists in the loan agreement

A loan agreement that is recognized by taxing authorities as straight debt has particular tax advantages and disadvantages. The buyer realizes a tax advantage because interest paid to the lender is used to reduce earnings and therefore reduces the tax liability on earnings. The lender realizes a tax disadvantage because interest payments are treated as earnings for the lender and are fully taxable.

Caution

Interest is recorded for tax liability on an accrual basis rather than on a cash basis. The interest can be deducted by the buyer and realized as earnings by the lender according to the payment schedule, and not when the lender receives payment. This means the buyer might skip a payment and the lender must still pay taxes on the interest as if it were received from the buyer.

A buyer that is a holding corporation could lose the deductibility of interest payments in state and local jurisdictions by the way in which the loan is structured. Let's say that a lender loans cash to a holding corporation. The holding corporation uses the cash to finance the operations of a subsidiary. The subsidiary distributes excess operating earnings to the holding corporation, which uses the cash to make payments to the lender on the loan.

Both the subsidiary and the holding corporation benefit from the tax deductibility of the interest payment because the holding corporation files a consolidated federal tax return reflecting both the holding corporation's and the subsidiary's earnings.

However, some state and local jurisdictions prohibit such consolidated returns and require subsidiaries located within its jurisdiction to file their own tax returns. The subsidiary in this example is unable to deduct interest payments made to the lender because the loan agreement is between the holding corporation and the lender—not between the subsidiary and the lender.

Therefore, the buyer that is a holding corporation must consult tax advisors before arranging a loan to determine the most advantageous structure for a debt. Failure to do this exposes the buyer to unnecessary tax liability.

Caution

A tax advisor must carefully examine exclusion provisions in tax regulations that either prohibit or limit interest deductibility from taxes. For example, some taxing authorities limit interest deductibility to the Federal Fund rate plus 5 percent.

Debt as Equity Consequences

A taxing authority might declare a loan as equity if the loan agreement fails to meet a reasonable test, such as that described in the previous section, that defines debt. If a loan is declared as equity, the buyer and lender must unravel payment of principal and interest already exchanged and recast those transactions as equity financing.

Recasting debt financing as equity financing has a far-reaching effect once the buyer and lender have begun to treat payments as repayment of a loan. For example, the debt might be declared preferred stock and the interest payments recast as dividends. Payments of principal might become a distribution of funds to stockholders.

Here are some of the repercussions:

- Debt that is redefined as preferred stock prevents the buyer from organizing as a Subchapter S corporation because a Subchapter S corporation is permitted to have one class of stock, which is usually common stock. Preferred stock is a second class of stock and disqualifies the buyer from declaring as a Subchapter S corporation. Stockholders are then exposed to double taxation of earnings.

- Other loans might be in default because loan agreements typically contain restrictive clauses that prohibit paying dividends and distributing cash to stockholders until the loans are retired.

- Previous taxable earnings for the buyer increase because the once deductible interest payment to the lender is now treated as dividends. Dividends are not tax deductible.

- Previous taxable earnings for the lender increase because payment on the principal of the loan is treated as distribution of the buyer to stockholders. This distribution is considered new money to the lender and is therefore taxable. Principal is considered the lender's existing money that is being repaid by the buyer, which is not taxable.

TAX-FREE TRANSACTIONS

There are several types of transactions used in an acquisition that, if properly organized, will reduce or eliminate tax liabilities on the transaction. The principle behind tax-free transactions is that the buyer and dotcom substitute stock in each other's corporations and thereby exchange stock of equal value. This is called a *reorganization* because there is no gain or loss and both parties to the transaction relatively remain unchanged. The reorganization must pass three tests to be qualified as tax-free. These are

1. The transaction must have a clear business purpose.
2. The buyer must continue the dotcom's business operation by using the dotcom's assets.
3. The buyer must maintain 50 percent interest in the dotcom after the acquisition.

There are three forms of tax-free acquisitions: stock-for-stock, assets-for-stock, and a merger. The stock-for-stock form of acquisition occurs when the buyer and dotcom exchange each other's stock. Stockholders in the dotcom haven't gained or lost on the acquisition because the dotcom's stockholders received equivalent shares in the buyer.

An assets-for-stock (see Chapter 3) occurs when the buyer acquires all the assets of the dotcom in return for shares in the buyer's corporation. The dotcom's stockholders indirectly still hold title to the assets by owning shares in the buyer's corporation.

A merger (see Chapter 3) occurs when the dotcom and buyer combine assets and liabilities. At least the buyer or the dotcom survives, and the other dies. In some mergers, both the buyer and dotcom die through the creation of a new corporation that contains assets and liabilities from both the buyer and dotcom.

These forms of tax-free acquisitions are created by using one of several reorganization methods, the most common of which are A, B, C, and D. The letters represent subchapters in Section 368 of the Internal Revenue Service code that explains the rules that govern those kinds of reorganization. The A-Reorganization is a merger of the buyer and dotcom in which both corporations are consolidated into one corporation. The merger must be either a tax-free forward merger or a tax-free forward triangular merger (see Chapter 3). Other forms of merger are not considered tax-free.

A tax-free forward merger occurs when the buyer's stockholders give the dotcom's stockholders stock in the buyer. The dotcom transfers its assets to the buyer. The dotcom retains title to the assets, since it owns shares of the buyer.

A tax-free forward triangular merger is a subsidiary merger in which the buyer gives the dotcom's stockholders shares in the buyer's holding corporation, and the dotcom's assets are transferred to the buyer's subsidiary.

The B-Reorganization is a stock-for-stock transaction, and the C-Reorganization is an assets-for-stock transaction. The D-Reorganization occurs when a corporation transfers title to an asset to a subsidiary.

Caution

A holding corporation can spin off a subsidiary to stockholders of the holding corporation by transferring shares of the subsidiary to the holding corporation's stockholders. This is a tax-free transaction. Value of the subsidiary, as represented in the holding corporation shares, reduces the value of the holding corporation's shares. However, that value is passed along to the holding corporation's stockholders in the form of shares in the subsidiary.

TAX STRATEGY

Prior to the acquisition, the buyer and dotcom should carefully develop a tax strategy in order to minimize tax exposure after the deal. A perfect tax strategy eliminates tax liabilities for both the buyer and the dotcom. This is possible using tax-free methods discussed earlier in this chapter. For example, a stock swap between buyer and dotcom results in an exchange of assets of equal value and avoids taxation. However, both the buyer and the dotcom must agree to accept each other's liabilities and agree to operate as one corporation.

Caution

Cash received from a stock purchase might be considered a cash distribution rather than a stock sale if a stockholder owns 50 percent of the share in both the buyer and the dotcom, since ownership in the dotcom assets hasn't materially changed hands. This means that the portion of the sale price that is considered as principal—nontaxable—is considered a cash distribution, which is fully taxable.

This is counter to the philosophy of many dotcom stockholders, who have a desire to cash out rather than retain material ownership in the dotcom after the deal. In this case, the dotcom needs to structure itself as a Subchapter S corporation prior to consummating the deal; otherwise, stockholders are faced with double taxation. This means the dotcom can have up to 75 shareholders and one class of stock, as described previously in this chapter.

Adjustments to the corporate structure are necessary if the dotcom is a Subchapter C corporation that is not qualified to become a Subchapter S corporation. The dotcom must eliminate those factors that disqualify it from becoming a Subchapter S corporation. Management of the dotcom should consult with a tax advisor to determine if a waiting period exists from the time these adjustments are made to the time when the dotcom declares itself as a Subchapter S corporation.

An asset purchase is preferred if the dotcom is not and cannot declare itself a Subchapter S corporation in time for the deal. An asset purchase exposes the dotcom's stockholders to double taxation if the dotcom is not a Subchapter S corporation, but does not expose them to liabilities found in a stock swap.

Caution

Asset purchases are commonly treated as a lump-sum payment between the buyer and dotcom rather than as the sale of each asset held by the dotcom. However, assets are treated as individual transactions for tax purposes.

A key to reducing tax liability is for the dotcom to postpone any gain on the deal. Typically in a cash-out strategy, stockholders in the dotcom receive a lump sum that is expected to be a substantially higher value than the purchase price of the shares. The difference is the gain, which is realized as a capital gain.

The capital gain from the dotcom deal is added to other income the stockholder received in the tax year. The stockholder pays tax on the entire income. The stockholder might be in a more favorable tax position by distributing the gain over several years, thereby postponing the tax liability.

Other income in those years might drop and place the stockholder into a lower tax bracket. This may become relevant should the stock in the dotcom be held less than the minimum time period required to receive reduced capital gains tax. Tax rates may also change during that time.

An installment sale is a common method used to postpone gains. Installment sales are used in an asset purchase or stock purchase as long as the stock is not traded on the open market. In an installment sale, the dotcom or its stockholders transfer assets or stock to the buyer in exchange for an installment loan.

The installment loan specifies the purchase price. The dotcom or its stockholders record the cost basis. The ratio between the purchase price and the cost basis is applied to each payment to calculate the gain received in the payment. Let's say the dotcom sold assets worth $10 million to the buyer as an installment sale. The assets have a cost basis of $5 million, and the installment loan specifies that the full price will be paid over 10 payments. Each payment is $1 million.

Half of the purchase price reflects the principal cost of the assets, and the other half is the gain. This ratio is applied to each payment. Therefore, the dotcom records a gain of $500,000 each time the buyer makes a payment. This gain is exposed to tax obligations.

Management Buyouts

A management buyout might pose unexpected tax liability to management. In a management buyout, managers of the dotcom form a new corporation, and with funds provided by a lender, acquire the dotcom typically as a forward or reverse merger (see Chapter 3). The lender can be the dotcom or a third party.

Management may also acquire the dotcom by using a stock purchase if the dotcom is a closely held, private corporation. Stock purchase of a public corporation might be hindered by regulations, as discussed in Chapter 6. For example, margin regulations limit a stockholder to borrowing half the value of the stock purchase. The other half must be cash. Typically, the full amount of a management buyout is borrowed.

The relationship between management and the dotcom exposes management to tax liabilities should the dotcom lend management funds to finance the deal. Management is an employee of the dotcom. The market value of stock that is transferred to management above the price management paid for the stock is treated as income and is exposed to income tax.

Let's say that as part of a management buyout deal, management pays $1,000 for 100 shares of stock in a dotcom, and the stock has a market value of $10,000. The difference between the amount paid and the market value, in this case $9,000, is treated as income and the dotcom is required to withhold income taxes as if the dotcom paid management $9,000 in salary. Furthermore, the tax basis for the stock is the purchase price plus the income—that is, the $1,000 price paid by management and the $9,000 income that brings the stock transaction to the full market value of the stock.

Caution

There is no income tax liability if management pays the full market value for the stock.

Restrictions can be placed on stock held by management as part of a management buyout. These restrictions prohibit the transfer of stock and expose management to forfeiture of ownership of the stock until a specific event occurs. For example, management may be required to remain with the corporation for at least five years after the acquisition. During that period, management does not have the right to sell or transfer the stock. Furthermore, management loses the stock entirely if it terminates employment before five years.

With these restrictions, the difference between the market value of the stock and the price paid for the stock by management are not treated as income until the restrictions are lifted. Once restrictions are removed from the stock, then the transaction is treated as income, even if management does not sell its shares.

This means that management is liable for income taxes on the difference between the market value and the purchase price. Management and the dotcom should tie liquidation of some or all of the stock to the event that removed restrictions from the stock. In this way, management will have the cash available to pay income taxes when they come due.

Caution

A gray area exists in a management buyout. Is management a member of an investor group who is acquiring the dotcom? Is management receiving stock as part of employment with the dotcom? A positive answer to the first question negates treatment of stock as income. The opposite is true if the second question is answer positively. Consult a tax advisor to determine how the Internal Revenue Service is likely to interpret the deal.

Management can avoid the risk that a management buyout is a treated as income by borrowing funds to purchase stock of the dotcom. The loan must be equal to the amount of the acquisition and give the lender recourse should the loan default. The loan must have an interest rate higher than the Federal Funds rate.

The recourse provision in a loan is critical to the way ownership is interpreted. A stock backed by a nonrecourse loan is considered a nonqualified option to buy the stock for tax purposes.

Caution

Recourse should be limited and exclude certain personal assets of management, such as a house and car. However, consult a tax advisor to determine if this exclusion reclassifies the loan as a nonrecourse loan.

SUMMARY

The dotcom, buyer, and stockholders of both corporations are exposed to taxes whenever there is a disbursement of assets. Taxes are applied to gains realized as the difference between the book value of an asset and the asset's sale price to the buyer.

Gains on the sale of assets are exposed to double taxation unless the dotcom is declared as a Subchapter S corporation or a partnership. Subchapter S corporations and a partnership pass through gains to stockholders and partners without any taxes applied at the corporate or partnership level. A corporation that is not declared as a Subchapter S corporation or a partnership pays taxes on the gain at the corporate level and at the stockholder level when the gain is distributed to stockholders as dividends.

At times, the buyer's and the dotcom's tax objectives are at opposing positions. The buyer takes a long-term tax strategy that sets out to minimize tax liabilities to acquire the dotcom, to operate the corporation following the acquisition, and to minimize tax liability when the acquisition is ultimately sold by the buyer to another buyer. The dotcom has a short-term tax strategy with the objective to minimize tax liability incurred by the deal.

Whenever tax strategies are in conflict, the dotcom and the buyer should develop a compromise tax strategy that minimizes aggregated tax liabilities for the entire deal. Adjustments are made to the deal price to reflect this higher tax expense. The acquisition price should also be adjusted to reflect any negative tax effects of tax credits, tax losses, earnings, and profits.

Taxes are calculated based on the way in which the buyer and dotcom record assets and liabilities on the day the deal closes. The two ways in which assets and liabilities are recorded are the purchase method and the pooling of interest method. The purchase method requires accountants to prepare a closing financial statement that describes assets, liabilities, earnings, and losses of the dotcom as of the day the deal closes. These are the values that are carried over and recorded on the buyer's books and records. The pooling of interest method treats the deal as a stock purchase or merger, and combines assets, liabilities, earnings, and losses of both the dotcom and the buyer. Once these values are combined, accountants for the buyer recreate previous financial statements to reflect the combination of both corporations.

QUESTIONS

1. What is the difference between a Subchapter S corporation and a Subchapter C corporation?

2. What is the difference between a Subchapter S corporation and a partnership?

3. When can a management buyout be considered as income to management?

4. What are the advantages and disadvantages of a carryover acquisition?

5. How does a buyer calculate a step-up adjusted basis for an acquired asset?

6. What is the impact if a taxing authority or court determines that a debt-financing plan is actually an equity-financing plan?

7. How can gains from a subsidiary be triple taxed?

8. How can interest paid on a loan not be deductible from earnings produced by a subsidiary?

9. What are the tax implications when a Subchapter S corporation offers an equity kicker to a lender?

10. What are the disadvantages of the pooling of interest?

CHAPTER 5

Employee Issues

Technology never can replace an employee.
—Anonymous

In This Chapter

- Compensation
- Combining Compensation Plans
- Benefit Plans
- Retirement Plans
- Health Benefits
- Assessing the Impact of Benefit Plans
- Extended Benefit Exposure
- Benefits Plan Funding
- Separating and Combining Benefit Plans
- Unions
- Employee Stock Ownership Plans

COMPENSATION

Compensation is the way in which employees are rewarded for providing service to a corporation. There are four ways in which employees are compensated: salary, incentive, bonus, and benefits. One or more of these methods is used in every corporation.

Salary is an annual sum paid to employees on a regular schedule during the year and represents the bulk of, and in some cases all of, their compensation. A bonus is normally a once-a-year payment and takes the form of cash or stock. In the financial industry and for corporate executives, a bonus represents the majority of their compensation.

A bonus can be deferred compensation that is guaranteed at the end of the year, which eases compensation cash flows during the year and encourages employees to remain with the corporation. A bonus can also be correlated to performance, in which case the bonus is called an incentive. Incentives are a way employees are rewarded for achieving a desired result, such as reaching a sales objective.

The bonus amount is calculated differently than an incentive amount. Salary and bonus are combined to arrive at a total compensation amount. Employees are typically hired based on total compensation rather than on salary only. For example, a manager is hired at a total compensation of $150,000, with $100,000 in base salary and $50,000 in guaranteed bonus paid in a lump sum at the end of the year.

An incentive is also combined with salary. However, the sum produces a range of total compensation rather than a guaranteed total compensation. Let's say the manager is hired with a base salary of $100,000. This amount is guaranteed. The incentive is $25,000 if the manager's division reaches its sales goal and another $25,000 if the corporation also reaches its sales goal. Total compensation for the manager can range from $100,000 if neither goal is met to $150,000 if the division and the corporation meet their sales objectives.

Bonuses and incentives are typically paid once a year, although some corporations may distribute quarterly bonuses or pay an incentive once the goal is achieved. Other times, these amounts are deferred to future years. In this case, the corporation places the bonus or incentive into an escrow account that is invested and that accumulates value until the employee withdraws the amount. Deferred compensation is a technique for lowering tax liability for the employee, since withdrawals are likely to occur after the employee retires and is in a lower tax bracket.

The fourth form of compensation is benefits. Benefits service is provided at no expense or reduced expense to an employee by an employer, and can range from health care and retirement benefits to use of the corporate plane. Common benefits are discussed later in this chapter.

Tech Talk

Escrow Account: An account overseen by a third party until terms of a contract are met, at which time the balance of the account is turned over to a party of the contract.

Compensation and Negotiations

Compensation is a key factor when negotiating a deal, because the success of the deal and the success of business operations following the deal are dependent upon adoption of fair compensation for key employees and fair compensation for other employees.

It is highly likely that the buyer and the dotcom have different compensation policies that must be addressed during negotiations. Although the buyer has full authority to set the compensation policy after the deal, two factors must be considered when discussing the compensation policy with the dotcom prior to the deal.

The first factor is that the dotcom might insist on a post-acquisition compensation policy that maintains the dotcom's existing compensation policy, especially for key management. The other factor is that employee contractual agreements may require that the dotcom's compensation policy remain enforced until the contract expires.

The buyer and dotcom typically approach the compensation issue at opposing positions. The dotcom seeks to impose restrictions that protect current employees from losing compensation. This is especially prevalent in closely held companies where a strong bond exists between the owners and employees.

The buyer wants the freedom to establish a new compensation policy that is in the best interest of business operations following the acquisition. Restrictions agreed to during negotiations that relate to postacquisition compensation will have a long-term effect on the buyer, and therefore the buyer should avoid such agreements, if possible.

Compensation must be discussed soon after negotiations begin, because the buyer can leverage restrictions imposed by the dotcom when negotiating terms of the acquisitions. For example, the cost of an expensive restriction might be deducted from the acquisition price.

The buyer's objective is to achieve a postacquisition compensation system that focuses on producing quality products and value to stockholders. To this end, the postacquisition compensation system must be directly associated with performance of the corporation, of the division, and of the workgroup, each of which has clearly defined goals that, if met, produce quality products and return stockholder value.

The buyer must evaluate a dotcom's compensation policy and compare the policy to the buyer's own compensation policy. The buyer may want to replace its own compensation policy with that of the dotcom, should the dotcom's compensation policy be more advantageous to the buyer. However, the dotcom's compensation policy should be terminated, or not carried over, after the acquisition should the compensation policy reward employees regardless of whether they meet corporate objectives. For example, a pattern of automatic pay increases and excessive bonuses for key employees that are paid regardless of the dotcom's performance will become a serious financial drain for the buyer if allowed to continue following the acquisition. Likewise, compensation that is higher than the local market also reduces cash that could otherwise be directed toward meeting the buyer's objectives.

Compensation Styles

Base salary, bonus, incentives, and benefits define the compensation style of both the buyer and the dotcom. Dotcom corporations are in a high-growth industry where most compensation is paid as incentives through stock options. In contrast, a brick-and-mortar corporation is likely to be in a mature industry where growth is relatively modest. Brick-and-mortar corporations have a tendency to bias compensation more toward base salary than incentives.

Industry practice also influences the compensation style of a buyer and dotcom. For example, the securities industry compensation style is to bias the bulk of compensation as a bonus. It is common that $200,000 is the highest salary paid to any employee at a major securities firm. However, the employee's bonus might be $10 million. Therefore, a buyer and dotcom may have conflicting compensation styles. It is critical to the success of the deal that both the buyer and the dotcom recognize these differences and assess its impact on postacquisition business operations; otherwise, the conflict might have a negative impact on the deal.

Let's say that A-Brick-and-Mortar wants to acquire A-Dotcom. A-Dotcom offers employees below-market pay and substantial stock options as a way to reduce a cash drain on the corporation. A-Brick-and-Mortar has a salary-based compensation style with a modest employee stock ownership plan.

A-Brick-and-Mortar and A-Dotcom compensation styles are at odds. Furthermore, A-Brick-and-Mortar risks losing employees once the deal is consummated because employees of A-Dotcom will expect to cash out their options, realize their incentive from the sale of the options, and move on to another dotcom that offers them compensation terms similar to A-Dotcom. Compensation therefore becomes a major issue for negotiations.

Tech Talk

Cash-Out: The technique used by employees who own stock options and exercise those options to realize cash.

Compensation is also affected by the structures of the deal. For example, an asset purchase breaks ties between A-Dotcom and the A-Brick-and-Mortar business operations because A-Brick-and-Mortar acquires A-Dotcom's assets, and not their employees. Therefore, A-Brick-and-Mortar does not have any obligation to A-Dotcom's employees.

In addition, an asset purchase could affect the value of A-Dotcom options held by its employees. Here's how this works. Let's say that A-Dotcom is a privately held corporation that is selling assets to A-Brick-and-Mortar in exchange for cash. A-Brick-and-Mortar and A-Dotcom negotiate an acquisition price, which becomes the market value of A-Dotcom.

A-Dotcom is liquidated by distributing cash received from A-Brick-and-Mortar to A-Dotcom stockholders. A-Dotcom acquires options from employees based on the liquidation value of shares of A-Dotcom.

However, the value of the options might be more or less than if the A-Dotcom became a public corporation and its shares were traded in the securities market. The value of a public corporation is determined by the marketplace rather than through negotiations between the buyer and dotcom.

A-Dotcom's employees have little, if any, say in the acquisition price because A-Dotcom's employees do not own shares of A-Dotcom and are unable to vote for or against the deal. A-Dotcom's employees own the right to purchase shares at a predetermined price that was established by A-Dotcom at the time the option was offered to the employee.

In contrast, a stock purchase continues ties between A-Dotcom's and A-Brick-and-Mortar's business operations. A-Brick-and-Mortar can operate A-Dotcom as a subsidiary or as an independent corporation. Stock purchase enables A-Dotcom employees who hold options to cash out by selling their options to A-Brick-and-Mortar.

A merger also continues ties between A-Dotcom's and A-Brick-and-Mortar's business operations. However, A-Dotcom employees who hold options are not cashing out because the merger typically involves a stock swap, and not a stock purchase.

Although the structure of the deal influences the value of stock options held by A-Dotcom's employees, A-Brick-and-Mortar will likely realize an advantage by continuing the services of A-Dotcom's employees after the acquisition. Therefore, A-Brick-and-Mortar still must resolve the conflict in compensation styles with A-Dotcom to be assured that the post-acquisition transition is smooth. The problem A-Brick-and-Mortar faces is that its compensation style might appear unattractive to A-Dotcom's employees. This conflict can have serious repercussions within A-Brick-and-Mortar's existing business operations after the deal is consummated, since A-Brick-and-Mortar's employees expect to be treated the same as former

A-Dotcom's employees. This dilemma must be resolved before the acquisition is consummated.

In this example, A-Brick-and-Mortar resolves the conflict by acquiring A-Dotcom through a merger, then operating A-Dotcom as a subsidiary. A-Brick-and-Mortar offers to acquire A-Dotcom's employees' options for cash or to swap for options on A-Brick-and-Mortar's stock. Furthermore, A-Dotcom's employees retain their corporate and compensation style without affecting other A-Brick-and-Mortar subsidiaries.

Key Employee Compensation

Expect to make special compensation arrangements for key employees, without whom the dotcom's business operation is likely to fail following the acquisition. Compensation arrangements take the form of an employment contract that is signed prior to, or as part of, consummation of the acquisition agreement.

Employment contracts are between the buyer and the employee. The dotcom is not a party to the contract or to contract negotiations, although an acquisition agreement between the buyer and dotcom might be contingent on signing of employment contracts.

There are generally two kinds of employment contracts for key employees: employee retention contracts and employee termination contracts. An employee retention contract is used to specify terms under which a dotcom's employee continues employment with the buyer after the acquisition. An employee termination contract specifies the terms under which a dotcom's key employee terminates employment with the buyer following the acquisition.

An employee retention contract, referred to as a golden handshake or golden handcuffs, contains terms that specify how the employee will be rewarded for continuing employment with the buyer. Terms vary, but usually include

- A signing bonus paid 30 days after the employee's start date with the buyer. Sometimes a signing bonus is paid in installments over a 12-month period.
- A noncompetitive clause, whereby the employee agrees not to work for a competitor within a specified period, such as five years after termination.
- Guaranteed employment for the life of the contract, even in the event that the buyer sells off the dotcom after the deal.

- A take-back clause that requires the employee to pay back to the buyer any bonus or incentive paid to the employee if the employee violates the employee agreement.
- A penalty clause that imposes a declining penalty on a take-back clause. For example, in a five-year contract, the penalty is 100 percent of a bonus or incentive paid to the employee. The penalty drops by 20 percent each succeeding year of the contract.

A termination employee contract, commonly called a golden parachute or tin parachute depending on the value of the terms, typically covers the following areas:

- A specified period of guaranteed employment, after which the employee terminates relations with the buyer.
- A termination bonus paid at the end of the contract period.
- Continuation of paid benefits such as health insurance for the contract period and for one year following the contract period.
- Outplacement services.
- Noncompetitive clause.
- Take-back clause.
- Penalty clause.

Caution

The Internal Revenue Service excludes deductions for excessive termination bonus and imposes a 20 percent excise tax on the employee if the termination bonus is three times higher than the previous five-year averaged compensation paid to the employee.

COMBINING COMPENSATION PLANS

Combining a buyer's and dotcom's compensation plans is a delicate operation, since failure to address the needs of employees could cause defection of talent. Typically, the buyer uses the services of compensation analysts, who survey both compensation plans and compensation levels in local markets, then devise a plan that meets the short-term and long-term needs of the buyer.

Initially, a compensation analyst develops a short-term compensation plan called a *bridge,* which is designed to address the immediate needs of the buyer, dotcom, and the employees of both companies during and shortly after the acquisition process. The bridge focuses on employee retention and termination contracts, and contains terms that are attractive to employees without exceeding local market compensation guidelines.

The primary objective of the compensation analyst is to develop an equal or more advantageous compensation plan than is realized currently by the dotcom's employees without jeopardizing the financial stability of the acquisition.

Let's say that a buyer whose compensation plan consists mainly of base salary and a minimum, if any, bonus acquires a dotcom that offers relatively minimal salary and a large bonus. The compensation analyst might recommend that the buyer roll up the previous year's bonus into the dotcom employees' salaries to determine the base salary after the acquisition. Employees would no longer receive a bonus going forward.

This bridge compensation plan might be implemented in phases, depending upon how well the plan is accepted by employees. For example, half the bonus might be paid and the other half rolled up into base salary in the first year following the acquisition. The remaining amount of the bonus is rolled up the next year. The compensation analyst may also recommend a signing bonus for selected employees whom the buyer requires to continue the dotcom's operation.

A long-term compensation plan is designed to assure that the buyer is offering sufficiently competitive compensation to retain and attract employees. A natural conflict arises whenever the buyer makes the dotcom a subsidiary. Managers of subsidiaries need autonomy to reach goals established by the holding corporation. Yet the holding corporation needs to assure a fair and equitable compensation plan is implemented throughout subsidiaries.

Compensation analysts resolve this conflict by dividing responsibility between the holding corporation and subsidiaries. The holding corporation determines a high-level compensation strategy and leaves the subsidiaries to interpret the strategy into low-level operating policy. For example, the holding corporation might determine the compensation mix among base salary, bonus, and incentives and the performance criteria for paying a bonus and incentive. Subsidiaries determine the amount of base salary, bonus, and incentives, and when to award bonus and incentives.

Compensation analysts use the structure of an acquisition as guidance when formulating a compensation plan. As a general rule, compensation should consist more of incentives—and stock options—than of base salary if the buyer is highly leveraged. This conserves cash.

Incentives should be linked to the retirement of loans so that cash flows used for debt service are available for payment of incentives. Incentives and stock options should make up less of the compensation if the buyer used cash or stock to acquire the dotcom.

Caution

Stock incentives dilute the value of existing shares. Therefore, avoid using stock incentives unless previously issued treasury stock is used to fund the incentive.

Employees affected by the acquisition are likely to resist a compensation plan that negatively impacts them or a compensation plan that is difficult to comprehend. It is critical that the buyer take every opportunity to ease employee anxiety by fully explaining the impact the new compensation plan has on employees.

If the compensation analyst developed a comprehensive compensation plan, then it is the responsibility of the buyer to sell the plan to employees.

- Point out to employees the advantages and disadvantages over the existing compensation plan.

- Explain why the existing compensation plan cannot be carried forward.

- Show how the compensation plan is fair and competitive.

- Highlight the similarities of the current compensation plan and the new compensation plan.

- Instill a sense of reality to compensation components that are not being carried forward. Some components, for example, might be perceived as important by employees but in reality were rarely used by any employee.

- Listen to employee concerns and attempt to resolve those concerns that meet the highest resistance. For example, a workday at the dotcom might be 9 A.M. to 5 P.M. The buyer's workday might be 8 A.M. to 6 P.M. The buyer may agree to the dotcom's workday as long as the dotcom remains a subsidiary and isn't merged with another subsidiary, and the dotcom's employees may work their regular hours unless they transfer to another subsidiary.

BENEFITS PLANS

Benefits have become a major component of compensation and a major expense to the buyer and dotcom. Benefits fall into three categories: retirement plans, health plans, and specialized plans. Retirement plans consists of pensions, 401K plans, and other forms of deferred taxed compensation. Health plans cover medical expenses that are incurred by employees and their families. Specialized plans run the gamut from discounts on products to paid vacations.

Nearly every corporation offers employees a benefits plan as a component of their compensation. However, terms of the benefits plan will likely be different from corporation to corporation. For example, some benefits plans are more generous than other benefits plans. There are benefits plans in which the employer pays the cost and extends benefits beyond termination of employment.

Tech Talk

Deferred Taxed Compensation: Untaxed cash earned by an employee and placed in a restricted fund that can be drawn down once qualifications, such as reaching retirement age, are met. Drawn-down cash is then taxed.

The buyer must become fully aware of the terms of the dotcom's benefits plan before an acquisition price is negotiated, otherwise the buyer might be saddled with unexpected expenses generated by the benefits plan. Once the details of the plan are known, then the acquisition price can be adjusted to reflect the cost of maintaining the plan.

The buyer should employ a benefits analyst to conduct a thorough review of the dotcom's benefits plan. This review generates a report that outlines:

- A comparison between the buyer's benefits plan and the dotcom's benefits plan
- Expense for adopting and maintaining the dotcom's benefits plan
- Expense and legal exposure to terminating the dotcom's benefits plan
- Hidden liabilities and expenses in the dotcom's benefits plan
- How well the dotcom's benefits plan is funded

The funding component of the benefits analyst's review determines whether or not the dotcom's benefits plan is funded properly, which directly impacts the expense of carrying over the benefits plan. Funding is determined by a statistical prediction of future demand for the benefit.

For example, a younger, more healthy workforce probably will not have chronic ongoing medical conditions, and therefore the demand for health services is less than that of an older workforce, which is reflected in the cost to provide the benefit.

An actuary is called upon by the benefits analyst to use statistics to forecast medical needs of a dotcom's workforce, and then the actuary establishes the size of a fund that is necessary to provide medical benefits. The dotcom and the buyer, if the benefits plan is carried over, finance the fund through premium payments.

The benefits analyst's report critiques the dotcom's existing funding for benefits. For example, the report may find that the actuary's forecast used by the dotcom is outdated and the fund is larger than it should be; therefore the dotcom's medical benefit plan is overfunded. The buyer will realize a lower cost and may recover a portion of existing premiums if the dotcom's medical benefits are maintained.

In contrast, the report may find that funding is too low, based upon the actuary's forecast. That is, the benefits plan is underfunded, which exposes the buyer to a higher cost to maintain the medical benefits.

The benefits analyst's report becomes the basis for allocating benefits plan exposure between the buyer and the dotcom. Based on the report, the buyer must determine if maintaining the dotcom's benefits plan is advantageous to the buyer once the deal is consummated. If it isn't, then the buyer must reassess the dotcom as a candidate for acquisition.

Caution

The dotcom's financial statement may not depict an accurate assessment of the liabilities of the dotcom's benefit plan. Typically, financial statements do not contain hidden costs or the statistical basis for the benefits plan expense.

Based on the benefits analyst's research, the buyer can request as a condition of acquisition that the dotcom modify the benefits plan prior to the acquisition, thereby creating a benefits plan that can be carried forward by the buyer.

The buyer should not underestimate the expense associated with benefits plans, because each year new federal, state, and local regulations are enacted that create an administrative nightmare for the buyer—and for the dotcom.

RETIREMENT PLANS

There are two kinds of retirement plans. These are qualified and nonqualified. Qualified means that the retirement plan is qualified for favorable treatment under Internal Revenue Service regulations.

Qualified retirement plans are divided into two categories: the defined benefit plan and the defined contribution plan. A defined benefit plan is a promise by the employer to pay a fixed amount of cash to an employee when the employee retires after a specified number of years of employment. An employer contributes regular payments to a fund that is invested tax-free in investments chosen by the employer. Once an employee is qualified to receive the benefit, regular fixed payments are made to the employee from the fund, which then becomes taxable as income to the employee.

A defined contribution plan requires a fixed level of contribution and a variable benefit based on the return on investments of the contribution. Employees contribute to the plan and an employer may or may not match contributions. Contributions and return on investments are tax deferred until the employee withdraws the funds. Employees control the choice of investments. The 401K plan is a popular version of a defined contribution plan.

Nonqualified retirement plans typically are used to defer compensation by placing funds in a trust. These plans do not receive favorable tax treatment and are therefore used as incentives for key personnel rather than offered to all employees.

Issues related to combining retirement plans, especially defined contribution plans, must be addressed prior to an acquisition, because the buyer might realize an expense to maintain the plan and may also be exposed to potential liabilities. These issues can be addressed by adjustments to the acquisition price.

Whether or not the dotcom's retirement plan is merged with the buyer's retirement plan depends on, among other things, the structure of the deal. A stock purchase or merger gives rise to a prima facie case for combining both plans. An asset purchase requires that both plans be maintained separately.

There are three options available to the buyer in a stock purchase or merger:

- Merge both plans.
- Maintain both plans separately.
- Terminate the dotcom's plan.

It is typical that a buyer maintains the dotcom's retirement plan for at least a year following the acquisition. This strategy gives the buyer time both to decide which of the three alternatives to take as a long-term strategy and to comply with regulations that govern retirement plans. These regulations include

- A one-year waiting period before the buyer can terminate the retirement plan.
- A buyer has until the anniversary date of the plan to bring the plan into compliance with regulations. This period might be less than a year, depending on the timing of the acquisition and the calendar year of the plan.
- The dotcom's qualified retirement plan becomes disqualified when, within a year after the acquisition, at least 2 percent of the employees join the buyer's retirement plan.

The major advantage of maintaining both retirement plans is that the dotcom's employees have an easy transition moving from the dotcom to the buyer, since their coverage remains unchanged.

The major disadvantage is that the buyer must maintain both the dotcom's plan and its own plan, which doubles the administrative cost for maintaining retirement plans.

HEALTH BENEFITS

Two types of health benefits are offered by corporations: indemnity healthcare plans and managed healthcare plans. An indemnity health care plan is one in which caregivers are paid a fee for each service that they provide to an employee or a member of an employee's family.

Managed healthcare plans take one of three forms: health maintenance organizations (HMO), point-of-service plans (POS), and preferred provider organizations (PPO). An HMO is the least costly to employers and employees, and is the most restrictive. A PPO is the most costly and least restrictive, and a POS is a middle ground between an HMO and a PPO both in cost and restrictions.

An HMO consists of a physician, called the primary care physician, who determines the care required to treat an employee, then either provides the care or refers the employee to other caregivers in the HMO network for treatment. Employees who belong to an HMO pay nothing for care as long as care is given by their primary care physician or a caregiver that is recommended by the primary care physician. Employees underwrite the complete cost of care given by non-HMO caregivers, in most cases. An HMO has contractual agreements with caregivers, whereby specified services are provided at a fixed cost during the life of the contract. This helps an HMO contain medical expenses.

POS offers employees cost containment similar to an HMO, but also pays for services rendered by caregivers outside of the POS network. As with an HMO, an employee selects a primary care physician who provides the same service as with an HMO. Except for a minor copayment by the employee for each visit to a caregiver, the employee is not charged for service given by a caregiver in the POS network. However, the employee pays a percentage of the cost for services provided by a caregiver that is not a participant in the POS network.

The PPO consists of a network of caregivers; however, employees are not required to use the services of a primary care physician. Instead, the employee can choose to consult with any caregiver that is a member of the network.

Funding Medical Benefits

Medical benefit plans are funded by employer contributions to a trust, by an employer buying an insurance policy, or by an employer being self-insured.

A trust-based medical benefit plan is called a funded medical benefit plan; contributions are made to a trust fund, which is drawn down to pay for employee medical coverage. The buyer has the option to transfer the trust from the dotcom to the buyer or to terminate the trust and replace the medical benefits plan with another plan. Contributions to a trust are tax deductible.

A medical benefits plan that is provided by a health insurance carrier or through self-insurance is called an unfunded medical benefit plan. An insurance company is used in both situations either to underwrite the health insurance plan or to provide administrative services to the corporation's self-insurance health insurance plan.

Premiums paid by corporations for a health insurance plan vary. The initial premium is established by an actuarial analysis of the corporation's workforce to determine the probability of the medical services required for the year. In addition, a reserve is created to cover unexpected expenses, then adjustments are made during the year to the reserve and premium to reflect actual outlays. This is called a *retrospective rating program* and exposes the corporation to unexpected expenses. For example, previously paid premiums can be increased to cover medical services required by the corporation's workforce that were outside of the actuary's projections. Likewise, the corporation might experience a refund if expenses decline.

Prior to arriving at a price for the acquisition, the buyer must have a full understanding of the medical benefits plan provided by the dotcom to its employees. Particular attention must be given to plans that permit adjustments to premiums and reserves, since the buyer might be liable to pay those adjustments after the acquisition is completed.

Caution

The buyer might be able to lower premiums when only a portion of the dotcom is acquired, since the dotcom's premium is likely to be based on the dotcom's entire workforce. Premiums must be adjusted to reflect on that portion of the dotcom's workforce that is transferring to the buyer.

ASSESSING THE IMPACT OF BENEFITS PLANS

The key to assessing the dotcom's benefits plan is to review the plan's actuarial valuation, which highlights the assets and liabilities of the benefits plan and the assumptions that are the foundation for calculating the plan's premiums.

Actuarial assumptions are the presumed facts the actuary used to calculate the probable use of the benefits by employees. The buyer cannot assume that these assumptions reflect current usage. The actuarial valuation might be outdated, or assumptions contained in the actuarial valuation may be unrealistic. An inaccurate actuarial assumption can lead to higher costs to maintain the benefits plan after the acquisition is consummated or can provide a hidden savings that directly benefits the buyer.

In addition to the actuarial valuation, the dotcom's financial statements should be reviewed for notes that discuss the valuation of the benefits plan and projected costs of retirement benefits. This information must be contained in financial statements. Actuarial assumptions include:

- Number of employees
- Age of employees
- Frequency of benefit claims
- Expense of medical claims
- Interests rates

Interests rates play a key role in determining the value of a dotcom's benefits plan. The value of a benefits plan is the plan's assets, which consist of funds provided by the corporation and by the employee contributions, where applicable.

The actuary determines the funding level that must be maintained to cover projected benefit claims. Amounts below the funding levels become a liability for the corporation. Interest payments received from investing funds and from premiums are used to maintain funding levels.

An assumption is made on the percentage of interest that the funds will accrue each year. Projection of a low interest rate infers a conservative view of the actuary. A high interest rate projection reflects an optimistic view.

The difference between the projected interest rate and the current interest rate is one way to determine the potential liability of a dotcom's benefits plan. A current interest rate that is lower than an optimistic rate in an actuary's assumption could underfund the benefits plan unless adjustments are made to the premium. In contrast, a current interest rate that is higher than a conservative rate in an actuary's assumption could overfund the benefits plan and become an advantage to the buyer. Adjustments can be made to reduce premiums or to refund to excess funds the buyer—not the dotcom—if the buyer acquires the dotcom and maintains the benefits plan.

Caution

Avoid accepting the dotcom's actuary's assumptions without independent verification when negotiating the deal, since those assumptions may not reflect the benefits plan's actual liabilities.

Caution

Defined contribution benefits plans are always 100 percent funded.

Special care must be taken whenever a buyer acquires a subsidiary of a dotcom through a stock purchase or merger, because the buyer also acquires the liabilities of the dotcom's benefits plan. This becomes material if the dotcom offers its employees a generous benefit plan as compared to that of the buyer.

The dotcom's benefits plan might be uneconomically sound for the buyer to maintain. Therefore, the buyer may require the dotcom to modify the benefits plan prior to the acquisition or to adjust the acquisition price to reflect that additional expense. The buyer must keep in mind that all of the dotcom's benefits plan, or a portion of it, may be carried forward for a period of up to a year before the buyer can terminate the plan.

EXTENDED BENEFIT EXPOSURE

A buyer must assess the liability exposure created by the dotcom's extended benefits plan. Extended benefits refer to benefits received by employees who have terminated employment with the dotcom. These benefits include retirement benefits, deferred compensation, and termination benefits.

Unless the buyer acquires the dotcom through an asset purchase that is not declared a de facto merger by the courts, the buyer is exposed to benefits obligations of the dotcom. In a typical dotcom acquisition, extended benefits are unlikely to become an issue, because compensation is generally based on a base salary plus stock options. Stock options are either exercised at the time of the acquisition or carried forward and recognized by the buyer at a later date.

However, corporations other than dotcoms in the e-commerce industry may have a brick-and-mortar heritage or may offer employees extended benefits, such as in the electronics manufacturing segment of the e-commerce industry. Therefore, the buyer cannot assume that a dotcom does not offer extended benefits to employees.

Extended benefits cannot be modified or terminated by either the dotcom or the buyer unless the dotcom's extended benefits policy clearly states that terms of extended benefits are not guaranteed. Barring such a policy, extended benefits remain a liability to the buyer. The buyer must retain a compensation analyst to evaluate extended benefits offered by the dotcom and to determine the coverage period and the anticipated cost each year during the coverage period. In many cases, the coverage period extends to the age at which the former employee receives Social Security benefits. In other cases, extended benefits carry forward until the death of the employee and the employee's spouse.

Extended Medical Benefits

Extended medical coverage exposes the buyer to an expensive liability, since the cost of medical coverage increases dramatically each year, especially with the aging population covered by extended medical benefits. The buyer should make an attempt to have the dotcom modify extended medical benefits to bring future costs of benefits into a manageable range. For example, the extended medical benefits offered by the dotcom should be subordinate to other medical coverage carried by the former employee.

Let's say that the former employee incurred $1,000 in medical expenses and is covered by another medical policy that pays $500 of the incurred medical expenses. The subordinate clause exposes the extended medical benefits to a $500 liability.

Potential expenses for extended medical benefits should be calculated, then used to adjust the acquisition price downward.

Deferred Compensation

Deferred compensation occurs whenever the dotcom awards bonuses and incentives to key employees. Bonuses and incentives are placed into a fund that is typically managed by trustees. The buyer might inherit the obligation to oversee such a fund even if bonuses and incentives are discontinued following the acquisition.

An analysis must be made to assess the buyer's obligation to the deferred compensation fund. For example, the buyer might have a fiduciary responsibility that makes the buyer liable to losses incurred if trustees mismanage the fund. Furthermore, the buyer might incur expenses to administrate the deferred compensation fund should those be related to reporting and disbursement of funds.

An effort should be made to have the dotcom turn over the deferred compensation fund to a third party, such as a financial institution, before the acquisition is consummated if the buyer does not intend to maintain the deferred compensation benefit.

This technique severs the obligation of the dotcom to employees covered by the deferred compensation fund by transferring management and fiduciary responsibility from the dotcom to the financial institution. Employees then interact directly with the financial institution to receive their benefits.

Termination Benefits

Termination benefits are another form of extended benefit that must be carefully examined by the buyer before considering the acquisition of the dotcom. Termination benefits take two forms: benefits specific to an individual employee as defined in an employment agreement and benefits defined as a general termination policy of the corporation.

The buyer must require the dotcom to disclose terms of all current and previous employment agreements so the buyer's attorney can examine these agreements to assess whether or not the benefits can be terminated.

Typically, termination benefits cover a three-month period following termination of employment with the dotcom. However, employment contracts might extend the coverage period to a year or more. In extraordinary cases, termination benefits could include lifetime medical benefits.

In assessing the termination clause in employment agreements, the buyer's attorney determines the duration of the coverage, the events that trigger the coverage, and the costs to the buyer that are associated with the coverage. Furthermore, the attorney determines if the employment contract is modifiable. For example, the employer initiating the employee's termination frequently triggers termination benefits. The employee loses the coverage if the employee leaves employment voluntarily. In this case, the buyer might take steps not to trigger the termination benefits. Other times, the employee is covered regardless of who initiates termination.

As with other extended benefits, the buyer must assess whether or not it is in the best interest of the buyer to carry forward termination benefits liabilities without compensation from the dotcom, which is usually in the form of an adjusted acquisition price.

An overfunded benefits plan can work to the favor of a buyer, because excess funds can be used to offset future funding requirements or can revert to the buyer once the benefits plan is terminated. Excess funds in a benefits plan generate an excise tax liability for the buyer. A buyer might also be able to borrow the excess funds from an overfunded benefits plan, should terms of the plan permit such loans.

Caution

Courts may invalidate termination of a benefits plan or may impose restrictions that make termination of a benefits plan not economically feasible. Therefore, it is critical that attorneys and compensation consultants advise the buyer prior to termination of a benefits plan.

BENEFITS PLANS FUNDING

Benefits plans must be properly funded to cover current and future obligations. However, the dotcom might underfund its benefit plan and therefore present potential liabilities for the buyer. A buyer that assumes the dotcom's benefits plan might be liable for the underfunded amount. Furthermore, laws might prohibit the buyer from terminating the dotcom's benefits plan until the benefits plan is fully funded.

A buyer can use the termination test to determine if a benefit plan is adequately funded. That is, the buyer determines if the benefits plan has sufficient assets to cover obligations if the benefits plan is terminated today.

An underfunded benefits plan on the surface should not inhibit an acquisition. Instead, the buyer needs to closely examine the financial condition of the dotcom to determine if the dotcom has sufficient assets to cover the underfunding. Dotcoms may have assets to fund a benefits plan, but may not have allocated those assets to the benefits plan. If this is the case, then the buyer can require proper asset allocation to fully fund the benefits plan.

However, the buyer must reconsider the viability of the dotcom as an acquisition candidate should there be insufficient assets to fund the benefits plan. The buyer must determine if adjustments in the acquisition price can offset the underfunded amount. If so, then underfunding should not impede the acquisition.

The buyer has three options regarding the dotcom's benefits plan. First, the buyer can adopt the benefits plan and become responsible for funding and liabilities that are associated with the plan. Second, the buyer can terminate the dotcom's benefits plan. In this case, the benefits plan must be fully funded even if it is at the buyer's expense. Once terminated, employees can be covered under the buyer's benefit plan. Third, the buyer can freeze the benefits plan. Freezing the benefits plan limits liabilities to obligations that exist at the time of the freeze. Future benefits and associated costs are not realized by the buyer.

SEPARATING AND COMBINING BENEFIT PLANS

There are two ways in which a buyer can separate itself from the dotcom's benefits plans. One is to hire the dotcom's employees, at which time they become new employees of the buyer and therefore fall within the buyer's current compensation and benefits plan. An alternative is for the buyer to carry forward assets and liabilities of the dotcom that are associated with the acquisition.

Hiring the dotcom's employees is a straightforward solution, as long as terms of employment are fair to the dotcom's employees. The dotcom is responsible for benefits that were incurred prior to the acquisition, including maintenance and distribution of retirement benefits. The buyer is not liable for preacquisition benefits agreed to by the dotcom.

Employment with the dotcom terminates as soon as the dotcom's employee begins employment with the buyer. Exposure to termination benefits, if any, becomes the liability of the dotcom, not the buyer.

A benefit split, however, transfers a portion of the dotcom's benefits obligation to the buyer. The portion that is transferred is proportioned to the business unit(s) acquired by the buyer. A benefit split limits the liability of the buyer, but introduces a degree of complexity to the deal.

The buyer and dotcom must employ accountants and actuaries to determine the benefits plan assets and liabilities that are directly associated with the acquisition. The buyer and dotcom must agree on the assumptions made by the actuaries, as previously discussed in this chapter, and must agree on how residuals from overfunded benefits are to be shared.

Caution

Avoid using actuarial data provided by the dotcom, since this typically places the dotcom in a favorable position in a benefit split. Instead, agree on actuarial data developed by an actuary hired by both the buyer and the dotcom.

There are many details that must be addressed when a buyer agrees to carry forward a dotcom's benefits plan, especially if that benefits plan is to be merged with the buyer's current benefits plan. A buyer can continue the dotcom's benefits plan without major administrative changes if the dotcom is operated as a subsidiary. In this way, the administrators, vendors, and trustees associated with the benefits plan remain in their current roles following the acquisition.

However, combining two benefits plans requires compensation analysts and accountants to review features of each plan to determine features that are similar and those that are different between the plans. The buyer then needs to decide if features offered by the dotcom, but not offered by the buyer, will carry forward after the acquisition. If not, then a strategy must be developed to terminate the features and resolve any administrative costs and disbursements necessary for the termination.

Those benefit features that will be carried forward and merged with the buyer's benefits plan must be transferred to the buyer. Transfer includes

- Title to assets such as reserve funds
- Employee benefits records
- Computer systems
- Administrative operations
- Adjustments in the basis for benefits such as actuarial assumptions
- Trustees who oversee benefits funds
- Transfer of assets in kind (i.e., cash-for-cash, stock-for-stock)

- Maintaining tax-differed treatment by transferring assets between trustees without distribution to employees
- Valuation of benefits assets between the agreement in principal and the date the acquisition closes
- Maintaining benefits and contributions during the transition period

---

Caution

Transfer and merger of benefits plans should be completed within a short time period to reduce the exposure to changes in the market that invalidate actuarial assumptions.

The buyer and dotcom must decide who maintains fiduciary and reporting responsibilities during the transfer of benefits. Typically, the dotcom retains fiduciary and reporting duties for actions that occur before the acquisition, and the buyer assumes fiduciary and reporting duties for actions that occur after the acquisition. However, both parties should agree to the division of responsibilities.

Caution

A transfer of some benefits requires both the dotcom and the buyer to report the transaction to regulatory authorities. Accountants and attorneys can advise on reporting requirements.

UNIONS

Although it is unusual for dotcom workers to be unionized, there are other corporations, such as telecommunications companies, that are unionized and that are players in the e-commerce marketplace. Therefore, there are factors a buyer and dotcom must consider whenever one or the other is a union shop.

A union is an organization that represents all or a class of employees during collective bargaining with the corporation. The liabilities imposed by an agreement with a union representing the dotcom's employees is inherited by the buyer if the buyer continues to operate the dotcom's business operations.

The only exception to this practice is if the dotcom's business operations cease for a material time period before the buyer restarts the dotcom's operation following the acquisition. The buyer is exposed to the liabilities of the dotcom's agreement with the union, even if the acquisition is an asset purchase, as long as the buyer employs a material number of the dotcom's employees.

The buyer is not a party to the agreement between the dotcom and the union. Instead, the buyer informally underwrites the dotcom's obligations in the agreement as part of the acquisition. The agreement remains enforced until the buyer and the union negotiate a new agreement, at which time the buyer becomes a direct party to the agreement.

The buyer must carefully examine existing union agreements to determine if the agreement contains a successor clause that specifies conditions imposed on the dotcom—and possibly on the buyer—should the dotcom be acquired. These conditions might limit the buyer's ability to reorganize the dotcom's operations following an acquisition. The buyer should anticipate that any change might need to be negotiated with the union.

For example, a successor clause might require notification of employees of a change in control of the dotcom before the acquisition is consummated. There could also be language that restricts changes that the buyer can introduce into the dotcom's operation without negotiating those changes with the union.

Caution

Be sure to consult with a labor attorney to determine the effect that terms of a union contract might have on compensation and benefits given to the buyer's nonunion employees. Discrimination regulations may require that enhanced compensation and benefits received by union workers be made available to nonunion workers.

Workforce Reductions

A reduction in workforce following an acquisition might trigger unwanted litigation for the buyer. Therefore, the buyer must take precautions to assure that such actions are perceived to be fairly executed and that they stay within the legal boundaries.

A workforce reduction must abide by contractual obligations of both the buyer and the dotcom should the dotcom's employees become the focus of the layoff. Federal regulations require that an employer who intends to lay off more than 100 employees must give employees 60 days notice of the layoff, regardless if employees are members of a union.

The buyer must avoid the perception of discrimination in terminating employees. Even if discrimination is not intended, a buyer might face litigation if the predominant number of laid off employees are over 40 years of age, members of recognized minority group, veterans, women, or disabled persons. The buyer must establish objective criteria, such as by seniority, for selecting employees to be laid off. This enables the criteria to be equally applied to all employees. Those selected should be given termination benefits that include medical coverage and financial compensation based on their years of service to the buyer or to the dotcom.

EMPLOYEE STOCK OWNERSHIP PLANS

An Employee Stock Ownership Plan (ESOP) is a benefits plan that encourages employees to purchase stock in the employer's corporation; at times, it is used to by employees to take over the corporation.

ESOP has multiple purposes. First, the employer can offer to sell stock at a discount from market value as an incentive for employees to purchase stock. It is common for employees to contribute a fixed amount each pay period to a fund that purchases the employer's stock on a schedule such as each quarter.

The fund invests in secure instruments, such as the money market, until it is time to purchase the stock. At that time, the employer sells shares held by the treasury to the employee, sometimes at as much as 15 percent below market value. The employer repurchases stock from the market at opportune times to supply the treasury with shares to resell to employees.

In this example, the ESOP is used as an incentive to give employees a feeling of ownership in the employer's business operations. Employee shares distributed as an ESOP is typically voting common stock that is restricted.

There are two kinds of restrictions commonly imposed on ESOP stock that is used as an employee benefit. Both establish rules for when and to whom employees can sell their ESOP stock.

ESOP stock can be part of a defined contribution benefits plan, in which case a penalty is imposed by the Internal Revenue Service if the shares are sold before the employee reaches an age threshold established by the Internal Revenue Service. The employee can transfer shares to a rollover Individual Retirement Account at a brokerage should the employee terminate employment.

ESOP stock that is not considered a defined contribution benefits plan might have a waiting period before the employee can sell the stock. For example, employees might be required to hold shares for five years before the shares can be sold. Furthermore, the employee is like to be required to sell the stock back to the employer at market value.

Another form of ESOP is when employees buy stock in the employer in a move to take control of the corporation. This is commonly referred to as a *management buyout*. In many cases, the employer encourages a management buyout, which is used to rescue a distressed corporation.

Employees use personal funds, retirement funds, and loans to acquire ESOP stock, after which they elect a board of directors who hire managers to run the corporation. Employees are likely to concede previous benefits and compensation in an effort to make the corporation profitable. If successful, the market value of the corporation's shares will increase and return a profit to employee stockholders. If the management buyout fails, then employees lose funds invested in the corporation's stock.

A third use of an ESOP is as a defense against a hostile takeover. An employer might view employees as a white knight who can own a material, although not controlling, interest in the corporation and who is against a hostile takeover.

A buyer looking to acquire the employer must purchase stock from employees if an ESOP exists. Employees are likely to cooperate only if the offer price is attractive and the buyer's postacquisition intent is advantageous to employees. Otherwise, employees will be encouraged by management to use their stock to block the acquisition.

Trustees of the ESOP and the employer have fiduciary responsibility to ESOP participants. That is, transactions between the employer and the ESOP must be conducted to the betterment of ESOP participants. Furthermore, such transactions must be fair to other investors; otherwise, regulatory authorities might rescind the transaction.

A key provision of fiduciary responsibility is for an independent appraiser to determine the value of privately held stock for the purpose of ESOP. An appraiser is not required for publicly traded stock, since the market determines stock value.

ESOP trustees take on a crucial role if shares are transferred by the employer to the ESOP, but are not distributed to participants. In this situation, the ESOP trustees make decisions regarding the shares, such as voting by consulting outside financial and legal advisors. Trustees are prohibited from taking directions from the employer. Actions taken by ESOP trustees must reflect the fiduciary responsibility to participants. Employees who are participants in the ESOP take over this role once shares are distributed to participants.

SUMMARY

The four ways in which employees are rewarded for providing service to an employer are through salary, incentives, bonuses, and benefits. One or more of these methods is used in every corporation. Salary is an annual sum paid to employees on a regular schedule during the year and represents the bulk of, and in some cases all of, their compensation. A bonus is normally a once-a-year payment and takes the form of cash or stock. A bonus that is correlated to performance is called an incentive and is paid when an employees achieve a desired result.

The success of postacquisition business operation is dependent upon fair compensation for key employees, among other things. A buyer must expect to make special compensation arrangements for key employees and that these terms are contained in an employment contract with the key employee.

There are generally two kinds of employment contracts for key employees: employee retention contracts and employee termination contracts. An employee retention contract specifies terms under which a dotcom's employee continues employment with the buyer after the acquisition. An employee termination contract specifies the terms under which an employee terminates employment with the buyer following the acquisition.

The buyer can combine compensation plans with the dotcom by assessing the similarities and differences in both plans, then arriving at a combination plan. A compensation analyst assesses each plan and devises a short-term and long-term combination plan. A short-term compensation plan, called a bridge, addresses the immediate needs of the buyer, the dotcom, and the dotcom's employees during and shortly after the acquisition. The bridge focuses on employee retention and termination contracts. The long-term compensation plan is a cohesive combination of both compensation plans.

The benefits component of the compensation plan falls into three categories: retirement plans, health plans, and specialized plans. Retirement plans consist of deferred taxed compensation. Health plans cover medical expenses that are incurred by employees and their families. Specialized plans run the gamut from discounts on products to paid vacations.

The two kinds of deferred taxed compensation are qualified and non-qualified. Qualified deferred taxed compensation means that the retirement plan is qualified for favorable treatment under the Internal Revenue Service regulations.

Qualified retirement plans are divided into two categories: the defined benefit plan and the defined contribution plan. A defined benefit plan is a promise by the employer to pay a fixed amount of cash to an employee when the employee retires after a specified number of years of employment.

Health benefits fall into two categories. These are indemnity healthcare plans and managed healthcare plans. An indemnity health care plan is one in which caregivers are paid a fee for each service that they provide to an employee or a member of an employee's family.

Managed healthcare plans take one of three forms: health maintenance organizations (HMO), point-of-service plans (POS), and preferred provider organizations (PPO). An HMO is the least costly to employers and employees, and is the most restrictive. A PPO is the most costly and least restrictive, and a POS is a middle ground between an HMO and a PPO both in cost and restrictions. Medical benefits plans are funded by employer contributions to a trust, by an employer buying an insurance policy, or by an employer being self-insured.

A review of the actuarial valuation of a plan is a way for the buyer to assess the dotcom's benefits plan. The actuarial valuation highlights the assets and liabilities of the benefits plan and the assumptions that are the foundation for calculating the plan's premiums.

Actuarial assumptions are the presumed facts the actuary used to calculate the probable use of the benefits by employees. An inaccurate actuarial assumption can lead to higher costs to maintain the benefits plan after the acquisition is consummated or can provide a hidden savings that directly benefits the buyer.

The dotcom's financial statements should also be reviewed for notes that discuss the valuation of the benefits plan and the projected costs of retirement benefits. This information must be contained in financial statements.

The dotcom's extended benefits plan can expose the buyer to liability because benefits such as retirement benefits, deferred compensation, and termination benefits are provided to employees who have left the corporation.

Benefits plans must be properly funded to cover current and future obligations; otherwise, the buyer assumes liability for the underfunded benefits plan. Furthermore, laws might prohibit the buyer from terminating the dotcom's benefits plan until the benefits plan is fully funded.

The buyer can separate itself from the dotcom's benefits plan by hiring the dotcom's employees, at which time they become new employees of the buyer and therefore fall within the buyer's current compensation and benefits plan.

QUESTIONS

1. What are the various forms of compensation?

2. What extended medical benefits might a buyer be exposed to?

3. How can a buyer determine if a benefits plan is overfunded?

4. How can a buyer reduce exposure to extended medical benefits?

5. What are the advantages of deferred compensation?

6. How does a buyer consolidate dissimilar benefits plans after an acquisition?

7. How do compensation and benefits affect acquisition price?

8. How does a buyer handle dotcom employee termination before the acquisition?

9. What are the dotcom's employee issues in an acquisition?

10. How do interest rates influence the outcome of an actuary's presumptions in funding a benefits plan?

CHAPTER 6

Public and Private Corporations

Public corporations hold a public trust.
—Anonymous

In This Chapter

- Public Corporations Basics
- Tender Offer
- Proxy Solicitation
- Public Disclosure
- Board of Directors Duties
- Defensive Strategies
- Restrictions
- Insider Conflicts
- Financing Issues
- Private Corporations Basics

PUBLIC CORPORATIONS BASICS

A corporation is an organization of stockholders that has been declared a legal entity by the state in which the organization was incorporated. The corporation's articles of incorporation, corporate charter, and bylaws, as well as state regulations, define the rules within which the corporation can operate.

A public corporation is a corporation in which some or all of its shares are registered with the appropriate agencies, shares are issued to the general public, and shares are likely to be traded in a stock exchange where the auction process dictates the current value of those shares.

State and federal agencies such as the Securities and Exchange Commission (SEC), which enforces the Securities Act and the Exchange Act, regulate public corporations. The primary objective of securities regulations is to assure a fair and open market for publicly traded securities without the influence of fraud and stock manipulation.

There are two key elements of these regulations. The first is to define the role of a public corporation's board of directors. The second is to establish guidelines for public disclosure of interest and intentions of parties associated with the public corporation.

The board of directors is empowered by stockholders to make business decisions on behalf of stockholders, except for material changes in the structure and control of the corporation—such as an acquisition. In those situations, the board of directors recommends a course of action to stockholders, who then accept or reject the proposal.

At times, a conflict can occur between the self-interest of the board of directors and the interests of stockholders. This is common whenever a move is made to acquire a corporation. The board of directors may negotiate a deal on terms that return gains to the board of directors rather than to the stockholder. This is especially true if members of the board of directors want to retain employment with the acquiring firm after the deal is consummated.

Regulators impose tight restrictions on the board of directors of public corporations when it relates to conflicts of interest such as in the case of an acquisition. Each member of the board of directors has fiduciary responsibility to stockholders and must make decisions that return the highest possible gain to stockholders. Failure to do so opens members of the board of directors to litigation by stockholders that could lead to nullification of the deal and imposed fines and other legal sanctions on individual board members.

Caution

Failure of a public corporation's board of directors to place self-interest second to the interests of stockholders could result in enforcement of the Racketeer Influenced and Corrupt Organizations Act (RICO). If a stockholder proves that a pattern of actions taken by a director harmed the stockholder, then the courts could impose up to a 20-year prison term on the director, freeze the director's assets, and award the stockholder treble damages.

The board of directors of a public corporation must remain neutral when it comes to potential buyers for the corporation. It is not within the discretion of the board to reject outright any creditable offer or to accept a creditable offer without investigating whether it is the best offer available.

A potential buyer might propose the acquisition to the dotcom's board of directors. However, the board must do everything in its power to encourage other potential buyers to make competing offers for the corporation. For example, the board must provide other potential buyers with information about other bids in an effort to entice more favorable terms.

Federal and state securities regulations require public corporations to disclose material financial information by filing disclosure forms with regulatory authorities such as the SEC. Likewise, certain stockholders and potential buyers must make public disclosure in the form of a filing. For example, a person or corporation that acquires 5 percent of the outstanding stock of a public corporation must disclose this position in a filing with the SEC.

Public disclosure is a way in which regulators assure that the public has pertinent information about the public corporation. The public then can assess the value of the information and make appropriate financial decisions, such as to sell or buy stock, regarding the corporation.

Pertinent information that is not disclosed to the public cannot be the basis for buying or selling a public corporation's stock; otherwise, the person undertaking the transaction might be found in violation of insider trading regulations.

Insider trading occurs whenever someone trades securities of a corporation based on information about a public corporation that is not widely known to the public or is not disclosed in a regulatory filing. For example, an employee might discover that earnings are substantially higher than earnings projected in the financial press. The employee is in violation of insider trading regulations if he or she purchases the corporation's stock before the earnings announcement or tips off another person about earnings and that tip results in a stock purchase.

The SEC and brokerage firms monitor any extraordinary trading activities days before the earnings announcement or announcement of any extraordinary event (i.e., acquisition announcement) to identify clues to insider trading. Regulatory authorities are able to trace the trading pattern of an individual to determine if there are reasonable grounds to suspect that insider trading has occurred.

A buyer wishing to acquire a public corporation must be aware of various regulations and restrictions that apply to the acquisition and to those individuals personally involved in the offer and transaction. Failure to do so could delay or kill a deal.

From Tim Miller, Webmergers.com

Acquire, Don't Build from Scratch

Building a B2B exchange is a massive undertaking. Most startups so far have chosen to build their B2B positions from the ground up. One exception is BuildNet, which has used a rapid-fire series of acquisitions to build up its B2B position over a period of less than a year.

BuildNet created the BuildNet Exchange to provide procurement, e-commerce, and information services to the $238 billion residential construction industry. The industry is highly fragmented. Building a critical mass of builders and suppliers from scratch would be an immense challenge. BuildNet has chosen to tackle it by quietly rolling up a half-dozen software companies that currently serve builders and suppliers. In so doing, BuildNet has amassed homebuilders that account for about 43 percent of 1999 U.S. single-family home closings, according to the S-1 filing.

Creating market-dominating B2B exchanges is much more challenging than B2C e-commerce plays for a number of reasons:

- It's a many-to-many marketplace. This means the startup must amass a critical mass of both buyers and sellers within roughly the same time period in order to provide value. The marketing effort to do this from scratch is daunting, to say the least.
- It's a "winner-take-most" game, making the stakes much higher.
- It typically involves the difficult task of changing the basic way that highly traditional companies currently do business.
- It's typically difficult to recruit talented, Internet-savvy employees from typically traditional business marketplaces.
- Existing players are often threatened and must be persuaded to participate.

For BuildNet, an acquisition strategy appears to solve many of the above problems. By snapping up the leading software providers, it acquires a critical mass of both buyers and sellers without changing the way they do business, and in so doing, acquires a pool of developers and co-opts some potential competitors.

BuildNet's strategy is this: Acquire market-leading builder and supplier management software products and link them into its Exchange. BuildNet says it has already integrated six products into the Exchange. BuildNet points out that this approach "gives us a significant competitive advantage since it connects builders and suppliers with minimal disruption to their existing systems and processes."

Though it hasn't divulged purchase prices for most of the deals, BuildNet paid stock worth about $32.5 million for NxTrend, which is equal to about one-half of expected revenues, or $87,000 per employee. BuildNet paid about $6.5 million for a homebuilder module from J.D. Edwards and $27 million for the e-commerce processing software of UniLink. While it's difficult to compare one to one, on a multiple-of-revenue basis, the NxTrend deal is a bargain compared with prevailing Internet company revenue multiples that range well above 10X.

The only other B2B company to date to use such an aggressive acquisition strategy is VerticalNet, which, unlike BuildNet and most other B2B companies, is expanding horizontally to create a family of B2B businesses.

Given the high stakes and the difficult road for build-from-scratch efforts, Webmergers.com predicts we will see M&A increasingly used as a tool to fast-forward creation of B2B marketplaces. The risks for the most part lie in the integration of the targets. While it looks great on paper diagrams, the actual integration process can be brutal.

TENDER OFFER

There are two common ways for a public corporation to be acquired. First is for the buyer to purchase shares of the corporation in the public market at the current market price. Another way shares are acquired is through a tender offer.

A tender offer is a publicly announced offer by the buyer to acquire shares of a single class of stock at a specified price. The price is substantially higher than the current market price as a way to entice stockholders to sell their shares to the buyer.

A buyer who announces a tender offer is exposed to greater regulatory restrictions than a buyer who purchases shares on the open market. However, those restrictions might also be imposed on a buyer acquiring shares on the open market if within a 45-day period the buyer directly acquires 5 percent of the outstanding shares within the same class of stock from stockholders without using a broker or securities exchange. The transaction is then considered a tender offer.

The tender offer process begins by the buyer organizing a team of experts who prepare the necessary legal documents for the tender offer, solicit shares, and process acquisition of those shares. The team typically consists of a deal manager who coordinates the team effort, attorneys who specialize in tender offerings, accountants who prepare the necessary financials, a solicitation organization that formally makes the tender offer to stockholders, and a bank who receives shares and pays stockholders.

The deal manager takes the initial lead and solicits stockholders who own large positions in the dotcom. This typically occurs before the tender offer is made to other stockholders. The buyer pays a premium above current market to acquire the shares, which assures the buyer of a large position in the dotcom without going to the open market and before the tender offer begins.

The team helps the buyer to determine the terms of the tender offer. Two critical factors contained in the terms of a tender offer are the date of the offer and the premium above current market value the buyer is willing to pay for shares.

The tender offer must be timed to coincide with favorable market conditions. For example, a tender offer is timed properly whenever the market price of the dotcom's shares is at a low value compared to earnings or potential earnings. However, the current market value of the dotcom's shares is a baseline above which the buyer offers stockholders a premium.

Tech Talk

Premium: An amount above the market price that the buyer will pay for outstanding shares of the dotcom.

There isn't a formula to determine a premium for a tender offer. The team usually forecasts the price of the dotcom's stock for 6 to 12 months from the tender offer date. The difference between the current market value and the forecasted market value is the premium for the tender offer. In essence, the buyer is telling stockholders that they can realize the future value of the shares today rather than wait for the future to arrive.

Let's say that shares are currently selling for $10 per share. The tender offer team determines that the shares are likely to be at $14 per share in 18 months. Their forecast is based on demand for shares and earning potential of the dotcom, excluding the effects the acquisition has on the dotcom's operation. The premium for the tender offer can be between \$1.00 and \$4.00 per share. The team must then decide what premium will be acceptable to stockholders. This is determined through informal discussions with key stockholders.

Caution

The tender offer team must anticipate an increase in current market value once the market informally learns about the forthcoming tender offer. This change in market value has a direct bearing on the premium.

Public Announcement

Once the date and premium for the tender offer is established and the legal documents are prepared, the tender offer team publicly announces the tender offer in advertisements and in a press release. The announcement identifies the buyer and the dotcom, the tender offer price that includes the premium, and the class of shares, such as common stock.

Typically, on the date of the public announcement, the buyer sends the formal tender offer document to the dotcom's stockholders and files appropriate disclosure forms with regulatory agencies. This date begins a 20-day freeze period during which the buyer can purchase shares only under the terms of the tender offer. The buyer cannot purchase shares outside the tender offer.

The tender offer team must decide whether or not it is in the best interest of the buyer to approach the dotcom before announcing the tender offer. The decision is dependent upon whether or not the buyer feels that this is a friendly acquisition.

In a friendly acquisition, the dotcom is cooperative and encourages stockholders to accept a tender offer as long as the proposed deal is the best proposal on the table. In this case, the buyer will find it advantageous to approach the dotcom prior to the tender offer announcement.

However, such a strategy gives the dotcom ample time to formulate and enact countermoves to fight off a takeover should the takeover been seen as a hostile action by the buyer. In this case, the buyer is better served by letting the dotcom learn about the tender offer when the tender offer is publicly announced, because the dotcom then has little time to react.

The tender offer team needs to carefully assess the dotcom's receptiveness to the tender offer before deciding on a strategy, because using the wrong approach could transform a friendly takeover into a hostile takeover.

For example, a dotcom that is favorable to a takeover may change its position if it feels the buyer is making an underhanded move by announcing the tender offer before consulting the dotcom.

Caution

The dotcom's management typically has a vested interest in the terms of a tender offer, since they too are stockholders. Management may try to withhold approval of the deal in an effort to increase the premium for the tender offer. The buyer can counter by decreasing the premium the longer it takes management to approve the deal.

The announcement of a tender offer is not the actual offer. Instead, the tender offer is contained in a transmittal letter and other documents that are sent to stockholders by the buyer. Stockholders who do not receive the transmittal letter can contact the buyer and request that the letter be sent to them. Some states require that a broker who works on behalf of the buyer make the offer to stockholders.

The tender offer must follow a prescribed timetable. The offer is available for 20 days from the date of the public announcement, although the buyer can cancel the offer within the first 5 days. Terms of the tender offer can change during the offer period. However, the offer must be extended for 10 days following the change, even if the time exceeds the 20-day offer period. The purpose of the extension is to allow time for the stockholders to receive the new terms for the tender offer.

Stockholders typically tender their shares in the dotcom to the buyer in response to the transmittal letter. However, the buyer must move quickly to compensate stockholders because stockholders retain the right for up to 60 days following the date of the tender offer to withdraw their shares. unless the stockholder received remuneration from the buyer.

Caution

The buyer must pay all stockholders who tender their shares the same compensation. Therefore, a buyer might raise the premium after receiving half the outstanding shares to encourage other stockholders to tender their shares. However, the new premium must be paid to stockholders who already tendered their shares.

Regulatory Filings

The buyer is required to file various regulatory forms that provide information about the buyer, the dotcom, and various aspects of the tender offer if the tender offer will result in a change in control of the dotcom's corporation or if the buyer can influence control over the dotcom's operation. For example, two weeks after the buyer becomes a beneficial owner of 5 percent of voting stock in the dotcom's corporation, the buyer must file the appropriate forms with the SEC and securities exchanges that trade in the dotcom's stock. A beneficial owner includes stockholders who have the right to take ownership of voting securities within 60 days.

Tech Talk

A beneficial owner is an individual or a group that has the ability to vote or sell shares, even if they do not directly own those shares.

The buyer becomes a beneficial owner when the buyer acquires 5 percent of the outstanding shares of the dotcom. Likewise, the buyer is a beneficial owner if it acquires shares or the right to acquire shares within the next 60 days if the accumulated shares equal 5 percent of the dotcom's stock.

Regulatory filings typically require the buyer to disclose

- The buyer's identity
- Background information on the buyer
- Plans for acquiring shares of the dotcom's corporation
- Plans for selling shares of the dotcom's corporation
- Plans for a merger or liquidation of the dotcom
- Changes in the dotcom's dividend policy
- Changes in the dotcom's management, including the board of directors
- Changes in the dotcom's capitalization
- Source of funding
- Previous violations of laws and regulations
- Relationships to the dotcom going back three years from the filing date
- Current market value of the dotcom's stock

- The number of shares of the dotcom held by the buyer 60 days before the filing date
- The buyer's financial statements

PROXY SOLICITATION

Election of members to the board of directors and material changes in a public corporation require the formal approval of a majority of stockholders. Approval comes in the form of a vote at a stockholder meeting.

The board of directors and/or any stockholder can propose changes, which are mailed to stockholders for their consideration. Depending on the bylaws of the corporation and state regulations, stockholders can mail their votes to the board of directors or cast their votes at the stockholder meeting.

It is common for the board of directors or any stockholder to ask other stockholders for the right to vote the other stockholders shares based on agreed-upon terms. This is called a *proxy,* and the solicitation to obtain the right to vote the shares is called a *proxy statement.*

A proxy statement must contain information that clearly describes the issue or issues that are the subject of the vote. This includes financial statements, projections, background information, and everything a stockholder requires to reach a decision on the issue. Furthermore, the proxy statement states the opinion of the issuer of the proxy statement on those issues and requests permission for the holder of the proxy statement to cast the vote for the stockholder in favor of the proxy statement issuer's position on the issue or issues.

One or a group of stockholders can attempt to materially change a corporation or membership of its board of directors by proposing changes, then engaging in a proxy fight with the board of directors to win over stockholders to their position. Both sides in a proxy fight have rights to the names and addresses of stockholders and the right to present their position to stockholders and solicit stockholder votes. It is advantageous to both sides to obtain a stockholder's proxy rather than permit the stockholder to vote directly on an issue, because the stockholder might change his or her mind when the vote is cast or might outright forget to vote.

Direct mail isn't the only way a proxy fight is conducted. As long as the shareholder files a proxy statement with the SEC, the shareholder can use mass media, such as publications and broadcasts, to solicit other stockholders.

PUBLIC DISCLOSURE

The board of directors of a public corporation is obligated to disclose to the public information about the corporation. One of the critical pieces of information that must be disclosed is a public corporation's involvement in an acquisition.

The objective of disclosure is to provide stockholders and the market with material information of an event that may change the structure or control of the corporation. Courts and regulatory agencies require the board of directors to use good business judgment when deciding if and when to disclose material information about an acquisition. The board of directors is expected to assure that the public has a fair knowledge of corporate activities. Therefore, they are not obligated to announce or respond to inquiries regarding rumors of an acquisition, nor are they obligated to announce or respond to every proposal for an acquisition they might receive. However, it is typical for a corporation to acknowledge or deny a possible acquisition if rumors of the corporate action are upsetting the market place or if a party to the acquisition has made the corporate action public knowledge, such as in the case of a tender offer.

The board of directors is obligated to make sure that public information is accurate and to correct inaccuracies through issuing a public announcement. Failure to do so might expose the board of directors and the corporation to litigation taken by stockholders and regulatory agencies.

Although a public announcement is left to the discretion of the board of directors, regulatory agencies such as the SEC or a stock exchange might direct the board to respond to conditions that create an erratic market for their stock. It is common that rumors of a potential acquisition will cause unusual swings in a corporation's stock price and cause disorder in the market for those shares. In an effort to bring order back to the market for the stock, the corporation might be ordered to deny or substantiate the rumor, then to provide the public with material information about the acquisition. The corporation risks having trading in its stock suspended for failure to comply with such an order.

The courts have been at odds over when a board of directors is required to publicly announce an acquisition or potential acquisition. Lower courts ruled that only when an agreement in principle is reached must a corporation announce an acquisition. However, higher courts narrowed the disclosure requirement to require corporations to announce when negotiations for an acquisition begin. Consult legal counsel for clarification of these rulings.

From Tim Miller, Webmergers.com

Buying E-Commerce Infrastructure

Department stores don't typically buy cash register manufacturers—they typically lease or license such infrastructure. But many Internet companies buy their e-commerce tools, lock, stock, and barrel. For example, iBoost Technology, Inc., an aggregator of Internet content and e-commerce Web sites, acquired BizBlast.com, a developer of automated e-tailing storefronts that, like iBoost, was backed by Softbank.

There are several reasons for Internet companies to buy infrastructure. In the case of iBoost, the objective was to gain control of its own destiny, says Chris Gonzalez, an executive vice president at the company. Gonzalez said that many other licensable solutions locked iBoost into their own framework and restricted modifications of the technology. "Besides," said Gonzalez, "at the end of the day, we still wouldn't own the solution."

Several other Internet companies in both B2C and B2B sectors have also acquired enabling technology. In the B2B sector, for example, VerticalNet acquired e-commerce software provider Isadra in 1999, well before it started making its own segue from Internet marketplace to infrastructure provider.

In addition to getting full control over product direction, there are other reasons that non-infrastructure companies acquire solutions:

- Buy service: If it's hard to get attention from service providers (and it is), buying the whole company is one way to get its full attention.
- Get it before it's gone: In some cases, acquirers appear to be snapping up solutions for fear all available properties will be locked up. There's a definite "me-too" dynamic in these acquisition frenzies.
- Leverage infrastructure in B2B sales: In some cases, B2C acquirers buy solutions with an eye toward reselling them to other Internet companies in the mold of such companies as InfoSpace.

Whatever its roots, the "serial mergers" phenomenon within Internet applications has proved to be a boon for startups. If you're lucky enough to be in the path of a serial mergers juggernaut, your chances of finding an exit are greatly enhanced. You no longer have to be first or second to market in order to find a decent exit; you can do okay even if you're third, fourth, fifth, or sixth to market.

Perhaps one of the best case studies of serial mergers is in the area of automated e-commerce price-gathering robots or "bots." In 1998, CNET kicked open the starting gate by acquiring PC-products price bot Computer/ESP for about $20 million.

BOARD OF DIRECTORS DUTIES

The board of directors has a fiduciary responsibility to stockholders to use good business judgment when making decisions about the corporation. These decisions include those that involve normal business operations and decisions regarding acquisitions. Failure of the board to reach a decision in good fairness and with the best interests of stockholders in mind exposes individual board members to stockholder litigation.

Every acquisition proposal received by the board of directors must be carefully evaluated, and not outright dismissed. The evaluation process must build a foundation with which the board can deliberate and can use as a basis for a decision.

Courts are unlikely to second-guess the business judgment used by a board of directors of a public corporation as long as the board used widely accepted procedures for reaching their decision. These procedures include consultation with advisors such as investment bankers, attorneys, accountants, and the corporation's own senior management. For example, stockholders can rightfully challenge a board for the outright rejection of a merger proposal that has merit. However, stockholders are on weak ground if the proposal was rejected after it was carefully explored and discussed by the board.

Here are guidelines directors can follow to assure they remain responsible to stockholders:

- All acquisition or merger proposals should be evaluated for merit by advisors.

- Request a fairness opinion from an investment banker, which is an objective opinion that determines if a proposal is beneficial to stockholders.
- An advisor's evaluation should contain a recommendation to the board and information about the proposal that supports the recommendation.
- All members of the board must review the proposal.
- The board must discuss the proposal and the advisor's evaluation and recommendation.
- A vote must be taken to reject the proposal or place the proposal before stockholders for a vote.
- Provide stockholders with material information that can be used to reach a decision on the issue.
- Employ expert advisors to assist in acquisition negotiations.
- Disseminate material changes to an acquisition proposal to the board and to advisors, then request a reevaluation of the proposal.
- A director whose personal interest conflicts with the interests of stockholders in this deal must remove himself from deliberations and from the proceedings.

Avoiding Conflicts

Special care must be taken to reassure stockholders that a fair and unbiased evaluation is conducted for any acquisition proposal received by the board of directors of a public corporation. This is especially true when some board members stand to gain or lose based on the outcome of the evaluation.

The board can avoid any perception of bias in its decision by forming an evaluation subcommittee of the board. The subcommittee should be comprised of directors, such as outside directors who have little or nothing to gain or lose by the acceptance or rejection of the proposal.

The subcommittee acts as a clearinghouse for proposals and buffers the full board against conflict of interests charges that might be advanced by some stockholders. The subcommittee must still follow prudent business practices to assess the proposal, as outlined earlier in this section.

To assure its independence from the full board of directors, the subcommittee must be empowered to retain the services of outside advisors who have not been employed by the full board or by the corporation for other projects. These advisors must include a financial consultant, such as an investment banker, and an attorney who specializes in acquisitions of public corporations. The financial consultant will examine the proposal, then issue a fairness opinion to the subcommittee. The fairness opinion states whether or not the proposal makes a fair offer to the board of directors. Furthermore, the opinion must present the financial consultant's rationale for reaching this conclusion.

Caution

The financial consultant should not be paid a contingency fee for rendering the fairness opinion, because this could give the impression that the financial consultant receives a greater reward for a positive opinion. Instead, a fixed fee needs to be established at the outset and be paid regardless of whether the board accepts or rejects the proposal.

The subcommittee must not accept the fairness opinion or any advice without challenging the advisor on the opinion or advice that is being given. Failure to explore the opinion might lead to legal action by stockholders who claim that the subcommittee and the full board failed to use good business judgment when considering the proposal. Members of the subcommittee can avoid unnecessary exposure to possible litigation related to business judgment by having legal counsel guide the subcommittee through the process. It is critical that legal counsel become a de facto, nonvoting member of the subcommittee and be directly involved in every aspect of the subcommittee's work. In this way, legal counsel can prevent the subcommittee from making inadvertent errors that could be costly in litigation.

The subcommittee makes a recommendation to the full board once the evaluation process is completed. The full board too must challenge subcommittee members on their conclusion before the board of directors formally votes to accept the subcommittee's recommendation. Failure to make such a challenge could be interpreted as failure of the board to use good business judgment.

DEFENSIVE STRATEGIES

Public corporations are vulnerable to attempted takeovers by unwanted suitors because most, if not all, the corporation's stock is traded freely on the open market. As long as the suitor stays within federal and state regulations, the suitor is free to purchase shares and acquire sufficient shares to transfer control of the corporation from current stockholders to the suitor.

Once the suitor has a controlling interest in the corporation, the suitor can vote to replace the existing board of directors, who in turn can replace the management of the corporation. Although the board of directors and stockholders cannot prohibit a suitor from purchasing shares of the corporation, actions can be taken by the board of directors to make the purchase practically and economically prohibitive.

There are several commonly used strategies for a board of directors to defend against an undesirable takeover:

- lockup option
- restructuring defense
- shareholder rights plan defense
- charter defense
- unattractive defense
- payment defense

These defenses can be deployed only if the board of directors feels the proposed acquisition of the corporation is not in the best interests of stockholders. The board is exposed to stockholder litigation unless the board can substantiate such a belief.

The primary reason for rejecting a suitor and taking on a defensive strategy is that the offer is appreciably less than the perceived value of the corporation. Current and forecasted corporate earnings determine the perceived value.

Lockup Option

Potential buyers use a tender offer to acquire a public corporation. The board of directors is obligated to stockholders to consider all offers and explain to stockholders why the board rejected an offer.

The board can take action to make the corporation a less attractive dotcom by using a lockup option. There are three kinds of lockup options: a stock lockup option, a reverse lockup option, and an asset lockup option.

A stock lockup option occurs when the board of directors enters into an agreement with a friendly investor, where the investor receives options to purchase unissued but authorized shares of the corporation at an attractive price. The investor is expected to exercise the option, then vote those shares only for an acquisition proposal that is recommended by the board of directors. The number of shares that are locked up by the option should be sufficient to hinder a successful tender offer because it adds a substantial block of shares to the market. However, should the lockup strategy fail, the investor can tender shares to the buyer and realize a material gain from the investment.

A reverse lockup option is where there is an agreement between the board of directors and existing stockholders who hold a large position in the corporation not to tender their shares in the event of a tender offer made by a buyer that is unacceptable to the board of directors. Similar to the lockup option strategy, the reverse lockup option in essence removes a substantial block of shares from the market. Should the buyer succeed in acquiring a material number of shares, however, the stockholder still has the option to tender his shares to the buyer.

An asset lockup occurs when the board of directors grants a friendly investor an option to purchase a key asset of the corporation. This strategy is particularly advantageous when the purpose of the acquisition is for the buyer to acquire a particular asset of the corporation. Let's say that a dotcom owns two Web sites, a travel site and an online theatre ticket service. A buyer might be interested in acquiring the travel site and care little about the theatre ticket service. Therefore, the buyer makes a tender offer for the entire dotcom company.

The board of directors of the dotcom company does not want to be acquired by the buyer. In a defensive move, the board sells an option to purchase the travel Web site to a friendly investor. There is an understanding between the board and the investor that the option will not be exercised unless the dotcom company is acquired by a buyer who is not approved by the board. In this case, the buyer could make a successful tender offer and acquire all the shares of the dotcom company. However, in doing so, the buyer loses the travel Web site because the investor exercises the option and purchases the travel Web site for the agreed-upon price. This is possible because the buyer acquires stock of the dotcom company and inherits the option contract between the dotcom company and its stockholders. Therefore, the buyer wins the dotcom company, but loses the real dotcom of the acquisition—the travel Web site. The dotcom is likely to make the buyer aware of the asset lockup option prior to the tender offer as a way to dissuade the buyer from pursuing the offer.

Lockup options are risky in that stockholders might challenge the strategy as a way for the board of directors to circumvent its fiduciary responsibility to stockholders. Some legal experts view such a strategy as not working in the best interests of stockholders. However, others disagree and point to the fact that those friendly investors—and not the board—block a buyer from completing a tender offer.

Generally, the courts tend to judge according to the impact a lockup option has on fostering a competitive environment for shares of the corporation. Courts are likely to look unfavorably at a lockup option that stifles offers from buyers. If the strategy encourages offers from several buyers, then the lockup option strategy will be seen as being within the board's fiduciary responsibilities to stockholders.

Caution

A board of directors might be exposed to litigation if a lockup option strategy is employed and the board rejects the highest offer for the corporation. In this case, the board must be prepared to prove that they used good business judgment when rejecting the highest offer.

Restructuring Defense

The restructuring defense is when the corporation buys back shares from the open market by using excess cash or receipts from debt to make the purchases. This is sometimes referred to as a *self-tender offer,* since the corporation is asking stockholders to tender their shares back to the corporation.

Another form of the restructuring defense is to encourage the corporation's Employee Stock Ownership Plan to acquire shares as an alternative to, or in conjunction with, the corporation's self-tender offer.

The objective of both forms of the restructuring defense is to control the number of shares available on the open market. The corporation and the employees, rather than the general public, control more shares following a successful restructuring defense. The restructuring defense is attractive to the board of directors because stockholder approval is not required to implement the defense. The board of directors has unilateral power to deploy the restructuring defense.

Three major disadvantages of this strategy are a reduction in public ownership of the corporation, potential litigation, and the expense to implement the restructuring defense. The market may take an unfavorable view of the corporation should the board of directors take action that gives the appearance of reduced liquidity of its shares. This can happen whenever there are few shares held by the public.

Potential litigation can arise from claims that the board violated its fiduciary responsibility to stockholders. Other stockholders, including the unwanted suitor, may charge that the board's self interest rather than stockholders' interest was the chief motivator for instituting the restructuring defense. In such a case, the board must be prepared to justify its position.

A restructuring defense is an expensive strategy to implement because the board of directors might find itself bidding against the unwanted suitor. The corporation could find itself in a high stakes game of poker, where the corporation must continually raise its opponent's last bid; otherwise, control of the corporation is transferred to the suitor.

Shareholder Rights Plan Defense

The shareholder rights plan defense occurs when the board of directors grants to existing stockholders the right to acquire additional shares in the corporation if a specific event occurs, such as a successful tender offer by an unwanted suitor. However, the corporation can repurchase these rights at a nominal price before they are triggered.

This defense is also known as the *poison pill defense* and can be deployed without stockholder approval because the right is granted as a dividend to stockholders, which does not require stockholder approval.

There are two flavors of the shareholder rights plan defense: the flip-over defense and the back-end defense. The flip-over defense grants a stockholder the right to purchase a share of the successor corporation following a hostile takeover.

The advantages of the flip-over defense are that it limits the unwanted suitor's position and gives the board of directors leverage when negotiating with the suitor. However, the event that triggers the issuance of the rights can occur in both a friendly and a hostile takeover. Therefore, the corporation may find itself at a disadvantage should a friendly suitor want to acquire the corporation. The board must phrase the terms of the shareholder rights defense so as not to trigger granting the rights in a favorable takeover.

The back-end defense grants stockholders the right to exchange their stock for a one-year note at a predetermined value should a hostile takeover occur. This defense strategy does not discourage a takeover. Instead, the strategy assures that stockholders are guaranteed a minimum price for their stock. The guaranteed price is specified as a literal value in the defense strategy, or a formula is used to calculate the price. The suitor has the right to bid at the predefined price or higher. Once an agreement is reached between the suitor and stockholders on the price for outstanding issues, then the back-end defense can no longer be deployed.

Charter Defense

The charter defense uses changes in the corporate charter and bylaws to inhibit the takeover of the corporation by an unwanted suitor. The charter is a document granted to the corporation by the state, authorizing the corporation to conduct specific activities, such as conducting business.

Bylaws are rules created by the board of directors and approved by stockholders that govern how the corporation conducts business. An important bylaw of every corporation defines the number of votes that constitute a majority, which is required to approve various structural changes to the corporation. Typically, a majority is defined as 51 percent of the voting shares of the corporation. However, the charter defense modifies the definition of a majority to a higher percentage when certain issues are to be considered, such as those involving a takeover.

Let's say that an unwanted suitor offers to acquire the dotcom. The suitor needs to receive a vote of 65 percent of the stockholders to receive stockholder approval for the move, should the board of directors increase the majority to 65 percent. This action does not prevent the suitor from acquiring the corporation, but does make it more difficult to succeed.

Another aspect of the charter defense is to inhibit a successful unwanted suitor from replacing the board of directors. In effect, this delays the suitor from unseating the entire board once the suitor gains controlling shares in the corporation. Here's how this works. The board of directors, with the approval of stockholders, adopts a staggered board clause whereby a third of the directors are elected each year for a three-year term. Directors cannot be removed until their term expires unless for cause. This means that two-thirds of the board remains in power during the first year the suitor acquires the corporation, assuming the suitor replaces one-third of the board. Three years will pass before the suitor can replace the entire board.

The staggered board clause is strengthened by the adoption of the cumulative voting clause. The cumulative voting clause defines the number of votes of each stockholder. Typically, a stockholder has one vote for each voting share of stock owned. The cumulative voting clause increases this vote when voting for the board of directors. The number of votes a stockholder can cast is determined by multiplying the number of shares held by the stockholder by the number of directors who are being elected. Let's say a stockholder owns 1,000 shares and therefore has 1,000 votes. There are nine members of the board of directors. Three seats are available; therefore the stockholder has 3,000 votes.

All the stockholder's votes can be cast for a single candidate or disbursed among three candidates. This means minority stockholders might pool their votes and elect a person not approved by the suitor to the board of directors, assuming that the suitor has not acquired all the outstanding shares of the corporation.

Another way in which the board of directors, with approval from stockholders, can inhibit an unwanted suitor's ability to make changes in the corporation is by removing the written consent clause from the corporation's bylaws. The written consent clause grants the board of directors the right to obtain approval from stockholders through a written consent rather than from votes at a stockholders meeting. The board forces the successful unwanted suitor to call a stockholders meeting to make changes to the charter and bylaws and to obtain stockholder approval on other matters. Deletion of the written consent clause does not prevent a hostile takeover, but will give the board of directors and minority stockholders time to present an opposing position to stockholders before a vote is taken at a stockholders meeting.

The major disadvantage of the charter defense is that the current board of directors and stockholders must live within those changes if the unwanted suitor breaks off pursuit or if a wanted suitor makes an offer for the corporation. For example, a friendly suitor will be hindered from replacing the entire board of directors and removing the various defense strategies should the board previously have adopted the staggered board clause and the cumulative voting clause, and have deleted the written consent clause. In fact, the friendly suitor and the current board of directors will find it cumbersome to remove these defenses because they must hold a stockholders meeting to assure themselves that changes and the election of new board members are not blocked by a minority of stockholders.

Unattractive Defense

Typically, a dotcom has attributes, such as a brand name or a product, that are attractive to a buyer. The unattractive defense is used to tarnish those attributes to make the dotcom less desirable to the buyer. There are three techniques used by a board of directors to implement the unattractive defense: creating antitrust issues, selling assets, and enlisting the services of a friendly suitor.

Government regulators will prohibit the acquisition of a corporation if the deal gives the successor corporation an anticompetitive advantage in the market. The dotcom can, through its own acquisition, purchase a competitor of the unwanted suitor, thereby raising the issue that the suitor would be violating antitrust laws by acquiring the dotcom.

Potential violation of antitrust laws isn't sufficient to prevent the acquisition of the dotcom, because the suitor can agree with regulatory agencies that the conflicting asset would be sold immediately following the merger. However, raising the antitrust issue might give the suitor second thoughts and may encourage the suitor to pursue a deal that is unlikely to bring close governmental review.

Selling assets is another way for a dotcom to make itself less attractive to an unwanted suitor. The dotcom's value to a suitor is likely to be based on at least one asset, and often a few assets, held by the corporation. The suitor is likely to pass up the opportunity to acquire the dotcom should those assets become unavailable. The board of directors can sell those assets either directly to another buyer or through a buyback arrangement in which title to the asset changes to the other buyer temporarily. Once the unwanted suitor has been dissuaded from acquiring the dotcom, the board repurchases the asset, thereby restoring the corporation to it whole again.

The third technique in the unattractive defense is to sell a major position in the dotcom to a friendly buyer. The buyer is sometimes referred to as a *white squire* or *white knight*. The friendly buyer is offered a premium for acquiring the position in the dotcom, which is expected to be held at least until the unwanted suitor loses interest in the dotcom.

The friendly buyer's position is restricted by a standstill agreement between the friendly buyer and the corporation. For example, the buyer may have limited voting rights and may be required to first offer the position back to the corporation before selling it on the open market. These restrictions assure the dotcom that the friendly buyer is unable to transfer the position to the unwanted suitor.

The disadvantage of the unattractive defense is that the board of directors lowers the value of the corporation to stockholders. Making the corporation unattractive to an unwanted suitor also makes the corporation less desirable to stockholders. The board must incorporate a restoration plan to bring back value to the corporation once the suitor is dissuaded from acquiring the dotcom.

Payment Defense

The payment defense is the simplest, yet most expensive, way to fend off an unwanted suitor. In this defense, the dotcom purchases at a high premium its own stock that is held by the unwanted suitor. This is sometimes referred to as *greenmail,* which is a form of black mail. Although the legality of greenmail is currently being debated, greenmail is still a practice. In fact, some suitors seek hostile takeovers as a way to extract a higher return from their investment through greenmail premiums. The unwanted suitor risks a stockholder lawsuit and a stiff excise tax by regulators on the proceeds from greenmail.

RESTRICTIONS

A buyer and a dotcom can enter into an agreement to restrict each other's options whenever a buyer makes a tender offer for a public corporation. These restrictions are a breakup fee clause, a topping fee clause, and a no-shopping clause.

The breakup fee clause, sometimes referred to as the *bust-up clause,* is an agreement between the buyer and dotcom in which the dotcom compensates the buyer for expenses, such as out-of-pocket expenses, should the deal with the buyer collapse. These fees can be as high as 4 percent of the proposed deal price.

A twist on the breakup fee clause is the topping fee clause. The topping fee clause requires the dotcom to compensate the buyer should the buyer's bid for the corporation be rejected because a higher bid was received from another buyer.

The purpose of the breakup fee clause and the *topping fee clause* is to make the acquisition of the dotcom costly and therefore less attractive to another suitor. Here's how this strategy works. A buyer who is friendly to the dotcom's board of directors makes a tender offer and signs an agreement with the dotcom that contains a breakup fee clause or a topping fee clause. The tender offer places the dotcom in play and attracts other unwanted suitors, who make a higher tender offer. The board of directors must seriously consider such an offer as a part of its fiduciary responsibility to stockholders.

However, the cost of acquiring the dotcom is the higher tender offer plus the breakup fee or topping fee to the original buyer. The dotcom, even after the unwanted suitor acquires the corporation, remains liable for the breakup fee or topping fee. Courts have upheld challenges to these fees as long as the fees are reasonable and haven't discouraged other suitors from entering a tender offer for the dotcom. Attorneys recommend that value-add, such as agreeing to permit the dotcom to seek other offers, be exchanged for the breakup fee clause or topping fee clause.

The no-shopping clause restricts the dotcom from seeking other offers for the corporation. Consult with an attorney before embarking on a no-shopping clause if the dotcom is a public corporation, because courts may see such an agreement as a violation of the dotcom's board of directors' fiduciary responsibility to stockholders. The no-shopping clause is favorably looked upon in closely held private corporations where the board of directors and management of the firm hold most of the outstanding shares.

INSIDER CONFLICTS

Officers and a wide breadth of associates of a publicly traded corporation are considered insiders by regulatory bodies and therefore are prohibited from receiving any benefit from corporate information that is not publicly known. An insider is a person who has possession of information about a public corporation that is unknown to the general public and that might affect the market price of the corporation. This information is commonly referred to as *inside information*. Insiders include employees of the corporation, consultants, accountants, investment bankers, attorneys, and any person who accumulates knowledge about the corporation that is not generally known by the public.

Legally, insiders cannot use this information to conduct transactions in the securities of the corporation and cannot provide this information to others who might buy or sell the security. Violating this regulation could bring criminal prosecution and civil penalties.

Insiders are released from restricted trading once the confidential information is released to the public and the public has time to digest the information. The time between the release of the information to the time when insiders are able to transact in the security varies from a few minutes to a couple of days, depending on the nature of the information and the market conditions.

The objective of regulators is to maintain a free and open market without the influence of manipulation of securities by insiders. To meet this objective, regulators review the timing of insider transactions in an attempt to identify a correlation between the transaction and the release of inside information. The insider is exposed to legal action from the regulators and from stockholders should such a correlation exist.

Federal and state regulators might require statutory insiders to identify themselves and to provide information about themselves. A statutory insider is a person who, by their position with a firm, is considered an insider. These include the board of directors, officers of the firm, senior executives who may not be officers, and any stockholder owning 10 percent or more shares.

Statutory insiders are prohibited from short-swing profits from certain transactions, such as a tender offer. A short-swing profit is defined as a profit earned from the buying and selling or selling and buying of the corporation's securities within six months of a tender offer.

An insider is exempt from this restriction if the insider does not have a controlling influence over the action (a tender offer, for example) or if the insider is not privy to inside information. Another exemption occurs in a merger where at least one corporation owns 85 percent of the assets.

An exemption also occurs if the insider divulges the inside information before entering a security transaction. However, this exemption is rarely satisfied, because only the corporation itself is typically in a position to publicly announce inside information. Furthermore, the insider is exposed to stockholder litigation if the information he or she publicly divulges is misleading.

An insider does not have to benefit directly from a security transaction based on inside information to be in violation of securities regulations.

A violation can also occur by the insider disclosing the information to another who benefits from a subsequent transaction.

The insider who provides the information is called a *tipper* and the person receiving the information is referred to as the *tippee*. The act of exchanging the information is called *tipping*. Tipping becomes a violation if the tipper received a benefit either directly or indirectly from tipping the information and if the tipper violates an obligation to the corporation and stockholders by tipping the information. Furthermore, the tipper and the tippee must know that the information being divulged is inside information.

Let's say that a financial printer tips a friend of a pending tender offer. The friend purchases stock in the dotcom's corporation, realizes a profit following the tender offer, and pays the printer a portion of the proceeds as a "thank you" for the tip. The financial printer has an obligation to the buyer who is issuing the tender offer to maintain confidentiality until the buyer announces the tender offer. Therefore, the printer violated this obligation. Furthermore, the printer indirectly benefited from tipping the information. The printer is clearly in violation of tipping regulations.

Although this is a clear example of a tipping violation, some tipping violations aren't as clear. Let's say that the tippee in the our example (that is, the friend who received information from the financial printer) did not purchase stock in the dotcom, but rather told his brother-in-law, and the brother-in-law purchased stock in the dotcom. The tippee becomes the tipper. However, because he is not an insider to the buyer, he does not have an obligation to maintain confidentiality. Furthermore, he may not receive material benefit from his brother-in-law. Therefore, regulators are likely to find it difficult to prosecute the tippee/tipper and his brother-in-law.

Caution

Benefits from tipping include status with the tippee and other nonmonetary benefits.

Caution

Both the tipper and the tippee can be held equally liable for violations of tipping regulations, even if the tippee does not have a fiduciary relationship with the corporation and does not profit from the tip.

FINANCING ISSUES

Financing an acquisition of a public corporation might become entangled in regulatory restrictions, depending upon the method used to acquire the dotcom. A buyer who uses the two-step acquisition method is exposed to margin regulations that limit the leverage used to acquire an equity position in the dotcom.

The two-step acquisition is used to facilitate the merger of a dotcom into the buyer's corporation. A merger requires the majority of the dotcom's stockholders approval. Rather than solicit votes, the buyer makes a tender offer for a majority of the dotcom's shares, then votes those shares in favor of the merger. Minority stockholders must abide by the majority vote.

Margin regulations require any purchase of a publicly traded security to collateralize no more than 50 percent of the value of the securities purchased. Here's how this works. Let's say a brick-and-mortar wants to acquire the outstanding shares of A-Dotcom. The brick-and-mortar borrows funds to finance the acquisition and uses the value of the shares as collateral for the loan.

However, only 50 percent of the shares can be used as collateral. The remaining 50 percent of the shares must be acquired as a cash purchase. The brick-and-mortar can use cash, funds collateralized by other assets (except assets of A-Dotcom), or unsecured debt such as revolving credit to acquire the other 50 percent of the shares of A-Dotcom.

The buyer must be careful not to construct an unsecured debt agreement that will trigger violation of the indirect margin regulation. The buyer can run afoul of this regulation by arranging an unsecured debt with a lender, the proceeds of which are used to acquire the dotcom's securities. As part of the unsecured debt agreement, the buyer agrees not to use the shares as collateral for other loans after the shares are acquired. If the shares become a substantial part of the buyer's assets, then regulators might charge that the agreement is an indirect violation of the margin rules. In this example, the buyer must liquidate the shares to repay the unsecured debt because the buyer has insufficient other assets to cover the unsecured debt. Therefore, the lender indirectly used the acquired shares as security in the event the buyer is forced to liquidate.

The exception to the margin regulation is if the buyer and dotcom formally agree to merge before the tender offer closes. In this case, the buyer can leverage more than 50 percent of the acquired shares, using the shares as collateral for the loan.

PRIVATE CORPORATIONS BASICS

A private corporation is a corporation whose securities are not registered with state and federal authorities and therefore are prohibited from being traded in the open securities market. The board of directors and the officers of a private corporation have a fiduciary responsibility to stockholders similar to that of their counterparts in a public corporation. However, securities of a private corporation are typically held by a very small group of investors, who may be members of the board of directors and officers of the corporation.

Public corporations have a private corporation in their genealogy. Typically, one or more investors form a private corporation. These investors manage the corporation to a level that attracts the general investment community. At that time, the board of directors of the private corporation, who are likely to hold a majority of shares in the corporation, enlists the services of an investment banker to make an initial public offering (IPO) of the corporation.

An investment banker organizes a team of underwriters, who purchase shares from the private corporation and place those shares with the initial group of public investors, who later sell them on a stock exchange.

Private corporations are exempt from many securities regulations that are imposed on public corporations because the general public is not exposed to fraudulent manipulation of the corporation's securities. The value of securities issued by a public corporation is determined by the marketplace. In contrast, a private corporation is valued according to standard accounting practices, since shares of the private corporate are not traded on the open market.

A private corporation is not required to provide any information to the public except when required by regulations such as licenses, permits, and other such rules. However, financial statements and offers to acquire another corporation or to be acquired remain confidential.

Acquiring a private corporation is a paradox when compared with the acquisition of a public corporation. It is easier than acquiring a public corporation, because the buyer deals with a small number of stockholders.

However, determining the acquisition price is more difficult than with a public corporation because the dotcom's financial information is not available and there isn't an open market that values the corporation.

Most acquisitions of a private corporation are friendly takeovers, although there are tactics that can be used to acquire a majority of shares in a private corporation where ownership is dispersed among many stockholders. The buyer requires the cooperation of majority shareholders, the board of directors, and officers of the private corporation, because only they have access to information about the corporation that is necessary to establish a fair market value for shares of the corporation. For example, the private corporation must furnish financial records and permit the buyer's auditors to audit the corporate records. This is unnecessary when acquiring a public corporation, because the financial records are already public and have been audited by outside auditors.

A buyer might find reluctance to sell on the part of major stockholders, because stockholders of a private corporation are likely to be founders who have built the business from when it was an idea drawn on a napkin. Therefore, there is a strong attachment to the business that is not commonly seen in a public corporation. Furthermore, these feelings might carry over to employees who have helped grow the corporation. The buyer must be sensitive to these needs and address them favorably.

Here are a few guidelines to help deal with a private corporation;

- Perform due diligence carefully, as described in Chapter 2, "Due Diligence."

- Begin an appraisal of the corporation and audit its records immediately following an agreement on principal by the private corporation to be acquired. The appraisal and audit provide the buyer's first independently derived value of the dotcom.

- Identify problem areas in the dotcom's operation, then determine if they can be fixed. If so, use this situation as leverage in negotiating terms of the deal.

- Negotiate with one person who holds majority stock or who is the most influential among the other stockholders. If possible, avoid negotiating with attorneys, investment bankers, and other professionals who might represent the private company, because it will be more difficult to win concessions than if negotiations are held directly with the major stockholders.

SUMMARY

A public corporation registers shares with the appropriate agencies and issues shares to the general public so the shares can be traded in a stock exchange where the auction process dictates the current value of those shares.

State agencies and federal agencies regulate public corporations to assure a fair and open market exists for publicly traded securities without the influence of fraud and stock manipulation. State and federal regulations define the role of a public corporation's board of directors and establish guidelines for public disclosure of interest and intentions of parties associated with the public corporation.

The board of directors of a public corporation has a fiduciary responsibility to stockholders to remain neutral in an acquisition bid for the corporation. The board is obligated not to reject outright any creditable offer nor to accept a creditable offer without investigating to determine if it is the best offer available.

There are two common ways for a public corporation to be acquired. The first is for the buyer to purchase shares of the corporation on the public market at the current market price. The second is through a tender offer.

A tender offer is a publicly announced offer by the buyer to acquire shares of a single class of stock at a specified price. The price is substantially higher than the current market price to entice stockholders to sell their shares to the buyer. A tender offer is initially publicly announced in advertisements and in a press release. A transmittal letter and other documents are then sent to stockholders by the buyer as the official tender offer.

The tender offer must follow a prescribed timetable. The offer is available for 20 days from the date of the public announcement and can be canceled within the first 5 days. Any change to the tender offer extends the tender offer for 10 days following the change, even if the time exceeds the 20-day offer period. This allows time for the stockholders to receive the new terms for the tender offer. Stockholders retain the right to withdraw their shares sold to the buyer for up to 60 days following the date of the tender offer, unless the stockholder received remuneration from the buyer.

Material changes to a public corporation must receive approval of a majority of stockholders at a stockholders meeting or through a written consent. The board of directors or any stockholder can ask other stockholders for the right to vote the other stockholder's shares based on agreed-upon terms. This is called a proxy and the solicitation to obtain the right to vote the shares is called a proxy statement. A proxy statement must contain information that clearly describes the issue or issues that are the subject of the vote and must state the opinion of the issuer of the proxy statement.

The board of directors of a public corporation is obligated to disclose to the public information about the corporation in an effort to provide stockholders and the market with material information of anything that may change the structure or control of the corporation. The board of directors is obligated to make sure that public information is accurate and to correct inaccuracies through issuing a public announcement. Failure to do so might expose the board of directors and the corporation to litigation taken by stockholders and regulatory agencies.

Public corporations are vulnerable to attempted takeovers by unwanted suitors, because most, if not all, of the corporation's stock is traded freely on the open market. Although the board of directors and stockholders cannot prohibit a suitor from purchasing shares of the corporation, actions can be taken by the board of directors to make the purchase practically and economically prohibitive. There are several commonly use strategies for a board of directors to defend against an undesirable takeover. These strategies are the lockup option, restructuring defense, shareholder rights plan defense, charter defense, unattractive defense, and payment defense.

A buyer and dotcom can enter into an agreement to restrict each other's options whenever a buyer makes a tender offer for a public corporation. These restrictions are a breakup fee clause, a topping fee clause, and a no-shopping clause.

Officers and a wide breadth of associates of a publicly trade corporation are considered insiders by regulatory bodies and therefore are prohibited from receiving any benefit from corporate information that is not publicly known.

A private corporation's securities are not registered with state and federal authorities and therefore are prohibited from being traded on the open securities market. The board of directors and the officers of a private corporation have a fiduciary responsibility to stockholders similar to that of their counterparts in a public corporation.

QUESTIONS

1. What are steps in a tender offer?

2. Who is an insider in a public corporation?

3. Why must public corporations make material information known to the public?

4. Is a private corporation obligated to make public announcements of material information?

5. What defenses are available to a public corporation that is involved in a hostile takeover?

6. What is the purpose of a staggered board of directors?

7. How does a buyer establish a premium for a tender offer?

8. What is the fiduciary responsibility of the board of directors?

9. What process is used to consider an acquisition bid by the board of directors of a public corporation?

10. Can shares in a private corporation be traded on a stock exchange?

CHAPTER 7

International Business

Oceans become smaller as international business grows.

—Anonymous

In This Chapter

- Acquiring a Business in the U.S.
- U.S. Taxes
- Acquiring a Business Outside the U.S.
- Foreign Taxes
- International Financing

ACQUIRING A BUSINESS IN THE U.S.

The United States is an attractive venue for acquiring and operating a business, because federal and state regulations foster a free economy. Federal regulations encourage foreign investors and corporations to conduct business in the U.S. by imposing few restrictions.

Any foreign corporation can easily acquire a U.S. corporation and conduct business in the U.S. without having to become a U.S. resident or a resident of the state within which the U.S. corporation is incorporated.

Generally, foreign ownership is restricted whenever the business has a strong influence on the U.S. economy and on international policies, as determined by the Federal Committee on Foreign Investment. This committee assesses the impact a business has on national interest, then recommends to the appropriate regulatory agencies whether or not to impose restrictions.

The regulatory agency has the authority to accept or reject the recommendations, although most recommendations are accepted. The regulatory agency then uses powers granted to it by the U.S. Congress to create regulations that limit or prohibit the participation of foreign ownership in the business.

These restrictions are sparsely imposed on Internet businesses unless the business is in the communications, banking, mining, merchant marine, or airlines industries. However, a foreign-owned U.S. business might be restricted if the business is a threat to the national security of the U.S.

Foreign owners of U.S. businesses are required to report to the Department of Commerce information about their ownership and about business activities if certain thresholds are met. For example, a foreigner who has acquired a business for $1 million or has become a beneficial owner of a U.S. business by owning 10 percent of the outstanding voting shares must notify the Department of Commerce.

Regulations regarding foreign ownership of a U.S. business frequently change. It is important that before considering the acquisition of a U.S. business, a foreign corporation consult with legal counsel who is familiar with the most recent restrictions and reporting requirements to assure that those requirements will not hinder the acquisition plans.

Caution

A U.S. citizen or resident who helps a foreigner acquire material ownership in a U.S. business also is required to report his or her activity to the Department of Commerce.

Although federal and local regulators impose few restrictions on foreign ownership of a U.S. business, there are other implications that a foreign corporation must consider. These include local country restrictions and taxation.

A foreign corporation should retain legal counsel within his or her own country to assess restrictions that the country might impose on its citizens owning a business in the U.S. Some countries dissuade its residents from investing outside the country by placing barriers that make it financially unattractive to acquire a U.S. business.

The foreign owner of a U.S. business must conform to tax regulations of both the U.S. and of the foreign owner's country of origin. These restrictions could make acquiring a business in the U.S. less attractive than if a resident of the U.S. acquired the same business. For example, the foreign owner might realize double taxation, once in the U.S. and again in the owner's own country.

From Tim Miller, Webmergers.com

Serial Acquisitions

CraftClickCraftClick.com is an interesting example of an Internet company that is using a series of small acquisitions to build a Web company almost literally overnight. The Bulletin-Board-traded firm has bought 11 small sites related to arts and crafts, in the process raking in 5 million monthly page views and 450,000 registered users. The company plans to stitch together (sorry) these sites into a leading "knowledge community" for the large and highly competitive arts and crafts marketplace (see table).

CraftClick Acquisitions

Target	Description
ToleNet.com	
CraftCoupons.com	Discount programs
MakeStuff.com	How-to
Crafter.com	Community
CraftNetVillage.com	E-commerce
TopCraftSites	Directory
Crafters Network	Community
Stamparoo.com	Rubber stamps
Art2Artonline.com	Crafts e-tailer
Stitches to Go	Needlework
CraftsSearch.com	Search engine

CraftClick pays in stock and has expended about 15 percent of its shares, spending on average just over half a million dollars in stock for the properties bought. Prices ranged from under $100,000 to just over $1.5 million based on current stock values.

CraftClick has a market cap of about $36 million and minimal sales. However, it projects a revenue run rate of $1 million per year, according to its primary funder, Venture Catalyst, Inc., a publicly traded consultancy and incubator. Venture Catalyst is largely responsible for persuading CraftClick to exit an auction business that it earlier operated and tackle the crafts market.

While the arts and crafts sector brings to mind little old ladies and knitting needles, it is actually a $20 billion U.S. retail business, according to Venture Catalyst. For evidence, one only needs to look at the success of Michael's Stores, a bricks-and-mortar arts and crafts chain that has about $2 billion in trailing-twelve-month sales and that currently sports a market cap of $1.23 billion.

Venture Catalyst counts more than nine competitors, including venture-funded heavies like CraftShop.com, Craftopia, and IdeaForests. CraftClick's plan is to beat the competition to the punch by quickly acquiring a critical mass of users—M&A as a marketing strategy, if you will. "Our wealthy competitors have bought, for boatloads of money, search engine keywords that are for the most part useless," says Venture Catalyst principal and CraftClick board member Sanjay Sabnani. "What we did is buy sites that already have users, that typically rank high in search engines."

The Web is a unique medium in that it allows acquirers like Craft-Click to assemble new companies out of a network of small sites. There are several reasons why this is uniquely possible on the Web:

- The Web fosters boutiques. Low distribution costs and a nearly infinite number of "channels" allows even hyper-specialized sites to have viable, albeit small, businesses.

- An acquirer can add tremendous value. By delivering both additional eyeballs and advertising sales across a network, an advertiser can build revenues far beyond what a standalone site could muster.

- Sites are "virtual." A buyer can link sites online no matter where they're located geographically.

- Little integration required. Cross-linkages may well be enough; there is little need to integrate these sites—cross-linkages work just fine.

- The price is right. Smaller sites are cheaper to buy and their founders typically have no other exit than M&A.

Of course, there are many potential complications in being a serial mergerer. It's a tremendous amount of work to do the negotiating and legal work—CraftClick's executives are working six days a week, 10 to 12 hours a day, to pull in deals. Also, it may be difficult to manage fiercely independent entrepreneurs, and the buyer risks losing its core assets if owners walk away. CraftClick lets founders run their sites as usual, and typically gives them a modest consulting contract to keep them around for a year or so. "Our M&A approach is more like a bricks-and-mortar [rollup]", said Sabnani, "...where you say to the seller 'why don't you maintain your current user experience...'and we consolidate the back end."

Valuations were initially something of a shot in the dark for Craft-Click, but a system is evolving. "The formula is almost shares per user per revenue dollars," said Sabnani

There are only two other companies to our knowledge that have had a focused serial acquisition strategy similar to CraftClick's, with vastly different success rates.

Most notable: Internet.com, Inc., the mother of serial acquirers. The company has strung together nearly 50 acquisitions to create a $1 billion-market-cap destination for users interested in anything related to the Internet—technology, development, marketing, investing, and more.

Most Notorious: Zapata, Corp., the fish-byproducts and food services company that in 1998 escorted more than two dozen smaller sites up to the M&A altar and then abruptly abandoned them when the stock market got rocky.

U.S. TAXES

A foreign owner of a U.S. business is liable for federal and local taxes for operations within the U.S. There are three kinds of federal taxes that a foreign business is required to pay: an income tax on net earnings, a tax on passive income, and a branch profits tax.

Tech Talk

Passive Income: Income generated by dividends, interest, royalties, and rents.

Income tax on net earnings is determined by the graduated tax rate as applied to any U.S. business. Tax on passive income is at a flat rate and is withheld by the person or company paying the passive income.

The branch profits tax is imposed on earnings from U.S. operations (branch) of a foreign corporation. The branch must be a foreign corporation that sends dividends and/or interest back to the parent corporation. The branch profits tax is at the standard income tax rate and is in addition to the regular income tax. The objective of the branch profits tax is to counteract taxes imposed by foreign governments on branches of U.S. corporations operating within their jurisdictions.

Caution

A foreign corporation can avoid the branch profits tax by forming the branch as a U.S. corporation.

A foreign corporation operating within the U.S. can reduce exposure to taxes if the foreign corporation's country has an income tax treaty with the U.S. An income tax treaty is an agreement that reduces double taxation on international corporations and establishes procedures for resolving income tax disputes. An income tax treaty is also used to impose informal economic policy among participating countries, which is later reaffirmed by formal policy decisions. Terms of an income tax treaty override tax law, including the branch profits tax.

Each income tax treaty defines residents who are covered under the treaty and the terms of the treaty. Terms vary depending on the terms negotiated by the Department of State. However, restrictions are imposed on foreign corporations who treaty-shop looking for the best tax deal.

Treaty-shopping is the technique used by international corporations whereby they enter into business operations in countries that have favorable tax treaties with the U.S. Let's say that a business in China wants to acquire a dotcom in the U.S. Furthermore, let's assume that China and the U.S. do not have an income tax treaty. Earnings from the dotcom are likely to be double taxed.

Assume that an income tax treaty exists between France and the U.S. The Chinese business might incorporate a business in France that acquires the dotcom in the U.S. In doing so, the Chinese business can take advantage of the income tax treaty.

Whenever the U.S. suspects that a business is inappropriately taking advantage of an income tax treaty, the U.S. attempts to restructure the treaty and impose terms that redefine the types of residents within the foreign country who are covered under the treaty. In extreme cases, the U.S. suspends or terminates the treaty.

Typically, a resident of the foreign country is considered a corporation if no less than 50 percent of the corporation's stock is owned by citizens or legal residents of the foreign country who is a signator to the income tax treaty. This permits minority stockholders to be noncitizens, or legal residents of the foreign country. In the previous example, the China business could take advantage of the French–U.S. income tax treaty as long as the China business did not own more than 50 percent of the French corporation that acquired the U.S. dotcom company.

Caution

Although a business cannot take advantage of an income tax treaty, the business is still able to open business operations in the foreign country as long as the business adheres to the foreign country's regulations.

The income-liability test is also used to define a foreign resident whom an income tax treaty covers. Under the income-liability test, earnings from branch operations in the treaty country must be redirected to the treaty country or the U.S. to be considered a resident under the treaty. Earnings that are repatriated to the home country disqualify the foreign corporation as a resident.

Let's say that the China business operates a branch in France. Since the branch is 100 percent owned by the China business, the China business cannot take advantage of the income tax treaty between France and the U.S. However, it can utilize the treaty if earnings from the branch in France are used to pay liabilities incurred doing business in France or in the U.S.

There are two additional ways in which an income tax treaty defines a resident. A foreign corporation whose stock is traded on a public exchange in the country who is a signator of the treaty is considered a resident and is covered under the terms of the treaty. For example, if the China business is a corporation and its shares are traded on the French stock exchange, then the China business is considered a resident of France under the treaty.

When a foreign corporation whose home country is a signator to an income tax treaty with the U.S. and who has a branch in another country that has a similar treaty, then the branch is considered a resident of that country. Here's how this works. Let's say a German corporation has a branch in France. Both Germany and France have separate income tax treaties with the U.S. The branch of the German corporation is considered a resident of France under the treaty because Germany has an income tax treaty with the U.S.

Caution

Individuals who are nonresident aliens of the U.S. are exempt from income taxes on passive income if they have not been resident in the U.S. for 183 days or more within the tax year.

ACQUIRING A BUSINESS OUTSIDE THE U.S.

Any U.S. corporation has the right to acquire a foreign corporation, although doing so involves greater risks than risks incurred when acquiring a U.S. corporation. Accounting standards, corporation regulations, and business operations are fairly standard throughout the U.S. However, these differ in each country and insert a degree of complexity into any international acquisition that could make a deal unattractive.

Before embarking on a foreign acquisition, the U.S. corporation must carefully review the standard business practices of the dotcom's country. These practices might be materially different than domestic business practices. U.S. accounting, law, and business operations do not apply in the international arena.

Here are some of the differences that might arise in an international acquisition by a U.S. corporation:

- The foreign government might be a minority owner of the dotcom (although a number of foreign governments are divesting their business operations).
- The dotcom's financials are based on the country's accounting rules, which are substantially different than U.S accounting rules.
- Terms used in the dotcom's financial are the same terms used on a U.S. corporation's financials, but their definitions are different. Therefore, the dotcom's financials must be restated according to U.S. accounting rules.

- Agreements between a U.S. corporation and a foreign dotcom might be exposed to changes implemented by the foreign government in an effort to protect its domestic businesses.
- A foreign country's cultural, religious, historical, language, law, and economic philosophies are different and might have stronger influence on business operations than do those philosophies in the U.S.
- Acquisition of the dotcom might require approval of the foreign government. Government regulations might prevent the U.S. corporation from acquiring controlling interest in the dotcom.

Caution

Efforts are underway to create an international accounting standard. However, these standards appear to be less stringent than U.S. standard accounting practices and therefore are unlikely to be adopted by the U.S.

Currency

Business operations in a foreign country generate earnings in local currency, which must be converted to U.S. dollars so that earnings can be properly reflected on the U.S. corporation's financial statements. Currency conversion introduces a hidden risk in conducting business outside of the U.S.

Currency must also be converted when the U.S. corporation acquires the foreign dotcom, because the dotcom's stockholders are likely to require payment in their local currency. Currency conversion might increase the price of the acquisition and make the deal unattractive.

The rate at which local currency is converted to U.S. dollars is dependent upon supply and demand for both currencies, as determined by the marketplace. Let's say that there is an equal demand by the U.S. for British goods and by the British for U.S. goods. In other words, the U.S. needs an equal amount of British pounds as the British requires U.S. dollars.

In theory, the exchange rate is 1:1. In the real world, however, these demands are not in balance, which causes the exchange rate between U.S. dollars and British pounds to change with relation to demand. A slight change in the exchange rate can have a dramatic effect on an acquisition price and on the financial results of a corporation. This is especially true in businesses that have low profit margins, where a change in exchange rate might erode the profit margin.

A U.S. corporation can lessen the risks of currency fluctuation by using forward purchase contracts and forward sales contracts. A forward purchase contract is an agreement between the U.S. corporation and usually a financial institution to exchange a specific amount of U.S. dollars for local currency at a fixed exchange rate, with the contract to be executed at a specific time in the future. A forward sales contract is similar to a forward purchase contract except that the U.S. corporation agrees to sell rather than purchase currency.

Let's say that a U.S. brick-and-mortar wants to acquire a British dotcom. Both firms reach a price based on British pounds. Once the closing date is established, the U.S. brick-and-mortar buys a forward purchase contract for the British pounds that are required to close the deal. The forward purchase contract guarantees a fixed currency rate to the U.S. brick-and-mortar corporation. This enables the U.S. brick-and-mortar corporation to eliminate the risk that currency fluctuations between the time of the agreement and the time of closing will make the acquisition unattractive.

However, there remains a risk that the currency rate, called the *spot rate,* at the time of the closing may be more favorable to the U.S. brick-and-mortar corporation than the forward purchase contract rate. In this situation, the U.S. brick-and-mortar is still locked into the forward purchase contract rate. Buying the forward purchase contract protects the U.S. corporation from unfavorable movements in the currency rate. In exchange for this protection, the U.S. corporation is giving up the opportunity to take advantage of a possible favorable swing in the currency rate at closing.

The forward purchase contract is also used whenever a U.S. corporation finances an acquisition through debt. The U.S. corporation might buy forward purchase contracts to correlate with the payment schedule and thereby reduce the effects of currency fluctuations.

Another way a U.S. corporation can deal with the currency rate risks is by purchasing options to purchase currency at a fixed rate. An option is different than a forward in that an option gives the U.S. corporation the right to either exercise the option or abandon the option, as compared to a forward, which cannot be abandoned by the U.S. corporation.

Here's how a currency option works. When the agreement to acquire the dotcom is reached, the U.S. corporation buys a currency option in the amount of the acquisition price at a fixed currency rate to be exercised on the closing date of the deal. If the spot rate at closing is less than the option's currency rate, then the U.S. corporation abandons the option and acquires currency at the spot rate. However, the option is exercised if the spot rate is higher than the option's currency rate.

Caution

A U.S. corporation that is acquiring a foreign corporation should consult financial advisors, such as accountants and investment bankers, who are familiar with leveraging forwards and options strategies.

Foreign Regulations

The U.S. corporation that acquires a foreign dotcom might face regulatory requirements imposed by the dotcom's country. These regulations typically include protection provisions that assure that the country's economy benefits from the acquisition.

A common protection provision is to limit the number of foreign employees that can be employed by the dotcom. The buyer is expected to employee local residents to operate the dotcom. Immigration and tax regulations are used to control the flow of foreign employees hired by the dotcom following the acquisition.

Likewise, certain assets of the dotcom, such as sophisticated encryption software, might be prohibited from leaving the dotcom's country. In this way, regulators are able to retain valuable assets that give their country a competitive edge in the international market place.

Probably the most important restriction that affects dotcom companies is import quotas. Dotcom companies might be limited in the amount of goods that they can bring into the country. This includes goods for the dotcom company's own consumption and for resale. For example, regulators might prohibit a dotcom company from importing servers and network components if similar products are available locally. This restriction might be an outright prohibition of receiving the product or the imposition of a very high duty that makes the cost of importing the product uneconomical when compared to purchasing local products.

Similarly, regulators may impose restrictions that discourage a dotcom company from selling certain goods manufactured outside the dotcom's country. This is especially true if the dotcom company is also the manufacturer of the product. This is called a *local content regulation* and is designed to protect local industry from international competition.

Before an agreement is reached to acquire the foreign dotcom, the U.S. corporation must determine if the dotcom's country has foreign exchange control regulations. Foreign exchange control regulations are laws that restrict the conversion of local currency to U.S. dollars or other currencies. Let's say a dotcom's foreign branch earned 100 million liras and the local government permits half the earnings to be converted into U.S. dollars. The other half must remain in lira. This means that the dotcom is limited in the amount of earnings that can be withdrawn from the branch operations.

The objective of foreign exchange control regulations is for the country to assure that earnings from local operations remain within the country and are not exported outside its borders. This helps to strengthen the local economy by indirectly requiring the foreign operation to reinvest earnings within the country rather than export the earnings to the corporation's home country.

Another area of regulatory interest of foreign governments is the way an employer relates to employees. Local regulations might grant employees rights that are not commonly given to employees in the U.S. For example, employees might have a statutory right to have a representative on the board of directors and the right to be consulted and to approve material changes in the corporation. Furthermore, regulations might restrict a corporation's ability to terminate an employee by requiring the corporation to pay higher unemployment benefits costs than is commonly experienced in the U.S.

Therefore, it is critical that a U.S. corporation carefully analyze the impact local regulations have on future operations of the dotcom before the deal is negotiated. Each regulation should be evaluated and assigned a cost value, which can be used to adjust the acquisition price. The buyer may discover after the analysis that a once attractive foreign dotcom becomes an unprofitable venture when the local regulations are considered.

Caution

An attempt should be made to negotiate terms of regulations with foreign government officials. Some regulations may be adjusted or waived, especially in countries that try to attract foreign investors.

U.S. Regulations

Regulations within the U.S. also govern the ability of a U.S. corporation to acquire a foreign dotcom. These regulations are minimal, but failure to comply can be costly to the U.S. corporation.

Any domestic corporation that owns at least 10 percent of a foreign corporation must file a report with the federal government that discloses information about both companies and their relationships. Furthermore, the books and records of the domestic corporation and the dotcom after the acquisition must follow generally accepted accounting practices. This is to assure that financial statements of the domestic corporation properly reflect the contribution of the foreign operation.

The U.S. corporation should expect to maintain two sets of books for the foreign operation. One set adheres to foreign accounting practices and the other set follows U.S. accounting practices.

Federal law prohibits the domestic corporation from making payments to foreign officials to gain favorable decisions. Bribery and influence peddling is a traditional practice in some foreign countries, but has become disfavored in domestic political circles. While federal authorities might lack the jurisdiction to enforce this law on a U.S. corporation-owned foreign operation, action can be taken against the domestic parent corporation.

U.S. regulations also prohibit a domestic corporation from actions that are against major U.S. policies, such as conducting business with a country considered an enemy to the U.S. Any domestic corporation that is considering acquiring a foreign dotcom must enlist the services of an attorney who is familiar with international federal regulations to assess the impact such regulations might have on the deal and on the operation of the dotcom once the deal is consummated.

FOREIGN TAXES

Operating a foreign business is likely to expose the U.S. corporation to tax liabilities both in the U.S. and in the foreign country. A foreign business operation is generally not liable for U.S. taxes because the operation is typically organized as a foreign corporation, and not as a U.S. corporation. In addition, the source of income is derived outside of the U.S.

Let's say that a U.S. corporation acquires a German dotcom. The German dotcom is incorporated in Germany, and the U.S. corporation owns the stock of the dotcom corporation. Earnings from the German dotcom operation are not taxable by the U.S., except when earnings are distributed by the dotcom to its stockholder, which is the U.S. corporation. However, earnings from the German dotcom are taxable by the German taxing authority.

The foreign tax rate applied to earnings of the foreign operation might vary depending on the country and whether or not the foreign operation is considered a resident of the country. A U.S. corporation might be considered a resident of a foreign country if the foreign subsidiary is managed and controlled within the country. This gives the corporation dual residency, both in the foreign country and in the U.S.

There are many exceptions to taxation rules; therefore, the U.S. corporation must carefully analyze the foreign and domestic tax consequences before an agreement is reached to acquire the foreign dotcom. Failure to perform a thorough review exposes the U.S. corporation to possible double taxation and nullifies the benefits of the deal.

An international tax specialist should be employed to evaluate the potential tax liabilities of the dotcom. The international tax specialist will chart the dotcom and its subsidiaries, carefully listing each tax jurisdiction.

The analysis will also reveal if the foreign dotcom falls within the jurisdiction of several countries based on the location of the dotcom's assets and if material owners reside in different countries. The tax consequences of each country must be evaluated along with the impact, if any, that U.S. taxes have on earnings following the acquisition.

Tech Talk

Material Owner: A person or corporation that controls 10 percent of the voting shares of a foreign corporation.

The international tax specialist also reports on the impact tax treaties and foreign tax credit have on operations. A tax treaty is an agreement between two or more countries that, among other things, reduces the likelihood that countries that are signators to the treaty will unfairly tax a foreign corporation. For example, some tax treaties exclude income that is to be taxed, while other tax treaties limit the tax rate.

Furthermore, U.S. taxing authorities might grant a U.S. corporation that owns a foreign business credit for taxes paid abroad. This is called a *foreign tax credit* and is designed to establish a ceiling on the tax rate to either the foreign tax rate or the U.S. tax rate, whichever is the higher. Applicable foreign taxes are deducted from gross income.

Caution

There are qualifications and exceptions to the use of tax treaties and tax credit; therefore, it is critical that an international tax specialist be brought in to the deal long before negotiations begin, since the tax implications might impact the price paid for the dotcom.

The U.S. corporation must determine the U.S. tax implications that occur should the corporation own more then 50 percent of the foreign dotcom. In this case, the foreign dotcom after the deal becomes a controlled foreign corporation of the U.S. corporation.

Stockholders of the U.S. corporation may be required to include specific classes of income amounts of the foreign operation as part of their gross income, even if these earnings were not brought back to the U.S. The income is prorated and might be offset by foreign tax credits.

Caution

Sole proprietorships, partnerships, and corporations may not have a comparable organizational form in the foreign country. Therefore, the international tax specialist must carefully assess the tax implications of the foreign dotcom's organizational structure.

INTERNATIONAL FINANCING

An international acquisition can be financed by financial institutions outside the U.S. Such financing is conducted in much the same way as domestic acquisitions are financed (see Chapter 3). However, international financing must weigh the impact that currency fluctuations and local regulations have on the lender, the buyer, and the dotcom.

Debt securities used to finance the acquisition are issued in the currency agreed upon by the lender and the buyer. The currency might be the currency domestically used by the lender, which could be different than the currency used to record the operating income from the acquisition. For example, an English bank might lend British pounds for a U.S. corporation's acquisition of a German dotcom. Stockholders of the dotcom expect to receive German marks in exchange for their stock. Therefore, the U.S. corporation must convert the pounds to marks to consummate the deal. The acquisition's operations will generate marks, which requires the U.S. corporation to convert marks to pounds to pay down the debt held by the English bank.

Interest on international debt is calculated using either the London Interbank Offered Rate (LIBOR) or the Singapore Interbank Offer Rate (SIBOR). These are the rates at which offshore banks are charged for loans. LIBOR or SIBOR is used as the base above which the interest is calculated. For example, the interest might be quoted as LIBOR plus 2 percent. If LIBOR is 5 percent, then the interest applied to the debt is 7 percent.

It is common in international finance for lending institutions to share the risk of financing an acquisition by forming a syndicate of financial institutions, each of which underwrites a percentage of the debt security. There are two kinds of syndicates: one in which the lead lender is liable for the full amount of the loan and the other in which each member of the syndicate is liable for its own piece of the loan.

In the first type of syndicate, the loan agreement is between the lead lender and the buyer. The lead lender commits to the full loan amount. Before closing the loan, the lead lender signs subscription agreements with other syndicate members that secure funds necessary to cover the loan. Each syndicate member is liable to the lead lender for the amount specified in his or her subscription agreement. Syndicate members, except for the lead lender, are not liable to the buyer, because the buyer's agreement is with the lead lender and not with the syndicate members.

In the other form of a syndicate, each syndicate member signs the loan agreement with the buyer for a specific portion of the loan and therefore is liable to the buyer for the specified loan amount.

Terms of the agreement are negotiated between the buyer and the syndicate manager, which is typically the lead lender. Terms include the interest rate, payback period, and other aspects commonly found in a domestic loan agreement. Additional terms include currencies issued to the buyer and currencies used to retire the debt.

The buyer makes loan payments to the lead lender, who distributes payment to the syndicate members. Liability of the buyer to each syndicate member is limited to the type of syndicate used to finance the deal.

In the first example, the buyer is liable for the principal and interest only to the lead lender, because the buyer does not have an agreement with each syndicate member. The buyer is liable to each syndicate member in the second example because all parties signed the loan agreement.

The buyer must be prepared to pay a variety of fees related to executing the loan. These include syndicate expenses, a syndicate management fee, a commitment fee, and an agent's fee. The syndicate management fee is compensation to the lead lender to organize the syndicate, and the agent's fee is compensation to the lead lender for negotiating the deal on behalf of members of the syndicate.

Caution

Investigate the opportunities made available by foreign countries who arrange loans and loan guarantees for firms expanding business into their country.

International financing of a deal requires careful coordination between the lender or syndicate and the buyer so that funds are available in the proper country at closing. This is especially important regarding the closing schedule, because local holidays, local financial regulations, and the time zone may hamper the schedule. Let's say that a U.S. corporation acquires a German dotcom and a British syndicate provides financing. What time of day is the closing? These seem relatively trivial points regarding a domestic deal, but can have serious repercussions in the international arena. For example, the time difference is critical, for noon in Los Angles is 8:00 p.m. in London and 9:00 p.m. in Zurich, which may be beyond the time the syndicate can transfer funds to meet the closing. Before the buyer, dotcom, and syndicate establish a closing date, they must consider the time factor required to complete all the necessary currency conversions and fund transfers.

SUMMARY

Any foreign corporation can easily acquire a U.S. corporation and conduct business in the U.S. without having to become a U.S. resident or a resident of the state within which the U.S. corporation is incorporated.

The Federal Committee on Foreign Investment assesses the impact a business has on national interest, then recommends to the appropriate regulatory agencies whether or not to impose restrictions. The regulatory agency has the authority to accept or reject the recommendations, although most recommendations are accepted. The regulatory agency then uses powers granted to it by the U.S. Congress to create regulations that limit or prohibit the participation of foreign ownership in the business.

Although federal and local regulators impose few restrictions on foreign ownership of a U.S. business, there are other implications that a foreign corporation must consider. These include local country restrictions and taxation.

There are three kinds of federal taxes that a foreign business is required to pay: an income tax on net earnings, a tax on passive income, and a branch profits tax. Income tax on net earnings is determined by the graduated tax rate as applied to any U.S. business. Tax on passive income is at a flat rate and is withheld by the person or company paying the passive income. The branch profits tax is imposed on earnings from U.S. operations (branch) of a foreign corporation.

A foreign corporation operating within the U.S. can reduce exposure to taxes if the foreign corporation's country has an income tax treaty with the U.S. An income tax treaty is an agreement that reduces double taxation on international corporations and establishes procedures for resolving income tax disputes. Each income tax treaty defines residents who are covered under the terms of the treaty. Terms vary depending on the terms negotiated by the Department of State. However, restrictions are imposed on foreign corporations who treaty-shop, looking for the best tax deal. Treaty-shopping is the technique used by international corporations whereby they enter into business operations in countries that have favorable tax treaties with the U.S.

The income-liability test is used to define a foreign resident whom an income tax treaty covers. Under the income-liability test, earnings from branch operations in the treaty country must be redirected to the treaty country or the U.S. to be considered a resident under the treaty. Earnings that are repatriated to the home country disqualify the foreign corporation as a resident.

A foreign corporation whose stock is traded on a public exchange in the country who is a signator of the treaty is also considered a resident and is covered under the terms of the treaty.

A resident is also a foreign corporation whose home country is a signator to an income tax treaty with the U.S. and who has a branch in another country that has a similar treaty; the branch is considered a resident of that country.

Any U.S. corporation has the right to acquire a foreign corporation, although doing so involves greater risks than risks incurred when acquiring a U.S. corporation. Accounting standards, corporation regulations, and business operations are fairly standard throughout the U.S. However, these differ in each country and insert a degree of complexity into any international acquisition that could make a deal unattractive.

Business operations in a foreign country generate earnings in local currency, which must be converted to U.S. dollars so that earnings can be properly reflected on the U.S. corporation's financial statements. Currency conversion introduces a hidden risk in conducting business outside of the U.S.

Currency must also be converted when the U.S. corporation acquires the foreign dotcom, because the dotcom's stockholders are likely to require payment in their local currency. Currency conversion might increase the price of the acquisition and make the deal unattractive.

A U.S. corporation can lessen the risks of currency fluctuation by using forward purchase contracts and forward sales contracts. A forward purchase contract is an agreement between the U.S. corporation and usually a financial institution to exchange a specific amount of U.S. dollars for local currency at a fixed exchange rate, with the contract to be executed at a specific time in the future. A forward sales contract is similar to a forward purchase contract, except that the U.S. corporation agrees to sell rather than purchase currency.

Another way a U.S. corporation can deal with the currency rate risks is by purchasing options to purchase currency at a fixed rate. An option is different than a forward in that an option gives the U.S. corporation the right to either exercise the option or abandon the option. In contrast, a forward is an agreement that cannot be abandoned by the U.S. corporation.

The U.S. corporation that acquires a foreign dotcom might face regulatory requirements imposed by the dotcom's country. These regulations typically include protection provisions that assure that the country's economy benefits from the acquisition.

Each regulation should be evaluated and assigned a cost value, which can be used to adjust the acquisition price. The buyer may discover after the analysis that a once attractive foreign dotcom becomes an unprofitable venture when the local regulations are considered.

Regulations within the U.S. also govern the ability of a U.S. corporation to acquire a foreign dotcom. These regulations are minimal, but failure to comply can be costly to the U.S. corporation.

There are many exceptions to taxation rules; therefore, the U.S. corporation must carefully analyze the foreign and domestic tax consequences before an agreement is reached to acquire the foreign dotcom. Failure to perform a thorough review exposes the U.S. corporation to possible double taxation and nullifies the benefits of the deal.

An international tax specialist should be employed to evaluate the potential tax liabilities of the dotcom. The international tax specialist will chart the dotcom and its subsidiaries, carefully listing each tax jurisdiction.

An international acquisition can be financed by financial institutions outside the U.S. Such financing is conducted in much the same way as domestic acquisitions are financed. However, international financing must weigh the impact that currency fluctuations and local regulations have on the lender, the buyer, and the dotcom.

It is common in international finance for lending institutions to share the risk of financing an acquisition by forming a syndicate of financial institutions, each of which underwrites a percentage of the debt security. There are two kinds of syndicates: one in which the lead lender is liable for the full amount of the loan and the other in which each member of the syndicate is liable for its own piece of the loan.

QUESTIONS

1. What are the two types of syndicates used in international finance?

2. How can a buyer minimize the currency fluctuation risk between a deal agreement and closing?

3. How does a tax treaty affect the acquisition of a foreign dotcom?

4. How do local accounting standards affect the valuation of a deal?

5. What is the purpose of a foreign tax credit?

6. How can earnings from a foreign operation be taxed in the U.S.?

7. What problems can you foresee when using international financial institutions to finance a deal?

8. When must a foreign owner of a U.S. corporation notify the federal government?

9. What factors must a U.S. corporation consider when contemplating the acquisition of a foreign dotcom?

10. What is the difference between a currency forward and a currency option?

CHAPTER 8

Pricing the Deal

The value of a business is the price paid for the business.

—Anonymous

In This Chapter

- Pricing Basics
- Buying Strategies
- Forecasting Cash Flow
- Ratio Valuation
- Risk Assessment
- Pricing Models
- Specifying Price in the Agreement

PRICING BASICS

The price paid for a dotcom is established through negotiations between the buyer and the dotcom and is based on the real value and the perceived value of the dotcom. Real value is a tangible amount that a party can rationalize through a formal valuation process. Perceived value is an amount derived from subjective rather than objective valuation. Instinctively, both the buyer and the dotcom have a perceived value of what the dotcom is worth when they initiate the deal. Their perceived value may or may not have any foundation in fact.

For the buyer, perceived value is arrived at through factors that attract the buyer to consider the dotcom as a candidate for acquisition. These factors include press notices, reputation, product line, organizational strengths, estimates of revenue and profit, and whether or not the dotcom is a fit with the buyer's organization.

For the dotcom, perceived value is based on management's impression of how the dotcom compares with competitors in the market, the quality of products and services offered to customers, clients' loyalty, and personal attachment to the organization. Although perceived value lacks a rational basis, it does play a critical role in negotiations, since a low perceived value by the dotcom can be an advantage to the buyer should the dotcom fail to properly assess its value. In essence, the buyer acquires the dotcom below the real value of the dotcom.

However, before either party acts on the perceived value, each should perform a formal valuation analysis of the dotcom to ascertain the dotcom's real value. Valuation analysis provides an objective foundation from which a fair market price can be established for the dotcom. Results from the valuation analysis are used in negotiations to justify a party's position and to convince the opposing party to adjust the bid or asking price for the dotcom to a more realistic amount. The results of the analysis are also used as supporting documents for financing the deal, since details required by lenders about the dotcom's operations are contained in the valuation analysis.

Tech Talk

Ask Price: The acquisition price proposed by the dotcom.
Bid Price: The acquisition price proposed by the buyer.

The valuation process is a multi-disciplined investigation into the dotcom's operations and determines how well the dotcom blends into the buyer's plans. Accountants, financial experts, industry analysts, and others with the appropriate special skills form a valuation team, which takes a critical look at the dotcom. Through the team members' knowledge of their specialties and of the industry, and with the use of analytical tools and some common sense, the valuation team collectively arrives at a real value of the dotcom.

The real value of the dotcom is an estimated amount rather than a precise amount, and estimates can vary greatly among the results of other valuation process of the same dotcom. These variations are largely caused by subjective influences in the valuation process, such as underlying assumptions.

The buyer must be sure to conduct a valuation that is independent of the dotcom, without relying on estimates and forecasts provided by the dotcom, because those figures tend to be distorted in an effort to present the dotcom in a better than realistic light.

A preferred approach to valuating a dotcom is for both the buyer and the dotcom to assemble independent valuation teams, each coordinated by a professional appraiser. One team reports to the buyer and the other to the dotcom.

The results of the valuation team must be fully understood and challenged, and the team must provide the rationale for its conclusions. Neither the buyer nor the dotcom should accept a valuation report at face value, because the buyer and the dotcom are ultimately responsible for fixing the value of the dotcom.

The buyer and dotcom should examine each other's valuation methodology to identify any material differences between the two. Adjustments can be agreed upon to bring the valuations in line with each other. However, expect that some differences between valuations will remain in disagreement and must be settled through the negotiation process.

The valuation should factor the volatility in the dotcom business, where there is a greater emphasis on earnings potential of the operation than on current earnings. New developments in technology and changes in market conditions occur seemingly overnight in the dotcom business and lead to rapid changes in both the perceived value and real value of a dotcom.

The valuation of a dotcom becomes the foundation for establishing a price for the dotcom. A number of methodologies are used to set the bid (these are discussed in the section "Pricing Models" in this chapter). The bid is the starting point for formal negotiations with the dotcom.

From Tim Miller, Webmergers.com

Pricing

The price of a deal can be based on a multiple of revenue where the multiple is based on market conditions. For example, we saw around 5 times TTM revenues for Lycos and 6 times current-year revenue for FreeRealTime's acquisition of RedChip.com, Inc.

Thomson Corp. paid about 2 times 1999 revenue, or just over 10 times TTM cash flow, for financial information provider Primark Corp., which sells information on a fee or subscription basis.

QXL's purchase of German auction leader Ricardo.de was announced at 11 times trailing revenue and $1,500 per subscriber. However, that deal eventually was given a severe haircut as a result of Ricardo missing its revenue targets and QXL's stock plummeting in value.

The renegotiated deal puts Ricardo at about 3 times revenue and almost $400 per subscriber. The WebVan consolidation with Homegrocer.com valued that company at 18 times TTM revenue, or just over a million dollars per employee.

BuyItNow's acquisition of technology e-tailer Netdirect Corp. was priced at about 1 times TTM revenues. Service-related e-commerce companies such as e-recruiters evidence a higher revenue multiple. TMP Worldwide's acquisition of Scottish online recruiter Recruitment Scotland.com was for 8 times expected current-year revenues.

BUYING STRATEGIES

The category of the buyer and the strategic objective of the acquisition influence the price at which a buyer will acquire a dotcom. Buyers fall into two categories: financial buyer and strategic buyer. A financial buyer sees a dotcom as a stream of cash that can be acquired through carefully orchestrated debt. In contrast, a strategic buyer seeks to use the dotcom to enhance the corporation's current organization through synergy of the existing corporation and the dotcom.

A financial buyer's primary objective is to use little cash and leverage the dotcom's assets to finance the deal. Once the deal is consummated a conscious effort is made by the buyer to reduce expenses and sell off-key assets of the dotcom, and then use the proceeds to retire the debt. This in effect increases the free cash stream generated by the dotcom's operation that can be diverted for other purposes, such as acquisitions of other dotcoms.

A dotcom can achieve a high price from a financial buyer if the dotcom structures its finances in such a way to make available assets that can be used for collateral or can be easily sold without jeopardizing the dotcom's cash flow.

A strategic buyer is less concerned about leveraging the dotcom's assets to finance the deal than it is with assuring that the dotcom is a good fit with the overall objectives of the corporation. The buyer is willing to pay a premium for a dotcom that complements the buyer's existing organization. Therefore, a dotcom can realize the high price by removing obstacles that inhibit synergy between the two corporations.

Both the financial buyer and the strategic buyer have a time horizon when they want to realize the full benefits of the deal. The time horizon for the financial buyer specifies when debt is retired and the cash stream is available for other objectives. The strategic buyer's time horizon specifies when the dotcom's operation is fully blended with that of the buyer's operation.

A time horizon is typically specified in years. For example, the financial buyer may anticipate that within three years following closing the deal, the dotcom's operation will generate $100 million annually in free cash. The price of the deal influences the time horizon in some cases, because the price might increase debt for the buyer.

Let's assume that a dotcom has assets of $200 million, some of which is free from debt and some that is used as collateral for debt. The buyer pays the dotcom $200 million, which is in part used to retire the debt and give free title of all the assets to the buyer. The dotcom did not profit from this deal; instead, it liquidated its assets.

The buyer has $200 million in assets, 80 percent of which can be used as collateral to finance the deal. Let's also assume that the cash flow from the operation and liquidation of some assets by the buyer retires the debt in two years. Therefore, the buyer fully realizes the benefit of the deal in a two-year horizon.

Instead of simply liquidating the business, the dotcom charges a price of $300 million, which gives the dotcom $100 million profit. The $100 million increases the time horizon for the deal to three years. This extension of the time horizon might make the deal unattractive to the buyer because the extension is unacceptable. Price and the time horizon then become points of negotiation.

In an ideal scenario, a buyer who has accumulated cash to acquire the dotcom approaches a dotcom, and therefore the issue of debt finances isn't a factor. However, in the real world, buyers tend to leverage some or nearly all of the deal and to require that the dotcom's operation produce a cash stream that is adequate to repay debt services and return a reasonable sum to stockholders.

The dotcom should determine the maximum leverage that can be supported by operating cash from the business. A financial advisor can provide the dotcom with factors that are used to assess the maximum leverage. These include

- Asset values
- The amount of the value that can be used as collateral
- Current interest rates that are applied to collateralized loans
- The annual debt service payment
- Projected cash flows that can be used to cover debt service
- Excess cash flow following debt service coverage

Excess cash flow can be used as a guideline for setting the deal price, since this is free cash that the buyer can postpone receiving for a time period and can apply towards the additional debt used to cover the purchase price.

FORECASTING CASH FLOW

A major reason to acquire a dotcom is to realize a new cash flow that is generated by the dotcom's business operations. Cash flow is the revenue produced by the dotcom in return for providing customers with products and services.

The amount of cash flow produced by the dotcom is a critical component in the valuation of the dotcom. A large cash flow makes the dotcom more valuable than a comparable dotcom with a low cash flow. Pricing methods, as discussed later in this chapter, use cash flow as a component to determine a fair price for the dotcom. Furthermore, once a dotcom's cash flow potential is identified, the buyer can use this information to formulate a financing plan that diverts cash flow to debt services. As discussed in Chapter 3, "Structuring and Financing the Deal," lenders look more favorably on a financing plan if the plan has free assets that can be used as collateral for the loan and cash flow to repay the debt.

The problem a buyer faces is to forecast the amount of cash flow a dotcom will realize following the acquisition. The process of forecasting cash flow begins with a thorough understanding of the dotcom's operations and of the marketplace for the dotcom's products and services. The initial step is to assess the demand in the market for each product and service that generates a cash flow for the dotcom. This is done by enlisting the services of a specialist, who will identify the demographics of customers and project the size of the customer population for each product and service. This becomes the universe of potential customers for the dotcom.

The size of this customer base is then forecast for a time horizon, the length of which is determined by the nature of the product or service. A short time horizon of a couple of years is used for products whose demands might be volatile, such as music, books, and similar products whose fundamentals are changing. The production and distribution of music and books (i.e., electronic books) online is new and dramatically different from the traditional manufacturing and distribution methods.

Less volatile products and services, such as fiber optic cable manufacturing and installation and telecommunications services, have a longer time horizon because their growth follows a more traditional pattern.

Once the potential customer base is identified for each year of the time horizon, the specialist examines the life cycle of products and services within the industry. In some industries, such as software applications and tools, products are typically out of date in 18 months. This information is generally available by reviewing the launch dates of new products or services in the industry in trade publications.

The specialist will plot out on the time horizon the estimated dates of product launches based on the estimated product life cycle. This provides a visual representation of when changes can be anticipated in the industry.

Tech Talk

Product Life Cycle: The duration beginning when a product is introduced to the market and ending when the product becomes unprofitable.

The next step is for the specialist to estimate the demand for each product and service for each year of the time horizon. Demand is recorded as units sold to the end customer. Services are noted as billable hours or definable job. For example, a Web site development company can bill customers by the hour or set a fixed price for a Web site. Demand for the latter is recorded as the number of Web site jobs. The result is plotted on the time horizon.

The specialist must take into consideration typical demand patterns based on the stage in the product life cycle. A product's life follows a normal bell curve in which there is a period of early acceptance followed by a rapid growth in demand that drops off at the end of the life cycle.

The length of the product life cycle is determined by the nature of the industry and the nature of the product or service. The length of each stage of the product life cycle is estimated by assessing the need for the product or service in the market. A new product that fills an unfilled demand is likely to have a short early acceptance stage and have a relatively longer growth stage until the market becomes saturated, at which time demand for the product rapidly diminishes.

However, a product that replaces an existing product may have a longer acceptance stage, because the existing customers are not in a rush to expense funds to replace a product that is working well. Furthermore, demand for the replacement product may not be as great as for the initial release, because a number of customers will not upgrade their products. This becomes a factor when the specialist plots the demand for the product on the time horizon.

After completing the market analysis, the specialist will have forecasted the potential demand for each of the dotcom's products and services. The forecast lists the number of units sold to customers, the number of billing hours, and the number of specific kinds of jobs that are in demand for each year of the time horizon.

The specialist turns his or her attention to the dotcom's relationship to the market by determining the dotcom's market share of each product and service. Market share is determined by calculating the percentage of total market sales accounted for by the dotcom's sales. Let's say we want to project the cash flow for the e-commerce line of books sold by a dotcom e-tailer. Market analysis indicates that the demand for e-commerce books is 100,000 books for the first year of the time horizon and 120,000 books for the second year. E-commerce books have an average price of $40. Therefore, the value of the market for e-commerce books for the first year of the time horizon is $4,000,000 and for the second year is $4,800,000.

Let's also say that the dotcom has a 30 percent market share based upon comparing previous sales to the overall market sales. By applying the percentage to the demand for e-commerce books, the specialist can forecast that the dotcom can expect to sell 30,000 e-commerce books in the first year and 30,600 in the second year. The value of these sales is $1,200,000 and $1,520,000 respectively.

The forecast presumes the market and the dotcom's operation will not radically change from the assumptions used by the specialist as the basis of the forecast. The buyer must realize that a forecast is an estimate and not a mathematical certainty. There is always a risk that errors or market changes, such as a new competitor or innovative technology, will invalidate the forecast.

The final step in forecasting cash flow for a dotcom is for the specialist to calculate net proceeds the dotcom will receive from sales. In our example, the average retail price of an e-commerce book is $40; it costs the dotcom $32 to acquire the book from the wholesaler, leaving the dotcom with a net income of $8 per book. This results in a net of $240,000 and $304,000 in the first and second years of the forecast.

By applying this methodology to all the product and services offered by a dotcom, the specialist is able to estimate the cash flow of the dotcom.

From Tim Miller, Webmergers.com

Valuation Metrics

Because many Web properties are immature and lack traditional revenue, cash flow, and earnings metrics, we have in the past chosen Monthly Unique Visitors (MUV) as our primary shorthand valuation metric for traffic-sensitive content and e-commerce properties.

However, a slumping stock market and other new Internet marketplace realities are causing investors and acquirers alike to take a much harder look at more traditional valuation metrics. Although for most Web targets, EBIDTA is still a pipe dream, buyers are certainly taking a closer look at cash flows or prospective of positive cash flows—and are most certainly casting a gimlet eye at cash burn rates.

Although we expect that we have moved into a new and permanent "return to basics" for dotcom valuations, we continue to believe that MUV is a useful general-purpose measure of a site's potential to create economic value. We maintain this for several reasons.

For one, MUV indicates a site's ability to attract visitors that can theoretically be "monetized" at some time in the future. While getting those visitors to "stick" and return and buy goods and services is a huge challenge, it is a challenge that is arguably more addressable than that of getting eyeballs in the first place.

In addition, MUV applies across both content and e-commerce sites. Also, MUV is relatively easily obtainable relative to revenues and other financial metrics that buyers and sellers often are unwilling to release.

For example, the Terra Networks purchase of Lycos went at the relatively steep MUV multiple of $380, or $2.80 per monthly page view. At the other end of the scale, smaller content deals like Pop-Mail.com's acquisition of low-end consumer fan clubs site Fan Asylum, Inc. went for $22.50 per MUV, or $2.50 per monthly page view.

In the college student content arena, Student Advantage's bid for Scholaraid.com equaled $14 per MUV and about $2.75 per monthly page view, and its purchase of College411.com came in at about a dollar per monthly page view and what we estimate to be about $6 per MUV.

Altrec.com's acquisition of the Greatoutdoors.com outdoor sports content site was priced at about $5.75 per monthly page view and TMP Interactive's acquisition of relocation content provider Virtual-Relocation.com was about $6 per monthly page view.

Palm, Inc.'s acquisition of e-calendar services provider AnyDay.com illustrates the typical premium paid for content-like applications (we call these companies "aptent" companies) that can be leveraged over a wide user base.

Although that deal went for $264 per MUV, or $47 per registered visitor, clearly the premium had more to do with the future potential of that application than with its current user base. Netzero, Inc. paid almost $23 million, or about $650,000 per employee, for development-stage advanced search engine Simpli.com, Inc.

RATIO VALUATION

The buyer and dotcom must derive a value of the dotcom that has a rational basis, which is at times difficult to achieve because of the emotional factor. Both the buyer and the dotcom have a value in mind when considering an acquisition. However, they need to substantiate the value.

A common approach to valuing a dotcom is to apply financial ratios to the dotcom's operations. Financial ratios define standard relationships that enable the buyer, dotcom, and financiers to objectively compare the dotcom with similar corporations. For example, debt to equity ratio is a common indicator of the cushion the owner provides creditors if the dotcom is liquidated. Let's say that total liabilities of the dotcom are $100 million and total equity is $50 million. The debt to equity ratio is calculated by dividing the total liabilities by the total stockholders' equity ($100 million/$50 million). The result is a ratio of 2:1. That is, there is one dollar in equity for every two dollars in liabilities.

We don't know if a debt to equity ratio of 2:1 is good or bad. A ratio by itself is meaningless unless compared with the same ratio of a similar corporation. In some industries, a debt to equity ratio of 2:1 is looked upon as favorable, while it might be a sign of trouble in a different industry.

Financial advisors will inform the buyer and dotcom as to which ratios are important to the acquisition of the dotcom. They will also calculate the ratios and provide a comparison with similar corporations. The results will give an indication of how well or how poorly the dotcom is performing compared with comparable corporations.

Ratios of similar corporations supplied by financial advisors may be estimates, because detailed financial and operating figures might not be available to the public. This is especially true in industries that contain many private corporations.

Ratios are used to assess the strengths and weaknesses of a dotcom before the buyer negotiates the deal. At times, ratios can indicate hidden value in the dotcom, such as is the case with the inventory turnover ratio for an e-tailer.

The inventory turnover ratio tells the buyer the number of times the e-tailer replenishes inventory in one year. An e-tailer should profit from each item sold from inventory. Therefore, a dotcom might have a higher prospect for increased profitability if the buyer can increase the inventory turnover ratio of the dotcom following the acquisition.

In this example, a low inventory turnover ratio, when compared with other corporations in the industry, may at first indicate that the dotcom is an unlikely prospect for an acquisition. However, this weakness is fixable by a clever buyer who can ultimately turn around the dotcom.

Ratios are also used to establish a price for a dotcom. A key value of any dotcom is the earnings that are generated from operations. Some buyers feel that cash flow generated by earnings is what the buyer is really acquiring, and they use the earnings ratio as a gauge. The earnings ratio is earnings for one year.

Therefore, earnings can become the basis to set the price of the deal by stating the price as a multiplier of earnings, such as two times. In essence, the buyer is saying to the dotcom, I will give you next year's earnings today if you sell me your company. The buyer and dotcom then focus negotiations on determining the multiplier.

Sophisticated buyers fine-tune the earnings ratio and calculate the free cash flow ratio. Free cash flow is earnings from business operations that exclude deductions for depreciation, interest, and taxes and include deductions for capital expenditures. This is the amount of cash that can be freely used by the buyer after the acquisition. The price paid for the dotcom becomes a multiplier of free cash flow.

The advantage of using ratio analysis for valuation and pricing is that buyers, dotcoms, and financiers find it practical to apply ratios on anticipated sales to forecast earnings, free cash flows, and other financial indicators.

A major disadvantage of using ratios is that the underlying assumption that what has happened in the past will happen in the future is flawed. Economic turns and the growth cycle of a corporation rarely are reflected in ratio analysis. This is especially true in dotcom corporations that are pioneers in an industry that does not have a history. Furthermore, many have low earnings compared with debt. The market value of some public dotcom corporations is many times higher than revenue produced from operations.

This means the public is willing to pay $10 for a company that has earnings of $1, in some cases. On the surface, paying $10 for $1 is nonsensical. However, investors are really paying for the prospect of future earnings that may or may not be realized.

Without a history that provides reliable patterns of activity, ratio analysis may not be the best tool to use to evaluate an Internet company or to establish value or a price for the dotcom. There is simply insufficient stable information from which to infer a conclusion based on the application of standard ratios.

RISK ASSESSMENT

The buyer of a dotcom is willing to pay a purchase price that is higher than the current earnings of the dotcom. This means that the buyer is anticipating that earnings will at least continue at the current level or will increase. There is no guarantee that either will occur, because no one can predict the future with any degree of accuracy. Therefore, the buyer, in paying a price higher than current earnings, is taking a risk that the dotcom will not meet the buyer's expectations. The dotcom too is taking a risk that future earnings will be substantially higher than current earnings. This means that the dotcom sold the business at a low price when compared with future higher earnings.

Both the buyer and the dotcom must evaluate the risk that is associated with the acquisition in an effort to factor the risk into the valuation of the dotcom and ultimately into the price paid by the buyer. Risk is defined in degrees, as some investments are more of a risk than other investments. The acquisition of the dotcom might be a total loss should the dotcom cease operations without returning any earnings to the buyer. The question the buyer must answer is, Can the buyer withstand a total loss of the investment made in acquiring the dotcom in case the dotcom fails?

The due diligence process should identify risky issues of the deal, many of which can be remedied through warranties by the dotcom prior to closing or through adjustments made to the acquisition price. However, there are inherent risk factors, such as economic downturns, technological obsolescence, and termination of key staff, that are not easily remedied.

A number of buyers assess the risks of a public dotcom by using the dotcom's beta to determine how the public reacts to the dotcom's stock. The dotcom's beta is a value between zero and one that indicates whether the dotcom's stock price moves in tandem with the Standard & Poor's 500 stock index. The value of Standard & Poor's 500 represents more than 75 percent of all publicly traded stocks. A beta value of one means both the Standard & Poor's 500 and the dotcom's stock price movements are synchronized. This means the dotcom is no more and no less risky than the corporations that comprise the Standard & Poor's 500. The further the beta value is from one, the more risky the dotcom is considered to be.

While the beta seems to be a convenient tool to use to assess risk, there are disadvantages to using the beta. Betas are available for publicly traded corporations and are not available for private corporations. Therefore, betas cannot be used to assess the risk when a private corporation is being acquired. Furthermore, a beta is an indicator of stock movement that may or may not have anything to do with the operations of the dotcom. For example, the dotcom's price could rapidly decline based on speculative trades. This could cause the beta to fall out of sync with the Standard & Poor's 500, even though the dotcom isn't any riskier than the Standard & Poor's 500. Therefore, the buyer should consider the dotcom's beta as a component of assessing risk, but not as the only assessment tool. The buyer must also rely on due diligence and an overall comfort factor to determine if the acquisition price is representative of the risk exposure.

PRICING MODELS

Once a value has been placed on a dotcom, the buyer and the dotcom must determine a price that the buyer is willing to pay to acquire the dotcom. The price reflects the buyer's perceived value of the dotcom, the risk that the buyer is taking, and the ability of the buyer to negotiate a good deal. The price also reflects the dotcom's own perceived value, risk undertaken by the dotcom, and the dotcom's negotiating skills.

Although a dotcom may think it is a unique entity, buyers tend to view a dotcom using the commodity pricing theory. The underlying premise of the commodity pricing theory is that all corporations are fundamentally the same. That is, a corporation is an economic unit that exposes an investment to risk while seeking to produce a cash flow stream.

A buyer, according to the commodity pricing theory, can realize a satisfactory cash flow from any corporation as long as the investment (price) in the dotcom generates an expected cash flow level within the risk tolerance of the buyer.

With this understanding, the buyer is expected to seek out dotcoms that meet a buyer's cash flow requirements, then apply one of the common pricing models to set a price for the dotcom. There are five pricing models used to acquire a dotcom:

- payback pricing model
- market value pricing model
- replacement value pricing model
- discounted cash flow pricing model
- average rate of return model

The Payback Pricing Model

The payback pricing model requires that the price paid for the dotcom be recovered by the dotcom's operations following the acquisition within a specified timeframe. For example, the buyer might be attracted to opportunities where the acquisition price of a dotcom is paid back within three years of consummating the deal. Through a valuation analysis, the buyer is able to project the total free cash flow that will likely be generated by the dotcom in the three years following closing. This forecast then becomes the foundation for setting the price. That is, the price cannot be more than three years' total free cash flow generated by the dotcom.

The three-year timeframe used in this example is an arbitrary period of time. Typically, a buyer has a philosophy about when a deal should pay back the investment, which then becomes a variable in the payback pricing model.

Many buyers find that this method is the easiest to understand and apply, although the payback pricing model does not reflect the time value of money, because there isn't any reference to the rate of return on the investment.

The Market Value Pricing Model

The market value pricing model is a common technique used to set the price of a publicly traded dotcom. The underlying philosophy is that the marketplace has all the information to properly evaluate and establish a price for the dotcom.

The initial step is for the buyer to identify publicly traded corporations that are similar to the dotcom. Next, the buyer notes the price earnings ratios for these companies. The price earnings ratio is the price of the stock divided by the corporation's earnings per share. This gives the buyer an idea of how much the market is paying for a corporation's earning power. The group of comparable corporations provides the buyer with a range of price earnings ratios that can be applied to the dotcom. The actual price is of course negotiable, but the range establishes a framework within which to hold the negotiations.

Although buyers use the market value pricing model to establish an acquisition price, the model does have its dissenters. Some point to the realization that the market tends at times to become emotional and pay a premium price for an issue. This optimism is reflected in the price earnings ratio, which artificially inflates the price.

Another concern when using the market value pricing model is that the model requires that the buyer identify comparable corporations. Unfortunately, this isn't an easy task because no two corporations are exactly the same. This requires the buyer to restate financial statements to make comparisons, which by its nature exposes the buyer to errors.

The Replacement Value Pricing Model

The replacement value pricing model requires the buyer to determine the cost of recreating the dotcom. The buyer is required to fully understand all the facets of the dotcom; otherwise, the buyer will not have sufficient information with which to develop a replacement cost.

The result of the replacement study is used to justify the acquisition of the dotcom, because traditionally buyers find that building a corporation is more costly than acquiring an existing corporation. Furthermore, the replacement cost can be used as a price ceiling for negotiations with the dotcom. Generally, the closer the dotcom pushes the price to the replacement ceiling, the more the buyer will consider starting its own business—and give the dotcom competition.

The major disadvantage of the replacement value pricing model is the time and expertise required to complete the replacement study. The buyer must reconstruct every aspect of the dotcom, using current technology and prices.

Discounted Cash Flow Pricing Model

The discounted cash flow pricing model is used to determine the net present value of future earnings that are forecasted for the dotcom. Both the buyer and the dotcom can independently project earnings for the dotcom for an agreed-upon period, such as three to five years.

The buyer and dotcom can negotiate the discount rate, also known as the *hurdle rate,* that is used to determine the net present value of future earnings. The discount rate is typically the incremental cost of capital realized by the buyer. This rate also reflects the risk factor that the buyer or the dotcom will experience in the deal.

Another point for negotiation is the forecast period. Generally, the longer the forecast, the higher the likelihood of error. Therefore, the buyer is likely to want to use a shorter forecast period than the dotcom.

The net present value of future earnings becomes the basis from which the buyer decides whether or not to pay the dotcom a premium over the net present value to acquire the dotcom.

Average Rate of Return Model

The average rate of return model bases the price of an acquisition on the expected rate of return on the investment. Analysis of the dotcom's operations by the buyer generates a profit projection for each year in the forecast period. The price paid by the buyer for the dotcom is the investment that is applied to the profit to derive the rate of return for each year in the forecast period. The rate is then compared to the buyer's desired return and the returns offered by other opportunities.

Assuming the buyer and dotcom can agree on profit forecast, price negotiations are focused on the average rate of return. Returns offered by similar risky opportunities become the price floor. That is, the buyer is unlikely to agree to a price that returns a rate less than alternative opportunities.

Tech Talk

Price Floor: The lowest price a buyer will pay for a dotcom.
Price Ceiling: The highest price a buyer will pay for a dotcom.

The price floor is also influenced by the buyer's desired rate of return. Let's say that alternative investment opportunities to acquiring the dotcom have an average rate of return of 8 percent. However, the buyer has a desired rate of return of 10 percent. Therefore, the price floor for acquiring the dotcom is likely to be raised to a price that returns the buyer an average rate of return of 10 percent.

The price ceiling is determined by the dotcom's expected average rate of return on funds already invested in the corporation. The buyer should estimate the net investment made by the dotcom and the term of the investment to project the dotcom's average rate of return based on a price for the acquisition.

Projected rates of return for the buyer and dotcom become the framework within which both parties negotiate a price. Typically, the lower the price is, the higher the rate of return is for the buyer and the lower the rate of return is for the dotcom.

SPECIFYING PRICE IN THE AGREEMENT

An agreed-upon price for a dotcom is based upon conditions that exist at the time of the agreement or conditions that are expected to exist some time in the future. For example, the buyer might agree to acquire the dotcom as long as liens against assets are removed by the time the deal is closed. If conditions are not met, then the buyer has the option of abandoning the deal.

The buyer typically expects that the dotcom's operation remain intact during the period between when the price is set and when the acquisition is consummated at closing. Changes in the dotcom's operation that can lead to a material loss in revenue or profit could occur during this period. Therefore, the buyer and the dotcom must carefully word the price and conditions in the acquisition agreement; otherwise, the dotcom might lose value, resulting in the buyer overpaying for the dotcom.

The agreement should contain verifiable benchmarks that clearly delineate when the buyer or the dotcom has the option to back out of the deal should the dotcom's operations fall below the benchmarks. Benchmarks are specific cash flows, revenues, earnings, profit, the number of customers, the number of employees, and other critical factors that influence the continuing operation of the dotcom.

In addition to listing the expectations of the buyer and seller, the acquisition agreement should contain any formulas that are used to determine the price of either the entire acquisition or key components of the acquisition. Let's say part of the purchase price includes compensation for each unique visitor to the dotcom's operation—for example, $100 per unique visitor. The buyer, in conjunction with the dotcom, analyzes the previous year's log files and determines that the dotcom has 30,000 unique visitors for the previous 12 months. The buyer agrees to pay $3 million, which is included in the price of the acquisition.

However, six months pass between the agreement and closing, during which time the number of unique visitors to the dotcom's Web site could drop or increase significantly. By specifically including the price of $3 million in the contract, both the buyer and the dotcom are exposed to risk. The buyer could be paying $3 million and receive less than 30,000 unique visitors. The dotcom could be delivering 40,000 unique visitors and getting paid for 30,000.

Specifying the pricing formula rather than a fixed price in the acquisition agreement can dramatically reduce risk. In this case, the formula states that the buyer will pay $100 per unique visitor based on the last 12-month period prior to closing, using a specified method to analyze the dotcom's log files.

The agreement becomes less sensitized to an extended period between the agreement and the closing of the deal. Days before the closing, the buyer and/or the dotcom analyze the log files according to agreed-upon methods, then apply the formula to the results to arrive at this component of the acquisition price.

A similar approach can be taken using other pricing models. Let's say that the buyer is willing to pay the dotcom two times the previous 12 months' earnings. Instead of fixing the price at the time of the agreement, the pricing formula is agreed upon. The buyer's and dotcom's auditors can agree on the earnings figure shortly before closing the deal, at which time the price is set by using the formula that is contained in the agreement. In some situations, a price floor might be established at the time of the agreement, below which the price cannot fall when the formula is applied. This reduces the downside risk for the dotcom. A price ceiling can also be used in the agreement above which the price cannot exceed. This protects the buyer.

While formulas built into an acquisition agreement give the buyer and dotcom protection against material fluctuations in the dotcom's operating results prior to closing the deal, formulas also open new areas of disagreement between the buyer and dotcom. For example, there can be honest disagreement over the dotcom's earnings should earnings be a component of the pricing formula, which can delay the closing of the deal. The parties might not be able to avoid disagreements, but they should include in the acquisition agreement a procedure that will resolve disagreements.

Typically, a third party who is a recognizable expert in the field will be called to render a binding decision. The party who loses the disagreement pays the cost of the expert. Let's say that the dotcom disagrees with the earnings fixed by the buyer. The expert derives his or her own earnings figures. If the expert's figures are materially different than those of the buyer (e.g., plus or minus 10 percent), then the dotcom wins and the buyer must pay the expert. Conversely, if the expert's earnings are not materially different than the buyer, then the dotcom loses and must pay the expert's fee.

Price floors and ceilings can be applied in at least two ways. First, they can be used to establish a base and top price, which will be paid at closing. The other application of these benchmarks is to use them as triggers. That is, when the floor or ceiling is reached, the parties are no longer obligated to consummate the deal. Let's say that when the price formula is applied, the price falls below the price floor. This might trigger a clause in the agreement that gives the dotcom the option to walk away from the deal, renegotiate pricing terms, or accept the lower price. Similar options are available to the buyer if the formula raises the price above the price ceiling.

Buyers can also protect themselves from a dramatic change in the dotcom's performance immediately following the closing by incorporating an earned-out clause in the acquisition agreement. The earned-out clause specifies that the seller will receive a portion of compensation at the time of closing and the other portion sometime in the near future following the closing once certain benchmarks are reached. For example, the buyer really doesn't know the accuracy of the dotcom's operating information until after the buyer acquires the dotcom. This is typically after the dotcom has been compensated. Therefore, the buyer's only recourse should the operating results materially differ from representations made by the dotcom is to take legal action.

However, the buyer can reduce this risk by withholding a portion of the dotcom's compensation for a short period (e.g., six months) following the closing. As operating results are realized firsthand by the buyer, the buyer can release further payments to the dotcom based on a prescribed schedule contained in the acquisition agreement. As each benchmark, such as monthly earnings figures, is reached, the dotcom will have earned a portion of the withheld price.

SUMMARY

The price is based on real and perceived value of the dotcom, although perceived value may or may not have any foundation in fact. Both the buyer and the dotcom should perform a formal valuation analysis of the dotcom to ascertain the its real value. Valuation analysis provides an objective foundation from which a fair market price can be established for the dotcom.

The valuation process is a multidisciplined investigation conducted by the valuation team into the dotcom's operation and determines how well the dotcom blends into the buyer's plans. Accountants, financial experts, industry analysts, and others with the appropriate special skills form the valuation team. Through their knowledge of their specialties and of the industry, and with the use of analytical tools and some common sense, the valuation team collectively arrives at a real value of the dotcom.

A preferred approach to valuating a dotcom is for both the buyer and the dotcom to assemble independent valuation teams, each coordinated by a professional appraiser. One team reports to the buyer and the other to the dotcom.

The buyer and dotcom should examine each other's valuation methodology to identify any material differences between the two. Adjustments can be agreed upon to bring the valuations in line with each other. The valuation of a dotcom becomes the foundation for establishing a price for the dotcom.

Buyers fall into two categories. These are a financial buyer and a strategic buyer. A financial buyer sees a dotcom as a stream of cash that can be acquired through carefully orchestrated debt. In contrast, a strategic buyer seeks to use the dotcom to enhance the corporation's current organization through synergy of the existing corporation and the dotcom.

Both the financial buyer and the strategic buyer have a time horizon for when they want to realize the full benefits of the deal. The time horizon for the financial buyer specifies when debt is retired and the cash stream is available for other objectives. The strategic buyer's time horizon specifies when the dotcom's operation is fully blended with that of the buyer's operation.

The amount of cash flow produced by the dotcom is a critical component in the valuation of the dotcom. A large cash flow makes the dotcom more valuable than a comparable dotcom with a low cash flow. Furthermore, once a dotcom's cash flow potential is identified, the buyer can use this information to formulate a financing plan that diverts cash flow to debt services.

The process of forecasting cash flow begins with a thorough understanding of the dotcom's operations and of the marketplace for the dotcom's products and services. An analysis is conducted to assess the demand in the market for each product and service that generates a cash flow for the dotcom.

A common approach to valuing a dotcom is to apply financial ratios to the dotcom's operation. Financial ratios define standard relationships that enable the buyer, dotcom, and financiers to objectively compare the dotcom with similar corporations. Financial advisors will inform the buyer and dotcom which ratios are important to the acquisition of the dotcom. They will also calculate the ratios and provide a comparison with similar corporations. The results will give an indication of how well or how poorly the dotcom is performing with regard to comparable corporations.

Both the buyer and the dotcom must evaluate the risk that is associated with the acquisition in an effort to factor the risk into the valuation of the dotcom and ultimately into the price paid by the buyer. The due diligence process should identify risky issues of the deal, many of which can be remedied through warranties by the dotcom prior to closing or through adjustments made to the acquisition price.

The price of an acquisition reflects the buyer's perceived value of the dotcom, the risk that the buyer is taking, and the ability for the buyer to negotiate a good deal. The price also reflects the dotcom's own perceived value, risk undertaken by the dotcom, and the dotcom's negotiating skills.

The five pricing models used to acquire a dotcom are the payback pricing model, market value pricing model, replacement value pricing model, discounted cash flow pricing model, and average rate of return model.

The buyer and the dotcom must carefully word the price and conditions in the acquisition agreement; otherwise, the dotcom might lose value, resulting in the buyer overpaying for the dotcom. The agreement should contain verifiable benchmarks that clearly delineate when the buyer or the dotcom has the option to back out of the deal should the dotcom's operations fall below the benchmarks.

The acquisition agreement should contain any formulas that are used to determine the price of either the entire acquisition or key components of the acquisition. Formulas built into an acquisition agreement give the buyer and the dotcom protection against material fluctuations in the dotcom's operating results prior to closing the deal.

QUESTIONS

1. How is a valuation analysis conducted?

2. What is the relationship between price and value of a dotcom?

3. What role does a beta value have in pricing a dotcom?

4. What is the disadvantage of using the replacement value pricing model?

5. Why should pricing formulas be included in the deal agreement?

6. What risks can occur between signing the deal agreement and closing the deal?

7. What are the disadvantages of using financial ratios to value a dotcom?

8. What is the objective of a financial buyer?

9. How would you structure a dotcom to make the business attractive to a strategic buyer?

10. What role does the product life cycle of a dotcom's product have in setting an acquisition price for the dotcom?

CHAPTER 9

Negotiating the Deal

The art of persuasion is the key to successful negotiations.

—Anonymous

In This Chapter

- Setting the Stage for Negotiations
- The Negotiations Strategy
- Face-to-Face Negotiations
- The Letter of Intent
- The Acquisition Agreement
- Representations, Warranties, and Covenants
- Terms of Closing
- Termination Procedures
- Indemnity
- Public Companies

SETTING THE STAGE FOR NEGOTIATIONS

Negotiations is a game of strategy in which the buyer and dotcom assume adversarial positions in an effort to get the best deal possible. The prize for the buyer is the dotcom, and for the dotcom it is compensation. Some see negotiations as a war where each side tries to outwit the other by presenting favorable arguments based on interpretation of facts in an effort to persuade the opponent to give up dollars.

By nature, negotiations meetings are confrontational. Although both sides have agreed in principle that the dotcom will be acquired, battles are fought over warranties, covenants, representations, and price. Warranties, covenants, and representations are facts about the dotcom for which the dotcom will be held accountable should those facts be wrong. These are explored in detail later in the chapter.

The party who wins the most battles tends to win the war and receive the prize. However, long before confrontation begins, the buyer and dotcom gather intelligence information that enables winning strategies to be developed and implemented. The more intelligence gathered before negotiations begins, the better the party will be able to engage in face-to-face combat.

Self-Evaluation

The initial step is for each party to learn its own strengths and weaknesses by employing a team of consultants to perform a critical, objective, no-holds-barred evaluation of the party's operation. The objective is for the consultants to uncover information about the party that is likely to be uncovered by the opponent.

The evaluation begins with a thorough review of business operations and financials. This information is assessed for accuracy, competitiveness, and profitability. In essence, consultants ask

- Do the financials represent an accurate picture of the business?
- How do the corporation and its components compare to competitors?
- What components are profitable and not profitable?
- What investment is necessary to make components competitive and profitable?

Answers to these and similar questions reveal the strengths and weaknesses of the party's operation. The opposition will also be asking the same questions in an effort to find weaknesses that can be used as leverage in negotiations.

Each party's operation has weaknesses. Learning about them well in advance of negotiations gives the party time to rectify problems or devise counterarguments that lessen the importance of the weakness to the deal.

Next, the party must assess the value of itself. The valuation process is discussed in Chapter 8, "Pricing the Deal." The result determines the value of the party, which becomes the basis for establishing an acquisition price in the case of the dotcom and the basis for financing for the buyer. It is critical that the party conduct an objective self-valuation, because the opposing party will be conducting a similar study on the party. A self-valuation should produce results similar to the results of the opposition's valuation. This allows the party time to evaluate the results and develop a strategy for using the valuation to bolster its position in negotiations.

Based on the self-valuation, the dotcom should develop three prices: initial price, desired price, and minimum price. The initial price is sometimes considered a throwaway price because realistically the buyer will rarely agree to the price. Therefore, the initial price can be unreasonably high. The desired price is an amount that would make the dotcom feel that the deal is fair. The minimum price is an amount below which the dotcom refuses to continue negotiations. Establishing prices before negotiations begin gives the dotcom time to develop arguments to support each price level.

The buyer uses the self-valuation process to determine the buyer's ability to leverage current operations to finance the deal. Self-valuation identifies free cash flows from current operations that might be available to self-finance the deal without the need to use third-party lenders. Similarly, the self-valuation reveals the financial strength of the buyer that can be leveraged to acquire the dotcom.

From Tim Miller, Webmergers.com

Customer Base Highly Valued Asset

VeriSign, Inc., one of the Web's largest security services providers, made history when it bought domain name registrar Network Solutions, Inc. for $21 billion. It was one of the largest acquisitions of (but not by) a Web company. VeriSign is hoping to marry its secure e-commerce services with NSI's customer base of some eight million registered domains. Clearly one of the prizes VeriSign was after was Network Solutions' customer base, which is widely quoted at 8 million.

However, that number reflects only the number of registered domains. Using a very conservative estimate that 80 percent of domains are owned by unique customers leaves us with 6.4 million customers and a per-customer valuation of nearly $3,300.

Let's think more about the value of those customers. NSI reports that a whopping 35 percent of its customers, many of them domain name speculators, fail to pay for their domains (we assume these are not counted in the 8 million). That fact somewhat calls into question the value of these customers, however many there are.

What have other Web acquirers paid for subscribing customers? A glimpse at other transactions from the Webmergers.com database provides a huge range in valuations when measured on a per-subscriber basis.

One basis of comparison would be public valuations of Internet Service Providers (ISPs), which have recently been trading at about $2,400 per subscriber, according to Internet.com. However, several recent sales of smaller ISPs have gone at only about $500 per subscriber, according to the same source.

Among the factors influencing per-subscriber values are of course (a) price points, (b) attrition rates, (c) ability to sell up to additional service, and (d) growth rates. In the latter category, one of the better bargains in history may well have been Microsoft's 1997 acquisition of a totally free service, Hotmail.

After purchasing Hotmail for about $33 a subscriber, Microsoft has leveraged the viral marketing power of that applet to snag another 35 million subscribers, making the per-subscriber cost, minus marketing costs, about nine dollars a head, a bargain by anyone's standards today.

The following table provides a sampling of other per-subscriber valuations from the Web M&A Report.

Examples of Per-Subscriber M&A Valuations

Date	Target	Valuation
12/08/97	Hotmail	$33/subscriber
11/10/98	AtWeb, Inc.	$160/subscriber [a]
12/01/98	Simple Network Communications. (ISP)	$1,380/Web hosting account
02/02/99	DICE (job listings)	$17,500/advertiser
03/23/99	MicroHouse (tech reference)	$1,059/subscriber [c]
06/01/99	Telebanc Financial Corp.	$30,000/retail banking account
06/30/99	Greenberg News Network	$30,000/subscriber [b]
11/16/99	NECX (B2B exchange)	$5,800/trading partner

[a] Portion of Web services subscribers unpaid
[b] Subscribers pay $400 to $1,200/yr for content services
[c] Includes 2,000 actual and 6,000 intended subscribers to $300/yr service

Evaluating the Opponent

Once the self-assessment is completed, the same process is used to evaluate the opponent. A team of consultants is employed to learn the strengths, weaknesses, and valuation of the other party before negotiations begin.

The evaluation should also include due diligence to substantiate all claims made by the other party. Due diligence is explored in Chapter 2, "Due Diligence." Consultants must carefully list those claims that are substantiated and those that remain unconfirmed. This list plays an important role in negotiations, because unsubstantiated claims can be used as weaknesses in the opponent's case and leveraged to receive a more favorable price. In essence, unsubstantiated claims when presented during negotiations place the opponent on the defensive.

After gathering the intelligence, consultants are asked to participate in a role-playing exercise in which they become the opponent in a simulation of negotiations. It is important that consultants seriously take on their role and be as tough as possible in negotiations, because this is the only way the party can feel the heat of the battle before entering the real confrontation.

There are two critical questions that each party must answer: Why does the dotcom want to sell? Why does the buyer want to buy? Each party must answer both questions because the answers become a component in negotiations.

For example, a dotcom may want to cash out. Knowing this, the buyer may avoid offering top dollar for the business because the dotcom is likely to be looking for a quick sale. Many dotcom corporations started the business from the concept stage and built it to a sustainable operation in which the business is on the verge of turning a profit. A sharp economic downturn could result in a substantial loss in value for the dotcom. Therefore, a reasonable price satisfies the dotcom investors.

The dotcom might discover that the buyer's operation is in need of a quick fix to pick up flat sales. The fastest way to achieve this objective is to acquire the dotcom. Therefore, the dotcom is likely to hold out for top dollar especially if the dotcom's operations shows increasing and sustainable sales. In essence, the buyer needs the dotcom more than the dotcom needs the buyer.

Practical Side to Negotiations

Preliminary intelligence-gathering gives way to the practical aspects of negotiations, such as where and when to meet and who is going to attend the meetings. Although these seem to be routine issues, they play a strategic role in the negotiations process.

A neutral site, such as a hotel located a distance away from each party's facilities, should be selected to hold negotiations meetings. At least three meeting rooms should be available. Each party's negotiating team has its own meeting room, and the third room is set aside for face-to-face meetings. Typically, each team caucuses in its own room while negotiators informally meet to exchange positions.

During this time, team members tend to become restless and begin walking the hallways, and could bump into an opposing team member. This could lead to undesired conversations about the negotiations. Team members must remember that negotiations are a combative arena and both sides in the battle must follow the battle plan. A rogue conversation, regardless of how innocently it develops, could open an unplanned front in the battle. Placing rooms on separate floors precludes inadvertent discussions from occurring.

A representative from each party should review and approve the accommodations. Each party pays for its own room and shares the cost of the third meeting room. Generally, the accommodations should not be too comfortable; otherwise, negotiating teams won't be encouraged to complete the deal. A simple table and chairs are sufficient.

Negotiations meetings should be held shortly after both parties have completed their self-evaluation, opponent evaluation, and due diligence. Meeting before strengths and weaknesses are known only lengthens the negotiations process and can place a party at a disadvantage.

Let's say that the buyer has completed the evaluation process, but the dotcom still lags behind. The dotcom is at a disadvantage going into negotiations, because the buyer has more information than the dotcom about factors influencing the deal. Although both parties are anxious to complete negotiations, neither should go into battle until they are fully prepared; otherwise, they could easily fall prey to a better-prepared opponent.

Both parties should prepare to have their negotiations teams attend meetings. However, neither negotiating team should have authority to finalize the deal. That is, the decision-maker should not attend negotiating meetings.

Here's how this works. The decision-maker, which could consist of the board of directors or a subcommittee of the board, approves the party's position and the strategy that is to be implemented by the negotiating team. The negotiating team is authorized to agree in principle to the terms authorized by the decision-maker. However, the opposition is unlikely to agree to all these terms. Therefore, the negotiating team is typically not in a position to reach an agreement in principle. Instead, the team negotiates terms, then makes recommendations to the decision-maker. Both sides are aware of this arrangement, so it doesn't come as a surprise when the negotiating team says, I'll take this back to my board of directors.

In essence, this strategy gives the party time to digest and evaluate terms posed by the opponent. This evaluation period doesn't exist if the decision-maker attends negotiations, because the opposition expects the negotiating team to speak with the decision-maker and come back with a decision within a few hours.

In reality, decision-makers should be on standby and available by telephone during negotiations meetings. The negotiating team can call the decision-maker for authorization to agree in principle to terms should a good deal be placed on the table by the opposition, making further evaluation unnecessary.

From Tim Miller, Webmergers.com

The Earnout Strategy

Most sellers of dotcoms would gladly accept a bird in the hand, but all too often in this down market they feel they're being offered a drumstick. To bridge the often-large valuation gap between themselves and their buyers, some sellers are using earnout deals to claw back value that might otherwise be left on the table. Such deals take a "bird-in-the-bush" approach, providing future stock or cash payments to the seller if management meets certain revenue or other performance benchmarks.

Buyers have often used earnouts to reduce their risks and to spur sellers to maintain their performance. Earnouts were popular in the early 1980s, "primarily as a pricing bridge between the disparate valuations of small companies and large buyers," says David J. Cummings, managing partner of Agile Equity, LLC, a New York-based technology investment bank. The practice later fell out of favor, but has recently revived to cope with current valuation gaps and the spate of startups whose success depends on retaining key personnel, according to Cummings.

In addition, the near-certain demise of the so-called "pooling of interest" accounting practice, whose rules restricted contingency payments such as earnouts, will open the door to an array of increasingly creative earnouts and other deals. This is predicted by Michael S. Dorf, a partner in the San Francisco technology M&A practice of Wilson Sonsini Goodrich & Rosati. "With pooling going away, I think you're going to see a lot more flexibility from buyers on what you can do [in a deal structure]." The Financial Accounting Standards Board (FASB), the accounting standards-setting agency, is planning to repeal the popular practice by the end of this June.

At Webmergers we frequently encounter sellers whose valuation expectations vary widely from those of buyers. There are several causes for the valuation gap. For one, many sellers still have circa-1999 valuation expectations fixed in their heads like ghost images that remain in the eyeball after a flashbulb pop. But in other cases, company principals and founders truly believe they're on the cusp of a revenue breakout—and are willing to prove it to the buyer. In still other cases, a seller has partially developed a technology or application and has little other recourse than to take payment upon successful completion.

There's something Apple Pie, all-American, purely capitalistic, and downright Christian, darn it, about the idea of an earnout agreement. It's a meritocratic reward for people who perform. It's an honesty filter that forces sellers to put their money where their mouths are. An earnout discourages sellers from getting slothful after they've banked their acquisition bounties. And finally, an earnout can create a sense of upside energy and excitement for both buyer and seller.

In practice, however, earnouts can be ineffective and even detrimental if they're not structured correctly, according to experts. The following text addresses some of the issues involving earnouts.

Let's take a look at two earnouts. In one deal, cash-strapped College-Club.com, Inc. sold its college student portal to StudentAdvantage, Inc. (Nasdaq: STAD), taking about $6.6 million in cash and about $10.3 million in stock, with an additional potential earnout of $5 million in cash upon meeting performance thresholds. In this case, the buyer insisted on the earnout as part of compensation, not necessarily as upside.

NetSales, Inc. of Overland Park, KS, in order to focus its energies on a separate business, sold its software download unit to rival Digital River, Inc. for about $8 million in stock. The deal included an additional 25 percent earnout requested by the buyer to ensure that NetSales would successfully transition the software download deals (and associated revenue) that it had with more than 1,000 software publishers.

The deal left NetSales' chairman and founder Robert Fraser with a good feeling about earnouts. In his case, the earnout ensured an aggressive and smooth transfer of NetSales' partnerships to Digital River. Fraser plowed a bonus and a portion of the earnout back to employees, based on the revenue objective. He told us that employees, even those who knew they were to be laid off after the deal was complete, "worked their tails off" for bonuses that in some cases approached the six-figure mark.

At CollegeClub, while he is unable to comment on the performance of his current contingency agreement, the company's senior vice president of corporate development, Monte Brem, is a self-confessed earnouts bear. "In general, I recommend that entrepreneurs just avoid [earnouts]," said Brem, who is an attorney and former investment banker. "Earnouts restrict some of the nimbleness of the seller's business."

Cummings and other experts point to several kinds of businesses that are best suited to consider an earnout deal. Dotcoms and tech companies in many cases fit these descriptions.

- Development-Stage Companies: Smaller, early stage companies that have only a product prototype or minimal sales history may benefit from an earnout, says Cummings. If such companies anticipate that a buyer may bring explosive growth, an earnout may be the best measure of their value. Many tech sellers, especially those that have run into a funding brick wall just short of completing a product, fit into this category.

- The Product Line Is Discrete: When an acquirer is buying a separate product line, as in the case of CollegeClub and NetSales, revenues and earnouts are simpler to track and are less subject to manipulation, and thus lend themselves better to an earnout. Many content sites and other dotcoms that retain a separate identity after a merger fit the bill. Internet.com, for example, offers earnouts to most of the 70-plus Internet properties that it has acquired and tightly integrated into its network of technology content sites.

- Turnarounds: Again, if management feels it is on the cusp of a breakout, it may well opt to monetize its optimism in a contingent deal.
- Expensive Deals: Buyers may wish to use earnouts when purchasing targets that are in red-hot sectors that carry high valuation premiums. An earnout reduces the risk of over-paying by tagging the price to performance. However, competition for such properties may be so intense that the buyer does not need to accept the earnout.

Contingent arrangements like earnouts are subject to a variety of problems, many of them traceable to the flawed structure of the deal itself. "Ill-conceived or badly implemented earnouts," writes Cummings, can have the perverse effect of "demotivating management and actually reducing the seller's value to the buyer." It can also lead to litigation.

One core problem with earnouts is the difficulty of precisely measuring performance. "In a fast-moving economy with volatility in the markets, it's getting harder and harder for entrepreneurs who sell their business to properly monitor earnings," said Andrew Sherman, a capital partner with the Washington, DC office of law firm McDermott, Will & Emery. "With earnings down, they're often better off with a bird in the hand than with a bird in the bush."

CollegeClub's Brem agrees. "I don't really like earnouts," he said. "It's very difficult to align the interests of buyer and acquirers.…It's particularly a challenge in the Internet industry where things change so fast. It puts handcuffs on the business." For example, Brem said, a content company in the face of declining CPM rates might want to morph from selling advertising to syndicating content, a move that may involve a brief hiccup in revenue as the transition takes place. But with revenue-based earnout terms in place, he said "the sellers may continue to chase that original business model to the detriment of the company."

Our pick for the most creative earnout goes to the multibillion-dollar-capitalized public software company that purchased a smaller, struggling VC-backed software firm. The buyer made about 70 percent of that $50 million stock deal subject to a modified earnout, with 50 percent of the payment to be paid upon conversion of the software to a Linux platform and another 20 percent based on meeting performance goals.

Clearly, the definition of "conversion" was a key issue in such a deal. "We wanted a real loosey goosey definition of the functionality," said Brian Fraser, the Oakland, CA-based technology attorney who handled the deal, "but the buyer wanted it tied to a very specific definition." Since the seller was in a tight situation, it accepted the deal (in its final form the deal granted the seller the full price even if the conversion did not succeed, but forced the sellers to accrue it over an even-year vesting period).

THE NEGOTIATIONS STRATEGY

Negotiating any deal is a strategy game in which both parties position themselves to outwit their opponent. Before any bargaining begins, both sides must establish a game plan that clearly enunciates their three positions—initial, ideal, and minimum deal. The game plan must also outline how and when each of those positions will be made known to the other party.

Typically, parties spar for a few rounds before making their initial positions known. They may begin with fluff by saying how an acquisition is in the best interest of both organization and how pleased they are to begin serious talks about making the acquisition a reality.

The purpose of sparring is to avoid being the first party to place its initial position on the table, because there is a general rule that the person who states his or her position first is usually at a disadvantage.

At the beginning of negotiations, both sides have set a price range for the acquisition from the initial price, which is likely to be unrealistic, to the minimum price. However, neither party knows the other's price range. Therefore, the ranges can be dramatically different.

The dotcom, for example, might think a price range of $5 million to $10 million is suitable, especially since the dotcom is likely to want to cash out quickly. The buyer in contrast might feel the deal is workable in the $20 million to $25 million range.

The dotcom could lose between $10 million and $15 million if it makes its initial position of $10 million known to the buyer. Likewise, the buyer could lose the same amount if its initial position of $20 million is placed on the table first. Knowing that the initial position on the table establishes the price range for the deal, both sides avoid making their initial position known until the timing is right. Predictably, negotiations open with a stalemate. The buyer might ask, How much do you want for your company? The seller might respond, Make me an offer I can't refuse.

Gamesmanship then begins, and each side avoids answering the other's opening question. It is important to both parties that negotiations continue. For the moment, both parties postpone answering those questions and turn their attention to a more productive avenue.

Round One

Price negotiations are based upon facts that both sides uncovered during the prenegotiations evaluation process. Therefore, a good starting point for negotiations is for the parties to review and agree upon facts pertaining to the deal. Parties typically can agree on most facts, which gives the negotiations process positive momentum toward eventually negotiating the price.

The review should start with fundamental facts that are unlikely to be in dispute. Follow the paper trail, beginning with each party's incorporation documents, which authorize the corporations to exist. Continue with the articles of incorporation, which authorize the corporation to sell or buy the corporation. Chapter 2 contains a list of facts that should be included in this review.

Parties can discuss each fact as presented, then either agree to accept the information as fact or agree to disagree that the information is fact. It is critical that neither side spend too much time debating the accuracy of the information. The objective at this point in negotiations is to derive a list of facts agreed upon and a list that is in dispute.

Generally, both sides will agree to most facts. Only a small number of facts are typically disputed. Once the parties complete the review of all the facts, attention is focused on disputed facts. This is the point in negotiations where gamesmanship comes into play.

Round Two

Each side must determine for itself if each disputed fact is a deal-breaker. That is, if the other side does not agree to the fact, will you walk away from the deal? Very few disputes fall into the deal-breaker category.

Before making this determination, each side must consider the other party's rationale for its position on the issue. Each side must be given time to state its position, which is probed by the other side.

Good gamesmanship dictates that no determination be made on disputed issues at the bargaining table. Instead, the party that disagrees with a fact should simply state that the opponent's concerns will be considered. The negotiating team then caucuses outside the presence of the other party and freely discusses all of the disputed issues. It is at this time that the negotiating team assesses the importance of the disagreement to both sides. The team then needs to answer these questions:

- Is the dispute possibly a deal-breaker for the other party?
- Is the dispute a deal-breaker for the team?
- What, if anything, can the team receive from the opponent in return for conceding to the fact?

The last question assumes that the dispute is not a deal-breaker for the team. Rather than simply agreeing to the fact, the team should use the concession as a bargaining chip. The team can use the concession to offset a concession from the opponent on another disputed issue.

Gamesmanship requires that bargaining chips be held until the proper time when the team can leverage them to gain the most possible advantage during negotiations. For example, the dotcom may give the opponent concessions on an issue that the buyer considers important in exchange for a higher acquisition price. Therefore, the concession would not be revealed to the buyer until the acquisition price is on the table for negotiations.

A concession does not mean that the team agrees in full about an issue with an opponent. Instead, the team could offer alternatives that address the opponent's concerns without the team fully agreeing to the issue. Let's say that the buyer states that an analysis of the dotcom's log files shows that the dotcom's site receives 100,000 unique visitors each day on the average. The dotcom disagrees and states there is an average of 250,000 unique visitors.

The disagreement is material to the deal because the value of the dotcom is partly based on the number of unique visitors to its site. The dispute isn't in the deal-breaker category as yet, although the issue could break the deal if value negatively impacts the acquisition price.

However, the dotcom's negotiating team can avoid the issue by proposing that three auditors be employed to independently analyze the log file and come up with the average number of unique visitors to the Web site. The average of their results will become the factual number of average unique visitors to the site.

From Tim Miller, Webmergers.com

Liquidity Through M&A

The Internet has spawned an explosion of small properties unparalleled in the history of any distribution medium. Many of the members of this huge middle class face some interesting challenges if and when they seek liquidity through M&A. This series of analyses will explore the issues facing the Web's middle class.

The arrival of cable television awed us with the prospect of 500 channels. Now comes the Web, offering literally tens of thousands of properties thanks to its nearly infinite ability to support "narrow-casting." Low production, maintenance, and distribution costs have fostered development of Web destinations addressing any imaginable niche ranging from auto recycling to tole painting to Web mergers, for that matter. Many of these boutique properties are, or could be, financially viable while others are borderline or worse.

There's little good data about the number of middle-market Internet companies or Web sites. But let's work from the top down with what we do know.

- At the top of the heap, 600 venture-funded Internet startups went public or were acquired.
- About 3,000 to 5,000 Internet startups received venture capital.
- An additional 5,000 to 15,000 startups received angel, bank, corporate, or other financing in the period.
- Some 15,000 large Web destinations account for 80 percent of Internet traffic.
- An additional 3–4 million Web sites (not URLs, but discrete sites) account for the remaining 20 percent of the traffic. The "tail" is very long—for example, more than 70,000 North American Web sites rack up more than 100,000 page views a month.

- At the very base of the pyramid are domain names. More than 27 million domains have been registered worldwide to date, 17 million of them dotcom addresses, according to *www.domainstats.com.*

While it's not clear how many of these entities are viable "haute bourgeois" sites, clearly the upper ranks include tens of thousands of Web properties that have value to someone.

Not only is the Internet playing field well-populated, it is far from being closed. "What's interesting to me is the amount of turnover I see," said Matthew Work, vice president of Alexa Research, the data division of Alexa Internet, whose research provides a large sampling of middle-market traffic.

"In our monthly analysis of the top 2,500 sites we usually end up replacing 500 of them because others have taken their place," he said. "This is a volatile and dynamic market space where there's a lot of room for obscure sites to move up."

Thousands of small- to mid-sized Web sites that entered the marketplace are suddenly coming to a point in the journey where they're considering M&A as an option. They're driven by one of several things:

- The Fatigue Factor: What may have started out as a hobby has turned into a relentless hobgoblin that consumes increasing amounts of time and energy. Owners need a break, but revenues, if they exist at all, don't support hiring of additional resources.
- Need to Go to the Next Level: Owners see opportunity within their niche and want to move to the next stage in their evolution. They can't do it themselves, and finding funding or strategic partners becomes a necessity.
- Inefficient or Blockaded Funding Channels: Mid-sized Internet properties that do seek funding resources find that the current financing infrastructure isn't equipped to dole out the small tranches they need. And of course in the current dismal market, even venture-funded Internet startups are running into a very solid brick wall as they go out for second- or third-round financing.

Many players have little choice but to turn to M&A as an option. But it's tough for the little guys. Mid-market Internet properties face the same challenges in M&A that they have faced in funding—they're too small for the big leagues but too big for the peewees.

In the finance arena, smaller startups that needed WaterPik-like jets of capital came up against VCs that could only wield fire hoses. Similarly, mid-market startups that need some hands-on assistance are finding traditional intermediaries unable by dint of their overhead to handle smaller deals. The little guys are left between posting classified ads and hawking their own properties. Sometimes they end up accepting lowball offers as a result.

It's not that smaller dotcoms aren't finding buyers. More than half of the nearly 1,000 deals that Webmergers.com has tracked since 1998 were in the sub-$10 million dollar range, which is often the lower threshold of acceptance for larger M&A firms.

Round Three

Any issue that remains on the dispute list at the end of the second round of negotiations becomes a potential deal-breaker. Each side must decide whether or not its position on the issue is flexible, and that position must be communicated to the other party. The party must make it clear that the issue is a real impasse and not simply a strategy to extract concessions from the opposition. This feeling should be placed in writing to the other negotiating team, presented in a face-to-face meeting of the teams, and informally presented by the team's chief negotiator to the other team's chief negotiator. The communication should be followed up by action such as the negotiating team leaving the negotiating site.

Both parties must realized that some issues cannot be agreed to and will in fact become a deal-breaker. This simply means that the acquisition wasn't in the best interest of one or both parties. However, should there be no issues in dispute following round two of negotiations, then both parties return to the first issue, that is, setting a price for the acquisition. Chapter 8 discusses how to derive an acquisition price.

Each side begins to spar again, still trying to avoid being the first to place its position on the table, but this time both parties have invested much time and money to get to this point in negotiations. Momentum has already built to a point where they have agreed to everything except a price. Both negotiating teams want to complete the deal and are probably being pressured to do so by their boards of directors. Therefore, sparring is kept to a minimum, and one party reaches a frustration level that forces it to make the first move and place its initial acquisition price on the table. For example, the buyer might say, We think that your company is worth $20 million, half in cash and the other half in take-back debt.

The buyer in this case has set the price floor for the deal. The dotcom counters with a much higher price, such as $30 million, which becomes the price ceiling. Therefore, the actual acquisition price is some place between $20 million and $30 million.

Once the price range is established, hard negotiations begin by both sides. Each presents its rationale for its position on price. Next, they each attempt to show flaws in the rationale that, if remedied, will justify a change in price by the opposition.

Eventually a price is agreed upon, as long as each side makes reasonable adjustments to its position. Failure to do so ultimately becomes a deal-breaker.

FACE-TO-FACE NEGOTIATIONS

Regardless of how well either party prepares for negotiations, the success of a deal rests on the success of face-to-face negotiations. Both parties must sit down at the bargaining table and agree to terms that both parties feel are fair to each other.

A fair price is a perceived notion, since there isn't any broadly accepted formula that defines a fair price. Therefore, both parties go into face-to-face negotiations with an expectation of settling for a fair price. However, sometimes the expectation is not realistic. Therefore, either side has the responsibility to bring high expectations of the other party down to reality as soon as possible once negotiations begin.

Once an unrealistic demand is made, the other party must use a rational argument to persuade the other side to rethink its position. This may be difficult at times, because expectations are instinctively biased and the other party may not have the experience to properly form its position. The other party must convince the opposing party that instincts may not be correct.

Negotiations is a game of trust and mistrust. At the onset of negotiations, both parties mistrust the other until they have evidence that warrants trust. Trust can be earned by being honest and being an effective communicator.

Establish goals for each negotiations meeting. These goals must be achievable and reached at the end of the meeting. Achieving results creates a pattern of success that builds momentum towards a successful deal.

A position must be stated in easily understood terms and followed by a sound rational basis for the position. This fosters trust because the other party will clearly see the basis for the argument, although it may not concur with the position.

Typically, negotiations begin cordially but quickly become adversarial as demands are placed on the table. An adversarial stance does not necessarily raise a question of fidelity. It simply implies that both parties have an honest disagreement of facts and expectations.

Let's say that a brick-and-mortar wants to purchase a dotcom. Both sides might disagree on the method for auditing the dotcom's Web site log. However, both methods might be acceptable accounting practices. Therefore there is no attempt to misrepresent the number of visitors to the Web site.

However, a serious problem arises if both auditing methods report substantially fewer visitors to the dotcom's Web site than originally purported by the dotcom. Even if the error was an honest mistake made by the dotcom, a lack of trust will quickly ensue, causing the brick-and-mortar to mistrust everything the dotcom represents as fact. Trust is very difficult to regain.

A party can lessen the impact of inadvertent misrepresentations by stating the basis for its conclusion. For example, the number of visitors to a Web site was calculated by using the ABC log audit software that was applied to log files of specific dates. The other party should be able to use the same software and log files and derive the same results. Again, they may disagree with the results and with the methodology used by the software, but that becomes a point for negotiation. As long as the results alleged by the dotcom can be reproduced, there should be no loss of trust between the parties.

Any factual errors must be placed on the table and explain the moment they are discovered by either party. This means that the buyer or dotcom can expect to be the bearer of bad news. The best way to deliver bad news is to avoid panicking and to present the news objectively. Avoid minimizing or embellishing the problem. Instead, simply state the facts, then explain what caused the problem. Most importantly, both parties should explore solutions and agree on a new course of action that prevents the problem from reoccurring.

It is critical to the success of negotiations that the adversarial relationship not inhibit a free dialogue. And to this end, both parties must develop rapport. Lead negotiators for each party must establish their relationships as being representatives of their party. This means the lead negotiator tries to help the other negotiator sell the deal to the decision-makers rather than make the decision himself or herself.

For example, a lead negotiator should look at his counterpart as a sounding board and advisor of what terms might be acceptable to the decision-maker. Neither negotiator is the decision-maker. This means neither is personally involved in the deal other than to facilitate the exchange of terms. Therefore, it is important that the lead negotiators develop a good rapport. There are several ways of creating rapport. First, they must find something in common. This includes anything that brings people closer together, such as sports and family. They need to converse using everyday language and remain as informal as possible based on the situation.

The rapport develops into a trusting relationship as they work toward the same objective, although they have competitive positions. This objective is to bring both parties around to agree to the same terms.

From Tim Miller, Webmergers.com

Earnouts Are to M&A Transactions What Leaky Buckets Are to Rowboats

Keep in mind that earnouts are to M&A transactions what leaky buckets are to rowboats—they work okay, but they've got lots of holes. When asked for his advice on structuring earnouts, attorney Andrew Friedman, no fan of the practice, says, "Don't do one. Earnout transactions are often cumbersome to manage, difficult to calculate, waste a lot of management time, and often end up in litigation," said Friedman who works in the Washington, DC-based M&A practice of McDermott, Will & Emery.

But in cases where it makes sense, either where there's a need to bridge a large valuations gap or there's a yet-to-be-proved technology being sold, an earnout may be useful. For those situations, here are some tips, primarily aimed at technology company sellers that wish to use earnouts to capture the value of their Internet companies.

1. BE REALISTIC FROM THE START

Earnouts pose an inherent conflict for sellers. On the one hand, in order to get the best offer for their company, founders tend to exaggerate the future potential of the business. But if the deal skews toward an earnout and the seller's management suddenly begins to backpedal on their projections, they either lose credibility or are forced to swallow projections they have no chance of meeting. And if it does become clear that the seller will miss its goals, sellers may lose motivation entirely, and when that happens it hurts both buyer and seller.

But realism doesn't come easy to entrepreneurs, who are often innately optimistic. "Most [Internet] companies have built-in expectations that in current market conditions really can't be achieved," commented one entrepreneur and earnout veteran, requesting anonymity.

2. KEEP THE EARNOUT PERIOD AS SHORT AS POSSIBLE

In general, the longer the earnout period, the higher the risk to the seller. The deal includes a six-month reevaluation to adjust performance goals in case the business environment changes, which, in the Internet marketplace, it is guaranteed to do with some frequency.

3. KEEP PERFORMANCE GOALS MEASURABLE

All experts agreed that it is absolutely critical to keep performance as concrete and as measurable as possible.

"The earnout formula should be as specific as possible in order to avoid disputes or uncertainty at the time that an earnout payment is due," says Andrew Friedman, an M&A attorney at McDermott, Will & Emery in Washington, DC. "If the buyer is reluctant to be specific up front as to what pieces go and do not go into the earnout puzzle, this is a sign that there will be issues on the back end with respect to the formulation of the earnout calculation," he advised.

Another reason to be specific is to protect against confusion in case the buyer executive who signed the deal leaves the company. "What begins as an unwritten understanding between two individuals," he said, "turns into a nightmare when such individuals are no longer with the companies and new parties are left to interpret the written documents."

Precision is as important for development milestones as it is for financial metrics. "You've got to be clear about what you need to achieve," said Michael S. Dorf, a partner in the San Francisco-based technology M&A practice of Wilson Sonsini Goodrich & Rosati. For example, he said, a recent deal for a telecommunications hardware product involved a 12-step checklist of such requirements as "simultaneously handle x number of telephone calls." Vague clauses such as "substantially in accordance" with a given metric only lead to disagreement, he said.

4. SHOOT FOR REVENUE, NOT EARNINGS, AS A METRIC

If the contingency is based on financial milestones, opt for top-line revenue rather than earnings, cash flow, or some other less easily measured quantity. In determining cash flow or earnings, it's far too easy for the buyer to place a thumb on the scale by tweaking overhead numbers. "You can get the Hollywood movie treatment," said Dorf. "You get a percentage of a movie's profits, but the production company sucks all the profit out.... If it's not topline number you've to be very, very precise."

On the other hand, a buyer may reasonably request minimum gross margins to keep the seller from gutting prices to boost the top line.

Sellers should make sure they're basing their financial projections on the same accounting system as the acquirer's.

5. SPECIFY THE BUYER'S ROLES

In revenue or earnings-driven deals, the buyer often controls the quantity and nature of resources that are devoted to the sales and marketing that drive revenues. A good earnout specifies the buyer's contribution.

Failure to specify the buyer's commitment can be painful. For example, one engineer consulted Oakland attorney Brian Fraser last year after he sold his technology hardware company to a large public company. The deal's earnout was tied to unit sales of his technology hardware product, but the seller had failed to negotiate anything more specific than some vague indications that the buyer would make a best effort to sell the product.

With no control over the sales process, the seller not surprisingly didn't hit his sales targets. "In a deal like that, you have to have direct control over the revenue," said Fraser, who specializes in working with startups.

Fraser, who also has an accounting background, doesn't hesitate to get into the nitty-gritty details of the buyer's commitment, going so far as to specify that a buyer will spend, for example, $1 million on specific kinds of sales and marketing campaigns. "It's difficult to negotiate those details because buyers don't want to be tied down," he said, "But to assign all the risk over to the seller isn't fair either."

6. MAKE THE DEAL LINEAR, NOT BINARY

Cummings urges sellers to make certain they get some reward along the line for partially meeting their goals, as opposed to an on-off relationship that puts 100 percent of the reward upon a single goal.

7. FIRST NEGOTIATE THE BASE DEAL, THEN PURSUE THE EARN-OUT AS UPSIDE

Just as you would negotiate a base price before deciding whether to buy or lease an auto, strike your best stock and cash deal first with the buyer and then try to get an upside bonus, suggests NYC technology attorney Scott Miller. "Build the box first, and then go from there," Miller said.

Brian Fraser agreed that most earnouts tend to get treated as penalties, rather than as bonuses. "You don't usually get a benefit for exceeding revenue targets, you just get dinged for not meeting them," he said.

8. PLAN FOR DISPUTE RESOLUTION

No matter how tightly it's crafted, an earnout agreement is often fodder for disagreements. Sellers should make sure to specify arbitration or some other efficient and minimally ugly dispute resolution process in advance to resolve both legal and accounting differences.

9. PROVIDE ADEQUATE INCENTIVE

Cummings pointed out that most earnouts range between 20 percent and 70 percent of the total. In general, he said if the earnout constitutes less than 20 percent of the deal, it may simply be better to agree on an up-front price while a deal at more than 70 percent may place too much risk on the seller.

If managers have little equity, Cummings advised, use an additional bonus pool of typically 10 to 25 percent of the total to motivate them, just as NetSales did to ensure its successful transition to Digital River.

10. "VEST" UPON SALE OR MERGER

Friedman cautions sellers to ensure that earnout agreement accounts for the "resale" of the seller, its division, or the entire company. If possible, he said, the seller should craft a provision that entitles it to its full earnout payment upon consummation of such a sale.

And, Friedman cautions, make sure the buyer has the financial resources to pay up. If possible, he advises, obtain a performance guarantee from the buyer's parent entity.

WHEN WORSE COMES TO WORST

Although an earnout may not be the perfect solution, it may be the
only game in town. "If it's only a choice between shutting down and
taking a lousy deal," said Fraser, an Oakland, CA-based independent
attorney who specializes in representing startups, "You'd better take
the lousy deal. It's still pretty much a bloodbath and you may just
have to swallow your pride and take what's available."

The Acceptance Process

Experienced lead negotiators carefully follow the stages of acceptances during negotiations so that neither party feels rushed into making a decision.
There are five stages of acceptances. These are awareness, exploration, examination, test, and adoption.

The awareness stage is when the negotiator is proposing a new idea.
The negotiator must get the other negotiator's attention and encourage him
or her to move into the exploration stage. Let's say that the dotcom has a
computerized distribution system that can easily be used by the brick-and-
mortar for its own distribution following the acquisition. The computerized
distribution system is an asset that might raise the purchase price of the dotcom if the brick-and-mortar sees it as a value.

The dotcom's lead negotiator might tell the buyer's lead negotiator
that the buyer could become more efficient by converting its distribution operation to the dotcom's computerized distribution system. This might be a
factor unknown to the buyer.

Once the buyer's lead negotiator is convinced of this possibility and
has raised the buyer's interests, the buyer moves into the exploration stage.
The exploration stage is when a party qualifies a proposal by asking general
questions in an effort to determine if the proposal might meet the party's
needs. In this case, the buyer is likely to review preliminary surveys of the
computerized distribution system that were developed as part of due diligence. If this shows promise, a closer look is taken and the buyer moves to
the examination stage.

The examination stage is where the party reviews the details of the proposal to determine if the proposal truly meets its needs. The buyer of the dotcom, for example, may create a detailed feasibility plan that merges current distribution operations with the dotcom's computerized distribution system. The plan contains the cost, effort and benefit that the buyer should realize should the proposal be adopted following the acquisition.

The examination stage leads to the test stage, where the proposal is tested in an effort to determine whether the party should accept or reject the proposal. It is at this stage that the party is nearly sold on the idea, but is looking for possible last-minute reasons why the proposal may not be right.

In the case of the buyer of the dotcom, the buyer might send engineers to the dotcom facilities to test the computerized distribution system. For example, the engineers might place one of the buyer's products into the system, then try to order the product to determine if processing is more efficient than on the buyer's current system.

When the test stage is completed and the buyer hasn't found a reason for rejecting the proposal, then the buyer is likely to adopt the proposal. In this example, the buyer determines that the dotcom's computerized distribution system is a valuable asset, which will be reflected in a higher acquisition price.

It is critical that the party has sufficient time to complete each stage of the acceptance process. Failure to allow adequate time will give the perception that the party is being rushed into a decision, leading them to believe the other party has something to hide.

Dealing with Angry Participants

The frustrations of negotiation can anger participants both on the buyer's team and on the dotcom's team. Typically, the anger is directed at the lead negotiators because they are the persons who are perceived responsible for negotiations.

Anger hinders negotiations because it focuses attention away from finding solutions to problems and instead directs everyone's energies to making accusations or defending actions. The lead negotiator has the responsibility to manage a hostile climate by controlling confrontation with angry participants. The lead negotiator must remain calm and remember that that anger is really directed at the situation rather than at the negotiator. The person must be given time to vent his or her anger; during that time the lead negotiator must make it known that he or she is sincerely interested in the person's concerns.

Once the anger subsides, the lead negotiator must explore the perceived nature of the problem by asking the person questions that isolate the issues that caused the anger. The lead negotiator's job is first to bring the person back to reality before attempting to address the issue. Keep in mind that people who are close to negotiations tend to lose sight of the significance of a problem. The lead negotiator must help the person redefine the importance of the problem by listening carefully and identifying the facts and misunderstandings that led to the anger.

The lead negotiator must become an advisor and help the person differentiate facts from myths. Acknowledge facts brought out by the person, then provide a rationale for defusing misperceptions. The objective is to have the person agree with the lead negotiator's view of the situation.

Don't be afraid to admit a problem exists, since this helps to give credence to the person's anger. Likewise, point out where the person's rationale is wrong, because this shows that the problem isn't as important or as impossible to solve as the person might think.

In doing this, make sure that the person saves face. For example, the lead negotiator might say "I thought the same way until someone presented me with another reading of the facts." Even if this isn't true, this gives the person a reason for being angry and a way of reversing his or her anger without being embarrassed. After the person has returned to reality, the lead negotiator works with him or her to devise a solution to the problem. Usually, it is at this point that negotiations get back on track.

The lead negotiator must realize that anger displayed by a party to the negotiations is many times based on fear. The deal is likely to have a disrupting effect on the person's life and he or she may be unsure of the future. Furthermore, the person's success following the acquisition is in the hands of others, some of whom are strangers.

The lead negotiator can stem fears by realizing they exist, then addressing the cause of fears before they manifest into anger that disrupts negotiations. Clearly identify each phase of the acquisition process early on so everyone knows what to expect and when.

Next, anticipate personal concerns such as employment and compensation, then take steps to address them. Let each person know how he or she might be affected by the acquisition. Address such issues as position and compensation for those who remain with the corporation and the termination benefits for those who don't remain.

Conducting a Successful Negotiations Meeting

The objective of a face-to-face meeting is for parties to exchange information, identify facts, and agree to terms of the deal. For this to occur, lead negotiators must use the semistructured meeting format, where there isn't a formal agenda but parties are aware of the topics to be discussed and the goal of the meeting. This allows for free flow of ideas without having a loss of focus, which is typical of an ad hoc meeting.

Information pertinent to the meeting should be shared with participants a reasonable time before the meeting to give them an opportunity to prepare for the meeting. Only those who can contribute to the objective of the meeting should attend; those who cannot contribute tend to be ill prepared and are more a distraction than a positive influence.

Lead negotiators should set the tone of the meeting so that participants are placed at ease. Negotiators should do most, if not all, of the talking. This gives each party one voice in the negotiations process. Neither lead negotiator should dominate the conversation. Each should be given time to present his or her thoughts while the other listens carefully and takes notes. The conversation should be kept moving to avoid getting bogged down in details that are unnecessary to the objective of the meeting.

Feedback is critical. After a lead negotiator completes his or her thought, the other lead negotiator should restate what was said. In this way, both negotiators are assured that the correct information was exchanged. When restating, it is important for the negotiator to see the information from the other negotiator's perspective in order to accurately relay the negotiator's position to the negotiations team for a response.

Avoid at all cost discussing matters that are not the topic of the meeting. Whenever the meeting moves off track, one of the lead negotiators should suggest that the matter become a topic of another meeting.

Always end the meeting on a positive note by having all participants agree on something. This helps to foster a feeling of accomplishment.

THE LETTER OF INTENT

The initial negotiations occur when both parties are brought together to discuss the concept of the acquisition. Typically, a party makes an overture to the other, floating a trial balloon to determine if there is any interest in pursuing the acquisition.

An inkling of interest sets into motion a series of events that might eventually lead to closing the deal. However, there are prescribed steps that most negotiations follow before closing occurs. The first of these steps is an informal conversation between parties that determines the feasibility of the acquisition. These are exploratory discussions in which the parties are generally acceptable to the notion of an acquisition and no major obstacles such as finances or legal issues stand in the way of consummating a deal.

Parties conduct preliminary due diligence in an effort to identify major financial deficits and to value the deal to establish a price. A thorough due diligence that includes a litigation review is conducted after the parties agree in principle to work towards a deal.

Typically, each party raises major concerns during this period, which are negotiated in a nonbinding agreement. For example, management of a dotcom may want to continue operating the dotcom as a subsidiary of the buyer rather than become a fully integrated component of the corporation. A rejection of this concept becomes a deal-breaker. An agreement to these terms encourages the dotcom to move to the next step in the process.

Once all the major concerns are discussed and agreed to, then the parties move to the next stage of negotiations, which is the letter of intent. A letter of intent is a document signed by both parties that contains the general terms of acquisition.

As the name implies, the document is to convey intent of both parties, and except in extreme situations, the document is not binding. This is called a nonbinding memorandum of understanding, which is clearly specified in the letter.

The letter of intent contains the type of deal (such as a merger or acquisition) and the price, among other factors that might be pertinent to the specific deal. For example, the buyer might require a no-shopping clause to restrict the dotcom from seeking other suitors in an effort to raise the price of the acquisition. Parties can agree that a no-shop clause and other similar restrictions that appear in the letter of intent are binding.

The price contained in the letter of intent is negotiable in that negative conditions uncovered during a complete due diligence process can be remedied by adjusting the previously negotiated price. The letter of intent becomes the framework within which parties negotiate the details of the acquisition. The letter also morally obligates parties to expend time and money to pursue the deal. Failure to consummate the deal can be viewed as a failure of management of both firms, which is something neither party takes lightly.

Also contained in the letter of intent are conditions that must be fulfilled before the parties move on to the acquisition agreement. These conditions might include financing and verifications of representations made by the other party. Failure to meet these conditions terminates the deal.

The parties should also address reimbursement of expenses in the event they don't consummate the deal. Extraordinary expenses are incurred in pursuit of the deal once the letter of intent is signed. Therefore, a question might be raised as to who is responsible for paying these expenses should negotiations break down and the deal never becomes a reality. Generally, each party expends funds knowing there is a risk that the deal may not materialize. However, those funds are expended based on facts known to both parties, such as conditions specified in the letter of intent.

A liability question is raised if all conditions in the letter of intent are met, yet one party decides to back away from the deal. Should the party that breaks off the deal reimburse the other party's expenses? Parties should address this issue in the letter of intent rather than leave this question to be resolved at the time negotiations break down.

THE ACQUISITION AGREEMENT

Once the letter of intent is negotiated and signed, negotiations focus on the acquisition agreement. The acquisition agreement is the binding contract that specifies the terms of the acquisition and contains representations, covenants, warranties, and indemnities made by the dotcom in exchange for the acquisition price. Representations, covenants, warranties, and indemnities are discussed in detail later in this chapter.

Failure to abide by terms of the acquisition agreement exposes a party to the agreement to litigation, which is not a risk taken by signing a letter of intent. In essence, the acquisition agreement is the document that initiates the transfer of ownership of assets from the dotcom to the buyer. Actual transfer of ownership occurs at closing, when legal title of assets is signed over to the buyer using several documents such as deeds and stock transfer documents.

Acquisition price and title transfer of assets is the simplest aspect of an acquisition agreement to negotiate. The more challenging terms to address are those involving risk allocation.

Accepting Risk

Typically, the dotcom is a complex operation that is fraught with risk-taking. For example, there isn't any guarantee that the operations will continue to run at the same level as they have in the past. This means the employees may leave employment, customers may move to a competitor, and morale among employees may drop. These and other conditions can have a dramatic effect on cash flow and profitability.

The question that must be answered through negotiations is which party accepts these risks. Let's say a buyer acquires a dotcom and key marketing employees quit the dotcom shortly after the acquisition, which lowers the operating revenue of the dotcom, exposing the buyer to the risk of lower revenue. The acquisition price paid by the buyer reflects the value of the dotcom prior to the defection of key marketing employees. Should the acquisition price be adjusted following the close of the deal, since the dotcom has dropped in value? If so, then the dotcom shoulders the risk of losing key employees. If not, then the buyer is solely exposed to this risk.

In another example, let's say that a customer of the dotcom initiates litigation after the closing for actions or inactions of the dotcom prior to closing. The litigation is new and would not have been revealed in due diligence because neither the dotcom nor the buyer knew anything about the possibility of litigation.

Furthermore, let's assume that acquisition is in the form of a stock purchase in which the buyer acquired outstanding stock of the dotcom. Should the buyer underwrite the expense of litigation, since the buyer now owns the dotcom? Should this burden shift to the dotcom, since the underlying action that initiated the litigation occurred prior to the acquisition?

The buyer and dotcom should anticipate risks associated with the acquisition, then negotiate how the risk will be shouldered. Risks can be borne by the buyer or the dotcom, or they can be shared. Risks can be limited, as well. For example, the buyer might assume a risk unless the liability for the risk exceeds a specific amount. Afterwards, the dotcom assumes the liability.

Risk is normally offset by the expense to insure a party against losses that are associated with a risk. In most situations, an insurance company will issue a policy to cover liability. The expense of the policy is used to adjust the acquisition price. The price rises if the dotcom agrees to underwrite the risk and the price decreases if the buyer assumes the risk.

The acquisition agreement contains verbiage that documents any verbal agreements that may have been made between the parties. The selection of words used to describe the terms of the agreement has a dramatic impact on the effectiveness of the agreement. Only terms specified in the acquisition agreement are binding. Oral agreements that occur as part of negotiations are voided once the acquisition agreement is signed. Therefore, it is critical that the parties fully understand the meaning of each word of the agreement and that any ambiguities are resolved in writing before the document is signed.

Let's say that the dotcom opened its books and records to the buyer as part of due diligence and that the company's records reflected a steady, predictable cash flow. Negotiations are completed and the buyer writes up the acquisition agreement.

The buyer documents the cash flow in a clause that states that the dotcom represents a specific cash flow for operations that the dotcom expects to continue through the first year following the acquisition. However, the dotcom is likely to object to that clause because the statement goes beyond the intent of the dotcom. By opening its books and records, the dotcom simply represents that the books and records show the previous and current state of the business. The dotcom had no intention to represent that the figures can be used to predict the future operations of the corporation.

This is a representative example of the conflicts that arise when oral understandings are documented in an acquisition agreement. The party that drafts the acquisition agreement can use verbiage to interpret the oral agreement in terms more favorable to it.

It is not unusual for parties to battle over who is going to create the first draft of the acquisition agreement. The party who wins this battle can phrase portions of the text to its advantage.

Both the buyer and the dotcom can expect attorneys to spend days negotiating the verbiage of the acquisition agreement. Attorneys will seek to either generalize terms of the agreement or narrow the agreement to specific conditions, depending on whether or not it is in the best interest of their client.

While haggling over words seems to be meaningless and a way for attorneys to charge more for their services, it is this detail that can encourage or hinder future litigation, which is likely to be more expensive than the cost to settle on the language of the agreement.

The dotcom's objective is to transfer ownership of the corporation to the buyer in an as-is state, then receive payment that is nonrefundable under any condition. An as-is state is where the buyer is aware of all the facets of the dotcom's operation prior to signing the acquisition agreement. The buyer is assumed to know all the benefits and risks that are associated with the dotcom and assumes those risks by signing the acquisition agreement.

The buyer's objective is to get what its is paying for, which is a revenue stream. The dotcom should remedy any condition that disrupts the revenue stream that is directly linked to the dotcom. This is because the disruption lowers the value of the dotcom and was within the dotcom's power to either remedy prior to closing or to make the potential condition known to the buyer before an acquisition price was established. In this case, the buyer could have adjusted the acquisition price downward to reflect the lower value of the dotcom.

Parties find a middle ground through negotiations. Typically, the buyer and dotcom will sincerely work toward uncovering any situation that might become a material issue from the time parties sign a letter of intent until a reasonable time following closing. Once those issues are on the table, both sides can negotiate a fair acquisition price for the dotcom.

The fair acquisition price will represent how well each party feels they can manage known risks and unknown risks of the deal. For example, the buyer might feel comfortable assuming the risk of retaining employees because the buyer can offer incentives to encourage them to stay after the acquisition. The dotcom would not be in a position to underwrite such a risk because the dotcom will no longer have influence over employees once the deal is consummated.

Likewise, the dotcom might be willing to absorb the risk for six months following the deal that there might be a sharp downturn in the market that reduces the value of the dotcom. The dotcom is well versed in the dynamics of the industry and doesn't anticipate a downturn during that period.

The reward for balancing the risk is the acquisition price. The buyer can expect to pay a high acquisition price if the dotcom underwrites the risks. The dotcom will receive a low price if the buyer absorbs all the risk. By accepting more risk, the buyer receives a higher price and if the liability doesn't materialize, then the dotcom gets to keep more of the price.

Structure

The acquisition agreement takes on a traditional structure that organizes information into nine sections:

- Introduction
- Price
- Asset transfer procedure
- Representations
- Warranties
- Covenants
- Indemnification
- Terms of closing the deal
- Terms to terminate a deal and legal remedies should closing not occur

The introduction sets the tone of the agreement and explains the objectives of each party, such as that the buyer will merge with the dotcom or the buyer will purchase assets of the dotcom. The price section simply sets the price, which can be a fixed amount or a pricing formula used to set the fixed amount at closing. For example, the formula might state that the acquisition price is calculated by multiplying earnings by two. Earnings are agreed upon at the time of closing.

The asset transfer procedure identifies assets and specifies steps that will be followed to transfer the title of the dotcom to the buyer. Also included in this section are any downpayments or deposits necessary to prove intent to go forward with the deal. It is here that risk allocation is also specified.

The representation section contains statements made by the buyer and dotcom relating to their operations, such as that each corporation was legally formed and is authorized to enter into the agreement. The warranty section basically asserts that the party making the representation assures that the statements are true.

The covenant section is where the parties agree to avoid changing anything that materially alters the representations and warranties. The indemnification section specifically states what either party will do to remedy a misrepresentation or violation of a covenant.

The terms of closing the deal outline the steps that must be completed for the parties to close the deal. The termination section delineates the terms whereby either party can terminate the agreement and avoid closing the deal. This section also contains the legal remedies, such as recouping certain expenses should the deal terminate.

These sections are discussed in more detail later in this chapter.

REPRESENTATIONS, WARRANTIES, AND COVENANTS

A buyer relies heavily on the information presented by the dotcom that describes the assets, liabilities, and revenue stream generated by a dotcom's operations, because the buyer is not privy to the details of the dotcom's business.

The buyer spot-checks the accuracy of information provided by the dotcom during due diligence. However, even a thorough due diligence can fail to examine every aspect of the dotcom and therefore there will be some information that the buyer must accept at face value.

There is an inherent danger in not independently verifying information the dotcom supplied because of possible inaccuracies and misreading of the information. A buyer can protect itself against exposure to being misinformed by requiring that the dotcom include in the acquisition agreement facts that the dotcom purports to be true. The section of the agreement that contains these statements is called the representation and warranty clause.

The representation and warranty clause has two components. The first is the representation of financial, legal, and other facts about the dotcom on the date the acquisition agreement is signed. The warranty is the second component and states that the dotcom will repair or remedy any misrepresentations made in the acquisition agreement.

The dotcom is likely to include as part of the representation clause a listing of current and potential litigation, financial records, and contracts with customers and suppliers. Furthermore, the dotcom stipulates basic information such as that the dotcom is a legal entity organized under state law and has the legal capacity to enter into and consummate the acquisition agreement.

Likewise, the buyer should be prepared to include in the representation clause information about its own business operations, since the dotcom is likely to know little factual information about the buyer. The buyer's representations should cover the same areas of business as does the dotcom's representations. In this way, both parties are identifying similar information about themselves.

Inclusion of a representation clause can become an obstacle in negotiations because the party who makes the representation is liable for the accuracy of the information. Many dotcoms prefer not to make any representations as a way to avoid any liability following the consummation of the deal.

Generally, the dotcom permits the buyer to examine any and all aspects of the dotcom's business before signing the acquisition agreement. It is assumed that the buyer will uncover the information necessary to have an accurate depiction of the dotcom. If this is true, then there is no reason for the dotcom to make any representation, since all the information about the dotcom is known by the buyer. The dotcom can then sell the business "as is."

The dotcom has the underlying concern that negative information might exist in the dotcom's organization that is unknown to the board of directors due to the complexity of the dotcom's business operations.

When the acquisition process reaches the final stages, the dotcom must search its records for relative information that would affect the deal. Critical information can easily be inadvertently overlooked and therefore invalidate any representations made to the buyer in the acquisition agreement.

Let's say that lower management of a dotcom discovered that its computer system has been miscalculating sales taxes for tens of thousands of customers over the past five years. The dotcom is liable for millions of dollars in taxes, but the liability does not appear on the books and records of the firm because lower management kept the problem away from higher management. The system was quietly fixed.

The buyer's due diligence didn't uncover the problem because they examined the dotcom's system and saw that the system was properly handling taxes. Recent sales were spot-checked and appeared to be in order, so they had no suspicion that a massive liability existed.

The dotcom listed all the liabilities and potential liabilities known to higher management in the representation clause of the acquisition agreement. Of course, the tax liability wasn't listed because lower management never let the problem rise to the level of top management.

Nearly a year following the acquisition, a disgruntled employee notified the taxing authority that the dotcom owed substantial sums in back taxes. An investigation ensued and resulted in litigation that attempted to collect back taxes and penalties.

The buyer was named as the defendant. The buyer took legal action against the dotcom for breach of the acquisitions agreement, since the dotcom misrepresented a material fact in the dotcom's operation. The dotcom represented that all liabilities and potential liabilities were listed in the acquisition agreement when in fact this was not the case.

A dotcom tries to avoid such exposure by avoiding, wherever possible, making any representation in the acquisition agreement. In contrast, the buyer wants the dotcom to make extensive representations for a number of reasons.

First, the buyer wants to pressure the dotcom to reveal information that enables the buyer to properly assess the value of the dotcom. The dotcom should be encouraged to examine every detail of its operation and not rely solely on the buyer's due diligence to uncover information.

Next, the buyer wants legal recourse should information purported to be true isn't true. The buyer is paying for a business that produces a revenue stream. Information that lowers the revenue stream in the future alters the business that is being bought by the buyer.

Finally, the lenders who are financing the deal want to be assured that revenue stream that the buyer is depending on to repay debt will exist following the consummation of the deal. Lenders will often specify the types of representations the buyer needs from the dotcom before lenders will finance the deal.

Narrowing the Scope of Representations

The buyer and dotcom can find themselves at opposing positions when it comes to representations in the acquisition agreement. The buyer wants complete representation while the dotcom does not want to give any representation.

In reality, both sides reach a compromise position in which the dotcom provides limited representation. A common limitation is to represent only facts that are material to the acquisition. Following the list of material facts, the dotcom typically includes a statement to the effect that the dotcom knows of no other material matters that would affect business operations.

While inserting the materiality statement in the acquisition agreement narrows the scope of the representation, it also presents another problem, that is, the definition of material. The dotcom and the buyer can honestly disagree on whether a fact is material to the dotcom's operation.

There is no easy solution to this dilemma. Courts tend to use the reasonable man rule whereby the judge determines whether or not a reasonable person—in this case, an investor—would consider a fact material to the dotcom's business operation.

Rather than leave a court to define material, both parties can agree to the definition and include the definition as a component of the acquisition agreement. Typically, a dollar amount of liability, for example, $500,000, is used to define material. Any factor that exposes the dotcom's business to less than $500,000 is not considered material.

Another statement that narrows representations made by the dotcom is the best of knowledge clause. The best of knowledge clause includes verbiage in the acquisition agreement that stipulates that the information is represented as accurate to the best knowledge of the dotcom. This means that the dotcom is not liable for negative information that arises after the deal if the dotcom did not know the information when the acquisition agreement was signed. This clause seems to narrow the dotcom's liability, but in reality the clause doesn't preclude litigation between the dotcom and the buyer.

The question that the best of knowledge clause leaves unanswered is whether or not the dotcom knew of the negative information at the time the acquisition agreement was signed. The buyer can search the records of the dotcom—including emails—looking for clues that the information was known to the dotcom's management. Once evidence is uncovered, then the buyer can sue the dotcom for breach of the representation clause of the acquisition agreement.

Another way the dotcom can limit the representation clause is to avoid making any statements about certain facts. For example, the dotcom may refuse to make any statements whatsoever regarding potential litigation. If litigation occurs following the consummation of the deal and the litigation is related to actions that happened before the acquisition agreement was signed, then the buyer has no recourse against the dotcom. The buyer must handle the litigation directly.

In the case of the dotcom that inadvertently hid the fact that the company owed millions of dollars in taxes due to a system error, limiting verbiage may not protect the dotcom from liability. The tax liability materially affects the operations of the dotcom. The buyer could prove that the dotcom knew about the problem because it fixed the system. This is true even if higher management were unaware of the situation. The only way the dotcom could avoid liability to the buyer is if the dotcom made no representations about the tax status of the company prior to signing of the acquisition agreement.

Covenants

The period between the time the buyer and dotcom sign the acquisition agreement and the time the deal closes (see Chapter 10, "After the Deal"), the dotcom has the opportunity to make alterations in the operations of its business operations. For example, there is nothing preventing the dotcom from changing its Web-hosting vendor after the acquisition agreement is signed and before the buyer consummates the acquisition. Such a change may not violate representations if the Web-hosting vendor is not explicitly identified in the acquisition agreement.

However, the change of vendor is likely to be considered a material modification of current business operations, exposing the dotcom and the buyer to risks that were not anticipated during due diligence and not reflected in the acquisition price. Transfer of the Web-host to new vendor might cause disruption in service to customers, which can directly impact the dotcom's revenue stream, without the buyer's knowledge or consent.

The buyer can reduce the risk that the dotcom will materially change its business operations between the signing of the acquisitions agreement and closing by requiring that the dotcom include a covenant section in the acquisition agreement.

A covenant is an agreement between the buyer and dotcom stating that the dotcom will not materially alter the dotcom's business operations from the date that the acquisition agreement is signed. An exception to this provision is that the dotcom will seek the buyer's permission to make such alterations as deemed necessary in the best interest of the dotcom's business.

Let's say that the dotcom's current Web-hosting vendor is unable to provide the dotcom with the level of service demanded by the business. The dotcom should relocate the Web site to another Web-hosting facility. However, the dotcom, working within the terms of the covenant, must receive permission from the buyer before making this change.

The buyer also agrees as part of the covenant not to withhold permission to make any material change as long as those changes are reasonable and necessary to maintain the dotcom's business.

This is an important aspect of the covenant section of the acquisition agreement because the dotcom is permitted to maintain the integrity of the business prior to closing. The dotcom can then survive should the deal be terminated by the buyer or dotcom. Without the withhold permission clause, the dotcom is hampered from reasonably implementing business decisions by the buyer's failure to agree to material changes in the business.

TERMS OF CLOSING

The acquisition agreement must list the terms that each party must fulfill before the dotcom is legally transferred to the buyer and the dotcom receives compensation from the buyer. These conditions serve as a checklist; when the checklist is completed, the deal is considered closed.

The terms of closing contain item such as reaching a clean title search on real property owned by the dotcom; approval of regulators, if required; and a final audit report of the dotcom's operation. The final audit report is used to set the acquisition price should price be based on a formula. Any item that is material to the deal and is pending at the time the acquisition agreement is signed should be included in the terms for closing.

If a term is not satisfied at closing, the opposing party has the right to terminate the deal without being liable for damages or to waive the term as a requirement to close the deal. Let's say that the buyer doesn't receive the official copy of the final auditor's report by the closing date. However, the buyer's financial advisors have seen and approved the final draft of the auditor's report. Technically, the dotcom is in violation of a closing term. Therefore, the buyer legally has the right to terminate the deal. The buyer may decide to waive this right to terminate, since its own auditors verified that nothing material has changed in the dotcom's operations since the acquisition agreement was signed.

It is also in the terms of closing that both parties include clauses that define when either party can terminate the agreement. For example, failure to comply with closing terms is an important reason for termination.

Another critical reason for termination that should be clearly explained in the closing terms is a breach of the representation, warranties, and covenants clause. The acquisition agreement explicitly contains the representations made by the dotcom. At the time of closing, the representative of the dotcom, who is usually an officer of the corporation, certifies to the buyer that nothing has materially changed with the dotcom since the signing of the acquisition agreement.

The buyer has legal grounds for termination should the certification be inaccurate. That is, changes have occurred in the dotcom's operation that invalidate the representations made in the acquisition agreement. In this case, a breach occurs. The buyer can always waive the right to terminate and is likely to renegotiate the acquisition price to reflect the change.

The buyer can also use the terms of closing as protection against the possibility that the buyer is unable to finance the deal. This is sometimes called the financial out clause. Dotcoms are rarely willing to agree to the financial out clause because the buyer has had sufficient time prior to the signing of the acquisition agreement to arrange financing.

It is not uncommon that the letter of intent require that the buyer has in place financing commitments at the time the acquisition agreement is signed. However, this does not eliminate the risk that the buyer is unable to finance the deal.

Typically, a financing commitment comes with contingencies that are not met until the time of closing. For example, the buyer is required to have clean title to certain of the dotcom's assets so that it can be used as collateral to secure financing. One or more contingencies may not be met and can lead to exercising the financial out clause of the acquisition agreement.

The dotcom can protect itself from the financial out clause by requiring that the dotcom agree to the contingency terms of financing commitment. The dotcom might reject a contingency if it thinks that there is a high probability that the contingency will not be met on the closing date. Likewise, the dotcom should include verbiage in the acquisition agreement that holds the buyer financially liable for liquidation damages should the buyer fail to meet a financing contingency that is within its control to fulfill.

Let's say that the dotcom is unable to give clean title to real estate property it owns and this causes financing to be denied. The dotcom shouldn't expect any liquidating damage from the buyer, although the buyer might hold the dotcom liable and require the dotcom to pay damages. On the other hand, the dotcom may seek damages if the buyer fails to grant a lien on the assets, thereby violating a contingency of the lender.

The dotcom should avoid agreeing to any closing terms that are beyond its control. There have been cases when a buyer wants the dotcom to guarantee a particular level of sales at the closing date. Sales are dependent upon market conditions as well as on the dotcom's business operating policies. The dotcom is not in a position to warrant performance of the market. Market conditions are a risk that the buyer undertakes without recourse against the dotcom.

Caution

Closing the deal in essence waives any right to terminate the deal. That is, the buyer and dotcom must carefully confirm that all representations, covenants, and terms of closing are met at closing.

TERMINATION PROCEDURES

The acquisition agreement should contain a termination section within which the parties set forth conditions under which either party has the option to back out of the deal. In addition, this section specifies any penalties or liabilities, if any, that either party incurs should the deal terminate.

The objective of the termination section is to clearly state each party's expectations and acknowledge the remedy should either party fail to live up to the obligation to close the deal. This section also establishes ceilings on the liability of the terminating party and therefore potentially avoids litigation.

For example, as a requirement to closing the deal, a dotcom agrees to arrange for an outside auditor to report on the status of the dotcom's assets and liabilities a week before closing. Information in the report is applied to an agreed-upon formula stipulated in the acquisition agreement to determine the acquisition price.

Let's say that the dotcom failed to enlist the services of the auditor. The dotcom's inaction causes a breach in the acquisition agreement. The termination section of the acquisition agreement addresses this issue by specifying that the party who did not breach the agreement has the option to terminate the deal. Furthermore, the section states that if termination took place, then the party who breached the agreement will compensate the other party for all cost incurred in pursuing the deal.

When the dotcom failed to produce the report according to schedule, the buyer had the option of sending to the dotcom notification of termination, followed by an invoice for expenses. In this case, the buyer likely explored the reasons why the dotcom breached the agreement. If both parties determined that the report would be available a reasonable time after the closing, then a clause could be inserted into the acquisition agreement that set the date for receiving the auditor's report, at which time the acquisition price would be established.

Arbitration

The arbitration clause is commonly found in the termination section. The arbitration clause stipulates that disputes will be handled by an arbitrator rather than through action with the courts. An arbitrator is a private individual who takes the role of a judge, establishes the facts in the case, and then recommends a solution to the conflict.

There are two forms of arbitration. These are nonbinding arbitration and binding arbitration. In a nonbinding arbitration, the arbitrator's role is to recommend a remedy and convince both sides to accept the decision. Either side reserves the right to reject the remedy, then has the right to take the matter through the legal system. Binding arbitration does not give either party the option to reject the remedy. Both sides, when agreeing to the arbitration clause, also agree to accept the decision of the arbitrator without recourse.

Arbitrators are lawyers, retired judges, and/or experts in a particular field. Such expertise can be advantageous when technical issues involving the dotcom's operations are in dispute—for example, if the dotcom's capacity to handle high-volume online inquiries is questioned.

The power of an arbitrator is based on contract law rather than directly authorized by statute, which is the source of the judiciary's power. Both parties to the arbitration sign a binding contract that states that they will enlist the services of an arbitrator and that the arbitrator's recommendation will be either nonbinding or binding.

The American Arbitration Association establishes rules for the arbitration proceedings. These rules provide guidelines for every aspect of arbitration and include the selection of an arbitrator and the rights of each party to present its case to the arbitrator.

Arbitration offers parties fast resolution of disagreements because there are far more arbitrators available to hear the case than there are judges. However, there are disadvantages. For example, the list of arbitrators made available by the American Arbitration Association may not contain anyone the parties feel is qualified to decide their case. Furthermore, there may not be a discovery period or the right to issue a subpoena. And parties lose the right to traditional legal remedies.

It is best to avoid an all-encompassing arbitration clause because the disadvantages of arbitration can have a dramatic limiting effect on rectifying a breach of contract. A preferred approach is to specify situations in which the parties will go to arbitration rather than to court to resolve a disagreement.

Typically, arbitration is agreed to for technical and noneconomical disputes, such as whether or not database software is designed to handle high-volume cyber traffic. A dotcom might have made such a representation in the acquisition agreement, yet the buyer might disagree should a backlog of visitors occur during the first few weeks following the acquisition.

The arbitration clause should stipulate that each party will choose an arbitrator from a list of arbitrators provided by the American Arbitration Association, then both arbitrators will pick another arbitrator to hear the case and render a decision. This tends to make the selection process objective and remove the chance that the arbitrator will be bias to a party.

Parties should stipulate that the arbitrator has the right to discovery whereby parties make available all their records to the arbitrator for review. Typically, the buyer and dotcom will not object to this stipulation because due diligence is a form of discovery and has been completed by both sides by the time the acquisition agreement is signed.

Parties should further stipulate that each party limits its right to seek traditional legal intervention in the disagreement. This includes subpoena power and injunctive relief. Local jurisdiction might define the subpoena powers of parties to arbitration. Some jurisdictions give subpoena power to the arbitrator to the exclusion of parties to the dispute. In other jurisdictions, the disputing parties, not the arbitrator, have subpoena powers. Therefore, it is important that both sides agree to the jurisdiction that will govern the arbitration and to who has subpoena powers.

In addition, parties must determine if a law of the local jurisdiction makes available injunctive relief if arbitration is included in the acquisition agreement. Parties may stipulate as part of the arbitration clause that both sides will cease the offending action until the arbitrator renders a ruling.

This generally has the same effect as an injunction in that the offending action is held in abeyance until the hearing is completed. However, it lacks the judicial teeth to force a party to comply with the agreement.

INDEMNITY

The indemnity section of the acquisition agreement specifies the procedures and litigation rights a party has to seek claims against the other for breaches of representation, covenants, and warranties. Parties rely on the indemnity section to expand their rights under laws that govern the acquisition agreement. For example, case law within a jurisdiction may not typically grant the plaintiff legal expenses if a breach of representation occurs. However, parties may stipulate to reimbursement of legal expenses in the indemnity section of the acquisition agreement. This agreement overrules case law because the basis of case law in this circumstance is that parties have not agreed to a remedy of legal expenses.

The indemnity section is also used to set time limits on representation, covenants, and warranties. The buyer can expect the dotcom to stand behind statements made as part of the acquisition agreement for a reasonable time following closing the deal. Both parties can agree to the definition of reasonable, which is clarified in the indemnity section of the acquisition agreement. Failure to define reasonable can lead to litigation should the buyer seek to recover damages beyond a period considered reasonable by the dotcom.

There is a judicial period within which the buyer or dotcom can take action against the other for a breach of the acquisition agreement. This is called the *statute of limitations,* which varies by jurisdiction. The statute of limitations sets forth the number of months from the signing of the acquisition agreement that litigation can begin. Terms of the indemnity section can modify the statute of limitations by both parties agreeing to either a longer or shorter time period than that granted to them by the statute of limitations.

Typically, the buyer and dotcom set the limitation of the indemnity section of the acquisition agreement to a fiscal year of operations. Once the buyer receives the audit report for the fiscal year, then representations, covenants, and warranties have elapsed and no claims can be made against the other party.

There is an exception to this limitation. It is common for the dotcom to agree to indemnify the buyer for litigation brought by a third party before the limitation deadline but resolved after the deadline. Let's say customers bring a class action suit during the limitation deadline. The suit claims that the dotcom misled customers by stating that customers were offered the lowest price for a product when in fact they were not. The dotcom is sold. The suit isn't settled for two years, which is well beyond the fiscal year of operations. The buyer is likely to attempt to recover losses and expenses from the dotcom, because the action was brought before the limitation period expired.

However, the verbiage used in the indemnity section governs whether or not such action is successful. For example, if the indemnity section contains wording such as "losses within the limitation period," then recovery by the buyer might be extremely difficult to achieve. The dotcom could argue that the loss didn't occur during the limitation period.

In contrast, the indemnity section could contain wording such as "claims made within the limitation period." In this case, the buyer stands a good chance of recovery, since the claim occurred during the limitation period.

Caution

Claims made by governing bodies against the dotcom are exempt from conditions stated in the indemnity section. This includes actions for any violation of the law.

Indemnity Basket

It is wise for the dotcom to insist that an indemnity basket be stipulated in the indemnity section of the acquisition agreement. An indemnity basket is the term given to the minimum loss that the buyer incurs before other terms of the indemnity section take effect. In essence, the amount of the indemnity basket defines a material loss. Losses below this amount become immaterial as defined by the indemnity basket of the acquisition agreement. This means that unless losses reach the indemnity basket threshold, the buyer agrees not to recover the losses from the dotcom.

An indemnity basket helps the dotcom avoid small claims yet reduces the buyer's exposure to more meaningful amounts. The amount of the indemnity basket is negotiated. Typically, the amount is defined as a percentage of the purchase price, usually below 5 percent.

In addition to the amount of the indemnity basket, the buyer and dotcom must agree to how the indemnity basket is administered. That is, they must determine whether, once the threshold is reached, the dotcom is liable for the entire loss or just for losses that exceed the threshold.

Let's say that the dotcom is sold for an acquisition price of $10 million. Parties agree that the indemnity basket is $3 million. They also agree that once the $3 million threshold is reached, the dotcom will cover all the losses, including the $3 million. The dotcom could have reduced its exposure by changing the terms of the indemnity basket clause to state that it will liable for losses above the $3 million threshold. In this case, the buyer underwrites the $3 million loss.

It is also wise for the dotcom to establish a minimum claim amount in an effort to avoid being involved in immaterial claims. These claims may not apply to the indemnity basket, based on negotiations.

Caution

Terms of the indemnity section are unenforceable should the dotcom lack the financial resources to sustain claims made by the buyer. Therefore, the buyer should insist that a portion of the acquisition price be held in escrow during the indemnification period.

PUBLIC COMPANIES

The acquisition of a public corporation is slightly different than that of a private corporation because information about a public corporation must be made public according to law. A public corporation must disclose material information, including materially inaccurate information of previous filing. Otherwise, the corporation and officers are exposed to criminal and civil action that can be brought by the government.

Disclosure regulations nullify the representations, covenants, warranties, and indemnification sections of an acquisition agreement. All the relative information that is covered under these sections is part of the disclosure required of a public corporation. However, these sections do serve as statements of understanding. It can be stipulated that should any of these understandings be breached, the other party has a right to terminate the agreement without any recourse of the other party.

The acquisition agreement should stipulate that the dotcom has complied with disclosure regulations and specify which party will file the necessary legal documents with the Security and Exchange Commission and other legal entities that govern acquisition of a public corporation.

SUMMARY

The initial step in negotiations is for each party to learn its own strengths and weaknesses by employing a team of consultants to perform a critical, objective, no-holds-barred evaluation of the party's operation. The objective is for the consultants to uncover information about the party that is likely to be uncovered by the opponent.

Next, the party must assess the value of itself. The result determines the value of the party, which becomes the basis for establishing an acquisition price in the case of the dotcom and the basis for financing for the buyer.

Based on the self-valuation, the dotcom should develop three prices: initial price, desired price, and minimum price. The initial price is sometimes considered a throwaway price because realistically the buyer will rarely agree to the price. Therefore, the initial price can be unreasonably high. The desired price is amount that would make the dotcom feel that the deal is fair. The minimum price is an amount below which the dotcom refuses to continue negotiations. Establishing prices before negotiations begins gives the dotcom time to develop arguments to support each price level.

Once the self-assessment is completed, the same process is used to evaluate the opponent. A team of consultants is employed to learn the strengths, weaknesses, and valuation of the other party before negotiations begin.

The evaluation should also include due diligence in an effort to substantiate all claims made by the other party. Consultants must carefully list those claims that are substantiated and those that remain unconfirmed. Unsubstantiated claims can be used as weaknesses in the opponent's case and leveraged to receive a more favorable price.

A neutral site, such as a hotel located a distance away from each party's facilities, should be selected to hold negotiations meetings. At least three meeting rooms should be available. Each party's negotiating team has its own meeting room, and the third room is set aside for face-to-face meetings. All rooms should be on different floors.

Negotiating any deal is a strategy game in which both parties position themselves to outwit the opponent. Before any bargaining begins, both sides must establish a game plan that clearly enunciates their three positions—initial, ideal, and minimum deal. The game plan must also outline how and when each of those positions will be made known to the other party. The first party who states its position is usually at a disadvantage.

A good starting point for negotiations is for the parties to review and agree upon facts pertaining to the deal. Parties typically can agree on most facts, which gives the negotiations process positive momentum towards eventually negotiating the price. Generally, both sides will agree to most facts. Only a small number of facts are typically disputed.

Each side must determine for itself if each disputed fact is a dealbreaker. That is, if the other side does not agree to the fact, will you walk away from the deal? Very few disputes fall into the deal-breaker category. Before making this determination, each side must consider the other party's rationale for its position on the issue.

Any issue that remains on the dispute list becomes a potential dealbreaker. Each side must decide whether or not its position on the issue is flexible, and that position must be communicated to the other party. Should there be no issues in dispute, then both parties set a price for the acquisition.

Regardless of how well either party prepares for negotiations, the success of a deal rests on the success of face-to-face negotiations. Both parties must sit down at the bargaining table and agree to terms that both parties feel are fair to each other. Experienced lead negotiators carefully follow the stages of acceptance during negotiations so that neither party feels rushed into making a decision.

Once all the major concerns are discussed and agreed to, then the parties move to the next stage of negotiations, which is the letter of intent. A letter of intent is a document signed by both parties that contains the general terms of acquisition.

As the name implies, the document is to convey intent of both parties, and except in extreme situations, the document is not binding. This is called a nonbinding memorandum of understanding, which is clearly specified in the letter.

Once the letter of intent is negotiated and signed, negotiations focus on the acquisition agreement. The acquisition agreement is the binding contract that specifies the terms of the acquisition and contains representations, covenants, warranties, and indemnities made by the dotcom in exchange for the acquisition price.

The acquisition agreement takes on a traditional structure that organizes information into nine sections: introduction, price, asset transfer procedure, representations, warranties, covenants, indemnification, terms of closing the deal, and terms to terminate a deal (including legal remedies) should the closing not occur.

The acquisition of a public corporation is slightly different than that of a private corporation because information about a public corporation must be made public according to law. A public corporation must disclose material information, including materially inaccurate information of previous filing. Otherwise, the corporation and officers are exposed to criminal and civil action that can be brought by the government.

Disclosure regulations nullify the representations, covenants, warranties, and indemnification sections of an acquisition agreement. All the relative information that is covered under these sections is part of the disclosure required of a public corporation.

QUESTIONS

1. What is the purpose of the indemnity basket?

2. How would you move negotiations away from a stalemate over acquisition price?

3. What are the advantages of including an arbitration clause in the acquisition agreement?

4. How would you handle an angry opponent?

5. What is the purpose of the letter of intent?

6. How would you begin the negotiations process?

7. What are the advantages of a dotcom narrowing the scope of representation in the acquisition agreement?

8. How would you approach facts that are in disagreement?

9. What are the disadvantages of face-to-face negotiations?

10. How would you create a pricing strategy for negotiations?

CHAPTER 10

After the Deal

A deal is never done until the fat man signs the agreement.

—Anonymous

In This Chapter

- Closing the Deal
- Before the Closing
- Closing Day
- Payment
- After the Closing
- The Integration Plan

CLOSING THE DEAL

All the efforts to locate a dotcom and negotiate satisfactory acquisition terms culminates when the buyer and the dotcom close the deal. Closing is when all components of the deal come together and title to the dotcom transfers to the buyer. In exchange, the dotcom receives compensation from the buyer. The closing is also when the parties sign the acquisition agreement and the buyer signs loan agreements with lenders in return for funding the deal.

A successful closing requires that a sequence of events occur in a particular order, because of the domino effect. Events are dependent on other events happening.

In a typical closing, the dotcom withholds signing the acquisition agreement and related title documents until the dotcom receives compensation from the buyer. The buyer is unable to provide compensation until loan agreements are signed with lenders. Lenders will not transfer funds to the buyer until loan agreements are signed and liens are placed on assets used as collateral for the loans.

The sequence of events that must occur to close the deal appears obvious. First, the buyer signs the lien and loan agreements. Next, the lenders transfer funds to the buyer. Simultaneously, the buyer forwards funds to the dotcom, which signs the acquisition agreement and title documents.

However, in a number of acquisitions there is a twist to what seems to be a straightforward process. The buyer might use acquired assets of the dotcom as collateral for the loan. However, the buyer cannot agree with lenders to place a lien on those assets, since the buyer does not have title until closing is completed. The buyer is in a dilemma. Without funds provided by the lender, the buyer is unable to acquire the assets necessary to collateralize the loan.

And here is another twist. The dotcom requires proceeds from the acquisition to retire debt and free title to assets used as collateral for its loans. Title cannot transfer to the buyer without first removing liens on the assets.

This catch-22 is resolved by the dotcom, the buyer, and lenders agreeing that all the necessary documents to close the deal occur simultaneously. All documents are executed and dated at the same date and time. In this way, each party has the necessary legal right to execute the agreements to close the deal.

The Practical Side to Closing

Closing a deal is a complex process, because many documents must be signed and filed with regulatory and legal authorities at the same time. A delay in the execution or filing of any document exposes one or more parties to risk.

Let's say a buyer purchases a dotcom. The dotcom is an online retailer that owns warehouses in three states. The buyer acquires titles to the warehouses. However, titles must be transferred from the dotcom to the buyer in three different locations at the same time. The buyer is exposed to risk because the buyer is not the recorded owner of the warehouses until the documents are filed.

Closing is further complicated if the dotcom used each warehouse as collateral for loans. In this case, the lender must abate liens against the warehouses by filing necessary documents with authorities in three states before the dotcom and the buyer can file the title transfer documents.

Furthermore, let's say the warehouses are to be used by the buyer as collateral for loans, the proceeds of which are to be used to consummate the deal. The new lenders must file new liens against the warehouses in all three local jurisdictions. Until these liens are filed, new lenders are exposed to the risk that the buyer will sell the warehouses once the buyer has free title from the dotcom.

What at first seems to be a simple closing process becomes a logistical nightmare for everyone involved in the deal. The only way for each party to minimize exposure to risk is for the closing process to be carefully orchestrated. The buyer, dotcom, and lenders must decide in advance of closing the documents that must be signed and filed, and where filings must occur.

Once documents and filing requirements are identified, the parties determine who should attend the closing and where the closing should take place. Portions of the closing might occur at multiple locations, including the locations where filings are required. Present at the closing should be those who have signing authority, those who technically review documents before signing, and those who administrate the closing process.

Caution

The chief negotiator for each side should be present at the closing, since it is common that one or both parties will introduce new terms minutes before signing. The pressure of closing is leverage for extracting additional favorable terms from the other side. The chief negotiators have the skills to address these issues.

There is usually one central location for closing, and satellite closing sites are arranged if documents must be signed and filed at remote locations. Parties typically gather at a place that is convenient to all, in a location that has accommodations for the closing process. The attorney's office for either the buyer or the dotcom or the offices of the lead lender is a common place to hold a closing.

Accommodations required for closing include facilities to replicate or modify documents and at least three rooms: two rooms for the buyer and dotcom to caucus and the third room where parties meet face-to-face to execute the closing documents.

Satellite closing sites do not need to have similar accommodations, since they are used mainly to facilitate filing documents such as titles and liens at remote locations. Each satellite site should have personnel to sign and file necessary documents. For example, the dotcom may give power of attorney to local attorneys in each state where the three warehouses are located to sign deeds to the warehouses. Likewise, the buyer and lenders may give local attorneys power to file the new deed and liens against the warehouses.

Parties at the central closing location must be in constant contact with personnel at the satellite closing sites. Once documents are signed at the central closing location, authorization is given to each satellite closing site to execute and file the documents. All parties remain until the satellite closing sites report that documents have been duly filed.

Caution

The date and time of the closing must coincide with the availability of government offices to receive documents for filing. Failure to properly coordinate the closing schedule might postpone filing for days.

It is advisable that the buyer distance lenders from each other and from the dotcom at closing. This helps to minimize the exchange of information among them, which could reopen negotiations between the buyer and the lender. For example, the dotcom might inadvertently mention a point that makes a lender apprehensive about funding the deal. The lender might share this concern with other lenders, and the financing unravels. Each lender should be placed in separate rooms at the central closing site, then called in when it is time to sign the loan documents and transfer the funds to the buyer.

Expect to spend a few hours closing the deal, unless a party tries to renegotiate terms in the final minutes, in which case closing can continue for days until negotiations are completed. The closing process can be kept on scheduled by following the standard stages of closing. These are preclosing, closing, and postclosing, each of which is discussed in this chapter.

BEFORE THE CLOSING

The closing process begins several days before the closing date. During this period the buyer and the dotcom make last minute preparations to assure that everything scheduled for the closing date occurs as planned, without a problem.

The objective of the preclosing process is to identify and resolve any open issues that might break the deal at closing. In addition, the dotcom, buyer, and lender execute as many documents as is legally permissible so that only key documents are executed on closing day. For example, the buyer is responsible for arranging and execute all financing documents, except for the final loan agreement with the lender, prior to closing. This includes the commitment letter from the lender and the lender's term sheet (see Chapter 3, "Structuring and Financing the Deal").

Likewise, the dotcom and the buyer should obtain all governmental approvals prior to closing. Rarely will government agencies work within the closing schedule. Therefore, the parties must work around the government agencies' review schedule to assure that the necessary approvals are at hand on closing day.

The only items that are left to be executed at the closing are verification that documents such as title between the buyer and dotcom are in order, signing the loan agreement, and the transfer of funds from the lender to the buyer.

The buyer should work with the dotcom to satisfy any lender's requirements, such as assessing the value of the dotcom's assets that are to be used by the buyer as collateral for the loan. This should be completed prior to closing the deal.

Plan to hold several meetings during the preclosing process, during which parties exchange final versions of closing documents, such as the acquisition agreement and audit reports. Attorneys and financial advisors carefully examine these documents to assure that the buyer and dotcom can still fulfill the terms of those agreements.

Months might pass between the time the documents are negotiated and the closing date. Conditions of either party could have changed during that time, placing the party in a less advantageous position than at the time the agreements were negotiated.

Last-Minute Negotiations

Final review of the documents gives each party the opportunity to renegotiate the deal and, in extreme situations, to break the deal. Both sides must be aware that last-minute renegotiations are a common strategy in merger and acquisition deals.

The buyer or the dotcom might leverage the pressure of imminent closing to extract favorable terms that otherwise would have been rejected. There is a straightforward basis for this strategy: The opposition is presented with the implied ultimatum to agree to the new terms or the deal is broken.

A careful assessment must be made before embarking on this last-minute strategy. The term that is sought must be a point that on the surface is not a deal-breaker for the opposition. The objective is to force the opposition to weigh within a short time the advantages and disadvantages of agreeing to the term. In doing so, the opposition should not be able to conclude that accepting the term would make the deal undoable.

Neither side wants to walk away from the deal days prior to closing unless there is material reason for breaking the deal. An opponent tends to accept terms even if it is bitter to swallow, simply to close the deal on time.

Review the Closing Checklist

Prior to the closing, parties must reconcile the closing checklist that is negotiated as part of the deal agreement (see Chapter 9, "Negotiating the Deal"). Both sides must be assured that nothing is outstanding. The checklist will be reviewed again on closing day. Any outstanding item might prevent the deal from closing on schedule.

Typically, representatives of each party, such as attorneys and financial advisors, meet to review the closing checklist. Documents such as governmental approvals and the final audit report are inventoried and exchanged. Appropriate experts assess these documents following the pre-closing meeting.

Any discrepancies in the inventory and the acceptability of the documents are reported to all parties, who determine if the problem is a deal-breaker. If so, then a determination is made whether the deficit can be remedied prior to closing or whether the deficit can be resolved at all.

The parties can agree to waive an outstanding issue and leave it unresolved until after closing or simply disregard the issue. These steps should be take only when an issue is of little consequence to the success of the deal. For example, the closing checklist may require the dotcom to receive from its management employment contracts that retain management for two years following the acquisition. However, some of the managers may have yet to sign the agreement when the parties review the closing checklist. The buyer may waive the issue entirely, depending on which managers have not agreed to the terms. For example, a manager whose position is replicated in the buyer's organization and who has failed to sign the agreement is not a key player in the acquisition. Therefore, the lack of a signed agreement is immaterial to the deal.

Both sides should seriously reconsider closing should any material issue remain outstanding. No material issue should be unresolved after closing the deal, because it is harder to walk away from a deal after closing than it is before closing the deal.

The Walk-Through

The preclosing process culminates with the walk-through of the closing the day before closing day. A walk-through is more than a dress rehearsal, because documents are actually executed at this meeting. Parties meet at the site of the closing and assemble and review the final deal book.

The deal book contains all the documents pertinent to the deal, including the letter of intent, acquisition agreement, final audit report, final due diligence results, and the deal checklist. The deal book becomes the historical record of the deal.

Each side provides the other with closing opinions of attorneys and financial advisors that the operating and financial conditions have not materially changed since the deal was negotiated. Let's say that the auditor gave an opinion as to the financial condition of the dotcom at the time of negotiations. At closing, the auditor is expected to render another opinion, which reflects that the financial condition has not materially changed since the auditor's last opinion. Likewise, attorneys provide an updated opinion on actual and possible litigation the dotcom faces. Representatives of the buyer present similar opinions. Closing should be postponed if updated opinions are not presented at the walk-through. Otherwise, underlying conditions of the deal might have changed and invalidated negotiations.

Any documents that will not expose either side to unnecessary risk should be signed at the walk-through. Executing routine documents prior to closing enables parties more time to focus on key issues at closing.

Also common at the walk-through is for the buyer to initiate fund transfers by executing documents at the buyer's financial institution that assure funds will arrive at the dotcom's accounts once agreements are signed at closing.

Some financial institutions require a lead-time to transfer funds to give the financial institutions time to receive internal approvals before funds are wired to the dotcom. Similar arrangements must be made with lenders, since they too need time to transfer funds to the buyer or directly to the dotcom on behalf of the buyer. A further discussion about fund transfer is in the section "Payment" in this chapter.

CLOSING DAY

Expect a minimum of activities on the day the deal closes, assuming that issues that could be resolved prior to closing have been addressed. At closing, all documents are reviewed by attorneys for the buyer, attorneys for the dotcom, and when necessary, attorneys for the lenders. This is the final review before all parties execute the documents.

Parties also review the closing checklist to assure that all the necessary opinions, reports, and other material to support the acquisition agreement are received in good condition. All missing supportive material must be addressed before the closing continues.

In reality, a supporting document might inadvertently be misplaced or somehow fail to be present at the closing. If the document is a representation or opinion rather than a material aspect of the closing, then the buyer and dotcom can agree to proceed with the closing in the absence of a supporting document. In doing so, the side who failed to provide the document can having its attorney sign a stipulation or render a written opinion that the missing document exists and contains no information that hampers closing the deal. The attorney also agrees to submit the missing document shortly following the closing.

However, closing must be postponed if the missing document plays a material role in closing the deal. For example, the acquisition agreement might contain a formula used to set the acquisition price. The formula states that the buyer will pay the dotcom a multiple of earnings. Earnings are stipulated in an independent auditor's report that is presented at closing. If the auditor's report is delayed, then parties must delay the closing.

Documents presented at the closing must reflect any last-minute changes that were identified during the walk-through. Once counsel for the buyer and dotcom approves the wording in the documents, the person designated by the board of directors for each corporation signs and dates the documents.

Fund and Title Transfer

Next, the buyer instructs its financial institution to electronically transfer funds to the account designated by the dotcom, if this hasn't been authorized prior to closing day. The dotcom waits to receive confirmation that funds were received by its financial institution.

Fund transfer is a more efficient method of payment than using a check. A check must be carried to the financial institution for processing, which exposes the dotcom to unnecessary risk, and the dotcom may not have access to the funds for several days. In contrast, funds are immediately available to the dotcom following the electronic fund transfer.

The fund transfer process becomes complex whenever a lender is involved, because the lender typically forwards funds to the buyer before the buyer transfers funds to the dotcom. This additional step should require a minimum of delay if all parties have their financial institutions on standby for the closing. You can learn the details of making payment for the deal in the next section of this chapter.

The buyer and dotcom also authorize any satellite closing sites to execute their documents, which includes title transfers and title recordings. The dotcom representative executes the documents and the buyer's representative confirms to the buyer that the process is completed.

The final step in closing is for the parties to review the checklist for the last time and compare each item against the executed document. The deal is official once the parties determine that all the documents are executed properly.

The buyer, dotcom, or the lender can easily postpone a closing because of an oversight. There are many documents required to close a deal. Likewise, many people are directly involved in the closing. And the closing must be coordinated with outside parties, such as government agencies for filings and approvals and financial institutions for fund transfers. Each document, person, and third party is a point of failure. Therefore, it is critical that a representative from both the buyer and the dotcom be appointed to coordinate all the aspects of closing to assure that all participants are synchronized with the closing schedule. For example, each financial institution that is involved in fund transfers must be notified well in advanced of closing and asked to have appropriate personnel on standby during the closing. Failure to do this might find that the person at the financial institution who can authorize large fund transfers is unavailable when it is time to transfer funds.

PAYMENT

Rarely are dotcoms paid by check for the acquisition of their company by the buyer. A preferred method of payment is through an electronic transfer of funds. This is called a *wire transfer*. A wire transfers consists of a series of book entries in which the buyer's financial institution debits the buyer's account for the amount of the transfer and the dotcom's financial institution credits the dotcom's account for the same amount. No actual money transfers. All the cash remains in the banking system. There are two kinds of wire transfer: domestic wire transfer and international foreign transfer.

Domestic Wire Transfers

The domestic wire transfer is executed within the Federal Reserve System of banks. There are 12 district Federal Reserve banks throughout the United States. Each district bank has many branches within the district. You might say that Federal Reserve banks are banks for financial institutions. Each financial institution that is a member of the Federal Reserve System has an account at a Federal Reserve Bank.

Financial institutions are identified to the Federal Reserve System by an American Banking Association number. This is a unique number that is assigned to a financial institution by the American Banking Association.

Wire transfer consists of a series of instructions that are transmitted from one financial institution to the Federal Reserve Bank and from the Federal Reserve Bank to another financial institution. Instructions travel over a private computer network, commonly referred to as the Fed Wire.

Here's what happens when funds are transferred from the buyer to the dotcom on the day the deal closes (see Figure 10–1). The buyer authorized its financial institution to wire funds to the dotcom by providing the financial institution with the amount of the transfer, the buyer's account, the dotcom's account, and the dotcom's financial institution's American Banking Association number.

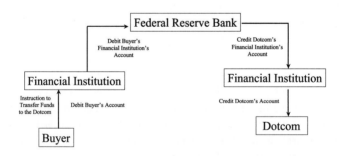

Figure 10–1 Domestic fund transfer over Fed Wire.

The buyer's financial institution debits the buyer's account for the amount of the transfer and issues instructions to the Federal Reserve Bank. These instructions tell the Federal Reserve Bank to transfer the same amount from the buyer's financial institution's Federal Reserve Bank account to the dotcom's financial institution's Federal Reserve Bank account.

The Federal Reserve Bank debits the buyer's financial institution's Federal Reserve Bank account and credits the dotcom's financial institution's Federal Reserve Bank account. Finally, the dotcom's financial institution credits the dotcom's account, then notifies the dotcom that the funds are available.

Caution

The financial institution used by the buyer and the dotcom must be a member of the Federal Reserve banking system and have accounts with the Federal Reserve Bank. Otherwise, the financial institution must arrange with a Federal Reserve banking system member to fulfill the transfer, which could incur additional expense for the buyer.

The buyer's financial institution has the right to request that the wire transfer be rescinded if the revocation request is made within a reasonable time following the wire transfer request. Let's say that through a clerical error and late renegotiations, an inaccurate amount was ordered transferred from the buyer's account to the dotcom. The error can be remedied by rescinding the request. The request will be honored if the Federal Reserve System has sufficient time to retrieve the funds—for example, if the original transfer was still processing and had yet to reach the dotcom's account.

Revocation does not have to be honored by the Federal Reserve System. The Federal Reserve System is only required to use good faith when attempting to execute the revocation request—or any request, including the request to transfer funds. Furthermore, the dotcom has the right to refuse to return the funds if the transfer is completed prior to the revocation request.

However, the Federal Reserve Bank is liable for transferring funds under normal business conditions once the transfer request is received from the buyer's institution. This assures the dotcom that it will have the proceeds of the deal available to use on closing day.

The dotcom must review terms of its account with the financial institution to determine when the dotcom's account will be credited with the transferred funds. Although the Federal Reserve System credits the dotcom's financial institution's Federal Reserve System account with the funds, the dotcom's financial institution must credit the dotcom's account before funds are available to the dotcom.

Under federal banking law, the dotcom's financial institution must credit the account promptly. However, the definition of promptly is left to the discretion of the financial institution. The agreement between the dotcom and the financial institution typically contains the definition of promptly and specifies when funds will become available to the dotcom.

Caution

Transfer all funds before 3:00 p.m.. Otherwise, the transfer may not be completed the same day due to Federal Reserve processing deadlines. Deadlines can be extended, however, in extraordinary conditions. The financial institution must contact the Federal Reserve Bank and request an extension of the deadline. The Federal Reserve Bank has the option to comply with such a request.

International Wire Transfer

An international wire transfer follows a similar procedure, except the Federal Reserve Bank is not used. Instead, the buyer and dotcom use correspondent banks. A correspondent bank is a financial institution that holds accounts for corporations and for other financial institutions, such as other correspondent banks.

Instructions to transfer funds are sent via telex. The telex is an electronic communiqué that is similar to instructions that flow over the Fed Wire. It differs from the Fed Wire in that more than one correspondent bank might be involved in the transfer.

Here's how it works (see Figure 10–2). The buyer instructs its financial institution to transfer funds to the dotcom's financial institution. As with domestic wire transfers, the financial institution debits the buyer's account and instructs the financial institution's correspondent bank to transfer funds from the financial institution's account at the correspondent bank to the dotcom's financial institution.

The buyer's financial institution's correspondent bank might be the same correspondent bank as is used by the dotcom's financial institution. In this case, the correspondent bank debits the buyer's financial institution's account and credits the dotcom's financial institution's account. The dotcom's financial institution is also instructed to credit the dotcom's account.

However, the dotcom's financial institution may use a different correspondent bank. Therefore, another step is added to the transfer. That is, each correspondent bank debits and credits the other correspondent bank's account. Correspondent banks typically have accounts at each other's bank. Figure 10–3 illustrates this process.

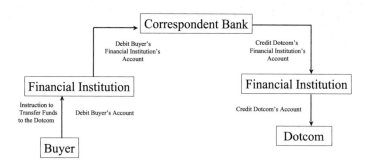

Figure 10–2 International fund transfer using telex and the different correspondent bank.

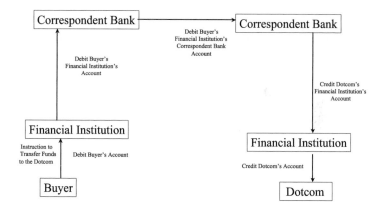

Figure 10–3 International fund transfer using telex and the different correspondent bank.

Caution

Typically, there is a 12:30 p.m. deadline on all international wire transfers.

International wire transfers can be recalled by the buyer's financial institution, such as in the case when the buyer's account lacks funds.

Checks

In rare circumstances, the acquisition price of a deal is paid by check. A check is a written document that instructs a specified financial institution to debit the buyer's account by a specific amount and give the payee of the check cash.

Dotcoms who agree to receive a check as payment in lieu of a fund transfer should only accept a bank check. A bank check is a check issued or certified by a bank rather by the buyer. Bank checks have the full backing of the issuing or certifying bank, which is generally considered low risk. There are three types of bank checks: a bank check, a certified check, and a cashier's check. A bank check is a checked issued by a bank and is considered the equivalent of cash. Payment of the check can be stopped only at the request of the buyer and only for reasons of theft and fraud. Otherwise, the bank must honor the check when presented by the dotcom. The bank must pay the amount stated on the check whenever the check is presented to the bank.

A certified check is a check issued by the buyer that the bank certifies as having sufficient funds in the buyer's account to cover payment of the check. A certified check cannot be stopped, although a bank can fail to honor the check. In this case, the bank is directly liable to the dotcom for failure to pay funds upon presentment of the certified check to the bank.

Let's say that a buyer gives a dotcom a certified check in the amount of $10 million to consummate the deal. The dotcom presents the certified check to the bank for collection; however, the bank refuses to honor the check. The dotcom can take legal action directly against the bank for failure to pay. Furthermore, the buyer can become the target in a secondary legal action.

A cashier's check is a check issued by the bank. The bank must honor the check, and failure to do so exposes the bank to similar liabilities as with a certified check. However, only the bank is liable, since the bank, not the buyer, issued the check. There is minimal risk to the dotcom, since only a bank failure prevents the check from being honored by the bank. Furthermore, the cashier's check is insured under the FDIC for up to $100,000, assuming the bank is a member of the FDIC.

Typically, checks are deposited into the dotcom's account and the dotcom's financial institution presents the check to the issuing bank for collection. This process can delay access to the funds for several weeks, depending on the arrangements the dotcom has with its financial institution.

AFTER THE CLOSING

Once the deal is closed, the dotcom becomes a legal component of the buyer's corporation. The dotcom and the buyer turn their attention to two tasks. These are to clean up the loose ends of the closing processing and to integrate both corporations into the buyer's organization.

Cleanup involves the assembly of all the documents that reflect the closing, then the distribution of those documents to the appropriate parties. Although cleanup is considered an administrative task, neither the buyer nor the dotcom should minimize the effort required to complete this job.

There are many documents that are executed prior to and at closing. These include the

- Agreement in principal
- Acquisition agreement
- Audit report
- Legal and expert opinions
- Titles to assets such as real property
- Certification of insurance
- Financing agreements
- Stipulations
- Representations
- Warranties
- Covenants

Each party to the deal, including lenders and attorneys, receives either original or copies of some or all of the documents. An important facet of the cleanup process is for each party to identify its requirements for documents and for the closing team to furnish those documents.

Not all documents are available in one location at closing. For example, filing title transfers might occur at several remote locations. Although the filings are confirmed the day of closing, written confirmation, such as a dated, stamped copy of the filing, is not available until days following the closing. On closing, the parties are likely to receive only faxed copies of these documents, which are no substitute for the original copies. Therefore, the closing team must plan to extend the cleanup process beyond the closing day. This typically does not present a problem, because final documentation of the deal is usually contained in a deal book that is prepared and distributed weeks following the closing.

A deal book is a formal, bound presentation of all the material that documents the deal. The deal book contains a table of contents and is indexed, which makes it easy for the parties to reference supporting documents or terms of the acquisition agreement. In addition to being a repository of documents relating to the deal, a deal book can also become a narrative of the deal itself, documenting major events in the life of the deal.

THE INTEGRATION PLAN

Following the cleanup of the deal closing, the buyer must focus on integrating the dotcom's operation with its own operation. The success or failure of the integration process determines whether or not the buyer will realize the benefits of the deal.

The integration process begins by the buyer forming an integration team consisting of key personnel from the buyer's and the dotcom's organizations. The integration team should consist of a management core who is responsible to see the integration process through to the end and of transient members who join the team as their expertise is required and leave when they are no longer needed for the integration process. There should be at least one member who is designated as the chief planner and team leader.

The initial objective of the integration team is to develop a formal plan, called the integration plan, that identifies the tasks that must be completed to achieve integration of the buyer and the dotcom. Subsequent objectives are to perform each task and, if necessary, revise the list of future tasks that must be performed.

It is important that the integration team consider the resources needed to perform each task and to establish the deadlines for completing each task; otherwise, the postacquisition process can lose the momentum it had following the closing. Formal project planning must be used to assure that integration is achieved within a reasonable time period.

The planning process begins by the integration team analyzing the financial and operating information of both the buyer and dotcom to determine if the dotcom should be operated as a subsidiary or as a fully integrated component of an existing operating unit. The analysis takes into consideration tax advantages and disadvantages, litigation exposure, and the synergy of both corporate cultures. Various outside and internal professionals are employed by the integration team to evaluate issues that surround integrating both operations.

The scope of the integration plan is dramatically reduced should the analysis conclude that the dotcom will operate as a subsidiary. In this case, the integration team focus moves from operating issues to financial reporting and oversight control.

Subsidiary Integration

In a subsidiary integration, the dotcom continues operations as if the acquisition had not occured. However, the integration team may intervene if an aspect of the dotcom's operations requires support from the buyer.

Let's say that a brick-and-mortar corporation acquired an online retailer. The online retailer began as a startup operation and is lacking a well-oiled distribution and customer support operation. The brick-and-mortar corporation complements this weakness, which was a key reason for the acquisition. The integration team may conclude that the online retailer should continue as a subsidiary of the brick-and-mortar, but the brick-and-mortar should handle distribution and customer support for the dotcom. Therefore, the integration plan includes tasks to provide financial reporting and oversight control along with tasks that are required to move distribution and customer support from the dotcom and to the existing brick-and-mortar operation.

Financial reporting from the dotcom requires that the books and records of the dotcom be translated into the format of the buyer's books and records. The simplest way to achieve this goal is to allow the dotcom's accounting method to remain unchanged. A conversion program is developed that translates results from the dotcom's accounting system to the buyer's accounting system format.

The integration plan should develop a two-pronged approach to integrate financial reporting. The first part of the approach is an interim plan that establishes a temporary method whereby the buyer's financial results for the first quarter following the acquisition can properly reflect the dotcom's operations. The second part of the approach is to devise a permanent method of integrating financial reporting.

Oversight control is a way in which the buyer manages the dotcom's operations. It is not uncommon for the buyer to leave intact the management that runs the dotcom if it has been successful and continues to be loyal to the dotcom business following the acquisition.

In this case, the buyer assigns the dotcom operations to one of its senior-level managers, who becomes the buyer's representative in all of the dotcom operations. Typically, this senior-level manager must approve any material change in the dotcom's business that deviates from standard operating procedures. Otherwise, the dotcom's management is held responsible for bottom-line operations.

Full Integration

The integration team should expect to develop a more involved integration plan if the dotcom is not going to be operated as a subsidiary of the buyer, but will become fully integrated with the buyer's operation. The initial task of a full integration plan is for the integration team to identify operating units both of the dotcom and of the buyer, then compare the detailed operations of each unit. An operating unit consists of profit centers within each organization and support operations that work as internal vendors to profit centers.

For example, a dotcom book reseller might organize profit centers around categories of books such as professional and reference books, consumer computer books, and fiction. The executive responsible for a profit center operates as a chief operating officer and has the freedom within reason to do anything to earn profits for his or her operation. Profit center executives might use common support operations, such as warehousing, advertising, and computers, to run the profit center. The costs of those operations are charged backed to each profit center based on the amount of service used by the profit center. The profit center and each service operation should be considered an operating unit.

Reviewing and comparing the operating units involves several objectives. First, the integration team needs to recognize the strengths and weaknesses of each operating unit, including the cost effectiveness of its operations. The objective is to identify complementary operations and redundancies that exist within the new organization. Next, the integration team must take operating units and reassemble them on paper into a more competitive organization. The first draft of the reorganization considers efficiency and redundancy.

In an ideal world, these are the only two factors the integration team needs to consider. Realistically, however, the integration team must examine other factors that assure the synergy of the reorganization. Operating units of both the dotcom and the buyer must be able and willing to work together; otherwise, the reconstituted organization is bound for failure.

A clue to whether or not the reorganization will socially and politically work is found in the negotiation process. If negotiations were not hostile and management of the dotcom and the buyer built mutual trust, then these feelings are likely to permeate each organization. However, antagonism occurring during negotiations tends to have negative repercussions when companies integrate following consummation of the deal.

Corporate culture tends to differ between the online world and the brick-and-mortar world. Dotcom companies usually have loose personal regulation as compared to more traditional businesses. This difference can cause friction among employees when the buyer attempts to integrate operations. Dotcom employees are likely to reject stricter regulations, and key employees might leave the new organization for another dotcom. The integration team must carefully examine both corporate cultures and identify potential problems before the integration plan is presented to management and to employees. Furthermore, the integration team must derive a solid procedure for addressing cultural differences; otherwise, the integration will not flow smoothly.

All possible and probable problems facing the integration of both companies must be identified and addressed, and solutions to those problems must become a material part of the integration plan. Failure to focus on the details of each problem and to resolve those problems almost guarantees failure.

Asset Integration

The buyer's financial statements must reflect the integration of the dotcom's assets into the buyer's organization. To achieve this result, the integration team must first focus on consolidating the financial assets of the dotcom with the buyer's financial assets. This includes accounts receivables, securities, and cash.

Next, the integration team must determine the value of the dotcom's tangible assets so they can be consolidated on the buyer's balance sheet. This valuation process is made simpler if the buyer purchased the assets of the dotcom, since the purchase price is the market value of the assets. The buyer receives a hidden benefit, because the purchase price is likely to be higher than the book value of the asset carried on the dotcom's balance sheet. Therefore, the buyer realizes a higher value than that reflected on the dotcom's financial statements, and that higher value can be depreciated.

However, acquisitions other than a straight purchase of assets involve a more complex valuation process and require advice from tax accountants as to whether the buyer must use the book value or market value of the asset when consolidating the asset in the buyer's balance sheet.

The integration team must also search for and remove duplicate assets from the dotcom's balance sheet before beginning the consolidation process. For example, the dotcom might have a wholly owned subsidiary. The balance sheet of the dotcom records the asset as a security and the subsidiary records the asset as equity. These are duplicate assets because both refer to the same asset. Therefore, accountants will offset duplicate assets and not include them on the consolidated balance sheet.

Personnel Integration

Personnel integration is the most delicate aspect of any deal because employees make the business flourish, and without them, the buyer has simply purchased equipment. The integration team must keep in mind that an acquisition is a volatile event in the lives of most employees, because their livelihood is in question.

Employees will look for clues from any source on whether or not they will retain their positions with the firm, be terminated, or work under conditions that are different from their current job—and possibly unacceptable. Expect that employees will associate any action taken by the company—even normal operating procedures—with how they will be treated following the integration.

The integration team can expect a grace period during which employees will carefully weigh their options of staying with the firm or leaving for better opportunities. However, the longer the integration team waits to announce its plans, the higher the risk that desired employees will leave the firm.

Prior to closing the deal, the buyer should identify key employees and open a dialogue with them to assure them that their needs will be addressed following the acquisition. This action has a stabilizing effect on key employees and on their developing relationships with the buyer. This relationship also provides a sounding board for the integration team for determining how other employees view the acquisition.

The integration team must quickly move to open communications with key employees on all levels. These are employees who operate critical areas of the business and who can train others. Each key employee should be spoken to personally and reassured that he or she has a position following the integration and that working conditions will be acceptable. In some cases, the integration team might offer key employees a short-term employment contract that will solidify the relationship between the employee and the company.

Once the needs of key employees are addressed, the integration team must determine which employees remain with the firm following integration. This is accomplished by focusing on the reorganization of operating units.

- The first objective is to create an efficient business organization.
- The second objective is to determine the personnel resources required to run each operating unit. Each personnel resource is a position that has a job description and job skills.

- The third objective is for the integration team to evaluate existing personnel both in the dotcom's and in the buyer's organizations in an effort to match current employees with positions. Current employees will not fill all the positions because their job skills will not match every position. Employees who cannot be matched with a position will be designated for termination.

The integration team must devise a fair and equitable termination package before announcing any terminations. Termination is a traumatic experience for an employee and can have lingering repercussions. The terminated employee might become disgruntled and bring litigation. Remaining employees see how the company treated the terminated employee, then decide whether they want to be treated in the same way. If not, then they may look for other opportunities.

Most, if not all, of these problems can be avoided by addressing the needs of the terminated employee. For example, the terminated employee might be offered three months pay that can be distributed in a lump sum or over the period similar to regular pay. The termination date should be recorded as of the date the employee received his or her last compensation, which might be three months following termination notice. This gives the terminated employee three months to find employment. And if he or she is successful, then there isn't an employment gap on his or her resume.

Medical insurance is another factor the integration team should consider extending to terminated employees. Ideally, the company continues coverage at least during the three-month period. In extraordinary cases, medical coverage may be extended for a full year following termination.

The integration plan must contain procedures for termination. For example, the plan is likely to stipulate that all termination notices will occur on a Friday morning and be completed by noontime. Furthermore, employees will be called to the personnel department one at time, then asked to leave the building without returning to their desks. Their personal belongings will be packed and delivered to their homes.

Caution

Counsel should be consulted prior to announcing termination to assure that the company isn't violating any federal or state laws.

Three Integration Plans

The integration team should devise three plans. These are an interim integration plan, a short-term integration plan, and a long-term integration plan. An interim integration plan specifies the strategy the corporation will use to continue operations in the immediate future, such as for conducting business in the days following the closing. For example, interim managers might be appointed to act as caretakers and to handle day-to-day operations.

The short-term integration plan focuses on a five-year strategy and should contain the reconstituted organization plan that reflects political, cultural, and similar concerns. Also included in the short-term integration plan are operating units that are to be sold and disbanded and operating units that must be acquired or created.

Let's say that the dotcom distribution operations are taken over by the buyer's distribution operation. Dotcom employees are either absorbed by the existing operation or are terminated. Likewise, warehouses and other physical assets of the dotcom that are associated with the distribution operation are either absorbed or sold.

The integration team might find that the new operations require a large customer service department, but neither the dotcom nor the buyer has such a department. Therefore, the integration team must plan to either create such a department or purchase a corporation that has a complementary customer service department.

The long-term plan extends beyond five years and depicts the long-range strategy of where the corporation wants to be in the future and how it plans to reach its objectives.

Once each plan is fully developed, the integration team presents the plan to senior management for approval. Next, appropriate portions of the plans are presented to employees, lenders, stockholders, key customers, and vendors.

Each plan should contain a statement that predicts the future performance of the reorganized corporation. However, the statement must be followed by a disclaimer to prevent any misunderstandings should the performance of the corporation not meet the predictions.

SUMMARY

Closing is when all components of the deal come together and title to the dotcom transfers to the buyer. In exchange, the dotcom receives compensation from the buyer.

All documents are executed and dated at the same date and time. In this way, each party has the necessary legal right to execute the agreements to close the deal.

Many documents must be signed and filed with regulatory and legal authorities at the same time. A delay in the execution or filing of any document exposes one or more parties to risk. The buyer, dotcom, and lenders must decide in advance of closing the documents that must be signed and filed, and where the filings must occur.

Present at the closing should be those who have signing authority, those who technically review documents before signing, and those who administrate the closing process.

There is usually one central location for closing, and satellite closing sites are arranged if documents must be signed and filed at remote locations.

Accommodations required for closing include facilities to replicate or modify documents and at least three rooms: two rooms for the buyer and dotcom to caucus and a third room where parties meet face to face to execute the closing documents. Satellite closing sites do not need to have similar accommodations, since they are used mainly to facilitate filing documents such as title and liens at remote locations. Each satellite site should have personnel to sign and file necessary documents.

Parties at the central closing location must be in constant contact with personnel at the satellite closing sites. Once documents are signed at the central closing location, authorization is given to each satellite closing site to execute and file its documents. All parties remain until the satellite closing sites report that documents have been duly filed.

The closing process can be kept on schedule by following the standard stages of closing: preclosing, closing, and postclosing.

The objective of the preclosing process is to identify and resolve any open issues that might break the deal at closing. In addition, the dotcom, buyer, and lender execute as many documents as are legally permissible so that only key documents are executed on closing day.

Prior to the closing, parties must reconcile the closing checklist that is negotiated as part of the deal agreement. Both sides must be assured that nothing is outstanding. Any outstanding item might prevent the deal from closing on schedule.

The preclosing process culminates with the walk-through of the closing the day before closing day. A walk-through is more than a dress rehearsal, because documents are actually executed at this meeting. Parties meet at the site of the closing and assemble and review the final deal book.

Expect a minimum of activities on the day the deal closes, assuming that issues that could be resolved prior to closing have been addressed. At closing, all documents are reviewed by attorneys for the buyer, attorneys for the dotcom, and when necessary, attorneys for the lenders. This is the final review before all parties execute the documents.

Next, the buyer instructs its financial institution to electronically transfer funds to the account designated by the dotcom, if this hasn't been authorized prior to closing day. The dotcom waits to receive confirmation that funds were received by its financial institution.

The buyer and dotcom also authorize any satellite-closing sites to execute their documents, which include title transfers and title recordings. The dotcom representative executes the documents and the buyer's representative confirms to the buyer that the process is completed.

Rarely are dotcoms paid by check for the acquisition of their company by the buyer. A preferred method of payment is through an electronic transfer of funds, called a wire transfer. A wire transfers consists of a series of book entries in which the buyer's financial institution debits the buyer's account for the amount of the transfer and the dotcom's financial institution credits the dotcom's account for the same amount. No actual money transfers. All the cash remains in the banking system.

Once the deal is closed, the dotcom becomes a legal component of the buyer's corporation. The dotcom and the buyer turn their attention to two tasks. These are to clean up the loose ends of the closing processing and to integrate both corporations into the buyer's organization.

Following the cleanup of the deal closing, the buyer must focus on integrating the dotcom's operation with its own operation. The integration process begins by the buyer forming an integration team consisting of key personnel from both the buyer's and the dotcom's organizations.

The initial objective of the integration team is to develop a formal plan, called the integration plan, that identifies the tasks that must be completed to achieve integration of the buyer and the dotcom. Subsequent objectives are to perform each task and, if necessary, revise the list of future tasks that must be performed.

The planning process begins by the integration team analyzing the financial and operating information of both the buyer and the dotcom to determine if the dotcom should be operated as a subsidiary or as a fully integrated component of an existing operating unit.

The integration team should expect to develop a more involved integration plan if the dotcom is not going to be operated as a subsidiary of the buyer, but will become fully integrated with the buyer's operation. The initial task of a full integration plan is for the integration team to identify operating units both of the dotcom and of the buyer, then compare the detailed operations of each unit.

The integration team needs to recognize the strengths and weaknesses of each operating unit, including the cost effectiveness of its operations. The integration team must take operating units and reassemble them on paper into a more competitive organization. The first draft of the reorganization considers efficiency and redundancy. The integration team must examine other factors that assure the synergy of the reorganization.

All possible and probable problems facing the integration of both companies must be identified and addressed, and solutions to those problems must become a material part of the integration plan. The integration team should devise an interim integration plan, a short-term integration plan, and a long-term integration plan.

QUESTIONS

1. How do you determine which employees to terminate?

2. What is the purpose of an integration team?

3. How does an integration team go about reorganizing the firm?

4. What personnel problems would you foresee in integrating the dotcom into the buyer?

5. Why is it important to have three separate rooms at the central closing site?

6. What role do satellite closing sites play in a closing?

7. How are funds paid to the dotcom at closing?

8. What is the difference between the Fed Wire and telexes?

9. Must all items on the closing checklist be addressed before closing?

10. Why is it a good practice to keep parties, including lenders, apart at closing until they are needed to execute a document?

CHAPTER 11

Business Alliances

Sharing a problem is the fastest solution to the problem.

— Anonymous

In This Chapter...

- Fundamentals
- Outsourcing Alliances
- Strategic Alliances
- Joint Ventures

FUNDAMENTALS

The Internet has created a new business climate within which economic power and control has shifted from product manufacturers and service providers to the customer. No longer can businesses decide what products are built or what services are offered; nor can businesses decide the market prices set on these products and services. Instead, the customer makes these decisions.

Competition to find and keep customers is keen. Customers are smart buyers and have little loyalty to vendors. They are no longer predictable. Customers want goods and services that exactly meet their needs at or below market value. And they want it now. Failure to meet this demand causes a business to lose the customer.

The new business climate is also more competitive—competitors are quick to offer similar or better products at or below another company's price. A corporation's lock on a product is short-lived because competitors are organized to replicate and enhance innovative products and services.

Years ago a corporation could easily spend time and money developing and thoroughly testing a product before introducing it to the market. The cost of research and development presented a barrier for competitors. Only large corporations could afford to compete.

Today the marketplace demands that consumer needs be fulfilled immediately. There is little, if any, time for research, development, and test marketing. Businesses must have a rush-to-market attitude to survive.

There are thousands of businesses that offer basically the same products and services, causing their offerings to become a commodity where price is the only difference between businesses. Commodity pricing has a ripple effect on business. Customers push businesses to compete on price alone, which dramatically reduces margins. Companies look at cost-cutting as a method to give them the competitive edge in the market. Some companies have gone to the extreme if buying customers by offering them incentives to become customers, offering products or services at below cost for a limited time.

Partnering

A common method used by dotcoms to meet market demands is to create business alliances, sometimes referred to as *partnering*. An alliance occurs when two or more businesses join to offer products and services to the customer.

Corporations that have a mutual market segment and whose operations are complementary form alliances. For example, a dotcom might form a home improvement Web site where customers visit to receive answers to their home improvement questions and learn how to make repairs themselves. The dotcom may want to offer design services, contracting services, and do-it-yourself merchandise. Rather than expand the business into these areas, the dotcom can locate other companies that are already in these businesses and with which the dotcom can create alliances.

An alliance enables a dotcom to rapidly expand its offerings to customers without spending the time and money to develop or acquire those offerings. A dotcom that wants to offer a design service need only enter into a business alliance with a firm that already offers such a service.

A business alliance uses a single interface with the customer to provide a breadth of product and service offerings that meets the customers' every need. However, behind this unified front, each member of the alliance is responsible for providing its product or service either independently or in coordination with other alliance members. A dotcom is able to quickly adjust to competition and new demands of the marketplace by forming and dissolving business alliances.

Let's say that an office supply dotcom has a steady clientele who enter orders through the company's Web site. However, a competitor challenges the dotcom by offering business customers the capability of internally approving orders before they are placed with the vendor. Customers' employees can order supplies on the vendor's Web site from a preselected inventory list, which is determined by the customer. The vendor holds up the order until an authorized person from the customer's company approves the order over the vendor's Web site.

In essence, the competitor offers business customers internal management controls over purchasing supplies. This value-added feature quickly causes the dotcom's customers to defect. The fastest way to stem the outflow of customers is for the dotcom to create an alliance with another dotcom that has a similar system.

Products offered by the dotcom office supply company are added to the alliance member's management control system and the system is linked to the dotcom's Web site. This alliance enables the dotcom office supply company to incorporate the online management control system as part of its offering to customers.

From Tim Miller, Webmergers.com

Consolidation Strategy

Two fast-growing online payment players decided they could grow faster together and merged in a merger of equals intended to form a "category killer" in the electronic payments marketplace. Closely held X.com merged with PayPal.com, yielding a combined customer base of about 600,000 users. Each company will have 50 percent of the combined entity and X.com CEO Bill Harris will remain in charge. Harris was formerly CEO of Intuit, Inc.

Both companies offer free payment services that allow people to send money instantly via email. Also, both companies have been seeing tremendous growth, attracting more than 10,000 users a day. PayPal's visitors grew 1400 percent from December 1999 to January 2000, while X.com's grew nearly 400 percent in the same period.

The announcement came just days after the mother of all person-to-person payment marketplaces, Ebay, announced it was working with Wells Fargo and Co. to develop its own system to allow auction sellers to accept payment by credit card. Ebay's move no doubt put additional pressure on PayPal and X.com to join forces.

Finding a Partner

An alliance is a long-term business relationship that is similar to a marriage in that each partner is committed to the other. It is critical that each member of the alliance shares a common objective and have the trust and respect of other alliance members. Each member brings something of value to the table that enhances the alliance's ability to satisfy its customers' entire needs. Members of the alliance remain interdependent corporations: each depends on the other to succeed.

An alliance has ups and downs like any marriage. Members won't agree on every aspect of the business, but they will agree to disagree, then work toward common goals. These are to make money for the customer, save money for the customer, or provide goods or services that enhance the value of their offerings to their customers.

There is a blur among organizations that form the alliance. Alliance members must share information on all levels and across organizations in an effort to solve business problems. Each member must have the integrity and competency to contribute to the goal, and the openness to have free flow of information among the alliance. Each alliance member is accountable to other members and to the customer. Failure to fulfill this commitment will cause a member to be dropped from the alliance and replaced by a competitor.

Flexibility to adjust membership in the alliance is a strong advantage an alliance has over other forms of business. The right blend of products and services can quickly be assembled—and disassembled, if necessary—by changing alliance members.

Members of alliances operate as separate corporations. They have their own facilities, employees, and financial statements. Each benefits from membership by sharing customers and receiving financial incentives such as finders' fees from other members. A finder's fee is a modest amount paid to an alliance member by another alliance member for referring a customer. For example, a corporation might permit a dotcom to offer its design services as part of the dotcom's Web site. The dotcom receives a percentage of each sale that passes through the Web site to the design service corporation as a finder's fee.

From Tim Miller, Webmergers.com

Brick-to-Click Strategy

An important deal was a classic bricks-to-clicks deal—Kinko's purchase of a majority of liveprint.com, an online printing services company that Kinko's will use to jumpstart its Web efforts. Kinko's and other investors capitalized the property at about $40 million.

At Webmergers.com we keep getting asked when we will see a major wave of bricks-and-mortar companies buying dotcoms to energize their Internet efforts. Our answer is always the same—when prices come down to something approximating sanity. In the case of liveprint.com, it may well be that the large number of competitors in this space forced the valuation down to where Kinko's could believe that a "buy" was as good as a "build."

OUTSOURCING ALLIANCES

A business alliance traditionally begins as a close vendor–client relationship where the success of a vendor's operation is closely dependent on the success of the client's operation. In a close vendor–client relationship, the client has a strong influence over how the vendor operates the vendor's business. For example, the client may dictate personnel recruitment, selection of suppliers, and the procedures used by the vendor to provide the client with product or services. The vendor in a close vendor–client relationship has little latitude in dealing with the client, because the client may be one of only a few clients that are serviced by the vendor.

Outsourcing is a common close vendor–client relationship model. Outsourcing is a business alliance in which a client turns over the operation of a portion of its business to an outsourcing firm. The operation is run within the procedures established by the client, but under the direction of the vendor. In essence, the outsourced operation is an extension of the client's business.

In an outsourcing alliance, the vendor is paid a regular fixed fee in exchange for providing a definable level of service to the client. Employees of the vendor interact with the client's employees as if they were working for the same corporation.

Let's say that a dotcom is in a rapid growth period where it needs to quadruple its warehouse operation within the year. Management of the dotcom lacks the experience to successfully undertake such growth. In a strategic move, management engages an outsourcing firm who takes over the dotcom's entire fulfillment operations. The dotcom and the outsourcing firm sign a five-year agreement whereby the outsourcing firm hires the dotcom's current fulfillment staff and leases the current warehouse and fulfillment equipment from the dotcom. In addition, the outsourcing firm leases additional warehouse space and hires its own staff to meet the growth demands of the dotcom.

From an accounting stance, the dotcom treats the outsourcing firm as a vendor and pays a fixed monthly expense, in exchange for which the dotcom is assured that its fulfillment operation runs smoothly and will maintain an acceptable performance level as demand increases for the dotcom's products and services. The dotcom also receives monthly revenue from the lease payment for use of the dotcom's warehouse.

From an operational stance, dotcom employees and systems are fully integrated with those of the outsourcing firm. Employees from both firms have access to each other's systems and facilities, and they have the same objectives.

Advantages

The advantages of an outsourcing alliance are to expand business operations quickly, acquire hard-to-find expertise, acquire the use of assets, provide cost containment, and reduce risk. Dotcoms can experience overwhelming customer demand that can outstrip the capabilities of the company. Outsourcing is a viable solution that enables a dotcom to expand operations and fulfill customer needs quickly.

However, the dotcom must be assured that the outsourcing firm has the capability to fill the void left by the dotcom; otherwise, customer frustration will result from a lack of response by the dotcom and will ultimately be the downfall of the company.

Outsourcing firms are also a resource for employees and assets that are in high demand. For example, the dotcom might require the services of several Java programmers or the use of high-performance Web hosting equipment. The market for these resources is tight. Rather than compete to acquire them, the dotcom will find it wise to create an alliance with an outsourcing company that provides programming and Web hosting services. In addition to utilizing scarce resources, the dotcom also benefits from cost containment in that the dotcom pays for just the service required to satisfy its operational needs.

Cost containment is also realized by the dotcom by agreeing to pay the outsourcing firm a fixed monthly payment for services. Services rendered by the outsourcing firm are predictable, as is payment for these services.

Minimizing risk is another advantage of outsourcing. The dotcom establishes measurable goals, which management of the outsourcing firm agrees to meet within the agreed-upon price. Risks experienced while attempting to achieve the goals is borne by the outsourcing firm. Employee termination, equipment malfunctions, and execution of the operational plan are just some of the risks to which the outsourcing firm is exposed.

Disadvantages

The disadvantages of outsourcing are unclear contractual terms, loss of expertise, loss of motivation by the outsourcing firm, and dependency on another company. The dotcom and the outsourcing company define their obligations in the outsourcing contract. Activities not covered in the outsourcing contract may not occur or may be negotiated at a later date at a premium expense.

It is difficult for attorneys to draft an outsourcing contract that considers every aspect of the outsourced operation, because business operations are difficult to define in clear and concise terms. Therefore, even the best outsourcing contracts fail to cover every facet of an outsourced operation. This leaves the dotcom exposed to services that will not be performed or to service that will be performed at a high cost, which might exceed the dotcom's outsourcing budget.

Another disadvantage of outsourcing is that the dotcom doesn't gain expertise in area operated by the outsourcing firm. The outsourcing firm's employees, not the dotcom's employees, master the outsourced operations. Once the relationship between the dotcom and the outsourcing firm is broken, the expertise remains with the outsourcing firm, and not with the dotcom.

Pressure to contain cost by the outsourcing firm is another disadvantage of outsourcing. The payment for the outsourcing service reflects anticipated expenses incurred by the outsourcing firm plus a profit for the outsourcing firm. Profit is the motive for the outsourcing firm to enter into the agreement with the dotcom. However, the outsourcing firm might underestimate the cost of providing outsourced services. Over-budgeted expenses reduce the outsourcing firm's profit, leading the outsourcing firm to cut costs, which ultimately reduces the level of service to the dotcom.

Failure to maintain an acceptable level of service by the outsourcing firm exposes the outsourcing firm to litigation by the dotcom. However, litigation doesn't address the immediate needs of the dotcom, which is to fulfill its customers' needs. The inability of the outsourcing firm to meet its obligation to the dotcom places the dotcom's operations at risk. In reality, the dotcom finds it more advantageous to increase payment to the outsourcing firm than to litigate the matter.

A dotcom's operation is dependent on the outsourcing firm, which is another disadvantage of outsourcing. Operational and financial disruptions of the outsourcing firm directly place the dotcom's operation at risk. Therefore, it is critical that the dotcom conduct a thorough due diligence of the outsourcing firm, as described in Chapter 2, "Due Diligence," and carefully negotiate outsourcing terms using the techniques described in Chapter 9, "Negotiating the Deal." Failure to do this will reflect on the dotcom's ability to service its customers.

From Tim Miller, Webmergers.com

Search for Partners Early

Based on our interactions with several hundred Internet companies that have contacted us in search of advice, Webmergers believes many struggling Internet companies could avoid shutdown by starting much earlier in their life cycle to seek strategic partners or acquirers.

We advise startups to begin planning for M&A as an exit option from the very beginning, at the business plan stage.

We suggest that principals start a concerted search for strategic partners or acquirers at least six to nine months before they are scheduled to burn through current cash reserves.

- The acquisitions search should be concurrent with attempts to obtain additional rounds of venture or angel funding.
- Waiting too long to seek an acquirer is invariably disastrous if funding sources do not emerge. Once the marketplace perceives that a seller is running out of money, the company loses leverage with buyers and is often forced to sell at a fire sale valuation or, worse, to shut down and have its bones picked over by its creditors.

We also advise most sellers to cast their nets widely for potential acquirers in order to accelerate the search and to ensure they fully address the highly diffuse pool of potential buyers. Prospective buyers of dotcoms range from Internet companies to bricks-and-mortar companies to "financial" buyers such as buyout firms. In addition, buyers of "virtual" properties can as easily as not be based in another country or geographic region.

STRATEGIC ALLIANCES

A strategic alliance is a substitution for a merger or acquisition. Parties to a strategic alliance agree to work together to achieve the same goal. Each party in a strategic alliance provides value and is exposed to risk. In return for participation in the strategic alliance, each party receives a proportion of revenues that are generated by the strategic alliance.

For example, a dotcom might create a strategic alliance with a news wire service. The wire service provides news content to the dotcom's Web site. The dotcom operates the Web site and sells and displays banner ads on the site. Both the wire service and the dotcom share the revenue generated by the banner ads.

In this example, the wire service underwrites the expense of gathering and delivering news to the dotcom. This is the value the wire service contributes to the strategic alliance. The dotcom absorbs the expense of operating the Web site, attracting visitors, and selling banner ads. Each company risks losing its investment in providing these services.

A strategic alliance is an economical way to acquire products and services without incurring a capital investment, since each participant in the alliance underwrites a portion of the expense for the opportunity to participate in the revenue stream generated by the venture. Partners in a strategic alliance typically have the expertise in the products and services that they contribute to the alliance that tends to minimize their risk. In addition, partners leverage their expertise with other ventures, which lessens the impact a strategic alliance has on a partner's business.

Let's say that a dotcom wants to offer books and other merchandise to visitors to its Web site as a collateral service. The dotcom has the option of investing heavily in inventory and a distribution system to transform the dotcom into an online reseller. The risks are enormous, especially if the dotcom has little or no experience in online reselling.

Another option is for the dotcom to enter into a strategic alliance with a seller of books and merchandise, preferably one that has an online presence. The online reseller already has an established operation that includes all the facets the dotcom requires to sell online. Furthermore, the online reseller has experience to guide both its own operations and that of the dotcom to a successful business venture.

The dotcom's value to the strategic alliance is to bring customers to the online reseller by placing a link to the reseller's Web site on the dotcom's Web site. The reseller's value to the strategic alliance is the operation required to sell and fulfill orders.

In this example, the dotcom's risk is minimal because the link to the reseller's Web site is very inexpensive. The dotcom is investing into programs that attract and maintain visitors to the dotcom's Web site. However, this expense is incurred as standard operating procedures for the Web site rather than as an additional function it must provide to attract customers for the reseller. Therefore, the dotcom is leveraging existing investments to bring value to the strategic alliance.

The online reseller brings most of the value to the strategic alliance, since it underwrites the operation of the online store. However, the expense and the risk are spread across strategic alliances with other dotcoms in addition to the reseller's operation of its own online store.

The reseller's investment to enter the strategic alliance is minimal because nearly all the investment is already made to operate the reseller's online store. The additional cost to connect to strategic alliance partners is incidental to the reseller's operation. Both the dotcom and the online reseller can possibly generate additional revenue with a minimal investment and little risk by entering into a strategic alliance.

Creating a Strategic Alliance

The impact of a strategic alliance on a business is similar to the impact of a merger or acquisition on a business. Whether a strategic alliance or a merger or acquisition, parties to the deal come together to increase their revenue potential.

Any cooperative operation is fraught with potential problems. Parties must agree on a common goal and a common strategy to obtain the goal. Conflicts can easily arise unless the operations and management styles of both parties are complementary.

Furthermore, the fiscal soundness of each party is critical to the success of the strategic alliance, because a failure of one party to adhere to the terms of the strategic alliance hinders strategic alliance partners in realizing potential revenue. Therefore, any company that desires to enter into a strategic alliance should carefully select strategic alliance partners and perform due diligence before entering into the strategic alliance agreement. Failure to adhere to such a prudent business practice exposes a business to undue risks.

Each strategic alliance partner must weigh the time and expense of a thorough due diligence against the risks involved in participating in a strategic alliance. Less stringent due diligence (see Chapter 2) is acceptable when the strategic alliance exposes the company to minimal risk. A complete due diligence must be conducted if strategic alliance partners are fiscally dependent upon each other. For example, an online reseller who forms a strategic alliance with a dotcom to allow the dotcom visitors to purchase books online exposes itself to minimal risk. Customers are basically using the dotcom's Web site to link to the online reseller's Web site. The transactions, fulfillment, display of merchandise, and customer service is handled directly by the online reseller. The dotcom does not receive inventory nor does it receive proceeds from the sale of merchandise except for a percentage of each sale, which is paid to the dotcom monthly by the online reseller.

In this case, the online reseller's only risk is the potential that the dotcom might injure the online reseller's reputation. Therefore, the online reseller is likely to focus due diligence on the public persona of the dotcom's Web site. The online reseller may not want to enter into a strategic alliance if the focus of the dotcom's Web site isn't complementary to the merchandise sold by the online reseller.

Due diligence in this example does not need to be concerned with the financial stability of the dotcom, since the online reseller is not exposed to any financial risks should the dotcom become fiscally unstable.

Terms of the strategic alliance must be carefully negotiated, as discussed in Chapter 9. The strategic alliance agreement must clearly specify tasks that each partner will perform and the compensation each will receive for participating. In addition, the strategic alliance agreement should set forth termination terms, which delineate the conditions under which a party may terminate the alliance.

The complexity of negotiations and of the strategic alliance agreement is dependent upon the risk exposure. A simple alliance, such as linking dotcom's Web site to an online reseller, does not require a sophisticated strategic alliance agreement. This agreement need only to set compensation and liability terms. More complex alliances should follow guidelines used for mergers and acquisitions.

Before parties enter into a strategic alliance, they must evaluate any government regulations that might prohibit such an alliance. Strategic alliances are considered a substitution for a merger or acquisition, and therefore fall under the same regulatory constraints.

JOINT VENTURES

A joint venture is a corporation formed by two or more independent corporations to achieve a mutually beneficial goal. A joint venture usually has a single objective and is dissolved once the goal is achieved. The joint venture is called a *consortium* if more than two independent corporations participate in the joint venture.

The goals of a joint venture can range from capitalizing on a market opportunity to development of new technology that would enhance the products and services of the industry. For example, telecommunications corporations might form a joint venture to create Internet packet transfer technology that is used by participants to efficiently transfer Internet packets.

Tech Talk

Internet Packet: An electronic envelope that contains a small piece of information that is being sent over the Internet. Internet packets are reassembled into the information at their destination.

In this case, Internet packet transfer must use the same technology regardless of which telecommunications corporation sends or receives the packet. Therefore, all the telecommunications corporations share in the benefits of the joint venture's new technology.

Joint ventures are commonly formed when the goal of the venture is to produce a product or service that is not used as a competitive edge to win market position over other members of the joint venture, such as technology that is shared among industry members.

Members of the joint venture contribute resources to the new corporation, such as capital, skilled employees, and assets that are necessary for the joint venture to reach its goal. For their participation, members of the joint venture share in the profits or free use of products and services developed by the joint venture. Let's say that telecommunications corporations form a joint venture to develop more efficient Internet packet-switching technology. Those corporations that contribute to the joint venture will have access to the new technology at no cost.

Other corporations in the industry who have not participated in the joint venture have the right to license the technology for a fee. The fee becomes revenue for the joint venture and is either reinvested into the new corporation or returned to participants in the joint venture as profit.

The joint venture agreement specifies the arrangements made with participants. This agreement itemizes each participant's contribution to the new corporation and its right to share in the technology and profit generated by the joint venture.

Advantages and Disadvantages

The advantage of forming a joint venture is to share expenses and risk, especially when the goal of the joint venture is to enhance the marketplace. For example, software and computer manufacturers might form a joint venture to perfect voice recognition technology. The results of the joint venture's efforts are a standardized voice recognition technology that can be implemented by companies in the software and computer industries. Competition is focused on how to better implement voice recognition technology in products rather than on development of the basic technology itself.

The disadvantage of a joint venture is that one approach is taken to achieve the goal of the joint venture and that approach is controlled by a single group of companies. Some participants might focus the efforts of the joint venture into a direction that is self-serving for a few companies rather than for the marketplace as a whole.

The joint venture might stifle explorations into alternative technologies that might have been developed had the joint venture not been formed. For example, a smaller firm might be intimidated and therefore not pursue the development of new technology when faced with a joint venture created by large firms to develop similar technology.

The dynamics of a joint venture and of its participants tend to work against achieving the joint venture's objective. It is common that participants temporarily assign professional employees to the joint venture as a way to share knowledge and manage the process efficiently. These employees are competitors who come together for a short time period to achieve a mutually beneficial goal. Afterwards, they return to their respective corporations and resume their competitive stance. Employees may lack the enthusiasm to fully cooperate with the joint venture because they were and will again be competitors. Instead, they will provide minimal assistance to fellow joint venture employees. With poor dynamics between coworkers, a joint venture can easily fail.

Therefore, a dotcom that considers becoming a member of a joint venture must carefully weigh the impact the joint venture will have on its business. A more advantageous approach might be to let other firms participate. If the joint venture succeeds, then the dotcom benefits by licensing the new technology.

SUMMARY

A common method used by dotcoms to meet market demands is to create business alliances, sometimes referred to as partnering. An alliance occurs when two or more businesses join to offer products and services to the customer. An alliance enables a dotcom to rapidly expand its offerings to customers without spending the time and money to develop or acquire those offerings. A dotcom that wants to offer a design service need only to enter into a business alliance with a firm that already offers such a service.

A business alliance uses a single interface with the customer to provide a breadth of product and service offerings that meets the customers' every need. However, behind this unified front, each member of the alliance is responsible for providing its product or service either independently or in coordination with other alliance members. A dotcom is able to quickly adjust to competition and new demands of the marketplace by forming and dissolving business alliances.

Each member brings something of value to the table that enhances the alliance's ability to satisfy the customers' entire needs. Members of the alliance remain interdependent corporations: each depends on the other to succeed. Each alliance member is accountable to other members and to the customer. Failure to fulfill this commitment will cause a member to be dropped from the alliance and replaced by a competitor.

A business alliance traditionally begins as a close vendor–client relationship where the success of a vendor's operation is closely dependent on the success of the client's operation. In a close vendor–client relationship, the client has a strong influence over how the vendor operates the vendor's business.

Outsourcing is a common close vendor–client-relationship model. Outsourcing is a business alliance in which a client turns over the operation of a portion of its business to an outsourcing firm. The operation is run within the procedures established by the client, but under the direction of the vendor. In essence, the outsourced operation is an extension of the client's business.

In an outsourcing alliance, the vendor is paid a regular fixed fee in exchange for providing a definable level of service to the client. Employees of the vendor interact with the client's employees as if they were working for the same corporation.

The advantages of an outsourcing alliance are to expand business operations quickly, acquire hard-to-find expertise, acquire the use of assets, provide cost containment, and reduce risk.

The disadvantages of outsourcing are unclear contractual terms, loss of expertise, loss of motivation by the outsourcing firm, and dependency on another company.

A strategic alliance is a substitution for a merger or acquisition. Parties to a strategic alliance agree to work together to achieve the same goal. Each party in a strategic alliance provides value and is exposed to risk. In return for participation in the strategic alliance, each party receives a proportion of revenues that are generated by the strategic alliance.

A strategic alliance is an economical way to acquire products and services without incurring a capital investment, since each participant in the alliance underwrites a portion of the expense for the opportunity to participate in the revenue stream generated by the venture.

Any company that desires to enter into a strategic alliance should carefully select strategic alliance partners and perform due diligence before entering into the strategic alliance agreement. Failure to adhere to such a prudent business practice exposes a business to undo risks.

Each strategic alliance partner must weigh the time and expense of thorough due diligence against the risk involved in participating in a strategic alliance. Less stringent due diligence is acceptable when the strategic alliance exposes the company to minimal risk. A complete due diligence must be conducted if strategic alliance partners are fiscally dependent upon each other.

A joint venture is a corporation formed by two or more independent corporations to achieve a mutually beneficial goal. A joint venture usually has a single objective and is dissolved once the goal is achieved. The joint venture is called a consortium if more than two independent corporations participate in the joint venture. The goals of a joint venture can range from capitalizing on a market opportunity to development of new technology that would enhance the products and services of the industry.

The advantage of forming a joint venture is to share expenses and risk, especially when the goal of the joint venture is to enhance the marketplace.

The disadvantage of a joint venture is that one approach is taken to achieve the goal of the joint venture and that approach is controlled by a single group of companies. Some participants might focus the efforts of the joint venture into a direction that is self-serving for a few companies rather than for the marketplace as a whole.

QUESTIONS

1. What are the advantages of outsourcing?

2. When would it be advantageous to form a joint venture?

3. How does a joint venture compare with a merger or acquisition?

4. What are the advantages of a business alliance?

5. What are the risks for a company to outsource a portion of its business?

6. What kind of due diligence would you perform before entering into a strategic alliance?

7. What are the disadvantages of forming a business alliance?

8. How do members of strategic alliances reduce their risk in participating in the strategic alliance?

9. What do members of a joint venture contribute to the joint venture?

10. What types of returns can a member of a joint venture expect for participating in the joint venture?

acquisition   Occurs when one corporation buys the stock or assets of another corporation.

acquisition agreement   The binding contract that specifies the terms of an acquisition and contains representations, covenants, warranties, and indemnities made by a the target company in exchange for the acquisition price.

acquisition agreement: asset transfer procedure section   Identifies assets and specifies steps that will be followed to transfer the title of a target company to a buyer.

acquisition agreement: covenant section   Provides for the parties to agree to avoid changing anything that materially alters the representations and warranties.

acquisition agreement: indemnification section   States what each party will do to remedy a misrepresentation or violation of a covenant.

acquisition agreement: introduction section   Sets the tone of the agreement and explains the objectives of each party.

acquisition agreement: price section   Sets the price that can be a fixed amount or a pricing formula used to set the fixed amount at closing.

acquisition agreement: representation section   Contains statements made by the buyer and dotcom relating to their operations, such as that each corporation was legally formed and is authorized to enter into the agreement.

acquisition agreement: termination section   States terms whereby either party can terminate the agreement and avoid closing the deal. This section also contains the legal remedies, such as recouping certain expenses should the deal terminate.

acquisition agreement: terms of closing section   Outlines the steps that must be completed for the parties to close the deal.

acquisition agreement: warranty section   Asserts that the party making the representation assures that the statements are true.

acquisition of property for stock merger   Occurs when a buyer exchanges stock for assets of a dotcom.

actuary   A person who uses statistics to forecast the medical needs of a dot-com's workforce and who establishes the size of a fund necessary to provide medical benefits to cover the medical needs of the workforce.

adjusted basis   Calculated by subtracting depreciation, amortization, and related charges from the initial basis of the asset.

adoption stage   The stage at which a buyer accepts a proposal.

approval clause   Grants a party who has an agreement with the seller the right to renegotiate terms whenever control of the corporation changes.

arbitration clause   Stipulates that disputes will be handled by an arbitrator rather than through action with the courts.

arbitrator   A private individual who takes the role of a judge, establishes the facts in the case, and then recommends a solution to the conflict.

A-reorganization   When a buyer's stockholders give a dotcom's stockholders stock in the buyer. The dotcom transfers its assets to the buyer.

articles of incorporation   A public document that explicitly defines a corporation's purpose and rules under which the corporation operates.

ask price   The acquisition price proposed by a dotcom.

asset lockup   Occurs when a board of directors grants a friendly investor an option to purchase a key asset of a corporation.

asset price   The current market price for an asset, adjusted for exposure to liabilities such as pending litigation that carry over after a deal, and the cost of acquiring the asset.

asset purchase   A buyer acquires all rights of the seller of an asset in exchange for consideration.

average rate of return model   Bases the price of an acquisition on the expected rate of return on the investment.

awareness stage   The stage at which a negotiator proposes a new idea.

back-end defense   Grants stockholders the right to exchange their stock for a one-year note at a predetermined value should a hostile takeover occur.

backward integration   Acquiring a supplier.

bank check   A checked issued by a bank and considered the equivalent of cash.

bankbook   A financing proposal created by a buyer and used to attract financial institutions and insurance companies into financing a deal.

beneficial owner   A stockholder who has 5 percent or more of the outstanding shares of a corporation.

benefit split   Transfers a portion of a dotcom's benefits obligation to the buyer. The portion that is transferred is proportionate to the business unit(s) acquired by the buyer. A benefit split limits the liability of the buyer, but introduces a degree of complexity to the deal.

benefits   Services provided at no expense or reduced expense to an employee by an employer; benefits can range from health care and retirement benefits to use of a corporate plane.

benefits analyst   A person who surveys benefits plans to determine if a benefits plan is economical.

best of knowledge clause   Verbiage in the acquisition agreement stipulating that the information is represented as accurate to the best knowledge of the dotcom.

beta value   The dotcom's stockprice and the Standard & Poor's 500 movements are synchronized.

bid price   The acquisition price proposed by a buyer.

binding arbitration   Both sides, when agreeing to the binding arbitration clause, also agree to accept the decision of the arbitrator without recourse.

bonus   A once-a-year payment that takes the form of cash or stock.

book value   The value of an asset minus depreciation.

branch profits tax   Tax imposed on earnings from United States operations (branch) of a foreign corporation.

breakup fee clause   An agreement between a buyer and dotcom in which the dotcom compensates the buyer for expenses such as out-of-pocket expenses should the deal with the buyer collapse.

B-reorganization   A stock-for-stock transaction

bridge   A short-term compensation plan that is designed to address the immediate needs of the buyer, the dotcom, and their employees during and shortly after the acquisition process.

bridge financing   Short-term debt used to finance an acquisition until a permanent debt is in place.

bridge loan   An obligation that finances a merger or acquisition to consummate a transaction before permanent financing is in place.

broker   Represents a company during the search and in the subsequent deal and follows prescribed rules when negotiating the best deal for the client. A broker is an agent who has a fiduciary responsibility to represent one party to the deal, but is not permitted to represent both parties.

bulk sales law   Requires that notice of the transfer of inventory be sent to creditors of the seller 10 days prior to the transfer if the asset is inventory.

business alliance   Two or more businesses join together to offer products and services to the customer.

bust-up clause   *See* breakup fee clause.

bylaws   Rules created by the board of directors and approved by stockholders that govern how a corporation conducts business.

carryover basis   The adjusted basis of an asset is transferred without change to the buyer following a stock purchase or merger.

cash financing method   When a buyer exchanges cash for stock or assets of a dotcom.

cash flow   A series of cash payments generated by business operations and/or investments.

cash-out   A dotcom sells to a buyer for cash only.

cashier's check   A check issued by a bank.

certificate of incorporation   A document that authorizes a corporation to exist.

certified check   A check issued by a buyer that the bank certifies as having sufficient funds in the buyer's account to cover payment of the check.

charter   A document granted to a corporation by the state, authorizing the corporation to conduct specific activities, such as conducting business.

charter defense   Uses changes in the corporate charter and bylaws to inhibit a takeover of the corporation by an unwanted suitor.

clayton act   Specifies among other factors that members of the board of directors cannot sit on the board of a competing company.

close vendor-client relationship   Where the success of a vendor's operation is closely dependent on the success of the client's operation.

closing   When all components of a deal come together and title to a dotcom transfers to a buyer.

commercial banker   Provides advisory services and does not underwrite securities for the deal.

commitment letter   A document that commit a lender to provide money at specified terms.

committee on Foreign Investment   The committee that assesses the impact a business has on national interest, then recommends to the appropriate regulator agencies whether or not to impose restrictions.

commodity pricing   Products and services are standardized and are priced according to supply and demand.

compensation   Defines the way in which employees are rewarded for providing service to a corporation.

compensation analyst   A person who surveys both compensation plans and compensation levels in local markets, then devises a plan that meets the short-term and long-term needs of the buyer.

compensation style   The percentage of compensation given as salary, bonus, incentives, and benefits.

confidence level   An indication of how sure you are that the information provided accurately represents the dotcom. A confidence level is noted as a percentage of confidence where 100 percent represents total confidence in the information.

consortium   More than two independent corporations participating in a joint venture.

contingency   A condition specified by the company that, if met by the dotcom, enables the company to consummate the deal.

corporation   An organization of stockholders that has been declared a legal entity by the state in which the organization was incorporated.

correspondent bank   A financial institution that holds accounts for corporations and for other financial institutions, such as other correspondent banks.

C-reorganization   When a buyer exchanges stock for assets of a dotcom.

cross default clause   Stipulates that default on any debt is default on all debt.

currency fluctuation   The change in the currency rate.

currency option   The right to purchase or sell a specific amount of currency at a specific exchange rate at a future date. Options can be exercised or abandoned.

currency rate   The ratio at which two currencies are exchanged.

current assets   Assets that can be converted into cash within a year.

current liabilities   Liabilities due within a year.

current ratio   Total current assets:total current liabilities.

deal agreement   The document agreed to by a company and dotcom that specifies details of the merger or acquisition.

deal book   Contains all the documents pertinent to the deal, including the letter of intent, acquisition agreement, final audit report, final due diligence results, and the deal checklist. The deal book becomes the historical record of the deal.

debt service   Repayment of outstanding debt.

deferred compensation   Earned compensation that is paid sometime in the future.

deferred taxed compensation   Untaxed cash earned by an employee that is placed in a restricted fund that can be drawn down once qualifications, such as reaching retirement age, are met. Drawn down cash is then taxed.

defined benefit plan   A promise by the employer to pay a fixed amount of cash to employees at retirement after a specified number of years of employment.

defined contribution plan   Requires a fixed level of contribution and a variable benefit based on the return on investments of the contribution. Employees contribute to the plan and an employer may or may not match contributions. Contributions and return on investments are tax deferred until the employee withdraws the funds. Employees control the choice of investments.

differed compensation   A technique for lowering tax liability for an employee, where a portion of earned compensation is paid to the employee at a later date, usually when the employee retires and is in a lower tax bracket.

disclosed liabilities   Liabilities the seller disclosed to the buyer when negotiating an acquisition.

discounted cash flow pricing model   Determines the net present value of future earnings that are forecasted for the dotcom.

diversification   Expansion into a different business that extends existing offerings to customers or operates in an entirely different industry.

domestic wire transfer   A wire transfer executed within the Federal Reserve System of banks.

D-reorganization   Occurs when a holding company transfers assets to a subsidiary.

due diligence   Independent verification of claims made by either the buyer or seller.

employee retention contract   Used to specify the terms under which a dotcom's employee continues employment with the buyer after the acquisition.

employee termination contract   Specifies the terms under which a dotcom's key employee terminates employment with the buyer following the acquisition.

environmental analysis   Reviews environmental regulations on the federal, state, and local levels to determine the environmental exposure of a dotcom.

equity kicker   Either a warrant to acquire shares in the buyer at a specific price or a transfer of stock to the lender.

escrow account   An account overseen by a third party until terms of a contract are met, at which time the balance of the account is turned over to a party of the contract.

examination stage   The state at which a party reviews the details of a proposal to determine if the proposal truly meets its needs.

exploration stage   The stage at which a party qualifies a proposal by asking general questions in an effort to determine if the proposal might meet the party's needs.

extended benefits   Benefits received by employees who have terminated employment with the dotcom.

Fed Wire   The electronic network used to for domestic wire transfers.

Federal Funds rate   The interest the Federal Reserve Bank charges banks for loans.

fiduciary responsibility   Exercising business judgment based on the best interests of stockholders.

financial buyer   Sees a dotcom as a stream of cash that can be acquired through carefully orchestrated debt.

financial ratio   Defines standard relationships that enable a buyer, dotcom, and financiers to objectively compare the dotcom with similar corporations.

finder   . Introduces both parties without representing either party, and does not negotiate the deal. There is no fiduciary responsibility and one or both parties compensate the finder. Typically, finders are not regulated and therefore don't require a license to operate.

fit chart   Is a tool that guides you through the process of identifying dotcoms that complement your company.

flip-over defense   Grants a stockholder the right to purchase a share of the successor corporation following a hostile takeover.

foreign tax credit   The deduction of foreign taxes from earnings on income for domestic tax reporting.

formal tentative value   An appraisal sufficient for a company to devise a financing plan and initiate formal negotiations with a dotcom.

forward integration   Acquiring a customer.

forward purchase contract   An agreement between two persons to purchase a specific amount of currency at a fixed exchange rate, with the contract to be executed at a specific time in the future.

forward sales contract   An agreement between two persons to sell a specific amount of currency at a fixed exchange rate, with the contract to be executed at a specific time in the future.

fraudulent conveyance   Occurs when title to assets, used as collateral for a loan, is not free and clear.

friendly acquisition   A transaction where both the buyer and seller agree to the acquisition.

friendly takeover   An acquisition of a corporation that is recommended by a dotcom's board of directors.

from-birth investigation   An investigation that documents the formation of a dotcom and documents events that have led to the dotcom's current status.

fund transfer   *See* wire transfer.

funded medical benefits plan   A trust-based medical benefit plan where contributions are made to a trust fund, which is drawn down upon to pay for employee medical coverage.

Glass Seagall Act   Federal law that prohibits commercial banks from underwriting securities.

golden handcuffs   Refers to an employee retention contract.

golden handshake   Refers to an employee retention contract.

golden parachute   Refers to an employee termination contract that contains a substantial buyout compensation.

goodwill   An intangible asset that takes into account the value added to a dotcom as a result of patronage and reputation.

green mail   *See* payment defense.

Hart Scott Rodino Antitrust Improvements Act   Requires that the company and the dotcom provide the Federal Trade Commission and the Department of Justice with notice of an impending merger or acquisition.

Health Maintenance Organization   Consists of a physician, called the primary care physician, who determines the care required to treat an employee, then either provides the care or refers the employee to other caregivers in the HMO network for treatment.

hidden cash   Cash and near cash assets that are not obvious during the initial examination of a dotcom's books and records.

HMO   *See* Health Maintenance Organization.

hold-and-pay clause   Requires subordinate lenders to hold in reserve amounts paid by the buyer to satisfy a debt until the senior lenders are paid.

holding corporation   A corporation that is a stockholder that holds at least 80 percent of the shares in affiliate corporations.

horizontal integration   Where a company expands its current business by acquiring a competitor or by moving existing operations into new territories.

hostile acquisition   A transaction in which the seller is against the acquisition.

hostile takeover   An acquisition of a corporation that is not recommended by the dotcom's board of directors.

immaterial litigation   Legal action, the success of which will not influence business operations.

in-house development   Using corporate resources to develop a business without acquiring an existing company in the desired market.

in-play   When a dotcom is known to be available for merger or acquisition.

incentive   A form of bonus that is correlated to performance.

income tax treaty   An agreement that reduces double taxation on international corporations and establishes procedures for resolving income tax disputes.

income-liability test   Used to determine if a company is considered a foreign resident whom an income tax treaty covers. Earnings from branch operations in the treaty country must be redirected to the treaty country or the United States to be considered a resident under the treaty.

indemnity basket   The term given to the minimum loss that a buyer incurs before other terms of the indemnity section take affect.

indemnity healthcare plan   Where caregivers are paid a fee for each service that they provide to an employee or a member of an employee's family.

initial tentative value   A rough appraisal used to narrow the field to a handful of dotcoms.

insider   A person who has possession of information about a public corporation that is unknown to the general public and that might affect the market price of the corporation.

insider trading   Occurs when someone trades securities of a corporation based on information about a public corporation that is not widely known to the public nor disclosed in a regulatory filing.

intangible asset   Things you cannot touch, but that have a value to the dotcom, such as goodwill, trademarks, copyrights, and patents.

integration plan   A plan that identifies the tasks the must be completed to achieve integration of the buyer and the dotcom operations.

integration team   Key personnel from the buyer's and the dotcom's organizations who is responsible for developing an integration plan.

inter-creditor agreement   An agreement among lenders that specifies how conflicts involving lenders are to be resolved.

international syndicate   A temporary organization of lenders who pool their resources to underwrite financing an international acquisition.

international wire transfer   Similar to a domestic wire transfer, except that correspondent banks are used instead of the Federal Reserve System.

internet packet   An electronic envelope that contains a small piece of information that is being sent over the Internet. Internet packets are reassembled into the information at their destination.

investment banker   Underwrites securities for the deal and provides advisory services.

joint venture   A corporation formed by two or more independent corporations to achieve a mutually beneficial goal. A joint venture usually has a single objective and is dissolved once the goal is achieved.

junk bonds   High yield bonds that hold the lowest priority of subordinate debt.

leaseback financing   Financing in which a third party purchases the asset, then leases the asset to the buyer.

lehman scale   Used to determine fees for a broker and/or finder, where the fee is 5 percent of the first million, 4 percent of the second million, 3 percent of the third million, 2 percent of the fourth million, and 1 percent of additional millions.

letter of intent   A document issued by the company to a dotcom, indicating an interest to merge or acquire the dotcom.

leveraged buyout   Where an acquiring company's capital structure is substantially higher debt than equity.

LIBOR   *See* London Interbank Offered Rate.

liquidate   Assets of a corporation are sold to a third party for cash. Cash is given to stockholders in exchange for their stock in the corporation.

liquidation value   The expected proceeds of the sale of an asset in the open market.

literature search   The task of reviewing all written, audio, and video documents pertaining to a dotcom or the dotcom's industry.

litigation analysis   The process of investigating previous, current, and potential litigation involving a dotcom.

London Interbank Offered Rate   An interest rate charged by banks to other banks for loans.

management buyout   Occurs when managers of a dotcom form a new corporation, and with funds provided by a lender, acquire the dotcom, typically as a forward or reverse merger.

market value   The value an asset will realize if sold in the current market.

market value pricing model   Underlying philosophy is that the marketplace has all the information to properly evaluate and establish a price for a dotcom.

material litigation   Legal action, the success of which will influence business operations.

material owner   A person or corporation that controls 10 percent of the voting shares of a foreign corporation.

maximum leveraged strategy   A strategy in which the acquiring company's capital structure is substantially higher debt than equity

merger   When two corporations combine assets and liabilities and only one corporation survives.

mezzanine debt   High yield bonds that hold the lowest priority of subordinate debt.

net present value   The value of tomorrow's cash flows in today's dollars.

no-shopping clause   A clause that prohibits the dotcom from seeking other offers during negotiations with the buyer.

nonbinding arbitration   The arbitrator's role is to recommend a remedy and convince both sides to accept the decision. Each side reserves the right to reject the remedy, then has the right to take the matter through the legal system.

noncompete clause   A clause in which an employee agrees not to work for a competitor within a specified period such as five years after termination

nondisclosure agreement   A document stating that information revealed during the due diligence process will be maintained confidential. Disclosure of information is actionable through litigation.

note financing method   When the dotcom or a third-party lender accepts a note from the buyer in lieu of cash or stock. In exchange, the dotcom transfers its assets or stock to the buyer.

operating expenses   Expenses incurred to operate the corporation.

operating unit   Consists of profit centers within each organization and support operations that work as internal vendors to profit centers.

option   The right to purchase stock at a predetermined amount and time.

outsourcing   A business alliance whereby a client turns over the operations of a portion of its business to an outsourcing firm.

overfunded benefits plan   The size of a fund to cover benefits obligations is higher than the forecasted obligation to cover the benefit.

partial acquisition   A buyer acquires a portion of a dotcom's operation rather than the dotcom's full operation.

partnering   *See* business alliance.

pass-through liabilities   A dotcom's liabilities are inherited by the buyer.

passive income   Income generated by dividends, interests, royalties, and rents.

payback-pricing model   Requires that the price paid for the dotcom be recovered by the dotcom's operations following the acquisition, within a specified timeframe.

payment defense   The dotcom purchases at a high premium its own stock that is held by the unwanted suitor.

perceived value   An amount derived from subjective rather than objective valuation.

perfect lien   One lien on an asset.

piggyback registration right   Restricts registration rights to a single security or to a class of securities.

point-of-Service Plan   Consists of a physician, called the primary care physician, who determines the care required to treat an employee, then either provides the care or refers the employee to other caregivers in the POS network for treatment. Employees have an option to be treated by a caregiver outside of the POS network. The POS plan and the employee share the cost of the outside-network caregiver.

poison pill defense   *See* shareholder rights plan defense.

pooling of interest method   Treats the deal as a stock purchase or merger and combines assets, liabilities, earnings, and losses of both the dotcom and the buyer.

POS   *See* Point-of-Service Plan

position threshold   Restores a balanced control by requiring 51 percent of the lenders of an outstanding debt to approve the exercise of a registration right.

PPO   *See* Preferred Provider Organization.

preclosing process   A meeting held before the closing day during which parties review documents and the details of closing the deal.

Preferred Provider Organization   Consists of a network of caregivers; however, employees are not required to use the services of a primary care physician. Instead, the employee can choose to consult with any caregiver that is a member of the network.

preferred stock   Confers certain preferences to dividend payments and distribution of corporate assets.

premium   An amount above the market price that the buyer will pay for outstanding shares of the dotcom.

prepayment clause   Prohibits prepayments except when cash flows earmarked for dividends are redirected to prepay subordinate debt.

price ceiling   The highest price a buyer will pay for a dotcom.

price floor   The lowest price a buyer will pay for a dotcom.

prima facie evidence   Facts that at first glance lead you to believe a dotcom is a fit for your company.

private corporation   A corporation whose securities are not registered with state and federal authorities, and therefore is prohibited from being traded in the open securities market.

procedural clause   Delineates steps lenders follow to initiate litigation if the buyer defaults on a debt.

product life cycle   The duration beginning when a product is introduced to the market and ending when the product becomes unprofitable.

proxy   A right to vote on behalf of a stockholder.

proxy fight   Competition among two or more parties for the proxy of a stockholder.

proxy statement   The formal solicitation of a stockholder's proxy.

public corporation   A corporation in which some or all of its shares are registered with the appropriate agencies, shares are issued to the general public, and shares are likely to be traded in a stock exchange where the auction process dictates the current value of those shares.

public disclosure   A way in which regulators assure that the public has pertinent information about a public corporation; used to assess the value of the information and make appropriate financial decisions regarding the corporation, such as to sell or buy stock.

purchase method   Records the current value of assets, liabilities, earnings, and losses of the dotcom as of the day the deal closes.

qualified retirement plan   A retirement plan that is qualified for favorable treatment under the Internal Revenue Service regulations.

quick ratio (Total current assets – inventory):total current liabilities.

real value A tangible amount that a party can rationalize through a formal valuation process.

reasonable man rule What a reasonable person would consider material or not material to the dotcom's business operation.

refinancing clause Stipulates that subordinate debt remain subordinate to senior debt in any refinancing plan instituted by the buyer.

registration right The right of a lender to require a buyer to register securities in the buyer.

regulatory audit A list of laws and regulations that cover a deal.

reorganization A restatement of financial conditions without any relative change in position.

replacement value-pricing model Requires the buyer to determine the cost of recreating the dotcom.

residual value The value of a fully depreciated asset that can be realized by selling the asset.

restructuring defense Where the corporation buys back shares from the open market by using excess cash or receipts from debt to make the purchases.

retrospective rating program An actuarial analysis that establishes a premium and reserves to cover medical expenses. Adjustments are made during the year to the reserve and premium to reflect actual outlays.

reverse lockup option An agreement between the board of directors and existing stockholders who hold a large position in the corporation not to tender their shares in the event of a tender offer made by a buyer that is unacceptable to the board of directors.

risk assessment Assessing the credit worthiness of the buyer.

salary An annual sum paid to employees on a regular basis during the year and which represents the bulk, and in some cases all, of their compensation.

sales leaseback Where a third party purchases the asset, then leases the asset to the buyer.

satellite closing site   Used mainly to facilitate filing documents such as title and liens at remote locations. Each satellite site should have personnel to sign and file necessary documents.

sell off   A buyer sells a portion of the dotcom's operation after the dotcom is acquired by the buyer.

senior debt   Obligations that receive the highest priority when a corporation is liquidated.

shareholder rights plan defense   Occurs when the board of directors grant to existing stockholders the right to acquire additional shares in the corporation if a specific event occurs, such as a successful tender offer by an unwanted suitor.

shell company   A corporation that no longer functions as a business.

short form merger   A merger in which a company acquires the stock of another company, after which the acquired company is merged with the acquirer.

SIBOR   *See* Singapore Interbank Offer Rate.

Singapore Interbank Offer Rate   An interest rate charged by banks to other banks for loans.

spot rate   The current exchange rate between two currencies.

stages of acceptance   The process by which a corporation adopts or rejects a proposal.

staggered board clause   A third of the directors are elected each year for a three-year term. Directors cannot be removed until their term expires until for cause.

statutory insider   A person who, by his or her position with a firm, is considered an insider.

step-up adjusted basis   The purchase price plus expenses associated with the purchase.

stock lockup option   Occurs when the board of directors enters into an agreement with a friendly investor in which the investor receives options to purchase unissued but authorized shares of the corporation at an attractive price.

stock purchase   A seller exchanges stock in the seller's corporation with a buyer for a negotiated payment.

stock purchase-merger strategy   A strategy in which buyer makes a stock purchase of a majority of stock in a dotcom before announcing merger plans. Once the controlling block of stock is acquired, the buyer proposes the merger, then votes the block of stock in the dotcom to approve the merger.

strategic alliance   A contractual arrangement between two companies, where one company provides a service to another for a percentage of each transaction.

strategic buyer   Seeks to use the dotcom to enhance the corporation's current organization through synergy of the existing corporation and the dotcom.

subordinate debt   Obligations that receive a lower priority than senior debt when a corporation is liquidated.

subordinate limitation clause   Limits the level of subordination to senior debt.

subsidiary   A corporation that is solely owned by another corporation.

substantive clause   Stipulates the order of payment among lenders.

successor liability   Where the liability of a dotcom is transferred to the company after a merger or acquisition.

syndicate   A group of lenders who organize to provide financing for a deal.

tail policy   Insurance that continues the coverage of an existing policy.

take-back clause   Requires the employee to pay back to the buyer any bonus or incentive paid to the employee if the employee violates the employee agreement.

take-back financing   When the dotcom accepts a note from the buyer in lieu of cash or stock. In exchange, the dotcom transfers its assets or stock to the buyer.

take-back financing   Is when a dotcom agrees to loan the company the proceeds of which are used to merge or acquire the dotcom

tangible asset   Physical property, such as software to run a Web site, real estate, and computer equipment.

target   A company that is the focus of a merger or acquisition.

tax-free acquisition of stock merger   A merger in which the buyer and dotcom exchange stock in each other's corporations.

tax-free forward merger   A merger in which the buyer's stockholders give the dotcom's stockholders stock in the buyer. The dotcom transfers its assets to the buyer.

tax-free forward triangular merger   A merger in which the buyer gives the dotcom's stockholders shares in the buyer's holding corporation and the dotcom's assets are transferred to the buyer's subsidiary.

taxable forward merger   A merger in which the buyer gives compensation, usually cash, to stockholders of a dotcom. The dotcom transfer title to its assets to the buyer.

taxable forward subsidiary merger   A merger in which the buyer gives cash to stockholders of the dotcom and the dotcom's assets are merged with a subsidiary of the buyer.

taxable reverse merger   A merger in which the buyer gives cash to stockholders of the dotcom. Shares of the dotcom are distributed to stockholders of the buyer.

telex   An electronic communiqué that is similar to instructions that flow over the Fed Wire.

tender offer   A publicly announced offer by the buyer to acquire shares of a single class of stock at a specified price.

test stage   The state at which the buyer looks for a reason for rejecting the proposal.

threshold   The minimum value that is considered material to a merger or acquisition.

tie-in   An arrangement by which a banker links together more than one service and requires a client to use the linked services regardless if these services are necessary.

time horizon   The date when the buyer wants to realize the full benefits of a deal.

tin parachute   An employee termination contract that has less favorable compensation than a golden parachute.

tippee   A person receiving information from a tipper.

tipper   An insider who divulges inside information.

tipping   The exchanging of inside information.

topping fee clause   Requires the dotcom to compensate the buyer should the buyer's bid for the corporation be rejected because a higher bid was received from another buyer.

total compensation   The sum of salary and bonus.

trade debt   Debt held by vendors.

trade debt clause   Specifies the subordination of vendor debt.

transmittal letter   A formal offer from a buyer to a stockholder to acquire the stockholder's shares in the corporation.

treasury stock   Shares of a corporation owned by the corporation.

treaty-shopping   The technique used by international corporations whereby they enter into business operations in countries that have favorable tax treaties with the United States.

unattractive defense   Used to tarnish certain attributes to make a dotcom less desirable to the buyer.

underfunded benefits plan   The size of a fund to cover benefits obligations is lower than the forecasted obligation to cover the benefit.

undisclosed liabilities   Liabilities the seller withholds from the buyer when negotiating an acquisition.

unfunded medical benefits plan   A medical benefit plan that is provided by a health insurance carrier or through self-insurance

Uniform Commercial Code (UCC)   A set of rules created by the National Conference of Commissioners of Uniform State Laws that govern the conduct of business.

valuation analysis   Provides an objective foundation from which a fair market price can be established for a dotcom.

vertical integration   Where a company expands by acquiring a supplier or customer.

walk-through   A dress rehearsal of the closing held the day before the closing, during which documents are assembled and reviewed, and routine documents are executed.

warrant   An agreement that specifies the number of shares in the buyer that can be redeemed by exercising the warrant.

wire transfer   A series of book entries in which the buyer's financial institution debits the buyer's account for the amount of the transfer and the dotcom's financial institution credits the dotcom's account for the same amount. No actual money transfers. All the cash remains in the banking system.

written consent clause   Grants the board of directors the right to obtain approval from stockholders through a written consent rather than from vote at a stockholders meeting.

wrongful termination   Occurs when an employer, after a consolidation, dismisses an employee for unjustifiable reasons such as age discrimination.

INDEX

webmergers.com

Webmergers.com is a data-driven hub for buyers and sellers of Internet and technology properties. Webmergers.com provides information, analysis and buyer-seller matching services for acquirers and sellers. The Webmergers hub provides the following services:

- A referral program that matches sellers with appropriate investment banks and intermediaries
- An online Marketplace of tech properties for sale, in partnership with BizBuySell, with distribution in such locations as Yahoo!, the *The Wall Street Journal*'s StartupJournal.com, Inc.com and others.
- An "Intensive Care Unit," which refers transitioning companies to turnaround firms or other strategic advisors
- Comparables reports that assist buyers and sellers in establishing valuations

Webmergers also produces reports and analysis based on its database of more than 3,000 Internet M&A transactions. Reports include the Web M&A Report, a 100-page quarterly analysis of merger and acquisition activity involving Internet companies, various special reports and custom reports on Internet-related deals. A free weekly newsletter provides updates on recent deals of note.

Webmergers.com data and interviews have recently appeared in more than 600 articles or broadcasts in such locations as *CNNfn, CNBC, CBS Evening News, C\Net, Fortune, Forbes, Barrons, Business Week, The Wall Street Journal, The Industry Standard, Reuters, Bloomberg* and in international press ranging from *Japan National Television to The Guardian, Les Echo* and others.

Tim Miller, President of Webmergers, Inc. previously headed New Media Resources, a consulting firm that provided advisory services to interactive media startups. Before starting New Media Resources, Miller spent five years in corporate development at Ziff Communications Co., assisting senior management in acquisitions research, strategic planning and development of online products. Miller has studied interactive services in a fellowship at the Gannett Center for Media at the Columbia University in New York. Miller maintains numerous contacts among the Silicon Valley new media community, serves on the program committee of the *MIT/Stanford Venture Laboratory* and has chaired several national conferences on Internet M&A topics.

Webmergers, Inc.
www.webmergers.com
1121 Clayton Street
San Francisco, CA 94117
(415)564-2500
Fax: (415)564-0500
Tmiller@webmergers.com

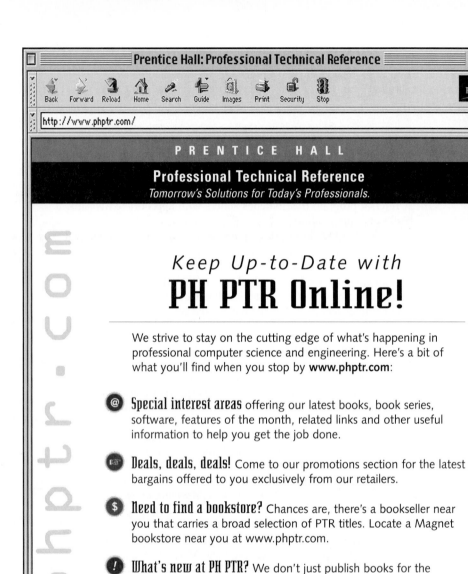

Prentice Hall: Professional Technical Reference

http://www.phptr.com/

PRENTICE HALL

Professional Technical Reference
Tomorrow's Solutions for Today's Professionals.

Keep Up-to-Date with

PH PTR Online!

We strive to stay on the cutting edge of what's happening in professional computer science and engineering. Here's a bit of what you'll find when you stop by **www.phptr.com**:

Special interest areas offering our latest books, book series, software, features of the month, related links and other useful information to help you get the job done.

Deals, deals, deals! Come to our promotions section for the latest bargains offered to you exclusively from our retailers.

Need to find a bookstore? Chances are, there's a bookseller near you that carries a broad selection of PTR titles. Locate a Magnet bookstore near you at www.phptr.com.

What's new at PH PTR? We don't just publish books for the professional community, we're a part of it. Check out our convention schedule, join an author chat, get the latest reviews and press releases on topics of interest to you.

Subscribe today! Join PH PTR's monthly email newsletter!

Want to be kept up-to-date on your area of interest? Choose a targeted category on our website, and we'll keep you informed of the latest PH PTR products, author events, reviews and conferences in your interest area.

Visit our mailroom to subscribe today! **http://www.phptr.com/mail_lists**

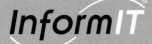

Solutions from experts you know and trust.

| Articles | Free Library | eBooks | Expert Q & A | Training | Career Center | Downloads | MyInformIT |

Login   Register   About InformIT

Topics

Operating Systems
Web Development
Programming
Networking
Certification
and more...

www.informit.com

Free, in-depth articles and supplements

Master the skills you need, when you need them

Choose from industry leading books, ebooks, and training products

Get answers when you need them - from live experts or InformIT's comprehensive library

Achieve industry certification and advance your career

Expert Access

Free Content

Visit _InformIT_ today
and get great content
from PH
PTR

Prentice Hall and InformIT are trademarks of Pearson plc /
Copyright © 2000 Pearson